THE RIVALRY

THE

BALLANTINE BOOKS NEW YORK

RIVALRY

Bill Russell, Wilt Chamberlain, and

the Golden Age of Basketball

JOHN TAYLOR

2006 Ballantine Books Trade Paperback Edition

Published in the United States by Ballantine
Books, an imprint of The Random House
Publishing Group, a division of Random House,
Inc., New York.

BALLANTINE and colophon are registered
trademarks of Random House, Inc.

Originally published in hardcover in the United
States by Random House, an imprint of The
Random House Publishing Group, a division of
Random House, Inc., in 2005.

Taylor, John.
The rivalry : Bill Russell, Wilt Chamberlain,
and the golden age of basketball / John Taylor.
p. cm.
Includes index.
ISBN 0-8129-7030-6
1. Russell, Bill, 1934– 2. Chamberlain, Wilt,
1936– 3. Basketball players—United States—
Biography. 4. Sports rivalries—United States—
History—20th century. I. Title.

GV884.A1T39 2005
796.323'092—dc22
[B]   2005042797

Printed in the United States of America

www.ballantinebooks.com

9 8 7 6 5 4 3 2

To my father,
for always insisting on fair play

THE RIVALRY

1

ON THE NIGHT of November 7, 1959, people lined up on the sidewalks outside Boston's North Station, a dingy yellow-brick building, and crowded along the bar at the Iron Horse, the old drinking-parlor inside. They stood in clusters on Causeway Street and Haverhill Street and Canal Street, their voices almost drowned out by the thundering traffic on the elevated highways and subway tracks that crossed above them on iron girders, and by the hiss and clang of the trains in the rail yards.

The citizens of Boston had much to debate that evening. In Washington, D.C., Charles Van Doren, the thirty-three-year-old Columbia University English professor, had just admitted to a congressional committee that the producers of *Twenty-One,* the television quiz show that had turned him into a national icon, had been secretly prepping him with the answers to questions. Senator John Kennedy, who had all but announced his intention to run for president the following year, had been touring California and Oregon the previous week, greeted by ecstatic crowds carrying signs saying "Viva Kennedy!" In Boston itself, a newspaper strike was under way, and just four days earlier, John Collins, the Suffolk County register of probate and a victim of paralytic polio who was confined to a wheelchair, had defeated Senate president John Powers for the Boston mayoralty. It was a stunning upset, brought about by an FBI raid on the headquarters of a gambling syndicate just one hundred yards from the East Boston police station and resulting in charges of widespread corruption in the city's government.

But the topic that consumed the crowds around North Station was neither the television scandal nor the impending administration of John Collins nor the presidential prospects of a young Irish American Catholic. It was instead basketball, specifically the game scheduled that night between the Boston Celtics and the Philadelphia Warriors. While Boston was a storied sports town, the sports that had always provoked the most passion were baseball and hockey, the sports of the Red Sox and the Bruins. These were sports with rich local histories, sports that had been played for generations in Boston and had, over the years, woven themselves so deeply into the fabric of the city that residence there seemed virtually synonymous with a rabid devotion to its baseball and hockey teams. Professional basketball, in contrast, was only thirteen years old in 1959. Walter Brown, the owner of the Bruins and leaseholder on the Boston Garden, had started the Celtics to fill seats at the arena on nights when his beloved hockey team was not playing and the big, drafty building, located above the train station, would otherwise sit dark and empty. In other words, the team was a purely commercial afterthought in a sport without strong roots in the city's culture, and for much of the fifties, attendance at its games reflected this. Rarely was the Garden more than half filled on the nights it played. Members of the Celtics joked that while Ted Williams could not get out of a car on Charles Street without being mobbed, their entire team could walk the length of the Common and no one would give them a second glance.

On the night of November 7, however, every one of the 13,909 seats in the Garden had long been sold out, even the hundreds of seats whose views became partially obstructed when the hockey arena was converted to a basketball court by raising the backboards, running guy wires out to the sides, and bolting the wooden parquet squares to the subflooring. Outside, along Causeway Street, scalpers were demanding upwards of $20 for tickets that usually went for $2.50. One New York sportswriter, arriving at North Station earlier that afternoon, was offered a ticket for $10 by a scalper who told him, "Just trying to do you a favor, Mac. I can get more for it at the Garden just before game time."

· The reason for the excitement was that twenty-three-year-old Wilt Chamberlain had joined the Philadelphia Warriors as a rookie that year and on this night Chamberlain would for the first time face the Celtics center, Bill Russell. The game was so eagerly anticipated that Red Auerbach, the Celtics coach, had been telling people that it would draw enough fans to fill Yankee Stadium. Sportswriters were calling the confrontation Battle of the Titans, Battle of the Giants, and Big Goliath vs. Little Goliath. They were speculating about what would happen when an "irresistible offensive force" encountered an "immovable defensive object." In an article anticipating the game, *Sport* magazine's headline was "The Big Collision," and it declared, "Pro basketball will be stepping into its golden age when Wilt Chamberlain, the rookie, clashes with Bill Russell, the leaping veteran."

Chamberlain had attracted national attention even while a student at Overbrook High School in Philadelphia, where his team won fifty-eight games and lost three in his three years there and where he set a statewide scoring record, averaging just under forty points per game. At the University of Kansas, he had proved to be such an overwhelming presence on the court that Jimmy Breslin, then a young sportswriter, wrote an article for *The Saturday Evening Post* entitled, "Can Basketball Survive Chamberlain?"

Basketball had had big men before. In the early fifties, George Mikan, the six-foot-ten-inch center of the Minneapolis Lakers, had dominated the game. But Mikan was a lurching, graceless man who wore metal-rimmed glasses and lumbered up and down the court, bashing aside opponents with his huge left arm. Chamberlain was more than seven feet tall and wore size fourteen-and-a-half shoes, but he was also quick, agile, strong, and smart. His legs were so long that he seemed part gazelle. And they were so powerful that when he leaped up, arms raised, toward the backboard, his hands at the apex of his jump were three feet above the rim, which he could look down into. He was so good that not only did no one seem to be able to beat him, few people seemed actually capable of playing against him.

Except maybe Bill Russell. Russell had led the Celtics to two championships since joining the team three years earlier. Never much of a shooter, Russell had nonetheless perfected a style of defensive play, blocking shots and rebounding ferociously by leaping so high into the air that he seemed to hang there in suspension. His size and athleticism had literally transformed professional basketball. Prior to Russell joining the National Basketball Association, the game had consisted of little more than men running up and down the court making layups. But because Russell blocked layups so effectively, players had been forced to create a wider range of offensive plays, passing back and forth and setting screens until one of them could make a mid-range jump shot. The game immediately became more complex, varied, and challenging for the players and more involving and fun to watch for the spectators, and the late fifties became known as the Russell Era.

But now, with Chamberlain in the league, sportswriters were wondering if the Russell Era was coming to an end, if the defensive style of play Russell personified would yield to the singularly muscular offensive style of Wilt Chamberlain, whose fadeaway jump shot was almost impossible to defend against and who amazed fans by leaping up to the rim, taking a pass over the outstretched hands of the defending team, and then, still rising into his jump, actually shoving the ball down into the basket. It was a feat so startling, requiring such a rare combination of timing, grace, and strength, that it seemed to have more to do with acrobatics than with basketball. Until then, the sport had been thought of as a game played well below the net. Now it was becoming a game played in the air.

Russell, sitting in the Celtics locker room before the game, had read the articles musing about an end of an era—his era, even though he was only twenty-six—and he wondered if they were true. Russell had eaten a steak that afternoon and then played cards with his teammates Maurice King and K. C. Jones, who had also been his teammate on the University of San Francisco Dons when he led it to two NCAA championships. Russell always got nervous before a game, so nervous that he routinely threw up. Night after night, sixty or seventy times a season, he was in the head before the game tossing the remains of his lunch. In fact, he did it with such regularity that to his teammates it became a ritualistic sign of good luck. If Russell wasn't in there puking, they got worried.

But on this night Russell was more nervous than usual, even after the obligatory trip to the head. Russell was tall, six-ten, but Chamberlain had three or four inches on him; Russell didn't know exactly how many inches, because while Chamberlain was officially listed at seven feet one and one-sixteenth inches, he also claimed that no one had measured him since he was in high school. Also, Russell knew, Chamberlain was a good forty to fifty pounds heavier than he was. He could jump just as high and he was just as quick up and down the court.

And Chamberlain was smart. Russell considered himself one of the most serious students and analysts of basketball ever to play the game. While at San Francisco, he had thought so systematically about the game's physics and geometry—the trajectories the ball drew between the horizontal plane of the court and the vertical planes of the backboards, the thrust of a 240-pound body hurtling at you at twenty miles an hour and the dynamics of deflecting that thrust—that he thought of himself as a scientist in sneakers. But Russell knew Chamberlain was just as smart as he was. The sportswriters were saying Chamberlain was even smarter. Russell wondered if tonight he was going to be outplayed and outthought by rookie Wilton Norman Chamberlain.

People had been feeding Russell information about Chamberlain for weeks: his moves and shots—particularly his fadeaway jumper—what worked against him, what didn't, how close to guard him. Prepared as he was, Russell still felt unprepared because Chamberlain, from what so many people were saying, sounded simply unstoppable, a man who was going to get his thirty points regardless of what you did. Russell decided one thing: he would not look up at Chamberlain. Russell was used to being the tallest person in the room or on the court, and there was nothing that a tall person, accustomed to looking down at everyone, found more intimidating than to come face-to-face with someone who was even taller.

Chamberlain had spent the afternoon before the game sprawled diagonally across two beds he'd pushed together in the Hotel Lenox, trying to rest. Basketball fans had learned where he was staying, and a small crowd of them badgered him for autographs when he emerged from the hotel in the early evening. After obliging, he caught a taxi to Boston Garden. Now, sitting in the cramped and overheated visitors' locker room with the rest of the Warriors, he was nervous as well. His transition into the pros had been more difficult than he'd thought it would be, given his commanding abilities and all the press he'd received. Pro ball was more violent than college ball, for one thing. He'd been elbowed in the mouth by Willie Naulls in a game against the Knicks. And Naulls had chased him up and down the court trying to tear off the rubber band he always wore on his wrist. It was like the guy was out to get him, like there was something *personal* going on. Also, Chamberlain had played exhibition ball with the Harlem Globetrotters for a year before turning pro, and since the actual games the Trotters played were little more than jokey pretexts for various basketball stunts, he'd picked up a few bad habits such as clowning around and walking with the ball.

But he was adjusting. A bigger problem for Chamberlain going into the game that night against the Celtics was that although he was surrounded by some good players such as Paul Arizin and Guy Rogers, the Warriors lacked Boston's overall talent. That meant that while Bill Russell could stick to rebounding and rely on Bob Cousy and Bill Sharman to score, Chamberlain would have to play both defense and offense. He'd managed to do this so far against other teams, and the Warriors had won their first three games of the season. But he wondered if he'd live up to all the advance billing, if he could hold his own against the greatest defensive player in the league.

The Celtics fans, overwhelmingly white and working-class, had tended to have conflicting feelings toward Bill Russell, their enthusiasm for him as an athlete undercut by their resentment at the fact that not only was the team dominated by a black man, but he was aloof in manner and from time to time gave voice to his indignation over his country's—and Boston's—racial inequities. As a result, the crowd tended to reserve its affection for Bob Cousy, the talented local boy who'd come from Holy Cross and was one of the best ball handlers in the league. But on this night, as the announcer introduced Russell to the almost 14,000 fans in the Garden, the applause, in anticipation of the matchup with Chamberlain, was thunderous. The Tall Man, as some sportswriters had taken to calling him, was finally getting a little appreciation in his adopted hometown.

In mid-court before the tip-off, Russell and Chamberlain shook hands. Russell, unable to help himself, broke his vow not to look at Chamberlain and glanced up. The man was *tall*. Ever since joining the league two and a half years ago, Russell had been able to do pretty much what he had wanted to do on the court. Now he was facing a man who not only towered over him but could jump and dunk, had huge hands and the strength of a wrestler, and knew how to rebound and could also hit from the outside. In fact, Chamberlain went up so high when he took that outside jumper of his that it was more or less impossible to prevent the shot. How, Russell wondered, was he supposed to play him?

The referee tossed the ball into the air and they both leaped. Russell, finding that he was quicker on his feet, went into the air first and got the tip-off. After that, the game quickly turned into a matchup between Russell and Chamberlain, almost as if it were a form of single combat. For the sportswriters sitting courtside, it was an amazing sight to behold. Those who had watched Russell and Chamberlain play individually before had never seen either man seriously challenged for control of the ball. But tonight was different. It was as if only now had each of them found an opponent worthy of his own talent, for each appeared to be forcing the other to work harder, to stretch further, to demand more of himself.

It seemed that every time Chamberlain rose up in the air to launch his fadeaway jump shot, Russell rose up with him, his arm reaching up and out and over Chamberlain, requiring Chamberlain to try to go even higher. At the apex of their leaps, with their arms raised, the two men were more than twelve feet in the air, towering above the people sitting courtside and moving together in what seemed almost like a form of ballet. Jimmy Breslin, it was clear, had it all wrong with his notion that Wilt Chamberlain somehow represented the end of basketball. What the sportswriters were seeing that night seemed more like the beginning of basketball, the discovery of infinite new possibilities—for drama, for maneuvers and combinations, for nakedly awesome athleticism—in a sport that until then had failed to inspire much public excitement.

All in all, Chamberlain took thirty-eight shots, but he scored only four baskets when paired man-to-man with Russell. Once—and this shocked the sportswriters and electrified the fans—Chamberlain leaped up to make a fadeaway jumper and Russell leaped up so much higher that he was actually able to block the shot of the taller man, reaching out with his hand and swatting down the ball. Chamberlain scored twenty-two points on tip-ins and dunk shots, but Russell had him so frustrated that in the second half he resorted to hook shots, a maneuver he had scorned since college as a disgracefully amateurish junk move. He looked awkward shooting them, standing flat-footed on the floor, tossing the ball over the side of his head, and every single one of those hook shots missed.

While Chamberlain ended up scoring more points than anyone else in the game—thirty to Russell's twenty-two—Boston won 115–106. When it was over, the Garden erupted. To Russell, standing on the court, the crowd's emotion was so powerful that the arena felt as if it were shaking. Far from Chamberlain making him irrelevant, Russell thought, his opponent had instead forced him, or inspired him, to play better basketball than he'd ever played before. He had a feeling that this could get interesting.

Red Auerbach, the Celtics coach, was sitting on the bench, and as the game drew to a close, he pulled out a cigar. Auerbach had first seen Chamberlain play back in 1953, when Wilt was still in high school, and Auerbach had become convinced even then that Wilt was going to be one of the best basketball players the game had ever seen, possibly the very best. But even before Wilt's rookie season began, the sportswriters had been acting as if it was a foregone conclusion that he and the Warriors would overrun every other team in the league. Auerbach had disagreed. His strategy going into the game that night had been to let Chamberlain get his thirty or forty points but to make sure that the Celtics smothered the rest of the Warriors, and it had worked. None of Chamberlain's teammates had ever really gotten into the game.

Auerbach removed the cigar's cellophane wrapping, pulled out his lighter, and fired it up. He puffed, smoke drifting upward, and then exhaled with an air of self-satisfaction. Auerbach smoked eight to ten cigars a day, but this one was always different, for this was the notorious Victory Cigar, the one he ceremonially lit once his team had put the game away, the one that drove opposing coaches mad with distraction, the one that seemed the ultimate embodiment of what they regarded as the man's unbearable arrogance. Auerbach was a stout, balding man with dark rings around his eyes and a cauliflower nose. He had a family, but his wife and two daughters lived in suburban Washington, D.C., while during the basketball season he stayed at the Hotel Lenox, in Boston's Back Bay. He rationalized this arrangement by saying that he traveled so much and worked such long hours during the season that he would have seen little of his family if they had moved to Boston. He always added that one of his daughters had asthma that would have made it difficult for her to live in Boston. But Boston's brisk sea air was much better for asthma than Washington's humid, pollen-thick climate, and some of the people who'd had exposure to Auerbach's frequently crude, obstreperous, primitive, intimidating personality believed it was a toss-up as to whether he couldn't stand to have his family around during the season or whether his family couldn't stand to be around him.

During games, Auerbach wore a dark suit or loud plaid sport coat and carried a rolled-up program in his left hand. His right hand was usually cupped around his wide-open mouth as he shouted in disgusted disbelief at the benighted officials. When a call particularly outraged him, he rose from the bench and raced along the sidelines shouting or ran onto the court and up to the offending official, thrust his face forward until they were standing nose to nose, arguing so heatedly it was almost impossible for the official to get a word in. He was, referees and rival coaches agreed, obnoxiousness personified. "He incites a murderous rage when he takes his place on the bench," one sportswriter declared. "When I first met Auerbach, I disliked him," an unnamed coach once told a reporter for the *Boston Record*. "But gradually it grew to hate."

One reason other coaches hated Auerbach was that he was becoming so successful. In the fall of 1959 he had won two NBA championships in the past three years. By the time he retired, in 1966, he had won seven more, a record unmatched by any professional team coach in any sport.* But Auerbach also had the improbable distinction of being one of professional basketball's most significant social pioneers. That first game between Bill Russell and Wilt Chamberlain was played just weeks before the dawn of what John Kennedy, in the upcoming presidential campaign, would call "the challenging, revolutionary sixties." At the time, the greatest turbulence in the country centered around race relations. Black migration out of the rural South had continued strong since the end of World War II, and the 1960 census found that in Washington, D.C., blacks for the first time had become a majority in a large American city. But segregation remained the rule throughout the Deep South, and in April 1959, seven months before the game, the most notorious lynching since the murder of Emmett Till took place when a group of hooded men kidnapped Mack Parker, the black suspect in the rape of a white woman, from a jail in Mississippi and left his mutilated body in the Pearl River.

As the civil rights movement gathered momentum in the early and midsixties, basketball, more than any other major sport, would find itself caught

*In 2002, Phil Jackson won his ninth championship as a coach, tying Auerbach's record, but he had done so with two teams, the Chicago Bulls and the Los Angeles Lakers.

up in the issue of race. Its integration was more sudden and complete than in football or baseball. Within a few short years after Chamberlain's arrival, four of the top five players in the league—Chamberlain, Russell, Elgin Baylor, and Oscar Robertson—were black. They became wealthy celebrities and, whether they liked it or not, role models. While the NBA in general integrated more quickly than any other team sport in the country, the Celtics set the pace within the league. They were the first team to field a majority of black players, the first to field an all-black team, and the first team in any major-league sport to hire a black coach. These developments were greeted with incredulity, skepticism, and outright resistance from some fans and sportswriters in the racially torn city of Boston, but they contributed to the Celtics' dominance of the NBA during the 1960s. While Auerbach was responsible for them, he was motivated not by any sense of social mission—he was so apolitical that he never even bothered to vote—but instead by a simple ruthless calculation in his desire to win. *Whatever it takes.*

ARNOLD AUERBACH grew up in Brooklyn's Williamsburg section, a thriving immigrant neighborhood of Poles, Ukrainians, Italians, and Eastern European Jews who lived in wood-shingled row houses—destroyed during the thirties in the federal government's first slum-clearing project—and worked in the sugar refineries, breweries, soda bottling plants, and kosher food factories on the East River waterfront. In Brooklyn in the twenties, just about everyone had a nickname. Auerbach's father, Hyman, a Russian immigrant from Minsk who owned a delicatessen and later operated a dry-cleaning establishment, was known as Hymie. Arnold Auerbach had red hair, and from an early age his inevitable street moniker was Red. In addition to providing him with the nickname by which he would be known long after he turned balding and gray, the rough, noisy, exuberant streets of Brooklyn stamped themselves on his personality. The borough forced boys to become tough and fearless and scrappy, to learn to work hard but also to take chances, to play the angles, and to appreciate the value of intimidation as a survival tool.

Red and his friends hustled for nickels by cleaning the windows of the cars that stopped at Williamsburg gas stations. They strapped on roller skates and grabbed the fenders of trolley cars, which pulled them through the streets. They sneaked into the movie palaces on Atlantic Avenue to watch

Gloria Swanson and Buster Keaton and into Ebbets Field to watch the Dodgers. But while rooting for center fielder Dixie Walker, known throughout the borough as "Da People's Cherce," Red Auerbach played little baseball because neighborhoods such as Williamsburg lacked the open space for fields. The games of choice in Williamsburg were punchball, handball, stickball, and basketball. Basketball had been invented less than three decades earlier, but because it was uncomplicated and fast-paced and could be played just about anywhere, it had proved wildly popular in schools and colleges around the country. In Brooklyn it was played on the black-tar rooftops of apartment buildings by the Irish, the Germans, the Italians, and the Jews— the inner-city ethnic groups of the times. The game, the *American Hebrew* observed, "requires a good deal of quick thinking, lightning-like rapidity of movement, and endurance; it does not call for brutality and brute strength."

At the Eastern District High School, Red made the varsity basketball team, and while he was neither tall, at five feet nine, nor particularly quick, he nonetheless played the game harder than anyone else—getting into fights, pushing and shoving, struggling for control of the ball—and consequently became the first boy from Eastern District High to be listed by sportswriter Lester Bromberg in the *New York World-Telegram*'s Schoolboy Hall of Fame. Even so, only one institution of higher learning offered Auerbach a scholarship: Seth Low Junior College, a Brooklyn branch of Columbia University so small that its 175 students did not even have their own campus. Seth Low's classes were taught in the Brooklyn Law School, and the basketball team played in the gym of the nearby Plymouth Church.

Gordon Ridings, the basketball coach at Seth Low, had gone to college at the University of Oregon, where he played under coach Bill Reinhart, who had just been hired to be the basketball coach at George Washington University. In the winter of Auerbach's freshman year, the George Washington team came up to New York to play Long Island University, and Ridings invited Reinhart and his players to take on tiny Seth Low in an informal scrimmage match in the Plymouth Church gym. George Washington overwhelmed Seth Low, but Auerbach played as if his team actually had a chance. In fact, his tough, aggressive but also smart moves—blocking, setting picks, using his elbows—made such an impression on Bill Reinhart that the coach, thinking Auerbach might bring some hard-edged city tactics to the simple run-and-shoot game favored by his players, offered him a scholarship to come to George Washington.

Some athletes and leaders are at an early age clearly destined for greatness. Red Auerbach at eighteen—the son of a dry cleaner, boisterous and quick with his fists but neither academically nor athletically distinguished—was not one of them. "He wasn't much as a player," recalled Moe Goldman, who played professional basketball in the thirties and who knew Auerbach from Eastern District High School. "He was lucky a lot of times." Indeed, if Bill Reinhart had not, as a favor to Gordon Ridings, allowed his team to play that scrimmage match at Plymouth Church, Auerbach might well have remained in Brooklyn all his life as a high school phys ed instructor, his ambition at the time. That he eventually became one of the greatest professional coaches in mid-century America owed more than a little to that chance encounter with Reinhart. The life of Auerbach's greatest player, Bill Russell, turned on a similarly fateful minor moment, and this gave both men a ferocious determination to fight to keep what chance had granted them—a determination that was missing in many men who, at the same point in their lives, were much more obviously talented.

WHILE NEVER a top-tier school, George Washington from time to time beat teams from much larger schools such as Ohio State, and in Auerbach's senior year he was made team captain. After graduating, he married the daughter of a local pediatrician, worked for two years as a high school teacher and coach, then joined the navy during World War II. He remained stateside, at the naval base in Norfolk, Virginia, and after the war, he prepared to return to his old job. A comfortable ,if utterly conventional and anonymous life seemed to stretch out before him. Then in the spring of 1946, Auerbach read a newspaper article about a meeting to be held in New York at the Hotel Commodore by Ned Irish, the general manager of Madison Square Garden. For a second time, chance was going to allow Auerbach an opportunity to change his life, if he had the audacity.

The Saturday Evening Post once called Ned Irish "Basketball's Big Wheel." Like Auerbach, Irish—the game's first truly successful promoter—was a man alert to opportunity. In 1933, while covering a basketball game at Manhattan College as a junior sports reporter for the *New York World-Telegram,* he found the doors to the small gym shut. He was forced to climb through a window, and in the process tore a hole in his suit pants. This convinced him that college basketball games needed larger venues, and the following year he persuaded the directors of Madison Square Garden to grant him the concession for college basketball by promising them a percentage of the gate, with a minimum of $4,000 a game. He didn't have to put up a cent of his own money; it was the middle of the Depression and on many nights the Garden was dark.

Basketball games rarely ran longer than ninety minutes, which did not strike most spectators as a satisfying return on their dollar, and so Irish came up with the idea of offering doubleheaders: four teams playing two games back-to-back for the price of one ticket. His first event, with a highlight game between New York University and Notre Dame, easily exceeded the $4,000 target, and Irish himself, who had been making forty-eight dollars a week at the *World-Telegram,* personally took home $1,100. By the end of the year, Irish had arranged eight doubleheaders that overall had drawn 99,528 paying fans. The idea caught on throughout the east, with dozens of college teams traveling a circuit of big-city arenas, and Irish soon was named executive vice president of Madison Square Garden, where he still owned the basketball concession. The hustling young newshound had been transformed into a haughty, calculating executive; it was said of him that he could move the Empire State Building if he thought there was a loose buck under it.

The meeting Irish organized at the Hotel Commodore took place nine months after the Japanese surrender aboard the U.S.S. *Missouri* officially ended World War II. Veterans were streaming home—245,000 a month from the navy alone—in search of work and diversion. At the time, baseball was the sport that mesmerized Americans. Stadium crowds had more than doubled since the beginning of World War II; the Yankees were drawing more than two million home spectators a season. But Ned Irish had made college basketball a large draw, and Max Kase, sports editor of the *Journal-American,* the largest afternoon newspaper in New York, had become convinced that professional basketball could prove just as successful. Kase had talked to the owners of several large arenas about starting a professional league. The Depression and the war had created a long stretch of lean years for the arena owners. With the war over, attendance was rising, but the no-strike agreements made by labor unions during the war were also over, and strikes were breaking out around the country; just the previous month, Harry Truman had signed an executive order seizing the railroads when a strike by rail workers threatened to cripple the country. The unions that had contracts with the arenas were demanding substantial raises, and Max Kase had argued that a professional basketball league could provide a new source of revenue to the arena owners without incurring a substantial new investment.

The country's first pro league, the American Basketball League, had been started in 1925, during the first great American sports explosion, with teams such as the New York Gothams and the Original Celtics, but it folded in the early years of the Depression. In 1937 the National Basketball League was formed, primarily in the Midwest, where companies such as Firestone and Goodyear and General Electric sponsored teams in their hometowns of Akron and Fort Wayne. The league, organized by promoters, limped along for years, but it lacked facilities and sports editors generally ignored it, and as a result it never developed much of a following.

The men meeting at the Hotel Commodore, by contrast, were arena owners, with connections to sports editors due to the hockey teams most of them owned and the horse shows, bicycle races, and boxing matches they booked. Their arenas were much larger than the ones in which the National Basketball League played, and since they were in bigger cities than the cities that were home to the NBL teams, they had the opportunity of drawing larger crowds. It seemed all upside. Max Kase had hoped to start the New York franchise himself and rent out Madison Square Garden, but Irish informed him that the Garden Corporation would need to own the team, and Kase had to be satisfied with a cash payment of several thousand dollars for his efforts to found the league. At the meeting, the owners drew up bylaws and established rules for the Basketball Association of America (BAA), named a commissioner, and created charter franchises in eleven cities.

When Red Auerbach read about the formation of the BAA, he thought it might actually work. The audience was there. After all, really good college players attracted passionate followings. But once they graduated there was no real league for them and so they vanished. Pro basketball for the previous twenty-odd years had been pretty lame, in Auerbach's view, but that was because it had been handled badly: bush teams playing in bush towns in a bush league. Handled correctly, it had genuine potential.

Auerbach's wife had just had a baby, but he was, at twenty-eight, still young. He could play it safe and remain a high school coach for the rest of his life, or he could take a gamble, try to get in on this new league at its launch, and see where—and how far—it would take him. Auerbach's father, who'd left Minsk at the age of thirteen and arrived in New York unable to speak English, was a man who understood that it was impossible to get ahead in the world without taking a chance, and so was his son. Despite the fact that he'd never played professional ball, coached a college team, or developed any sort of national reputation as a college player, Auerbach approached Mike Uline, the owner of the Washington Arena and one of the men at the meeting at the Hotel Commodore, and proposed himself as the coach for Uline's new team, the Washington Capitols.

Auerbach made his case to Uline by giving him a singular analysis of the state of basketball at the time and how he could exploit it to put together a winning team. Since the sport was intrinsically improvisational, and since television, then in its infancy, had yet to create a national audience with common expectations of how it should be played, the game of basketball had, in the five decades of its existence, evolved distinct regional differences. One outstanding player influenced how everyone else in town played. One forceful coach imprinted all the good players of one state with a certain style, and they passed it on to the kids they coached. As a result, for example, Midwesterners emphasized a running game while New Yorkers focused on perimeter set shots. Most of the professional teams being put together in the summer of 1946 hoped to capitalize on the popularity of local college players by drafting and featuring them. As a result, those teams would inevitably lean heavily on the prevailing local style of play.

However, Auerbach told Mike Uline that what no one seemed to understand was that the way to build a winning team was by hiring players from all regions of the country, each bringing with him the special skills that his region emphasized. Auerbach explained to Uline that he had firsthand experience of how successful such a team could be. While in the navy, he had been a chief petty officer in charge of recreation at the naval station in Norfolk, where he ran an intramural sports program and consequently got to know basketball players from around the country. Those men were now all being discharged and were in need of jobs. If he became coach, Auerbach told Uline, he could put together a talented, inexpensive team from that pool of ex-navy men, fielding backcourt players from New York, runners from the Midwest, rebounders from California. Most of the other franchise owners were hiring college coaches; Ned Irish brought in Neil Cohalan from Manhattan College to run his new team, the Knickerbockers; the Chicago investors signed Harold Olsen from Ohio State. But Mike Uline, an innovative

Dutchman who'd made his fortune patenting various types of ice-making machinery, liked Auerbach's idea and offered him a one-year contract for $5,000.

Going into his first season, Auerbach knew that no one had ever heard of him, that he had no reputation to speak of, and he was afraid the referees and the name coaches such as Cohalan and Olsen would dismiss him as nothing more than an overpromoted lightweight high school coach. He also wanted to establish his authority over his own players, since most of them were his age or older, and all of them were better basketball players than he'd ever been. "If you get obnoxious you build incentive," he once told one of his players. And so he turned himself into a courtside presence that everyone in the league would be forced to contend with. During games he did not so much feign rage as he allowed it to engulf him. He pounded his fists together so angrily that his knuckles became swollen, and so he began rolling up a program before each game and using it to smack his hand. He snarled at the opposing team's fans, shook his fist, sighed, waved his cigar, smacked his hand with his rolled-up program. He hated hearing the word *why* from his players—*Why'd you take me out?*—and none of them were allowed to question or ask for an explanation for any of his decisions. He protested virtually every call made against his team, storming over to the official in question, tapping cigar ashes on the man's shoes, and flecking his face with spittle as he shouted at him. He wanted to keep officials off balance and doubting themselves in the hope that, in the crucial closing minutes of the game, they might hesitate to rule against his team. And so he never gave ground, acting on the assumption that he was always right and everyone else was always wrong. He wanted it understood throughout the league that no one was going to hose Auerbach.

Auerbach's methods produced results. In their first year, the Capitols ran up a seventeen-game winning streak and had a record of 49–11, a winning percentage that would remain a record for twenty years. But, in what would come to be another signature Auerbach statistic, the Capitols also led the league in defense, becoming the team with the fewest points allowed. Auerbach produced two more winning seasons with the Capitols, ending up in the playoffs each year and making it to the finals in the third, where his team lost to the Minneapolis Lakers in six games.

Nonetheless, the Washington Capitols were barely afloat financially, and in the three years since its inception, the entire league had been floundering.

Four teams lasted only one season. None of the owners wanted to spend money on those that survived. Many early games were played on wooden floorboards laid over hockey ice; puddles formed on the court and the shivering players sitting on the bench wrapped themselves in blankets. Attendance was sparse. The audiences that did show up, accustomed to wrestling and boxing and hockey, expected some blood with their sport, and the early players, many of them brawling World War II veterans, were happy to comply. In one 1949 game between New York and the new Baltimore franchise, one hundred personal fouls were called and three bloody fistfights broke out on the court. In 1949, the National Basketball League collapsed altogether, and its five surviving franchises linked up with the BAA, which then changed its name to the National Basketball Association.

That same summer, Auerbach asked Mike Uline for a three-year contract. Some of the players, unhappy with Auerbach's hard style, had tried to persuade Uline to get rid of him, and Auerbach felt a three-year contract would establish his absolute authority. But Uline, afraid that his money-losing team might not last three years (and indeed it didn't), refused, and Auerbach quit. After a brief hiatus as an assistant coach at Duke University, Auerbach was hired by Ben Kerner, the owner of the Tri-Cities Blackhawks. "I'll give these customers a real show if you'll pay the fines," Auerbach told Kerner upon his arrival.

He also completely rebuilt the Blackhawks, making more than two dozen trades. By the end of the season only three of the original players remained, but the Blackhawks made it into the playoffs. Kerner had publicly promised Auerbach complete autonomy at the beginning of the season, but then in the spring, over Auerbach's objections, he traded John Mahnken, who'd played for Auerbach on the Caps, for Boston forward Gene Englund. Auerbach felt there was no point in being a coach unless he had total independence. Without it, he thought, his job would consist primarily of toadying up to the owner. There were coaches like that in the league, coaches who spent most of their time trying to placate the owner and anticipating his desires, but Auerbach had no interest in becoming one of them. When the season was over—the Blackhawks lost to the Anderson Packers in the playoffs—Auerbach told Kerner he was quitting. He had no immediate prospects. He had failed to get along with the two professional owners he'd worked for. But he had established a reputation as a coach who could win, and he was thinking he might return to college basketball, where he would at least enjoy the independence that had eluded him in the pros. And then, for the third time in his life, a critical opportunity presented itself.

THE BOSTON CELTICS had not made it into the playoffs that year. They had in fact finished in last place in the Eastern Division, and their coach, Alvin "Doggie" Julian, felt discouraged. Julian had a reputation as one of the best basketball coaches in the country, but that reputation had been made on the college level, when he won an NCAA title during his tenure at Holy Cross College. He had never been able to adjust his tactics to the aggressive pivot style of play that predominated in pro ball, and the NBA's grueling travel left him exhausted. Though he had one more year left on his contract with the Celtics, Dartmouth College had approached him about becoming its basketball coach, and he was inclined to accept. At the Celtics' breakup dinner on March 17, 1950, he turned to Walter Brown, the team's owner. "Walter, I think you better get yourself a new coach," he said. "Somebody else could probably do a better job, because I know I have made quite a few mistakes this year."

"Doggie, I'll repeat here what I've said so many times before," replied Brown, who was unaware that Julian was in discussions with Dartmouth. "As long as I have anything to do with the Celtics, you're going to be the coach."

But after thinking it through over the weekend, Julian told Brown the following Monday that he was quitting. The news dismayed and irritated Brown, who felt that a man he trusted had abandoned him, and now, with the college draft only a month away, he had to scramble around to find yet another coach. Brown's real passion being hockey, he didn't follow basketball closely, and had little idea of who might replace Julian. But he had the natural salesman's gift for seeing the promotional potential even in adversity. After Julian's departure was announced, he told Howie McHugh, the public relations man for the Celtics, to call some of the local sports reporters and invite them down to the Garden for a meeting. Brown wanted advice on whom he should hire to replace Julian. He also wanted a photographer present to record the event and provide a publicity boost in the wake of the dispiriting announcement of Julian's departure. McHugh called ten men: the *Patriot-Ledger*'s Roger Barry; Sam Brogna of the *Record;* Jack Conway, Jr., of the *Boston-American;* Joe Kelley of the Associated Press; Joe Looney of the

Herald; and the radio reporters Leo Egan, Jack Malloy, Red Marston, Les Smith, and Dinny Whitmarsh.

It was, even by the standards of the time, a surprising invitation. Joe Looney, the *Herald*'s dapper basketball reporter, considered it practically unprecedented. But no one regarded it as a conflict of interest. Sportswriters had a much more openly collaborative attitude toward owners then. Both the reporters and the owners understood that they were in the business of manufacturing excitement for fans. Owners, eager for coverage of teams, often paid for the travel expenses of reporters and provided other favors that in a later day would be regarded as outrageously unethical. The reporters, for their part, naturally favored the hometown franchises and some actually moonlighted for the teams they covered. At the time, it was seen as simple reciprocity.

Brown told the reporters the session needed to be off the record since they would be discussing coaches still under contract to other teams. He then explained that he could not afford another losing season. The Celtics had now gone through two coaches in four years. Julian's predecessor, John "Honey" Russell, had also been a college coach, at Seton Hall. Both Julian and Russell had been unable to duplicate their college success on the professional level, and Brown had no intention of making that mistake yet again. College coaches were ruled out. Nor could he afford to hire an untested coach who, like Julian, might prove not to have the stomach for the job. He needed to hire a coach with an established track record in the pros.

Some of the reporters suggested Art Spector, a Celtics player who'd been with the team since its formation four years earlier. But the problem with Spector was that, while he was a respected player, he had no coaching experience. Other reporters proposed Buddy Jeannette, a former coach of the Baltimore Bullets known for his colorful character. Roger Barry of the *Patriot-Ledger* suggested Red Auerbach. From his seat at the press table of the Garden, Barry was right next to the visitors' bench, and he'd had a good opportunity to watch Auerbach in action when the Washington Capitols had come to Boston. During one game Barry had covered, the Capitols had come back from a twenty-point deficit to win. The other reporters recalled similar experiences watching Auerbach's teams. The one thing about them, the reporters agreed, was that they never gave up.

The photograph of the meeting, captioned "Walter Brown and his Ten-Man Advisory Committee," appeared in the *Herald* the following day. But before Brown could determine whether or not he should try to pursue Auerbach or look for another coach, an even more critical problem cropped up, one that threatened the very survival of the Celtics. The team was owned by the Garden-Arena Corporation, which Brown managed but did not control. The corporation's directors had supported the decision to start the team four years ago, but in 1948, after two years of losses totaling $250,000, they had threatened to fold the team unless Brown could produce a "gimmick." The gimmick Brown had produced had been Doggie Julian, whose Holy Cross teams had sold out the Garden several times. Now, with Julian gone and the Garden's four-year losses reaching $460,000, the directors felt they could not keep throwing good money after bad. They had voted to fold the Celtics. Although the Celtics had not had a single winning season in their four-year existence, Brown was convinced the team would ultimately prove a financial success if it could only begin to win, and he decided to buy it himself from the Garden. It was a surprising act of faith considering that for many years Brown had thought that the idea of a professional basketball team in Boston was ludicrous.

Walter Brown was a big man, broad in the shoulders, ruddy in the cheeks, with a double chin and the bright blue eyes of his Irish forebears. He loved scotch, was quick to anger and quick to forgive, and could shrewdly take the measure of a man. His father, George V. Brown, had been one of the country's original sports businessmen, attending the first modern Olympic Games in Athens in 1896 and becoming so taken with the marathon that when he returned home to Boston he organized the Boston Marathon. For more than thirty years it was George Brown who fired the starting pistol that sent the runners on their way. George Brown was also the general manager of the Boston Arena, the city's primary indoor sports facility in the twenties, and his son Walter grew up around the place and fell in love with the sights, sounds, and raffish electricity of arena life. He played in the corridors as a child, saw the boxers and ice skaters and circus performers, inhaled the smells of sawdust and horse manure. He worked for his father taking tickets, painting seats, and writing programs. In the late twenties, the owners of Madison Square Garden in New York built the Boston Garden, but ticket sales dwindled during the Depression and in 1934 Boston's Arena Corporation acquired it and George Brown took over its management. At the age of twenty-eight, Walter Brown was made an assistant manager of the Garden, and when his father died, in 1939, he succeeded him as general manager.

At the time, Ned Irish, manager of Madison Square Garden, had become extraordinarily wealthy booking college basketball games into his arena, but Brown resisted imitating him. The way Brown saw it, Boston was a hockey town, not a basketball town. The local public high schools had stopped playing basketball in the twenties and didn't renew their programs until the late forties, which meant the city had little to offer in the way of local talent. When Arthur Sampson of the *Boston Herald* asked Brown why he didn't promote basketball, Brown replied, "I don't know anything about basketball, but it looks like a silly game to me. We can't afford to put on events that nobody will look at—and nobody watches basketball in New England."

But once Holy Cross became a nationally ranked team and began selling out Boston Garden when it played there, Brown recognized basketball's potential, and he had become one of the most enthusiastic supporters of a new professional league. But now, in 1950, many investors considered the idea a folly. The same month that the directors of Garden-Arena Corporation informed Brown that the company could no longer support the Celtics, four other teams—the Denver Nuggets, the Sheboygan (Wisconsin) Redskins, the Anderson (Indiana) Packers, and the Waterloo (Iowa) Hawks—all folded.

To cover the Celtics' ongoing losses, Brown took out a mortgage on his home and, with that and other loans, raised $200,000. Brown's wife, Marjorie, and many of his friends thought he was making a terrible mistake. "Walter, what's going to happen to us if it's all lost?" she asked him one day that year. But despite his wife's fears, Brown was willing to gamble everything he owned on the proposition that the Celtics could become commercially viable. He was motivated in part by Irish stubbornness and pride, but also by a simple love of the game and, most important, an instinctive feel—honed by the thousands of hours spent in the seats and behind the ticket window studying fans—for what brought out the crowds.

The directors of the company, aware of Brown's limited resources and hoping to help him avoid bankruptcy, had agreed to give him the team only on the condition that he find a partner to help him sustain the business through the inevitable short-term losses. Looking for leads on possible investors, Brown drove down to Providence, Rhode Island, to see a friend named Lou Pieri, owner of the Rhode Island Auditorium. Pieri was a short, corpulent Italian American who wore double-breasted suits and parted his slicked-back hair in the middle. He had owned a basketball franchise, the

Providence Steamrollers, before folding it in 1949 when it had compiled one of the worst win-loss records in the league and run up losses totaling $200,000.

Pieri surprised Brown by offering to invest $50,000 in the Celtics himself.

"Are you kidding me?" Brown asked. "You're the last man I thought would want back in after the losses you suffered."

"No," Pieri said. "I'm still sold on the game."

While Pieri believed in the future of professional basketball, he was convinced the Celtics needed to become a winning team in the next season in order to survive, and so he said he had one condition: that Brown hire Auerbach as coach. Pieri had met Auerbach a year earlier when looking for a coach for the Steamrollers. Auerbach had told Pieri that the team would have to be completely rebuilt, that it would take at least two years and that it would cost $400,000. Pieri decided instead to fold the team, but he appreciated Auerbach's brutal candor. "Get Red Auerbach as your coach," he told Brown, "and I'm your partner."

WALTER BROWN liked a man with a direct manner, and he took to Auerbach immediately. Auerbach was blunt, candid, and forceful, had coached both the Capitols and the Blackhawks to the playoffs, and in doing so had demonstrated that he could handle veteran players and withstand the rigors of the schedule. Brown saw no reason even to interview anyone else. Auerbach was as happy as Brown. He'd be living in a big East Coast city rather than a small prairie town, and he'd be much closer to his family. Most important, Brown, who professed his own ignorance of basketball, guaranteed him complete autonomy, and Brown was a man known for keeping his word.

As he'd done with Capitols owner Mike Uline, Auerbach asked for a three-year contract. Brown, like Uline, told Auerbach that this was out of the question. The team might fold in a year if it continued to lose money at its current rate. The most Brown said he could offer was $10,000 to coach the team for one year. "All I can promise you is you'll be treated fairly and I'll back you all the way," Brown said. "If we're still in business next year, we can talk about raises then. That's the picture. What do you say?" Auerbach agreed to Brown's terms, and the two shook hands. "How the hell can you say no to a man like that?" Auerbach would ask later.

Even before Auerbach's hiring was officially announced, he had to oversee Boston's picks in the 1950 college draft. Since the conventional wisdom among the pro teams was that the way to build a local following was to recruit the top local college players, most fans and sportswriters in New England assumed Auerbach would draft Bob Cousy, the region's most promising eligible player. For the past four years, Cousy had played for Holy Cross in Worcester, thirty-five miles from Boston. The team had made it into the NCAA national tournament three times in those four years, winning the championship in 1947, largely due to Cousy's talents.

Walter Brown also assumed that the Celtics should draft Cousy, but Auerbach disagreed with the notion that the best way to draw fans was to feature local favorites. After all, he pointed out to Brown, the Celtics had been recruiting hometown heroes for the last five years—Saul Mariaschin and Wyndol Gray from Harvard, Ed Leede from Dartmouth—and none of them had boosted attendance. Also, Auerbach had watched Cousy in action, in a game between the college all-stars and the Globetrotters, and he was unimpressed. "Walter, I've seen this kid play," Auerbach told Brown. "His defense stinks. On offense, he wants to be the star and tries to show off by always attempting to make the spectacular play."

But the most important consideration in Auerbach's mind was that Cousy, for all his prestidigitatious ballhandling, stood at only six feet one. The Minnesota Lakers were dominating the NBA because of George Mikan, their six-eleven center. Auerbach felt he had to begin rebuilding the Celtics by finding a similar big man, and Brown finally agreed. The college draft was held at the Biltmore Hotel in New York, and in the first round, Auerbach passed over Cousy and selected Charlie Share, a six-eleven center from Bowling Green. Another draft pick made by Auerbach and Brown that day was even more controversial. Auerbach was looking for a shooter and rebounder to complement Share at center. He thought he had found one in

Charles Cooper, a six-five graduate of Duquesne who'd helped his team make it to the semifinals of the National Invitational Tournament. But Cooper was black. While Branch Rickey and Jackie Robinson had integrated major-league baseball three years earlier, in 1947, the NBA remained all white. Plenty of talented black basketball players existed, but until now they had been confined to playing for all-black exhibition teams such as the Harlem Globetrotters and the Harlem Rens.

Still, the inevitability of an integrated league had been obvious ever since 1948, when Don Barksdale had become the first black to play on the American Olympic team. Auerbach did not think of himself as a social pioneer—he was simply looking for a rebounding forward. But he was certainly willing to make a breach in the league's segregated roster if it would give his team an edge, and so, at the meeting in the Biltmore, when it came time to announce the Celtics' second-round pick, Walter Brown said, "Boston takes Charles Cooper of Duquesne."

It was a momentous occasion. There had been no official discussions among the owners about integrating the NBA, and the development seemed certain to have repercussions. Eddie Gottlieb, the owner of the Philadelphia Warriors, leaned over to Sid Hartman, who worked in the front office of the Lakers, and said, "Abe's gonna go crazy." Abe was Abe Saperstein, the owner of the Harlem Globetrotters. The Trotters at the time were a much larger draw than any of the NBA teams; they played in many of the same arenas, with the Trotters often leading the bill in a doubleheader that featured two NBA teams in the second half. Saperstein had a proprietary interest in black basketball players and a virtual monopoly on them as well. And while he had been a powerful supporter of the NBA, he was afraid that if the league started recruiting black players, his talent pool might dry up, and NBA teams with black players might undercut fan interest in the Globetrotters.

The franchise owners, for their part, worried that if Saperstein felt the NBA was competing against him, he might boycott their arenas, and they made more money selling tickets for the Trotters than they did for their own money-losing teams. And whatever their private feelings about race, the owners had to contend with the fact that most basketball fans were the same blue-collar white males who showed up to watch hockey games, and as a whole, this was not a demographic that in 1950 had embraced a mixing of the races. For the owners, the operant phrase was, "It's a white dollar." They were uncertain whether the arrival of black players would enliven and strengthen the game or send an already tottering sport into collapse, and at least some of them did not want to find out.

"Do you realize Mr. Cooper is a Negro?" one of the owners asked Brown.

"I don't care if he's plaid!" Brown said. "All I know is this kid can play basketball and we want him on the team."

The owners called a recess but quickly realized that the league had no technical grounds to prevent Brown from drafting Cooper. They reconvened and there was no more dissent. In fact, once Brown had broken the color barrier, other owners were quick to follow. The Washington Capitols picked Earl Lloyd of Washington State in the draft's ninth round, and later in the summer the Knickerbockers lured Nat "Sweetwater" Clifton from the Harlem Globetrotters.* Abe Saperstein was in fact enraged and threatened Brown with a boycott of Boston Garden, but Brown did not back down. The day after Cooper learned he had been drafted by the Celtics, he sent Brown a telegram. "Thank you for offering me a chance in pro basketball. I hope I'll never give you cause to regret it."

A WEEK AFTER the draft, on April 27, 1950, Walter Brown hosted a luncheon at the Hotel Lenox to officially introduce Auerbach to the Boston press corps. One reporter observed that, despite Auerbach's nickname, his "hair is now somewhat sparse and dark brown after his harrowing experiences as a pro coach." Auerbach was barraged with questions about his decision to draft Charlie Share instead of Bob Cousy. He tried to explain that what would fill seats in the Garden was a winning team and that, as far as he was concerned, Bob Cousy had not demonstrated a talent that would help the Celtics win. And then, in comments that displayed to the reporters the new coach's boisterously confrontational manner, Auerbach said, "I don't give a damn for sentiment or names. That goes for Cousy and everybody else. The only thing that counts with me is ability, and Cousy still hasn't proven to me that he's got that ability. I'm not interested in drafting someone just because

---

*None of these untested players were of course starters. Lloyd was the first one of them to be sent into a game, and to him goes the honor of being the first African American to play in the sport that in the decades to come would create so many African American superstars.

he happens to be a local yokel." Auerbach turned to Walter Brown, who was standing next to him. "Am I supposed to win or am I supposed to please these guys?" he asked.

"Just win," Brown said.

The sportswriters were outraged. SENTIMENT OUT — AUERBACH was the headline in the next day's *Herald*. Cousy himself was stunned and humiliated. He'd expected, even assumed, he'd be drafted by the Celtics. After all, he was not just a talented local player but a genuine star, the leader of an NCAA championship team. And he was a proven draw at the Garden. When he was taken out of games, the Boston fans would chant his name—*Couseee! Couseee!*—until his coach sent him back in.

Raised in a tenement in the Yorkville section of Manhattan, Cousy was the son of a taxi driver who'd immigrated from the Alsace-Lorraine region of France. While only six-one and incredibly skinny, he had long arms, big hands, quick feet, and even quicker eyes. His high-bridged nose and narrow face afforded him such extraordinary peripheral vision that he could sit in a chair facing a wall and see enough of the wall behind him to at least identify its color. People joked he could look due east and enjoy a sunset, that he had the 360-degree vision of an insect, that his large, bulging eyes were so big that when he fell asleep his eyelids failed to cover them. Cousy's peripheral vision enabled him to pass the ball without seeming to look at the other player. He passed balls behind his back and over his shoulder. They came so unexpectedly his teammates sometimes missed them. In a moment of desperation in a game against Loyola, he improvised what would become the most famous of his signature moves—shifting the ball behind his back from hand to hand while dribbling. With eight seconds left and the game on the line, Cousy drove to the basket from the left side of the court, dribbling with his right hand, but the Loyola player guarding him boxed him in so tightly that he could not raise his right arm to shoot, so he spontaneously bounced the ball behind his back, caught it with his left hand, and dropped in a hook shot, which decided the game.

For all Cousy's pyrotechnics, Auerbach's view that he was overrated seemed to be shared by other franchises. Cousy became only the ninth pick in the draft, chosen by Auerbach's former boss Ben Kerner of the Tri-Cities Blackhawks. Cousy didn't even know where Tri-Cities was, and he went down to Boston Garden to see Walter Brown and plead to be given a chance to play for the Celtics. Brown explained apologetically that Chuck Share filled the Celtics' immediate requirements. "We need height," Brown said, "and Share gives it to us. I wish we could have gotten both of you, but it wasn't possible."

Cousy pointed out that he had already established his popularity with the Garden fans. Brown replied that time and again the Celtics had drafted popular New England college players, including three of Cousy's own former teammates at Holy Cross, only to have them fail to make the team or fail to draw fans once they did. Cousy asked Brown for his advice about playing for Tri-Cities. "You're the property of another team now," Brown said, "and it's against regulations for me to suggest anything. I shouldn't even be talking to you."

Accepting the fact that he was not going to become a Celtic, Cousy signed with Kerner to play for the Blackhawks.* But before the season started, the Chicago Stags folded, and on October 5, 1950, the league's commissioner, Maurice Podoloff, held a meeting of the owners at the Park-Sheraton Hotel in New York to determine the legal status of the players associated with the team. Podoloff, nicknamed Poodles Podoloff and Pumpernickel Podoloff, was a short, stout, thick-featured man, born in Russia, who had the delicate job of simultaneously representing the owners, who were his bosses, to the players and to the public and mediating the numerous and divisive differences between them. He seemed spineless and indecisive to many players and referees, and incompetent to some of the owners, but his power was hampered by his one-year contract and his lack of leverage with the owners. And despite his reputation for subservience, in the fall of 1950 he stood up to Ned Irish, the richest and the most powerful and arrogant of the owners, and made two crucial decisions that affected the course of the league for the next two decades. Before folding, the owners of the Chicago Stags had been secretly auctioning off the players—Irish being one of the most aggressive bidders—and Podoloff vetoed the results. "The secret auction was bad," he explained later. "The Chicago people were going to a team and saying, 'So-and-so bid so much. What is your offer?' Teams couldn't dare check with each other."

---

*Part of the Celtics legend, repeated by Cousy himself in his later years, was that he refused to sign with any team but Boston, but contemporaneous accounts and his own 1957 memoir, *Basketball Is My Life,* contradict him.

Next, Podoloff decreed that valuations be placed on the Stag players, to pay off the team's debt, and that to improve the level of the league overall, they be distributed to the teams that would benefit most from each player's specific talents. The Blackhawks' Ben Kerner insisted that Frankie Brian, a player on the Stags roster who was a friend of his, be allowed to join his Tri-Cities club, and Podoloff decided that if Kerner was going to acquire Brian, he would have to surrender his draft choice Bob Cousy to the pool of Stags players. Kerner agreed, and Cousy, who had been passed over by Walter Brown, was now rejected by a second owner.

At the end of the meeting in the Park-Sheraton, all the players had been disposed of except for Cousy, Andy Phillip, and Max Zaslofsky. Walter Brown wanted Zaslofsky, one of the league's perennial all-star players. He argued that because the last-place Celtics had had the first choice in the college draft, they should also have first choice of these final three players. Ned Irish, however, demanded that Zaslofsky go to New York because he had been born in New York, had gone to St. John's in Queens, and would help the Knicks draw Jewish fans. Eddie Gottlieb of the Philadelphia Warriors also wanted Zaslofsky, and he argued, even more creatively than Irish, that the Warriors deserved him because Gottlieb's minority partner was Abe Saperstein, who had acquired Zaslofsky in one of the secret trades with the Stags. None of the three men would relinquish their claims on Zaslofsky, and finally Podoloff lost his patience. "I'm sick and tired of all this," he said. "There's three of you and three players, all backcourt men, so I'm going to put the names in a hat and whoever you draw, that's who you got."

Podoloff wrote the names of the three players on three pieces of paper and placed the folded slips in the fedora of Danny Biasone, owner of the Syracuse Nationals. Walter Brown felt he had been euchred out of Zaslofsky, but even so, ever courteous, he offered Irish the chance to draw first, then he instantly regretted it, since he realized he had just given Irish the best odds of acquiring Zaslofsky. Irish picked out a slip, opened it, and gave a triumphant shout. He had in fact selected Zaslofsky. Andy Phillip, the second team member from the Stags, was an excellent and experienced playmaker, but when Brown, picking second, reached into the fedora, he drew the name of Bob Cousy, the untried rookie. As he read Cousy's name, he did not feel that this was somehow meant to be, that the crowd-pleasing local boy with the dazzling moves had all along been destined to play for the Celtics. To the contrary, what he felt was that he and his last-place team had once again gotten the dirty end of the stick.*

Cousy, staying with his parents on Long Island, was unaware of the meeting at the Park-Sheraton in New York, unaware even that Ben Kerner had traded him into the pool of Stags players, and he expected any day to hear from Kerner summoning him to the Blackhawks training camp in Illinois. Instead, after midnight, he received a call from Walter Brown, who told him to report to the Celtics office in Boston. Cousy, who was jubilant, drove up to Massachusetts the following day to talk to Auerbach. Like Walter Brown, Auerbach was disappointed that the Celtics had been stuck with Cousy. It also irritated Auerbach that the sportswriters and fans had tried to foist Cousy on him, and he wanted it made clear to all concerned that, despite his local-hero status, Cousy was going to have to prove himself. "To me, he's just another rookie who has to show me that he can play professionally," he told a reporter that morning.

The article appeared in that afternoon's newspapers. Cousy read the quote before his meeting with Auerbach, and its cold tone made him acutely aware of just how serious were the coach's reservations about him. Buster Sheary, Cousy's last coach at Holy Cross, had been an inspirational leader, but Red Auerbach, Cousy could tell as soon as they met, had absolutely no interest in inspiring people. He was hard and practical, with a direct, penetrating gaze—a man who assumed you probably weren't going to like him and didn't care. Auerbach told Cousy that his one disadvantage was his size. If he made the team, he'd be one of the six shortest men in the entire league. He was too small to play up front, Auerbach said; he would have to try for a position in the backcourt. "I hope you make this team," Auerbach said. "If you can, I'll be glad to have you. If you can't, don't blame me. A little guy always has two strikes on him in this business. It's a big man's game."

AUERBACH HAD rented a two-room corner suite on the ninth floor of the Hotel Lenox, on Boylston Street near the Boston Public Library. The suite,

---

*Another part of the Celtics legend, repeated without sourcing in numerous books, is that Brown drew third, but in a 1960 interview with *Sport* magazine, he stated that he drew second.

which had a refrigerator and a hot plate but no stove, was a spartan place, but since he had few friends and no interests outside of basketball, it suited him perfectly. Just as he had done with the Tri-Cities Blackhawks, Auerbach set about rebuilding the Celtics. He dropped Tony Lavelli, the legendary Yale player who scored only nine points a game but who performed on his accordion for the crowds at halftime. He then cut two local favorites, the Holy Cross stars George Kaftan and Joe Mullaney. By the time training camp was over, he'd decided to keep Cousy. Auerbach had been hard on the kid, but he took orders without sulking and he was now trying to make sure that the man who received his pass at least knew it was coming.

Eventually, Auerbach traded away all but two players—Ed Leede and Sonny Hertzberg—from the team that had played the previous season under Doggie Julian. As he engaged in his trades, Auerbach always kept in his mind the image of a unified, cohesive team. He was interested in a player only to the extent that the man could demonstrably perform a specific function within the team. Boston picked up a number of players from the five franchises that had folded at the end of the previous season. The most promising was Ed Macauley, who had been with St. Louis and who was considered a better center in the league than anyone except Minneapolis's George Mikan. Macauley played both center and forward, and at six feet eight, he was tall enough for Auerbach to designate him as the team's big man, which meant Auerbach no longer needed Chuck Share, the center he had opted to draft over Bob Cousy. So Auerbach traded the rights to Share to Fort Wayne in exchange for Bob Harris, the rights to Bill Sharman, and approximately $10,000, which Auerbach used to buy Bob Brannum from Sheboygan.

Both Harris and Brannum were big, bruising, sharp-elbowed players. Brannum, with fewer skills than Harris but more brute strength, became the team's enforcer, and the two of them together with Macauley formed the Celtics frontcourt. Sharman, who had played for the Washington Capitols and then was assigned to Fort Wayne when that team folded, was a gamble for Auerbach. A baseball player as well as a topflight shooting guard, Sharman was still playing on the Brooklyn Dodgers and had yet to decide whether he wanted to pursue basketball or baseball. If he had chosen to go with baseball, Auerbach would have traded away something for nothing. But he thought it was worth the risk. Sharman, a great natural athlete from central California, seemed more of a basketball player than a baseball player in his size and agility, and Auerbach sensed he had the potential to become one of the best shooters in the league. When Sharman did join the team the following year, he and Cousy formed one of the greatest backcourt combinations in league history, Cousy moving the ball around the floor with his startling maneuvers, spinning, twisting, creating opportunities, and Sharman the meticulous perfectionist, methodically lofting his shot from twenty feet out.

At the outset of that first season, Auerbach decided to allow sportswriters to attend the team's practice sessions. Any additional coverage he could generate would only help the team, and in the process he might be able to educate some of the sportswriters, whom he considered woefully uninformed about basketball, on the finer points of the game. Jack McCarthy of the *Boston Herald* attended one of the early sessions. Auerbach held up his hands in front of the reporter's face and wriggled his fingers. "This is what makes a basketball player, see?" he said. "Hands. You've got to have the touch. Max Zaslofsky has it. And so does Macauley. That's what makes Ed so good."

The Boston sportswriters of the day, who worked for six different papers that were engaged in unending circulation wars, were narrow-minded and sensationalistic and extremely competitive. But the men Ted Williams sardonically referred to as "the knights of the keyboard" were also sentimental in a particularly Irish way. They believed in loyalty, they loved the lost cause and the heroic gesture, and Auerbach struck many of them as singularly unromantic. They felt he had insulted the Boston fans by his lack of enthusiasm for Bob Cousy. And when, at weekly basketball lunches hosted by Walter Brown, Auerbach belittled the very notion of sportsmanship as a lot of crap and bragged of urging players to bend rules and fake injuries if that would help them win, it seemed an appalling violation of the ideals of honor and nobility that had always been a central justification for athletics.

Auerbach did find an ally, surprisingly enough, in "Colonel" Dave Egan, the sports columnist for the *Boston Record*. The *Record* was a Hearst tabloid, with a formula that relied heavily on scandal and sports, but it had a circulation of 500,000, and throughout New England, people bought it faithfully every day just to read the Colonel—though he never satisfactorily established what it was he'd been colonel of. A graduate of Harvard Law School, but also a hopeless alcoholic with a foul temper, Egan was the most talented, opinionated, and derisive sportswriter in the city. He had an ongoing feud with Ted Williams, whom he called "the inventor of the automatic choke," and he had proposed that a cab driver who once almost ran over Casey Stengel, when Stengel was managing the beleaguered Boston Braves, be given an MVP award.

But the incorrigible Egan, who loved to play the contrarian, sensed immense potential in Auerbach and his reconfigured Celtics, and went so far as to compare him to Frank Leahy, the idolized football coach of Boston College who had taken his team to victory in the Sugar Bowl. "We know now, as Syracuse, Fort Wayne and Minneapolis and the giants of the game come striding toward Boston, that a winner has been forced upon us in the person of Red Auerbach of the Celtics, and that he will do for professional basketball what Frank Leahy did for intercollegiate football," he wrote during Auerbach's first year. Auerbach, who called Egan "my boy," told an acquaintance, "I'd be dead without him." Egan also approved of the way Auerbach was restraining Cousy and integrating him into the team. "This is not a team of ballerinas and prima donnas and temperamental, selfish stars," he wrote. "They are young and hungry and full of heart, and they play the rambunctious, enthusiastic, blood-and-thunder basketball which only the young and the hungry and only the hearty can play."

Blood-and-thunder basketball. That was indeed how the game was played in those formative years of the league's existence, when basketball shared its rowdy fan base with the hockey teams playing in many of the same arenas, and as the owners all knew, hockey fans never felt a game was complete without one good fight. Many of the NBA games were played on so-called neutral courts in smaller towns in New England or upstate New York or central Pennsylvania, where the arenas had nicknames such as The Tub of Blood. Fans shook the basket when players were shooting, the ladies stuck their hairpins into the legs of players and smacked them with handbags, and miners heated pennies with their lamps before hurling them at the losers. The home courts were just as raucous. In Fort Wayne, where the Pistons played in a small north-side gym, spectators liked to reach out and pull the leg hairs of the opposing players when they were taking the ball out of bounds. The players retaliated by "accidentally" misfiring passes that sent the ball into the faces of the offending fans.

Through the early and mid-fifties, professional basketball proved most popular in the smaller cities that did not have either baseball or football teams. The Syracuse Nationals, who averaged more than 5,000 fans a game in the early fifties, sold more tickets than any other team. The rest of the league hated playing in Syracuse, in part because of the weather; they reached the town either by train or by DC-3, and in the depths of winter the cold and ice made the trip seem both grueling and dangerous. Players feigned illness so regularly to avoid the city that the condition became known as the "Syracuse flu." But it was not just the weather. Syracuse was a raucous, two-fisted, blue-collar town—the Carrier air-conditioning factory was one of the largest employers—and its fiercely proud inhabitants loathed the teams from the big cities. Egged on by the Nats coach, Al Cervi, who turned to the crowd and gesticulated in mock despair whenever a call went against his team, the Syracuse fans hurled candy bars, cups of soda, programs, and popcorn boxes down on the court and poured beer and spat on visiting players as they walked along the ramp into the locker room beneath the stands. Every time Bob Cousy went up that ramp, he ducked his head. One Syracuse fan, a huge, bald man known among visiting teams as the Strangler, would reach down as visiting players walked by and try to choke them. He once put a stranglehold on Philadelphia Warriors owner Eddie Gottlieb while Gottlieb was sitting on the visitors' bench. After fending him off, Gottlieb told the Strangler, "I'll put fifty dollars in an envelope in Philly and we'll get rid of you."

The Nats fans also went after officials. After one game that fans believed the Nats had lost because of officiating, an irate mob gathered outside the referees' changing room, and the officials, Sid Borgia and Johnny Nucatola, had to flee town on a late-night train. Nucatola was beaten up by fans after working another game in Syracuse, and on yet a different occasion, Charlie Eckman, an official who knew what had happened to Nucatola and became afraid from crowd noise that he might be similarly attacked, changed into his street clothes at halftime and simply disappeared. Nucatola believed that Nats coach Al Cervi and owner Danny Biasone, who screamed abuse from the sidelines, were responsible for inciting the violence against the officials in Syracuse. Nucatola publicly declared at a New York Basketball Writers luncheon that Cervi and Biasone should be reprimanded by the commissioner and fined up to $1,000, but when he brought the matter up with Podoloff, the commissioner, ever mindful of his own job security, told Nucatola, "We have to be careful. This is a funny bunch we're working for. One mistake and we can all be out on our ear tomorrow."

Biasone, who was not fined or reprimanded, responded to Nucatola's complaints by telling Podoloff to keep "those New York refs" out of Syracuse. The officials worked freelance at the time, for $45 a game, and after criticizing Biasone, Nucatola stopped receiving assignments from the NBA. It was clear that some if not all owners wanted referees susceptible to crowd intimidation. After all, a crowd that believed it could influence the referees was an involved crowd, and that was good for business. One referee was said to be so easily shaken by crowd hostility that the odds shifted four points in favor of the hometown team when he was officiating.

The odds. Gambling was a primary reason fans throughout the NBA were so noisy and uncontrolled. The league had avoided the point-shaving scandals that devastated college basketball in 1951; during the fifties, only two people, an official named Sol Levy and a Fort Wayne player named Jack Molinas, were ever found to be involved in gambling. But the fans bet heavily. Some were gamblers first and fans second, attending games because they knew that by screaming at referees and players, and by barraging the court with litter, they could influence the outcome. In fact, betting was such a prominent part of fans' attraction to the game that the cheering was at times louder at a shot that put a team ahead of the point spread than at a shot that won a game. In many arenas, bookies appeared under the stands at halftime, taking new bets. Johnny Kerr, a center for the Nats in the fifties, recalled that fans in Boston Garden would yell, "Hey, we doubled our bets on you shmucks, so you better beat the spread."

Despite the rambunctious fans, the game itself often seemed oddly unrealized, at times a confused morass of struggling bodies, at times stilted and lifeless. One problem players faced was congestion under the basket. Too many of them struggled for rebounds, the offensive players crowding in, creating the impression of a wild rugby scrimmage rather than deft individual maneuvering. Since the lane was only six feet wide, it extended only three feet on either side of the basket, which meant a giant like George Mikan could station himself, in his metal-rimmed glasses, a mere three feet from the basket and wait for the high pass, then sweep away defenders with his Herculean left arm and loft in a right-handed hook shot.

To ease the congestion under the basket, the franchise owners voted in 1951 to widen the lane from six feet to twelve feet, and this had an immediate effect, forcing the players to rely more on distance shooting. But the game was still frequently boring, degenerating all too often into what were known as "freeze-and-foul" contests, with the team in the lead playing possession ball to run out the clock and the losing team fouling to try to recover, the game stopping each time it succeeded. In one notorious example of "stall ball," as it was also known, on November 22, 1950, between the Minneapolis Lakers and the Fort Wayne Zollner Pistons, the final score was 19–18. The Pistons coach, Murray Mendenhall, had decided not to run the ball but simply to hold it and wait until the end of the game to score the winning point. He succeeded, but fans were reading newspapers in the stands; some walked out and demanded their money back, others swore never to buy another ticket to a professional basketball game.

By the spring of 1954, it was obvious to the owners that the rules needed to be rethought. "When fans are walking out on your show," Ned Irish told an acquaintance, "you don't have to be awfully smart to realize that you're doing something wrong." Danny Biasone, owner of the Syracuse Nationals, argued that the league needed to pick up the pace of the game by limiting the amount of time a team could hold the ball. Biasone was alternately feisty and dour, a slight man with a large head who wore a fedora, spoke in an Italian accent, and sat on the bench during games, a cigarette dangling perpetually from his lips. Ned Irish derided him as the prototypical small-town owner, and in many ways he was—his wife made his players pasta and even washed their uniforms—but he was responsible for the single most important innovation in basketball since James Naismith invented the game. Biasone had decided that the exciting games were the ones in which each team took at least sixty shots. He divided the length of the game, 48 minutes, by 120 shots, 60 for each team, and came up with 24 seconds per shot. He had his team play some college students in an exhibition game using a shot clock that required both teams to turn the ball over once twenty-four seconds had elapsed. At first the players, not used to any time limit, rushed their shots. "Take your time out there," Biasone called. "Twenty-four seconds is a long time." The players slowed their pace and found out that they indeed had plenty of time to set up and shoot.

All the owners agreed to the measure. Walter Brown immediately saw its potential to make the game more exciting. The new rule did have its opponents, including Red Auerbach, who felt that stall ball worked effectively for the Celtics. Even though the fans hated it, toward the end of a game he'd take out Cousy and put in Sonny Hertzberg, who'd simply stand there holding the ball. Some sportswriters also complained that the innovation robbed the game of complexity. "Movement is no longer necessary," wrote Milton Gross, the sports columnist for the *New York Post*. "Ballhandling now becomes a liability. The strategic freeze is outmoded. . . . It's become a game for mathematicians, statisticians, clock-watchers, and coaches who are afraid to attack their problem at its sources."

The new rule, which went into effect in the fall of 1954, was initially treated as an experiment. In the first games after the measure was adopted, someone simply stood on the sidelines with a stopwatch and after the twenty-four seconds expired yelled *Time!* But the new rule was such a success that by the end of the year all teams had invested in shot clocks. The owners without exception recognized the shot clock as a radical breakthrough that had completely reinvigorated professional basketball. The number of playoff games in which more than one hundred points were scored more than quadrupled. More important, over the next two years, attendance at NBA games increased by 50 percent.

IN THE FALL of 1954, when the twenty-four-second clock was officially introduced, the Boston Celtics were still a work in progress. Red Auerbach had been with the team for four years by then, and he had come to accept the fact that finding exactly the right players was an exercise in patience. Walter Brown was not as patient as Auerbach. The year he had hired Auerbach, the team had ended the season 25–16 and a rise in attendance cut his loss to a mere $11,000. But the following season attendance had fallen back, and the Celtics' losses again began to exceed $100,000 a year. The team had yet to make it to the finals, much less win a championship, and only a victory like that, Brown believed, would excite Boston's sports fans. The Celtics had an outsized payroll, and Brown began to feel he was not getting his money's worth. When Cousy, the highest-paid man in the entire league, scored only four points in a losing game against the Warriors, Brown told the writers at a basketball luncheon: "That's a lot of money per point. I don't need an expensive club to lose games. I can lose just as easily with a cheap one."

Brown blamed his coach as well, and after the 1954 playoffs ended with yet another loss to Syracuse, he cut Auerbach's salary. "I hold him partially responsible for the poor showing of our team this year," he said at the end of the season. Some sportswriters felt Brown should have gotten rid of Auerbach altogether. "Much to my sorrow, [Auerbach] will return to the Hub as chief of the Celtics," wrote Tom Carey of the *Worcester Gazette*. "For my two points, Auerbach is the most overrated coach in the business."

What Auerbach was trying to build was a team that excelled at fast-break basketball. In Cousy, his star, he had the man who could set the pace of the game, racing downcourt with the ball and then passing off or going in for the shot himself. In Sharman and Macauley, he had two terrific outside shots, while Bob Brannum provided him with some muscle. The problem was that Brannum, while strong, was just not very athletic, and Macauley, who had height, was simply too frail to muscle in for rebounds. The Celtics' best rebounder was Jack Nichols, but he played only part-time because he was a dental student at Tufts College. As a result, the Celtics were weak on defense. That day Bob Cousy had arrived in Boston to join the Celtics, Auerbach had told him it was a big man's game, and three years later Auerbach believed it more than ever. He knew that what the team still needed was one man who was tall and strong and could jump. The guy didn't even need to be able to shoot. All he had to do was get the ball.

A year before, in the summer of 1953, Auerbach had met a player he was convinced could be the solution to all his problems. Auerbach had spent the summer at Kutsher's Country Club, a resort in the Catskill Mountains of upstate New York. As part of their summer attractions, Milt Kutsher and some of the other resort owners hired the country's top college basketball players, who worked as bellhops during the day and played on the basketball teams the resorts fielded. To coach his team, Kutsher had brought in Auerbach. While Kutsher usually hired only college students, there was that summer a high school kid in Philadelphia named Wilt Chamberlain who was such a phenomenal player that after watching him, Haskell Cohen, the public relations man for the NBA, had persuaded Kutsher to make him a bellhop. The first time Auerbach saw Chamberlain, moving along briskly in his bellhop uniform—striped pants, short-sleeved white shirt, bow tie—he just stood there and watched him walk. Just watched him walk. The kid was huge, but what Auerbach thought was incredible was how graceful he was for someone his size. A little while later, when he saw him on the basketball court, he realized that even though the kid was still in high school, he was comparable to the best college players Auerbach had ever seen.

Auerbach pushed Chamberlain hard during practices and tried to work with him on his moves, like guarding the pivot man, but Chamberlain, he found, was not a receptive student. Wilt was only sixteen, but because of his size and ability and all the press attention he'd already received, people even then had begun to treat him with awe, and it had gone to his head. Still, his talent was phenomenal, and so was his hustle. Even off the court he hustled, carrying guests' luggage in and out of the hotel, pocketing tips, bringing trays of drinks to the patio. The NBA at the time had a territorial draft, which allowed each team to exploit the draw of local talent by giving it the right, regardless of its position in the regular draft, to acquire a top player graduating from a college within its territory. Which meant if Chamberlain went to a college in New England, Auerbach could claim him for the Celtics. "Why don't you go to Harvard, kid?" Auerbach asked Chamberlain one day.

Auerbach was serious. He called Walter Brown, who was at his vacation house on Cape Cod, and urged him to come up and take a look at Chamberlain. "This is the most fantastic player I've ever seen," Auerbach said. He added that it would be worth almost any amount of money to acquire him, and even suggested that Brown consider giving the Chamberlain family $25,000—just out and out bribe the mother and father—if Wilt would attend a college within the Celtics' territory. Auerbach argued that no league rules specifically forbade payments to a potential player's family, but Brown considered it underhanded. Then Eddie Gottlieb, owner of the Philadelphia Warriors, heard about Auerbach's scheme. He considered Chamberlain a Philadelphia talent and was determined to have him play for the Warriors. Gottlieb believed Chamberlain would be capable of playing for the NBA as soon as he graduated from high school. But if Chamberlain decided to go to college, that was fine with Gottlieb. If he had to, he was willing to wait six more years to get him. But one thing was certain, at least in Gottlieb's mind: Wilt Chamberlain *would* play for the Warriors. "If that kid even thinks about blowing town for Boston," Gottlieb told Milt Kutsher, "I'll turn your joint into a bowling alley."

BY THE TIME Chamberlain was ready to go to college, not just Auerbach and Gottlieb but every coach who had ever seen him play, and many more who hadn't, wanted to sign him. In early 1955, when a team of Philadelphia's high school all-stars featuring Chamberlain was traveling through the Northeast playing all-star teams from other cities, sportswriter Bill Libby and New York Knickerbockers coach Joe Lapchick went out to White Plains, a New York City suburb, to watch Wilt.

Lapchick was astounded by Chamberlain's performance. He was six feet five himself and had been one of the original tall men in the earliest days of pro basketball, back in the twenties, before becoming the coach at St. John's University and then taking over the Knicks. In all that time he'd never seen anyone dominate a game, both on offense and defense, as thoroughly as Chamberlain did. Afterward, he and Libby went down to the locker room to meet Chamberlain. Some dad was there with a camera, pestering Chamberlain to pose with his young son, and Chamberlain was graciously obliging. Lapchick figured he'd be doing a lot more of that in the years ahead.

"I'm Joe Lapchick," the coach said, "and it's been a pleasure to watch you perform."

"Thank you, Mr. Lapchick," Chamberlain said. "Coming from you, that's very nice."

"If I was still at St. John's, I'd be after you."

"That's all right," Chamberlain said. "Everyone else is anyway."

That was no exaggeration. "It was a manhunt probably unprecedented in the history of college athletics," Irv Goodman declared in *Sport*. More than two hundred colleges—Michigan State, Penn, Notre Dame, Ohio State, Holy Cross, Missouri, Oklahoma, Purdue, UCLA, to name just a few—expressed interest in recruiting Chamberlain. "About the only place I didn't hear from was Alaska," Chamberlain later recalled. Many people assumed this put Chamberlain in an enviable position, but in fact the deluge of interest—the pleas of desperate recruiters and the unsubtle insinuations of wealthy alumni—had a nightmarish quality, and made him feel both paranoid and megalomaniacal. "I couldn't walk into my house without finding someone waiting for me," Chamberlain remembered. "The telephone and doorbell never stopped ringing. Coaches were coming through the windows to get at me. Every mail brought more offers. I was hounded."

Wilt Chamberlain grew up in Haddington, a largely black neighborhood of West Philadelphia where small row houses were tightly packed on treeless streets. His parents, William and Olivia Chamberlain, had a total of eleven children, but two died in infancy, and Wilt and his two brothers and six sisters—he was the sixth child—were raised in a semidetached two-story gray brick house on North Salford Street. The house had four bedrooms, one for the parents and three for the nine children. It was extremely crowded, especially given his growing size, and while Chamberlain remained close to his family throughout his life, he never married, always living alone, and eventually built for himself in Los Angeles a huge, sprawling mansion that, among its many distinctive features, had only a single, if enormous, bedroom. Guests were consigned to a separate wing.

Chamberlain's father was originally from rural Virginia, had only a sixth-grade education, and worked as a janitor for the Curtis Publishing Company. He was taciturn but sober and responsible, the neighborhood handyman who could serve as an electrician, carpenter, mason, or plumber. Chamberlain's mother, more outgoing than her husband, worked as a maid, but also kept the Chamberlain household clean and the nine children in washed clothes. While the children never went hungry, the family had very little money, and Chamberlain and his brothers and sisters all worked, delivering groceries, shoveling snow, and collecting newspapers and scrap metal to sell to the junk dealer. "Wilt worked with the milkman, the iceman, and the ragman," recalled his sister Barbara Lewis.

While Wilt's father was only five feet eight, throughout his childhood Wilt was always a head taller than the other kids in the class photo. The milkman who'd hired him to help with deliveries when he was seven was under the impression he was twelve. He was also disproportionately long-legged, with an enormous stride, and at George Brooks Elementary School, he became the anchor leg and youngest member of the three-hundred-yard shuttle relay team. By the time he actually turned twelve, Wilt was six feet tall. That year Don Barksdale became the first black to play on the U.S. Olympic basketball team, and the sport seemed to hold out possibilities for young black boys in a way it had not before. The following year, the city built the Haddington Recreational Center a few blocks from the Chamberlain house, and Wilt began to spend long hours there playing pickup basketball games, tutored by Blinky Brown, the man who ran the center.

Brown thought Wilt's legs were so thin that he was surprised that they supported him. Wilt was also a timid kid who allowed other, shorter kids to shove him around. But Brown believed that all Wilt had to do was develop. He not only had his amazing height, but unlike most tall kids, who tended to be uncoordinated and slow, he was graceful and quick. Brown thought Chamberlain had such potential that sometimes in the summer, when Wilt and his friends begged him, he'd lock the rec-center gym and let them play undisturbed for hours at a time.

Once he reached adolescence, Chamberlain's growth rate, remarkable to begin with, accelerated dramatically. The summer he turned fourteen he grew four inches in two months, requiring a new pair of pants every four weeks, and reached a height of six feet seven with no sign of his growth leveling off. Jack Ryan, who covered high school sports for the *Philadelphia Bulletin,* watched Chamberlain play when he was still at Shoemaker Junior High School and was so struck by his heron-like legs that he nicknamed him Wilt the Stilt, a phrase Chamberlain always hated. He was also known as the Hook and Ladder and as Dipper—the only one nickname he ever liked—which came about because even before he became a teenager, he had to duck his head to get through a doorway.

By the age of sixteen, when he was at Overbrook High School, Chamberlain could stand flat-footed under the basket, reach up, and almost get a finger on the rim. His combination of height and athleticism made him so freakishly good—and the Overbrook victories such decisive routs—that opponents felt playing the school was not just challenging, it was pointless. The team regularly won by margins of fifty points or more. In his senior year, in a game against Roxborough High School, Chamberlain scored twenty-six points in the first half. Roxborough, hoping to avoid a record rout, tried to stall, passing the ball to run down the clock, but Chamberlain went on to score thirty-one points in the third quarter, and thirty-three in the fourth quarter—twenty-seven of them in the last four minutes. His total score, including free throws, came to ninety. The final game score was 123–21. Joe Goldenberg, a player on the West Philadelphia High School team, had been asked by his coach to scout Overbrook in the game against Roxborough. Afterward, Goldenberg told his coach that Chamberlain scored ninety points.

"Where does he shoot from?" the coach asked.

"Anywhere he wants," Goldenberg said.

Eddie Gottlieb, who ran the Warriors, had naturally gone out to Overbrook to watch Chamberlain play. Gottlieb figured Wilt was one of the few high school basketball players who could, if he wanted to, join the NBA right out of high school. He was ready. And it would have been good for the league, Gottlieb figured, since it did not in the mid-fifties have many truly big men. George Mikan was the best big man in the league, but he was past his prime. Wilt was faster and could jump higher. Gottlieb had Neil Johnston playing at center for the Warriors, but Gottlieb was certain that Wilt, even as a high school student, would make sliced bananas out of Johnston.

If the rules had permitted it, Gottlieb would have taken Chamberlain that very year and made him a starter. But that would have required changing the rule that players were eligible only after graduating from college, and he knew the other owners wouldn't go for it. "They didn't want to wreck their relationship with the colleges," Gottlieb later recalled. "The colleges were their minor leagues. They polished the prospects for us, and it didn't cost the pro teams a dime. But I'd have taken Wilt. Wilt was special. It was a waste of time for Wilt to go to college."

Gottlieb tried to persuade Chamberlain to go to college in the Philadelphia area so the Warriors could claim him in a territorial draft, but he learned that Wilt was determined to go out of state. So at a league meeting in early 1955, before Chamberlain had graduated from Overbrook High, Gottlieb proposed a rule extending the territorial draft to high school. To Gottlieb, it was entirely logical. The league was still struggling. Hometown boys, big at the box office, could make the difference between whether a team stayed afloat for another couple of years or sank. "This time, I benefit," he told the rest of the owners. "Next time it'll be your turn." Other owners with promising local talent supported him, and despite the opposition of Ned Irish, the rule was approved. Gottlieb then selected Chamberlain in the 1955 draft even though he would not be eligible to play for four more years.

Chamberlain spent much of his senior year flying around the country with his Overbrook coach, Cecil Mosenson, at the expense of various universities. The NCAA rules limited athletic scholarships to tuition, room and board, and $15 a month in laundry money. But alumni, ostensibly operating independently as freelance recruiters, approached Wilt in the hopes of luring him to their schools. They made tantalizing suggestions about the money that would come his way, oblique references to no-show jobs, to gifts from alumni of new cars, to pocket cash that could run as high as $100 a week, and to slush funds in the tens of thousands of dollars that would accrue interest while he was in college and then be his when he graduated. Some of the recruiters were so aggressive that they seemed willing, Jimmy Breslin wrote in *The Saturday Evening Post,* "to violate the Lindbergh kidnapping law to grab the Stilt for alma mater."

The desperation of so many coaches to recruit Chamberlain, and the shamelessness and alleged illegality of the offers, became the talk of the sports world. In fact, while still in high school, Chamberlain received a letter from the NCAA asking him to detail any illegal offers that had been made. Later, the NCAA sent an investigator to the Chamberlain family's house to question Wilt about offers from alumni. Around the same time, investigators for the Internal Revenue Service questioned him about any cash he might have received. No evidence had as yet emerged that any college had actually made Chamberlain illegal offers, but the assumption that such offers had been made was so widespread, and so widely discussed, that some colleges decided not to try to recruit him, because they feared that if they succeeded, it would be taken for granted that they had bribed him. "Nobody will believe he 'just came here,' " said Jerry Ford, the athletic director at the University of Pennsylvania, when he heard that various alumni were in pursuit of Chamberlain.

The two universities pursuing Chamberlain the most aggressively by then were Kansas and Indiana. The rivalry between the schools was intense. Two years earlier, Kansas had beaten Indiana for the NCAA title. Phog Allen, the Kansas coach, and Branch McCracken, the coach of Indiana, personally despised each other so much that they refused to schedule games between their two teams and met only in the playoffs. McCracken thought he had the edge in the competition for Chamberlain. He ran one of the top basketball programs in the country, having won two national collegiate titles, and Indiana had played a pathbreaking role in integrating college basketball: Bill Garrett, the team's center, was the first black to play basketball in the Big Ten. After Wilt visited the campus, McCracken became so convinced that he was going to come to Indiana that the coach actually announced it.

But McCracken had been outmaneuvered by Phog Allen. The Kansas coach had first heard of Chamberlain in 1952, when Don Pierce, the university's director of sports publicity, had seen a photograph of Chamberlain in a newspaper, clipped it, and forwarded it to Allen, who pinned it to his office door. The following year, he received a firsthand account of Chamberlain from one of his own players, all-American B. H. Born, who played in the summer on a Catskills team sponsored by Shawanga Lodge. Born had a national reputation, and before the players from Kutsher's Country Club took on his team, Auerbach warned Chamberlain, *Born is going to make chopped chicken liver out of you.* Chamberlain, however, scored some forty-five points while holding Born to eight, and when Born returned to Kansas, he told Allen that on a basketball court Wilt Chamberlain was in a league of his own.

Allen was a legendary figure, the man responsible for making basketball an Olympic sport. He had been the protégé of none other than the game's inventor, James Naismith, who had been hired by the University of Kansas in 1898, seven years after coming up with the idea for basketball at a YMCA in Springfield, Massachusetts. Naismith started the basketball program at Kansas, but he was a devout Christian, unassuming and gentlemanly, with an aversion to competition and a belief that the primary object of all sport should be enjoyment and exercise. Once competitive league play started in basketball, he lost his enthusiasm for the sport, and at Kansas he preferred to watch the university's gymnastics team.

As a student at Kansas, Phog Allen had been one of the Jayhawks' first outstanding players, comfortable at any position. He'd been hired as basketball coach in 1916, and had been there ever since. In fact, he was now sixty-nine, and the University of Kansas had a policy of mandatory retirement at seventy. But the Kansas Jayhawks were Allen's life, and he could not bear the thought of retiring. If he succeeded in recruiting Chamberlain, the freshman would have to wait a year until he was eligible to play, and Allen was convinced that the university's administrators would not force him to retire the very year that the greatest player in its history—a player he had personally brought in—joined the team. Chamberlain could mean a championship, even a string of championships. He would fill seats and drive fund-raising for the new arena the university was planning. But he would need a coach with Allen's stature to guide him. And so, Allen reasoned, if he was able to sign Chamberlain, he could postpone his retirement, enjoy a final run of glory with this tremendous player, and thrash Indiana, thereby sticking it to Branch McCracken.

Other colleges had approached Chamberlain when he was just a sophomore, but Allen held back until February of Wilt's senior year. When he did make his overture, he decided that a central element of his approach to Chamberlain would be to assure him that Lawrence, Kansas, offered a racially comfortable environment, and to that end he devised a strategy that he later described, with remarkable candor, as "the Negro talking to the Negro." Allen arranged for some of Lawrence's prominent blacks to court Chamberlain, including Lloyd Kerford, who owned a number of enormous limestone caves rented by the federal government as storage facilities. Allen also brought in Dowdal Davis, editor of the *Kansas City Call,* a black newspaper, and the concert singer Etta Moten. Kansas was not as rigidly segregated as the Deep South, but blacks were still treated as blatantly inferior by most whites. Davis, the newspaper editor, thought that if Chamberlain simply showed up in Kansas, played basketball, and behaved himself, his prominence and success could help the entire state make racial progress. "They wanted another Jackie Robinson out here," Allen later recalled. "And they wanted to win. Wilt was a way to kill two birds with one stone. I wanted to win. I didn't care about another Jackie Robinson. I played every angle I could think of to get him."

Allen visited the Chamberlain family in their West Philadelphia row house. He was courteous and considerate and emphasized Kansas's academic program and the superb education Wilt would get there. But he also treated Chamberlain like royalty. When Wilt visited the school, a reception committee met him at the airport, he was driven to the campus in a Cadillac, the head of a Negro fraternity supplied his own girlfriend as a date, and a group of alumni whom he later referred to as the "godfathers" privately assured him that he would be provided with some $4,000 a year in cold, hard cash.

On May 14, 1955, Chamberlain announced that he would be attending the University of Kansas on a basketball and track scholarship. Many Philadelphians felt betrayed and suspicious. After all, their city had four of the best basketball schools in the country. "Why does a Philadelphia boy have to travel halfway across the country to go to college?" one columnist wondered. The rumor had it that Chamberlain had received anywhere from $25,000 to $30,000 in cash from Kansas alumni. The joke going around was that all the money Kansas had promised to pay Chamberlain was hidden in Lloyd Kerford's limestone caves. "Isn't the NCAA investigating reports of a special trust fund due to mature on Wilt the Stilt's graduation?" demanded the *New York Journal-American*'s Max Kase. At Bloomington, Branch McCracken insinuated that Wilt had demanded a bribe to attend Indiana. "We couldn't afford that boy," McCracken joked to a reporter. "He was just too rich for our blood." The cynical humor was pervasive. "I feel sorry for the Stilt," wrote Leonard Lewin of the New York *Daily Mirror.* "When he enters the NBA four years from now he'll have to take a cut in salary."

4

THREE YEARS BEFORE Wilt Chamberlain, amid all the acclaim and controversy, announced he was going to the University of Kansas, a young man named Hal DeJulio decided to attend a basketball game at Oakland High School in California. DeJulio was an alumnus of and former basketball player for the University of San Francisco, a member of the USF team that won the National Invitational Tournament in 1949. After college, he began a career in insurance, but basketball remained his singular passion, and he spent much of his free time in high school gymnasiums as a volunteer scout for his alma mater, watching games with the hope of finding an undiscovered talent who could lift USF from the obscurity into which it had fallen since DeJulio's glory days.

DeJulio had gone to the game with the intent of scouting Truman Bruce, the all-city all-star center for Oakland High, and also to take a look at the three all-star players on the other team, which was from McClymonds High School. But instead he found himself closely watching the man playing opposite Bruce, a rail-thin black kid named Bill Russell. DeJulio had never heard of Russell. McClymonds played in the Oakland Athletic League, which had only six teams, and when each season was over, the local reporters produced a First All-League Team, a Second All-League Team, and a long string of honorable mentions, and Russell's name had never appeared on any of those lists.

During the game, Russell scored fourteen points, hardly an astonishing feat, but it was not the points themselves, it was the moments at which he scored them that caught DeJulio's attention. Russell ran up eight points just before the first half ended and another six at the tail end of the game. Russell struck DeJulio as a clutch player, someone who could make a decisive contribution at a critical moment. He could also jump like nothing DeJulio had ever seen. The first time he saw Russell's head rising above the other players, he thought it was a mirage, but then he saw it again. And on defense Russell showed glimmers of genuine originality. His fundamentals were atrocious, and he still seemed awkward, but DeJulio thought he had an extraordinary instinct for the game. He was one of those players who could anticipate where the ball was going to go.

After the game, DeJulio went over to talk to Russell's coach, George Powles. "I swear if we could train that kid, he'd make a great player," DeJulio said. "Is he as good as I think he is?"

"He's good," Powles said. ·

"Is he intelligent?"

"Yes, he is."

"Can he make Division One?"

"He's got a long way to go."·

DeJulio then talked to Phil Woolpert, San Francisco's basketball coach, emphasizing the fact that Russell seemed the type of player who would fit into the controlled, defensive game Woolpert favored. The university was a small school, with only three thousand students and a limited athletic budget, but it had a few scholarships available, and Woolpert told DeJulio that he was willing to give the scout's discovery a tryout. DeJulio drove over to the Russells' apartment in a project in largely black West Oakland. Russell answered the door.

"I'm Hal DeJulio from USF," DeJulio said.

"What's USF?" Russell asked.

He had never heard of the place. Nonetheless, as soon as DeJulio, somewhat irritably, described the university and the possibility of a basketball scholarship, Russell became so excited he almost started trembling. He was about to graduate, and he had not received even a letter of interest, much less an actual offer, from a single other school.

WEST MONROE, where Bill Russell was born and where he spent his early years, was across the Ouachita River from Monroe, the chief market town in northeastern Louisiana, a region of cotton, soybeans, timber, and cattle that was more similar to neighboring Mississippi than to the state's southern Cajun country. It was a drab, featureless city of feedlots and warehouses where segregation was rigidly enforced. A policeman once threatened to jail Russell's stylish mother, Katie, for dressing like a white woman, and one evening a group of white men, just for the fun of watching him run, took potshots at Russell's father, Charles, when he was walking home. Like blacks throughout the South at the time, Russell's father, who'd left school at the age of fifteen, had no choice but to work as a field hand or take a service job. He became a janitor in a factory that manufactured paper bags—what Russell would later refer to as a "Negro job." But then in the early forties, preparations for America's involvement in World War II created economic opportunities elsewhere in the country, and when Bill was nine, his father moved the family to Oakland, a gritty, noisy city with a thriving waterfront of cranes, docks, and shipyards.

Charles Russell became an independent trucker, hauling laborers out to the San Joaquin Valley and produce back to town. He was a stern, hard man who despised self-pity, and Russell counted on his mother for affection. But when Russell was twelve, and his mother was thirty-two, she came down with the flu and suddenly and unexpectedly died of kidney failure. The extended Russell family urged Russell's father to move back to Louisiana or at least send his two sons to live with relatives, but he refused. Instead, insisting on raising his boys himself, he gave up his trucking business, since it required that he spend too many hours on the road, and took a job pouring molten iron in a foundry for forty dollars a week.

Bill's brother Charlie, a promising athlete, was selected to enroll in Oakland Tech, a prestigious, predominantly white high school, but Russell was a gangly, awkward adolescent with poor grades who'd become moody and withdrawn after his mother's death, and he had no choice but to attend McClymonds High, a nominally integrated school that was in fact predominantly black, with some Japanese and Mexicans and a handful of whites. George Powles, the white coach of the junior varsity basketball team, sensed some potential in the sullen, defeated young man, and he suggested Russell try out for it.

Russell had absolutely no idea what to do with the ball and was the worst of the sixteen players who tried out for the team, but he could clearly run and jump, Powles saw, and he had extremely large hands, measuring ten and a half inches from wrist to fingertip. Although the team normally had only fifteen players—and fifteen uniforms for them to wear—Powles made Russell the sixteenth player. He and a kid named Roland Campbell shared a uniform, playing in one game and sitting in the stands the next.

At first, even when he was suited up, Russell spent most of his time on the bench. On the occasions that he did take the court, he moved so awkwardly that he provoked derisive cheers from the spectators. But Powles still had faith in Russell and encouraged him to join the Boys Club to get in more practice—even giving him the two-dollar membership fee. Russell began going there every day after school to shoot and scrimmage. That work, together with a delayed growth spurt, paid off, and Russell became an adequate if still undistinguished basketball player.

In his junior year, Powles was made coach of the varsity team. Russell tried out again for the junior varsity but was cut by the new coach. When Powles heard this, he suggested Russell try out for the varsity team.

"What good will it do?" Russell asked. "I can't even make the jayvees."

"I think you've got the makings of a good basketball player," Powles said, "and I want you to come out for the varsity."

"Those guys are better than I am," Russell said.

"Son, remember this," Powles said, "if you think the other guy is better than you are, he will be."

For the sixteen-year-old Russell, the coach's words had the force of revelation, and he never forgot them. Powles gave Russell a slot on the team. All but one of the players were black, and Powles told them that because of this, the white referees would hold them to a higher standard than white teams, and white players would try to provoke them into fights, confident that the officials would take their side. "If you play like the rest of the teams, you're going to be called roughnecks and dirty and worse," Powles said. "If another team has a fight, it will be called a melee. If you get into a fight, it's a riot. So we're not going to get into any fights. We're going to play good clean basketball."

No white person had ever spoken so candidly to him about race, and Powles's talk provided another lesson that Russell never forgot. He continued to develop, and to grow, so quickly in fact that he outgrew his clothes in four months and needed new ones. In his senior year, his team displayed enough talent to contend for, and eventually win, the city championship. Russell would not be there for the finals, however. He had been such a good student in Louisiana, back when his mother was alive and had supervised his homework, that he had been put half a year ahead when he moved to Oakland, which meant he graduated in January, in the middle of the basketball season. He had never scored more than ten points in a game, but then in the last match of his high school career, against Truman Bruce and Oakland High, with—though he had no way of knowing it—scout Hal DeJulio sitting in the stands, something clicked and he reeled off fourteen points in two clutch spurts.

EVERY YEAR, a man named Brick Swegle, with backing from the Oakland Jaycees, put together a team called the California High School All-Stars and took them on an exhibition tour of the Pacific Northwest and British Columbia. The month-long excursion occurred in January and consisted solely of high school seniors who were known as "splitters" because they were graduating in the middle of the year. Russell was the only splitter on his team and therefore the only one eligible to join the all-stars. Since McClymonds had one of the top teams in the region, Brick Swegle wanted a player from the school on his all-stars and so he invited Russell.

The team traveled by Greyhound bus, playing a game against a local high school or college team in one small town, then hiking to the bus station and waiting for the next scheduled bus to take them to the next town on the tour. For an entire month, Russell had nothing to do except play, talk, and think basketball. For all George Powles's encouragement, Russell's high school coach had not been a font of technical expertise, and Russell for the first time found himself seriously analyzing the game. One of his teammates, Bill Treu, was an accomplished ball handler, and another, Eural McKelvey, stood out for his rebounding. Russell spent hours talking with them about the way they played. In his mind, he broke down their moves into component parts until he could visualize the entire sequence. Once he'd done that he found he could go on the court and imitate them.

But Russell was not a ball handler, so he stopped imitating Treu's dribbling maneuvers and began instead to envision moves he could use to defend against the guy. The first time he tried out one of these moves he'd mapped out in his head—it was an original move, not one he'd seen another player perform—he was astounded by its success, and he realized that his best chance to distinguish himself as a player might be by concentrating on defense. He also realized that being left-handed gave him an additional defensive advantage. Since most players shot with their right hand, his left was naturally positioned to rise up and block the shot. Russell began blocking shots aggressively. It was a playground move discouraged by coaches because the man with the ball could fake, sending the shot blocker leaping into the air, and then spin around him toward the basket. Brick Swegle, however, let Russell try to block as many shots as he wanted.

Going up for blocked shots, Russell came to appreciate for the first time how high he could jump. He and a group of players would all go up for the ball at the same time, and a moment would come when Russell's head was above everyone else's, and when he was still rising into the air while they had begun to fall back to the ground. He began refining his jump, and by the end of the tour, he had developed such a distinctive way of playing the game that his teammates were referring to "Russell moves."

When Russell returned from his trip through the Pacific Northwest, he went down to the San Francisco Naval Shipyard and applied for a job as an apprentice sheet-metal worker. Russell's father had promised his mother that he would send his son to college, but Charles simply lacked the money to pay for the tuition and Bill's grades were not good enough for an academic scholarship. Then came the visit from Hal DeJulio and the invitation to try out for the University of San Francisco basketball team.

After Russell played a scrimmage game with the team, Phil Woolpert, San Francisco's coach, kept his feelings to himself, telling Russell only that the school would let him know if it could provide him a scholarship. In the meantime, Russell started working at the naval yard. He also played basketball in the evening and one night took part in a game between McClymonds alumni and the high school's varsity team. It was his first chance to demonstrate before a crowd the moves he'd developed on Brick Swegle's all-star tour. His adrenaline was pumping so strongly that at one point, standing under the backboard, he leaped up to take a jump shot and for the first time in his life he found himself, for an instant, looking down into the basket. He was so startled that he completely missed the shot. He thought it might have been a fluke, but then, in the second half, he did it again, intentionally this time. Looking down into the hoop, through the net, he saw hardwood.

Eventually, Russell received a letter from the University of San Francisco offering him a full scholarship. Unlike Wilt Chamberlain, who was to be deluged with offers, Russell received only this offer. "We didn't think much about Russell," recalled Bob Feerick, then the coach at the University of Santa Clara. "He was a kid over at McClymonds. He was small. He was nothing. He grew up *after* he got to college."

The offer from USF, Russell would always feel, was largely a fluke. In fact, what ultimately led to Russell enrolling in San Francisco was largely a series of flukes: his father's unconventional decision to raise his two sons himself instead of turning them over to relatives in Monroe, where Russell would probably never have learned to play basketball, or at least would never have been encouraged by a white coach and spotted by a white scout; junior varsity coach George Powles charitably allowing him to become the sixteenth man on a fifteen-man team; Hal DeJulio's decision to scout Truman Bruce in a game in which Russell just happened to score his career high of fourteen points. Had any of those decisions turned out differently, Russell would probably have become a sheet-metal worker instead of a professional basketball player. Unlike Chamberlain, who had been considered an extraordinary athlete ever since he was in fourth grade and had come to feel entitled to acclaim, Russell understood from the outset how lucky he was to be where he was, and he knew how hard he would have to work to stay there. San Francisco was his one chance, he realized, the one chance he'd ever get, and he was determined to make the most of it.

PHIL WOOLPERT, the San Francisco basketball coach, was a lean, fine-boned man with black-frame glasses and receding hair who chewed gum and had a nervous stomach and a dry, deadpan manner. He had been at San Francisco for three years when Russell enrolled, and though San Francisco had won the National Invitational Tournament in 1949 under Pete Newell, Woolpert's won-lost record was so discouraging that one alumnus had called him a "lousy coach" to his face and he had threatened to quit. The performance of his teams was not entirely his fault. While San Francisco, run by the Jesuits, was a small school, the budget for the athletic department was even less than might be expected. It had once been a football powerhouse, but in the late forties its coach had been forced to resign when it was discovered that twenty-two members of the football team had received illegal payments. The Jesuit administrators, concerned about the corrupting influence of sports on higher education, had discontinued the varsity football program and reduced the athletic budget.

Woolpert was unable to scout nationally or compete with bigger schools for the top players; his recruiting was restricted to the San Francisco Bay Area. His team, which had no auditorium of its own, practiced in an ancient gym with cracked windows and warped floorboards. When other teams visited, Woolpert rented the pavilion at Kezar Stadium, an aging facility run by the city, or the San Jose Auditorium or, if it was a high-profile team, the Cow Palace. The team's official name, in tribute to the Jesuits, was the Dons, but they were known as the "Homeless Dons." The team manager joked that on train trips he had to hide in the bathroom because the team couldn't afford his ticket.

But Woolpert, in another one of the small acts of fortune that marked Russell's career at this point, favored a basketball system ideally suited to his new player. Woolpert scorned a high-speed offensive game as "jackrabbit basketball." "To me, run-and-shoot, jackrabbit basketball is only half a game," he explained to an acquaintance. "It's like the Yankees taking batting practice and calling it a baseball game." Instead, Woolpert emphasized defense. He drilled his team to slow down their opponents, to crowd them, to cut off their patterns, to break up their drives, and to steal their balls. He believed that if his teams could do this they could destroy the confidence of their opponents, and that was a more sure route to victory than trying to keep pace basket for basket.

The university had offered Russell tuition, room and board, and a part-time job in the cafeteria. Regarding his athletic scholarship as little more than an unexpected opportunity to acquire a college education, he majored in accounting, then, because he'd been fascinated by the trains of the Southern Railways that had thundered through Monroe, switched to transportation. Basketball, he thought, was just an extracurricular activity. Even so, he was determined and eager to improve, and he had much to improve upon. When he first arrived, his basketball skills were so limited that he did not even have a hook shot. He spent hours a day working one-on-one with freshman coach Ross Guidice, who introduced him to basketball strategy, teaching him how to set screens, time passes, and toss in a hook shot. He often stayed in the gym until midnight or later, taking five hundred left-handed hook shots and another five hundred right-handed hook shots.

Russell was assigned to room with K. C. Jones, a sophomore who also had a basketball scholarship. Jones was a painfully shy, monosyllabic young man who had gone to San Francisco's Commerce High School, but the interest he and Russell shared in basketball soon made the two of them insep-arable. They broke down basketball into its geometrical components: points, lines, arcs, and angles. They decided that the horizontal aspects of the game, the lines up the court and down the court, were more important than the ver-tical aspects, the lines from the court to the baskets—that timing and speed trumped height. They talked about the mechanics of jumping, dribbling, re-bounding, and shooting. They analyzed other players and their weaknesses and discussed how to exploit them. They invented plays. Russell felt as if they were creating a large database, each discovery building on the one be-fore, improvising an extended formula for success on the court. He also read every newspaper and magazine article he could find on basketball, studied the photographs of players in action, pondered the remarks they made to re-porters, and absorbed the details of their routines and styles, filling his room in the process with stacks of *Sport* and *The Sporting News*.

To everyone's surprise, Russell continued to grow at a phenomenal rate. When he arrived at San Francisco, he had stood a tall but not startling six feet five and had weighed 158 pounds. "A real mass of muscles," he liked to joke. By the start of his sophomore year in college, when he first played on the varsity team, he had shot up to six feet nine, which meant—though Woolpert had no way of knowing this would turn out to be the case when he had offered him the scholarship—that he was now one of the tallest players in San Francisco's conference. "When Bill Russell registered for his first basketball practice," Woolpert said later, "I gave him only one instruction: 'Grow to seven feet and you'll be unbeatable.' He did and he was. I'm a coaching genius."

But Russell was still so thin that he lacked the strength to play the muscular offensive game defined by big centers such as George Mikan. Instead, Russell focused on the defensive strategy he had begun to develop on the all-stars tour with Brick Swegle. On defense, most centers simply guarded the other center, who usually stayed in the pivot at the top of the key. Russell did this, but he was also quick enough to drop back and cover the basket if one of the opposing forwards broke through. He trained himself to have what he thought of as "smart feet," moving as lightly and as quickly as a guard.

In the fall of 1953, when Russell joined the varsity, San Francisco played its first game of the season against the heavily favored University of California, the tenth-ranked team in the country, which had beaten San Francisco 64–33 in their last encounter. Russell was playing opposite California's lauded all-American center, Bob McKeen. Minutes after the game began, Russell blocked McKeen's first shot, smacking the ball into the third row of seats in the Berkeley Arena. "Now where in the world did he come from?" Pete Newell, the California coach, asked the player sitting next to him. The player had no answer, but from that moment on, the game was a rout, with Russell blocking thirteen shots and scoring twenty-three points while holding McKeen to fourteen.

K. C. Jones had felt ill during the game, and the next night he collapsed with a ruptured appendix. That put him out for the season, and San Francisco's opponents quickly learned to triple-team Russell, muffling the brilliant start. But then next season, with K. C. Jones back and Russell stronger and more experienced, the perennially neglected Dons won their first two games, lost their third to UCLA, and then did not lose another game for the next two years.

What was so extraordinary about San Francisco was that the team seemed to come out of nowhere, from a school so small it was completely off the radar, with a fretful, anonymous, bespectacled coach and a roster of players no basketball powerhouse had even deigned to consider recruiting. Of the sixteen members of Woolpert's team, twelve came from the San Francisco Bay Area, and only one was from out of state. None of them had achieved any true distinction in high school; had they done so they would not have gone to San Francisco. The coaches who ran the basketball programs at the powerhouse universities had the luxury of selecting from hundreds of hopeful players the chosen few whose skills matched exactly with the requirements of their specific systems. The San Francisco Dons that Bill Russell played with had been put together almost as haphazardly as a playground pickup team.

They were also more integrated than other teams. Three of Woolpert's starting players—K. C. Jones, Hal Perry, and Russell—were black, and so were three substitutes. In that day, many college coaches, even in California, would play only one black player at a time, and segregated Southern colleges never considered recruiting black players, regardless of talent. Once San Francisco became successful, Woolpert began receiving hate mail, fans in Southern arenas threw pennies at his players, and one USF alumnus told a reporter, "They are scarcely representative of the school. Perhaps a rule should be established that only three can be on the court at any one time." When another alumnus suggested to Woolpert that he reduce the number of black starters, the coach reacted angrily. "Anyone," he replied, "who claims there should be discrimination toward a Negro or a Protestant or a bricklayer's son on an athletic team or in a classroom is not representative of this school either."

As San Francisco's unbeaten record grew longer during the 1954–55 season, East Coast sportswriters considered it a statistical aberration that would be corrected once the team faced substantial, nationally ranked competition. When the Dons arrived in New York to play in the Holiday Festival at Madison Square Garden, it was expected that they would be trounced by Holy Cross, which had won the NIT championship the previous year with Tommy Heinsohn, who was to become Russell's teammate on the Celtics, playing center. But Russell completely shut down Heinsohn, keeping him scoreless throughout the second half, blocking his signature hook shot, and scoring himself in a play, altogether legal at the time, that astonished Heinsohn. K. C. Jones backed into a corner as if to make a long set shot, but then he hurled the ball up over the backboard, while Russell leaped into the air, caught it, and stuffed it through the hoop. Heinsohn, who had never seen anything like it, was flabbergasted.

By February 1955, when San Francisco's record was 18–1, the Dons overtook Adolph Rupp's legendary Kentucky to become the top-ranked team in the country in an Associated Press poll. The streak continued as the team sailed through the NCAA tournament. While the entire team was unexcelled in its balance of shooting, playmaking, coordination, and defense, it was Russell who received most of the attention. While watching one of Russell's spurts of shot blocking, a radio announcer declared, "This is like a one-man volleyball game."

In the regional finals, San Francisco faced Oregon State, which had seven-three Swede Halbrook, the country's tallest basketball player. Before the game, photographers had Halbrook and Russell pose together. Halbrook raised his right arm, a ball in his hand, as high as he could. Russell's wingspan, which had never been measured, was said to exceed seven feet, and though he was six inches shorter than Halbrook, he now raised his arm up over the ball Halbrook was holding and wrapped his fingers around the top of it. Red Auerbach had a theory that the one true way to measure a basketball player's height was not from the top of his head but from the top of his fully extended arms, and when Woolpert saw the way Russell's reach exceeded Halbrook's, he knew that his team could go all the way. In what was one of the greatest Cinderella stories in college sports, it did. Russell scored a record 118 points in the five NCAA games the team played. At one moment in the semifinals, in the game against Colorado, he had his back to the board but still managed to come down with the rebound. Then, his back still to the board, he jumped up above the defenders and, using both hands, swung the ball backward over his head and down into the hoop.

"Did you ever see anything like that?" a San Francisco reporter asked Harry Hanin, a scout for the Globetrotters.

"No," Hanin said, "and I never saw anything like *him,* either."

After the Holiday Festival in Madison Square Garden, a writer for *Sports Illustrated* had declared, "If [Russell] ever learns to hit the basket, they're going to have to rewrite the rules." And indeed, once the season was over, NCAA officials decided to do just that. They widened the free-throw lane from six to twelve feet, to inhibit Russell's ability to rebound on offense. "We weren't planning to make any changes in the foul lane," Doggie Julian, the Dartmouth (and former Celtics) coach told a reporter afterward. "But after some of the coaches saw Russell's performance, they got scared and pushed through the twelve-foot lane."

When Russell started his senior year, in the fall of 1955, other coaches expected San Francisco to dominate the season once again. "The rest of us might just as well stay home and weed the garden," one complained. Indeed, the Dons' streak continued, and on January 28, 1956, when they beat UCLA and won their fortieth straight game, they set an NCAA record. But Pittsburgh State in Kansas had once won forty-seven consecutive games in the small-school circuit, and the Dons, still surprised by their own success, began to realize that they might surpass Pittsburgh State's streak and make basketball history. Woolpert, by nature a nervous man, grew so anxious that he had trouble keeping down food and became unable to eat. Game by game, the string of victories grew longer, the magic number drew closer. And then on February 28, 1956, the Dons beat the College of the Pacific for its forty-eighth consecutive victory and a record in college basketball. By the end of the year, when the team beat Iowa for its second NCAA championship, it had a winning streak of fifty-five victories. After watching the final, Utah coach Jack Gardner said, "This is the greatest college basketball team ever assembled."

BY THE SPRING of 1956, when Russell and the Dons had become the most talked-about basketball team in the country, Red Auerbach was wrapping up his sixth year as coach of the Celtics. Attendance at Celtics games was now so dismal that when the 1955 playoffs were over, Walter Brown had been unable to pay the players their playoff bonuses. He had promised to make good on the debts, together with interest, at the start of the following season, and he was true to his word. But Auerbach felt uncertain enough about his future that he had begun supplementing his income by working as a sales representative for CelluCraft, a plastics company that manufactured flexible packaging like Jell-O bags and Kool Pop wrappers.

By then Auerbach had become convinced that Bill Russell was the big man who would finally allow the Celtics to break out as a club and start drawing fans. The question for him in the spring of 1956 was how to bring the player and the club together. Auerbach had been aware of Russell since 1953, the same year he first saw Chamberlain at Kutsher's Country Club. He had gone to see his old college coach Bill Reinhart. The George Washington basketball team had just returned from the All-American College Tournament in Oklahoma City, where it had been beaten by the University of San Francisco with Bill Russell playing center. It was the year K. C. Jones had burst his appendix, before the Dons began their record-breaking streak and when Russell was still an unknown. He had not scored many points in the game against George Washington, but he dominated under the basket, blocking shots and rebounding at will.

Over lunch in the university's Welling Hall, Reinhart told Auerbach he was convinced that Russell not only could play professional basketball but might well provide the crucial piece that was missing from the Boston Celtics. While Russell was still only a sophomore, Reinhart said, he was the fastest center in college, could outrebound taller players, and by thinking smarter was able to destroy the opposition's game plan. "Try to get this guy," Reinhart said, "no matter what you have to pay or who you have to trade."

It would be another year before Auerbach actually saw Russell play. In the mid-fifties, NBA teams did not have scouts who traveled the country evaluating potential talent. It was an era before videotape, and coaches such as Auerbach had to rely on the recommendations of people they knew and trusted. After talking to Reinhart, Auerbach periodically called Russell's coach, Phil Woolpert, who assured him that his player had professional potential and could fit into Boston's fast-break game. Auerbach also talked to Freddy Scolari, one of his own former players who was from the San Francisco area and had returned there.

"Red, he can't shoot to save his life, but he's the greatest thing I've ever seen in my life on a basketball court," Scolari told Auerbach.

Auerbach asked Scolari if he was sure.

"I told you," Scolari said. "You want an affidavit?"

A number of coaches and sportswriters believed Russell lacked pro potential. He had certain specific, if somewhat limited, skills, they believed, but he was too skinny and he was a poor shooter. He was certainly not the all-around phenomenon that Wilt Chamberlain, then still a high school student, was proving to be. But Auerbach's inquiries left him with the impression that, however limited Russell might be in general, in the areas of his strengths he was overwhelming. Russell was not the answer to every coach's prayers. But working with players whose skills complemented and extended his and whose talents covered for his weaknesses—players, that is, like the Celtics—he could be the linchpin of an indomitable team.

DURING THE SUMMER of 1955, after the Dons' first incredible season, Bill Russell had been invited to the White House for a meeting about physical fitness with President Dwight Eisenhower. Willie Mays, Gene Tunney, Hank Greenberg, Ford Frick, and Bob Cousy were all present. It was a remarkable honor for a mere college player to be included among professionals of such stature, and the president singled him out, reportedly asking him, as a favor to the country, not to turn pro until he'd played in the Olympics. With Russell were his father, his stepmother, and his fiancée, Rose Swisher, the niece of Earl Swisher, one of his teachers at McClymonds. They had all driven from California to the capital, and afterward, they decided to stop by Louisiana on their way home.

This trip through the Jim Crow South, after having just been feted at the White House and called "Mr. Russell" by the president of the United States, made a lasting impression on Russell. The travelers endured the humiliation and indignity of being forced to use "colored" bathrooms, drink at "colored" water fountains, and enter rooms through "colored" doors, of being unable to find a restaurant that would serve them and having to buy crackers and bologna at a general store and sit eating on the roadside as whites drove by snickering. Once Russell arrived in Monroe, he had to step off the sidewalk if a white man walked by, had to sit in the back of the bus and in the balcony of the movie theater. The glory and honors, the attention and publicity, the cheering fans, the acknowledgment of the president himself—it was all reduced to nothing in the state of Louisiana. "I was just another black boy, just so much dirt, with no rights, no element of human courtesy or decency shown to me or mine," he wrote in a 1966 memoir.

It was one of the central experiences in Russell's life, one that would stay with him forever. As an adolescent, Russell had been inordinately sensitive to the smallest slight, often imagining an insult when none was intended. He even thought that Phil Woolpert, who had fielded one of the most integrated teams in the NCAA, was racially insensitive, judging white players more leniently than black ones. Having achieved acclaim as a basketball star, he remained just as acutely, even morbidly, sensitive to slight, but now he was in a position to demand respect, and one of the first people to feel the sting of his icy disdain was Abe Saperstein.

The owner of the Harlem Globetrotters was a tiny, fast-talking man, the son of a Polish immigrant tailor, who was born in London and then had moved to Chicago with his family when he was a child. Although he was an enthusiastic athlete, he turned to coaching after he reached a height of five feet three and stopped growing. In 1926, he had an all-black team, the Savoy Big Five, that was based in the Savoy Ballroom on Chicago's South Side. When the ballroom's owners dropped their basketball program in favor of roller-skating, Saperstein decided to take the Savoys on the road to play local teams in small Midwestern towns. He renamed them the Harlem Globetrotters, to establish in advance that the team was entirely black and to suggest an international track record that was totally nonexistent, and he created new gold-starred uniforms in his father's tailor shop.

In 1927, the team set out in a used Model T that Saperstein had bought from a funeral director. In their first game, in Hinckley, Illinois, they earned seventy-five dollars. It was just enough money to encourage them to continue. The Globetrotters struggled through the thirties, with Saperstein serving as manager, ball boy, driver, and even, from time to time, substitute player. The team began to attract a real following only once World War II came to an end. Since the two professional basketball leagues were all-white, the Globetrotters provided the sole outlet for black athletes who wanted to earn a living from their basketball talents, and by the late forties the team had perfected its game, which was part vaudeville show, part circus act, and part sport. The Trotters, also called the Globies, dribbled between their feet, rolled the ball the length of their arms, passed behind their backs, double-faked and triple-faked, and ran up into the stands. Goose Tatum was their team clown, Marques Haynes the dazzling dribbler with the fancy footwork. In 1952, on their twenty-fifth anniversary, Saperstein took the team on a world tour that had them playing before crowds in Europe, Africa, the Middle East, and Asia.

In the spring of 1956, with San Francisco's record streak continuing, Bill Russell preparing to graduate, and the NBA college draft approaching, Saperstein let it be known to sportswriters that he might be willing to pay as much as $50,000 for Russell's services. Russell, who was nothing if not serious, was disinclined to play for a team of crowd-pleasing entertainers and clowns, but an offer of $50,000 was too rich to dismiss out of hand, so when USF was in Chicago playing at the DePaul Invitational, Russell, together with Phil Woolpert and assistant coach Ross Guidice, accepted an invitation to meet Saperstein, who arrived at Russell's hotel room with his assistant, Harry Hanna. Saperstein assumed he was negotiating with Woolpert, and, saying little to the prickly young man he wanted to sign, he talked to the coach about the benefits and rewards of playing for the Globetrotters while Hanna told jokes to Guidice and Russell. The slight enraged Russell, and as he listened to Saperstein make his case to Woolpert, he found himself thinking, *You want to talk to Woolpert, you just get Woolpert to sign a contract with you.*

RUSSELL HAD NATURALLY LEARNED of the calls Red Auerbach had been making to Phil Woolpert, and he knew the Celtics were interested in him. His personal preference was to play with George Mikan and the Minneapolis Lakers. In 1949, when he was a junior in high school, Russell had once gone to see the Lakers in an exhibition game in Oakland. Afterward, he hung around outside the locker room to meet Mikan, who said, "How ya doin', big fella?" and encouraged him to become a professional basketball player. But he was certain he would be drafted before the Lakers, the second-place team in the Western Division, got their pick, and he decided that if he ended up with the Celtics, he would play for them.

Auerbach, for his part, knew he would be unable to draft Russell. Boston completed the regular season with the second-best record in the league and was drafting seventh. Russell, for all the discussion of his limitations, was one of the strongest college players to become eligible that year, and he would certainly be one of the early picks in the first round. If Auerbach was going to get him, he would have to trade for him.

When the season came to an end, the Rochester Royals had the worst record in the league and were entitled to the first pick in the upcoming draft. Lester Harrison, who had owned the Royals since the time it was a franchise in the National Basketball League, was disinclined to draft Russell. Russell had committed to playing for the U.S. basketball team in the winter Olympics to be held that November in Melbourne, Australia, which meant he would not be able to join any professional team until December, well after the start of the season. Also, Harrison knew Abe Saperstein was itching to hire Russell, and while Russell had indicated his preference to play for the pros, it was expected that the NBA franchise that acquired him would at least have to approach the $50,000 Saperstein was reportedly offering. That would make Russell the highest-paid player in the NBA, and it represented a huge sum for the Royals, a money-losing franchise in a small city that, even with a big star, might not be able to draw enough fans to justify his salary.

Furthermore, Harrison had no idea whether Russell was really of professional caliber. He himself had seen him play once, at the East-West College All-Star Game in New York City, and had been unimpressed. In any event, what Harrison really needed was a shooter. His top player was center Maurice Stokes, a Rookie of the Year who had established himself as one of the best rebounders in the league. But the Royals backcourt was weak. Another prominent draft prospect, Sihugo Green, a guard from Duquesne, could shoot and handle the ball, and he made a better fit with the team than a tall man who would throw Stokes out of position.

Auerbach, trying to anticipate whom he would have to trade with to acquire Russell, asked Walter Brown to call Harrison and try to find out if the Royals intended to draft him. It was not ordinarily the sort of information one owner would share with another, but Brown and Harrison had a relationship based on the fact that the Ice Capades, of which Brown was part owner, had performed in the Rochester arena. Harrison told Brown that he could not compete with the offer the Globetrotters were expected to make for Russell. "I'm going to have to pass him up and go for Sihugo Green," Harrison said.

"That's all I wanted to know," Brown replied.*

*In later years, when the Russell trade had become encrusted with mythology, Harrison's failure to pick Russell would come to be seen as a colossal misjudgment that changed sport history, and Harrison himself, turning defensive, liked to claim, without any evidence, that Russell had intentionally played poorly during that all-star game because he knew Harrison was in the audience and hoped to avoid being drafted by the Royals. Auerbach, meanwhile, claimed that Walter Brown got Harrison to pledge not to draft Russell by promising to allow the Ice Capades to perform in Rochester two weeks a year. But Harrison always denied this, pointing out that the Ice Capades were already playing in Rochester, and Brown never mentioned it in interviews he gave over the years. What clearly happened is that Harrison had underrated Russell's ability after seeing him only once and, since he already had an excellent rebounder in Maurice Stokes, made the logical decision to opt instead for Sihugo Green.

• • •

With Harrison eliminated as an obstacle, Auerbach now focused on Ben Kerner, owner of the St. Louis Hawks, which had the second pick in the draft. The franchise had led a peripatetic existence in the six years since Auerbach had coached it in its incarnation as the Tri-Cities Blackhawks. The year after Auerbach left, Kerner had moved the team to Milwaukee and changed its name to the Hawks. They did well their first season, but then in March 1953 the Boston Braves unexpectedly moved to Milwaukee, completely eclipsing the Hawks in the affections of the city's sports fans, and in 1955 they moved on to St. Louis, a nomadic tribe in a plaintive quest for a home they could call their own.

Kerner knew St. Louis could prove fatal to sports teams. The city's previous professional basketball team, the Bombers, had folded in 1950, but Kerner had reason to hope his team might survive. The Hawks star forward, Bob Pettit, was from Louisiana. Playing in St. Louis, he was considered almost a local boy. KMOX, a 50,000-watt station that began broadcasting the Hawks games, could be heard in Louisiana, and fans began coming up from Pettit's home state to see him play.

Since Kerner already had, in the six-nine Pettit, one of the biggest men and best rebounders in the league, he was not seriously considering drafting Bill Russell. An unknown and unproven rookie from California, he would hardly be an immediate box-office draw in St. Louis. And if Russell missed the first six weeks of the season due to the Olympics, he might arrive too late to help the team break out in a crucial year. Kerner needed someone who could galvanize the gate on opening night.

Auerbach knew this as well, and he intended to propose that Kerner trade his second-place draft pick for a player who suited Kerner's needs perfectly: "Easy" Ed Macauley, the Celtics center. The idea of trading Macauley bothered Auerbach. Auerbach hated having to call a player—any player but particularly a talented, dedicated player such as Macauley—into his office and tell him he was trading him. It was the worst part of the job. Auerbach had done a lot of trading at first both when he took over the Blackhawks and when he took over the Celtics, but once he'd assembled his team and gotten to know the guys, it became more difficult, and as a result he traded players a lot less frequently than other coaches. Still, he did it when he had to. One of the main reasons he avoided becoming too close with his players—going to their houses for dinner, getting to know their wives and kids—was that he might need to trade them one day, and if it came to that, he didn't want to be tearing himself up about how the move would upset the player's pretty little wife and cute little kids.

But Auerbach thought that Macauley might actually welcome the trade. He had grown up in St. Louis and gone to St. Louis University, where he'd been a top player, and had played for the Bombers. He and his wife had kept their home there, and his one-year-old son, Patrick, had recently contracted spinal meningitis, leading to a high fever that brought on cerebral palsy, and was under the constant care of specialists in St. Louis. If Macauley was traded, he would be able to spend more time with his son.

When Ben Kerner heard from Auerbach proposing that the Hawks trade the Celtics their draft pick for Ed Macauley, he liked the idea. But he realized that it was, in effect, Boston's opening bid, and if Auerbach was that eager to acquire the second draft pick, he might get him to raise the ante. As it stood, the Celtics were already acquiring Tommy Heinsohn, the Holy Cross center, under the territorial draft. Kerner, figuring the Celtics could afford to give up another player, said he would agree to the deal if Auerbach threw in Cliff Hagan, an all-American whom Auerbach had drafted from Kentucky in 1953 but who had gone into the service and was only now being discharged. "Red, I need bodies," Kerner said. "You got the rights to Cliff Hagan when he comes out of the army, and I can use him, too. You're getting Tommy Heinsohn, and you got that gorilla Jim Loscutoff. You give me Hagan with Macauley, and you get Russell, and we're even up."

Auerbach instantly agreed, and the deal, which one historian would later declare was the most important trade of the decade in any sport, was struck.

THE U.S. OLYMPIC basketball team, with Bill Russell playing center, went on an exhibition tour that summer to raise money. One of the stops was Washington, D.C., where Auerbach always spent the summer with his family. Auerbach had seen Russell play only once, when San Francisco met Holy Cross at the Holiday Festival, and he'd paid more attention to Tommy Heinsohn, whom he was already planning to acquire in the territorial draft, so he went out to watch the Olympic squad take on an all-star team in College Park, Maryland. Russell played one of the worst games of his life. Auerbach thought he was awful, horrible in fact. He thought, *God, I've traded* *away Ed Macauley and Cliff Hagan for this guy.* He felt like holding his head in his hands. Later, Russell came over and apologized, saying that he'd never played so poorly but that he was suffering from a hernia. Auerbach said that he hoped that was the case because if it was not, then he, Auerbach, was a dead pigeon. Russell sounded sincere, and anyone could have an off night, but Auerbach couldn't help wondering if the people who said Russell was not cut out for the NBA had been right.

Russell had not yet signed with the Celtics, but the fact that he'd been drafted caused Avery Brundage, the head of the International Olympic Committee, to question whether he had lost his amateur status. "If he intends to turn professional, then he violates the ethics of amateurism," Brundage declared. "He should guarantee that he will continue as an amateur or he shouldn't compete in the Olympics." Russell insisted that he was in fact an amateur, that he had no control over whether the NBA drafted him, but some sportswriters argued that he was compromised by a Jim Thorpe taint, and as the Olympic games approached, this attack on his integrity put Russell in an angry mood.

Then, on the flight to Melbourne, one of the plane's engines caught fire and it had to return to Hawaii, precipitating a fear of flying that would dog Russell through the endless travel of his long professional career. Once Russell's team reached Australia, however, it won the gold medal, scarcely breaking a sweat in the process, and Russell flew home for his scheduled marriage to Rose Swisher. Walter Brown was so eager to court his prospective player that he flew out to San Francisco to attend the ceremony. And in a sign of the celebrity that Russell had already acquired, the San Francisco Police Department provided him with a police escort from the church to the reception.

THE CELTICS were out of town when Russell and his wife arrived in Boston, but Walter Brown and Bill Sharman, who was injured, were on hand to meet them. Russell had never in his life actually seen a regulation NBA game, and so, before his debut—scheduled for a Saturday afternoon game in the Garden that was to be televised nationally—Auerbach had him fly down to New York to watch a doubleheader in which first the St. Louis Hawks played the Fort Wayne Pistons and then the Celtics played the Knicks. As part of Russell's introduction to the major leagues, Auerbach invited Milton Gross, the sports columnist for the *New York Post,* to join them.

Gross was a dry, vinegary man, a chain-smoker who favored scotch and soda, had a master's degree in economics from Fordham University, and wrote a thousand-word column five days a week that was syndicated in one hundred newspapers in cities ranging from Atlanta to Jerusalem. Gross was also an unapologetic liberal at a paper then known, under its owner, Dorothy Schiff, for its liberal politics, and he had established himself as a writer who understood, sympathized with, and championed black athletes. At the time, he was the *Post*'s second sports columnist after Jimmy Cannon. Gross's column was anchored on the first inside page from the back, next to the crease, or splayed across the top of the back page itself if he had an especially hot exclusive. Cannon never had much of a feel for basketball, but Gross, who'd played the game in high school in the Brownsville section of Brooklyn, did. And in the mid-fifties he sensed the sport growing, felt the pro game was on the brink of becoming major-league, and he covered it energetically.

There were seven newspapers in New York at the time, and the competition was ferocious. The *Post*'s sports editor, Ike Gellis, was a gambler as well as a passionate sports fan, and he edited his section for men such as himself, making the *Post* the first newspaper to run the betting line on all games in all sports. Gellis wanted hard, exclusive sports news for insiders, and so Gross was not a poetic lyricist in the vein of Red Smith and Grantland Rice, not a Homer evoking the beauty and pathos of heroic competition. Instead, he was a hustling newshound, a "digger," as his colleague Dick Young called him, someone who could create a scoop out of a locker-room interview, getting good position right next to the athlete and murmuring his questions out of the side of his mouth so none of the other reporters could hear him—a type of question that became known as a Milty. He was always running off to catch a plane or tracking down a source in a distant hotel room, always searching for the scoop or angle that would be uniquely his, and sitting next to Russell as the Celtics' new young center watched his first regulation NBA game would provide just the sort of inside material that made for a prototypical Milton Gross column.

When the first game of the doubleheader began, Madison Square Garden, at Eighth Avenue and Fiftieth Street, was filled. Kids were packed into the fifty-cent-a-seat upper balconies, which on the sides extended so far out that they blocked the view of part of the court, while a smoky haze was rising to the rafters from the cigars of the swells in the top-dollar courtside seats. Russell was paying particular attention to the Hawks, since that was the team against whom he would make his debut the following Saturday. The speed and the bulk of the players impressed him, and so did the unremitting pace of the game. As he was watching, Willie Naulls, who had played against Russell when at the University of California and who was now with the Knicks, came by to welcome him to the NBA.

"This ain't possession basketball," Russell said.

"You got to run in this league," Naulls told him.

Auerbach explained the tactics and styles of the different players to Russell. Bob Pettit liked to fake his jump shot and go around you. Mel Hutchins had a long shot from the side but he could also drive in with power. Charley Share sometimes dribbled just to better his position.

At the end of the game, Gross asked Russell what he'd seen.

"Nothing I didn't expect," Russell said. "Good shooting. A lot of shooting and a lot of running."

At the time, Gross felt Auerbach may have been oversold on Russell. Gross thought that it would take Russell time to adjust to the pro game, that his rebounding would not amount to much until he did, that he would never be a serious scoring threat, and that the other Celtics would get upset with the fact that the rookie would be earning more than all of them except Cousy. It was entirely possible, he thought, that Bill Russell would turn out to be a big disappointment.

Auerbach was aware of Gross's skepticism, but he did not share it. After watching Russell's dreadful performance in College Park, which he kept reminding himself was the result of a hernia, he'd followed him in the Olympics and talked to more people, and he'd become a convert. Auerbach thought that Russell might actually turn out to be better than even his supporters believed he was. That was because Russell was essentially untested. Few of the teams he had faced in college truly challenged him, and he had not played any harder than had been necessary to win. When Russell joined the NBA, in Auerbach's view, it would be like taking off the wraps. Auerbach's only concern was whether Russell would be tough enough for the pros. He had the talent, no doubt about that. The question was: did he have the guts?

Russell had yet to sign his contract and was still not officially a Celtic, and when the game between the Hawks and the Pistons was over and the

Celtics prepared to take the floor, Auerbach asked the commissioner, Maurice Podoloff, who was sitting in the first row, if Boston's newest player could join the team on the bench.

"Why not?" Podoloff said. And then, as a joke, Podoloff added, "Every once in a while point out to the court and then point your finger at him. It will look good."

"Fine," Auerbach said and turned to Russell. "You'll sit with us."

"You won't mind, of course," Podoloff continued, "if I fine you twenty-five dollars for the privilege."

"After what you paid for Russell," Gross said to Auerbach, "what's another twenty-five dollars?"

"He'll make it up for us," Auerbach said.

Russell said nothing, but, Gross observed, he seemed to nod in agreement.

When the Celtics returned to Boston, Russell sat down with Auerbach in the coach's cluttered office to sign his contract. Russell was to be paid $24,000, only a bit less than Bob Cousy, the highest-paid player in the league, who earned a reported $25,000. But by going to the Olympics, Russell had missed more than a quarter of the regular season, so Auerbach agreed to pay him $17,000 plus a bonus, which at the time was considered an astonishing sum. "Not even pro baseball has ever paid a salary of that size to a rookie," wrote Arthur Daley in *The New York Times*.

Before Russell signed the contract, Auerbach wanted to reassure him that he shouldn't worry himself over the endless press stories speculating about whether he had the ability to score. Auerbach had hired him to control the ball, and that was all he needed to concentrate on doing.

"Russell, are you worried about scoring?" Auerbach asked.

Russell said that while he wasn't exactly worrying about it, he was indeed thinking about it.

"I'll make a deal with you," Auerbach said. "We'll never discuss statistics when we talk contract. I'll only discuss whether you played well. If you rebound and play good defense, I'll just consider whatever points you get a bonus."

Russell played his first game as a Celtic three days later, on December 22, 1956. His arrival had been a topic of discussion in Boston since the start of the basketball season. "Bill Russell's Buildup Rivals That of Ted Williams," one newspaper headline declared. The game was scheduled for a Saturday afternoon, and afternoon games as a rule drew the smallest number of fans, but the biggest crowd of the season so far showed up, some 11,000 fans— 4,000 more than appeared at a typical game—along with the city's major sportswriters and a television crew for NBC, which planned to air the game live.

The Celtics players usually arrived at the Garden two hours before game time, but Russell, still new to the city, became stuck in a Sumner Tunnel traffic jam, then got lost in the strange streets and reached the arena twenty minutes before the tip-off. He was so frustrated and angry when he appeared in the dressing room that Auerbach, angry himself over his new star's absence, had to calm him down. Auerbach assigned Russell to cover Bob Pettit. The league's leading scorer, Pettit was strong and fast. He could outrebound much taller men as well, setting up the Hawks' fast break, and he kept his team fired up by moving tirelessly up and down the court. Auerbach knew Pettit would get away from Russell and make him look bad by scoring, but he saw that as inevitable. The only way Russell would learn to play against men such as Pettit was by playing them. "Just try not to let him get away from you too often," Auerbach said. "And whatever happens, don't let it throw you."

Auerbach didn't start Russell. Instead, to give his debut some theater, he sent him in after five minutes, and when the announcer called out his name, the crowd gave him a window-rattling ovation. Russell was immediately startled by the violence of the professional level of play. Nothing he'd experienced in college had prepared him for it. When the Hawks' Charley Share knocked him across the chest with a forearm, Russell stopped to wait for the foul call, but it didn't come and the Hawks took off upcourt, leaving him to chase the play.

After his first quarter, Russell was also exhausted by the pace of the game, the sheer drain of running after Pettit, who never seemed to slow, much less stop. He was astonished that Pettit could keep it up. "Doesn't this guy ever get tired?" he asked his veteran teammate Arnie Risen.

"Sure, he gets tired," Risen said, "but he doesn't look tired."

Auerbach, watching from the sidelines, was a little disappointed in Russell. He seemed timid. The Hawks kept setting screens and blocks that hemmed him in while Pettit raced downcourt to score. The Hawks were pressing Russell, testing him, knocking him around, and he did not act as if he was willing to hit anyone back. Auerbach wondered if Russell's timidity was due to the fact that he'd just gotten married. That never did a guy any good—at least on the basketball court.

For all his timidity, Russell had some incredible moves—jumping for a rebound and, while still in the air, twirling around and rifling the ball over the opposing players to a teammate halfway down the court. No one had seen that before. But his most amazing move was his shot blocking. Pettit, one of the tallest players in the league, had a distinctive jump shot that powered him way up over the heads of his opponents before he released the ball. It had generally been considered an indefensible shot, but Russell was outjumping Pettit and had actually been able to block his jumper three separate times, swatting the ball out of the air after it had left Pettit's hand. And he did not knock the ball into the stands, the way some grandstanding shot blockers did—a crowd-pleasing move but one that gave the ball back to the other team. He reached under or around the ball and either tipped it up and caught it himself or deflected it to one of his teammates, making it a turnover as well.

Auerbach knew that all rookies had to be introduced to the pro game by degrees, and after twenty-one minutes, he took Russell out. Pettit had held Russell to six points, which was not bad considering Russell had been in the game for less than two quarters. But Russell also made sixteen rebounds, a figure that caught the attention of the sportswriters because it meant that while he was on the court he had controlled the backboards. Johnny Most, who called the Celtics games for the radio, had a gravelly voice that he liked to joke was due to the fact that he gargled with Sani-Flush. During the game, he had been shouting so excitedly about Russell that he'd actually grown hoarse. "You'll have to forgive me for losing my voice," he croaked to his audience. "But I think we just witnessed the birth of a star." Bud Collins, then with the *Herald,* reviewed Russell's performance as if it were a dance: "After waltzing effortlessly—though nervously—about Walter Brown's ballroom for twenty-one minutes, the willowy debutapper was adjudged a budding Brahmin for the NBA menagerie."

MILTON GROSS'S FEAR that Russell's salary would create envious discontent on the Celtics was unfounded. Whatever initial irritation his new teammates may have felt when they learned Russell's pay would exceed theirs—and none of them gave voice to any—it was quickly dispelled when Russell proved, as Auerbach had believed he would, to be an incredible draw at the gate. "It's certain that the increased receipts Big Bill brings to every box office will pay off the investment in him," a *New York Times* reporter predicted. Fans turned out in droves to see the new phenomenon. There was a blizzard in Syracuse the first time the Celtics played there with Russell, but attendance doubled. The Fort Wayne arena tripled its average attendance for his initial game against the Pistons. Record crowds watched him in St. Louis and Philadelphia, where ticket sellers had to turn away fans after the Arena sold out. Some 18,000 people showed up at Madison Square Garden, basketball's premier venue, for his New York debut. "Boston Forming 'Dynasty' with Russell as Gate Draw," a headline in the *New York Post* declared after Russell had played a mere five games. The paper's correspondent Leonard Koppett pronounced him "the biggest attraction in the game" and presciently observed that "he has the potential to give Boston the kind of 'dynasty' Minneapolis had with George Mikan."

Russell, however, was so miserable that he was ready to quit. Hostile fans screamed insults and racial epithets, an entirely new experience that left him brooding and hurt until Bob Cousy told him, "If you let the names people call you bother you, you don't belong in this business." Russell continued to be surprised by how much he was knocked around by opposing players, and at first he was unsure how to respond. Physical aggression was an accepted part of basketball, and the NBA's veterans made a point of testing the courage of every rookie who came into the league. Joe Lapchick, the coach of the Knicks, called it "putting the question." Just how brave was the rookie? Could he be intimidated? What sort of pain could he endure? Could a sharp elbow in the ribs rattle him? Would he fight back? And if he did fight back, would that throw off his game even more?

"What do you do when you get hit?" Russell asked one of his teammates.

"Very simple," his teammate said. "Hit back."

Still, Russell resisted. Then, at a doubleheader in Syracuse, Ray Felix, the six-eleven center for the Knicks, started harassing Russell, tripping, shouldering, elbowing, jabbing, and pushing. Auerbach, who could see what Felix was doing to Russell, knew that the rookie's career in the league would be short-lived unless he demonstrated that he was just as aggressive. "Russell, what's the matter with you?" he asked during a time-out. "Felix is murdering you out there. You don't have to take that." Back in the game, Felix continued with his tactics, but this time when Felix shoved with his elbow, Russell called him on it, pushing back. Felix, pretending to be the aggrieved party, drew his fist to hit Russell, but Russell was first, landing a crosscut to Felix's jaw that dropped him to the floor, where he lay sprawled on his back, stone-cold unconscious. Auerbach cheered from the sidelines. And Russell felt that the twenty-five-dollar fine he received was worth every penny.

But Russell also still felt like quitting, in part because he was mortified by the fact that he had the worst shooting record in the NBA. In one game against the Warriors, he missed fifteen consecutive shots. "Don't worry about it," Auerbach told him. "You're not paid to score points." Sportswriters, however, kept pointing out that other big men in the league, such as the Nats' Dolph Schayes and the Warriors' Neil Johnston, *could* shoot. As a result, Russell kept trying to raise his scoring totals, which irritated Auerbach. During one game, when Russell missed a long shot that he shouldn't have taken in the first place, Auerbach screamed, "What the hell are you doing shooting from way out there—besides making a fool of yourself?"

What Russell had no way of gauging, since he'd never played in the NBA before, was the impact he was having on the game. Years later, Auerbach would decide that Russell was one of the four men who had revolutionized basketball. Hank Luisetti had developed the one-handed running shot. George Mikan had turned the pivot into an offensive weapon. Bob Cousy made the game spontaneous, with split-second playmaking and the fast break. And Russell, with his blocked shot, created the modern defense.

When Russell joined the Celtics he was six-ten. He had towered over most every college player he had played, but in the NBA the average player was six-five. Many teams had one or two or three players who were Russell's height or close to it, and there were a few players actually taller than Russell. But in addition to his height, Russell had two other advantages. One was his reach. His wingspan—it had by now been measured—was seven feet four. And he was an amazing jumper who could kick the net and leap up and touch the top of the backboard. Sure, the Celtics reasoned among themselves, Russell had missed fifteen consecutive shots in that game against Philadelphia, but the important point was that Boston won the game. With Russell on the team, the Celtics finally became the fast-breaking club Auerbach had always wanted them to be. Auerbach hated to see a guard slowly dribbling the ball down the court—*thump, thump, thump*—while everyone else stood around watching. He wanted the entire team on the move all the time. One reason he liked the fast break was because the more you used it, the more the other team expected it, and that put them on the defensive even when they had the ball. Anticipating it, worried that they were leaving their own basket undefended, they backpedaled downcourt after shooting instead of moving in to the boards. Until Russell arrived, however, Auerbach's team had not been able to rebound consistently enough to make the fast break anything other than an occasional option. But with Russell now pulling down so many rebounds, the fast break became the central weapon in the Celtics' arsenal. Russell would come down with the rebound and immediately fire a line-drive outlet pass to Cousy, who would already be streaking to the far end of the court. If the man defending the basket moved toward Cousy, he passed off to Tommy Heinsohn or Bill Sharman for a jumper. If the defender stayed back to guard Cousy's teammates, Cousy went in for the layup. Such fast breaks, run one after another after another, literally changed the pace of the game.

The Celtics also began guarding the basket in a more aggressive style, one they called the " 'Hey, Bill,' defense." Cousy would play his man close, with a hand in his face, and shut down his outside shot. Then, if the man spun and beat him on the drive, Cousy would just yell, "Hey, Bill!," and Russell would move in to intercept the man. It was particularly effective because of the advent of the twenty-four-second clock. The rule had not been adopted in college at the time Russell had his great run with San Francisco, and on offense opponents could pass the ball around forever, wearing down the defense while waiting for an opening. But now, in the pros, Russell discovered to his delight that he had to maintain his defensive intensity for only ten to fifteen seconds before opponents would start to get nervous about running out the clock and take an off-balance shot.

Russell's most intimidating move, however, was his shot block. He would tell opponents he was going to make them eat the ball. He blocked so many shots, shoving them back down into the faces of the shooters, that the Celtics started referring to the balls Russell blocked as "Wilsonburgers." Teams throughout the league adjusted to Russell by changing the way they played the game. Previously, offense in basketball had focused on driving into the basket and then putting the ball in with a hook shot or layup. But because Russell was so effective defensively, teams started passing more and relying on the mid-range jump shot. Outside shooting came to the forefront of the game, and the layup, except on the fast break, all but disappeared. By the spring of Russell's rookie year, according to one calculation, 75 percent of all field goals were jump shots. "In one beautiful sweeping motion," the Boston sportswriter Joe Fitzgerald observed, "he was turning the game around." Of course, not everyone applauded the development. Shirley Povich, the gifted but contrarian sportswriter for *The Washington Post*, professed dismay. "In a single generation," he wrote, "there has been a revved-up degeneration of basketball from a game to a mess. It now offers a mad confection of absurdities, with ladder-sized groundlings stretching their gristle in aerial dogfights amid the whistle screeches of apoplectic referees trying to enforce ridiculous rules that empty the game of interest."

THE WEEK AFTER Milton Gross spent the afternoon with Bill Russell in Madison Square Garden, the *New York Post* columnist decided to fly out to Kansas City and meet the country's other phenomenal new black basketball player. It was late December, and Wilt Chamberlain and the University of Kansas Jayhawks had come to Kansas City to play in the Big Seven* tournament. In a poll of sportscasters conducted by the Associated Press earlier in the season, Kansas had been ranked the top team in the country, thanks to Chamberlain, who was now a sophomore. He had already become such a celebrity that, as the tournament got under way, a crowd gathered all day in

*Later it became the Big Eight.

the Muehlebach Hotel, where the Jayhawks were staying, hoping for a glimpse of the star. When he finally appeared they murmured in astonishment at how he'd had to duck to get through the elevator doors.

At the beginning of the season, *The Saturday Evening Post* had published Jimmy Breslin's article "Can Basketball Survive Chamberlain?," and many college coaches did not consider the question entirely rhetorical. Gross talked to a number of them during the Big Seven tournament, and there was a feeling that Chamberlain actually might be *too* good, that he so overwhelmed other players he could literally ruin the game. "When one player can louse up your offense because you can't go around him and can't go over him," one Big Seven coach complained to Gross, "and he scares you so much that you pay no attention to his teammates while concentrating completely on him, it ought to be illegal."

In the first game Gross saw, however, Chamberlain was surrounded by a collapsing four-man defense and scored only twelve points. Bill Russell, Gross thought, had been more impressive the first time Gross had seen him playing for San Francisco. But then Chamberlain scored thirty-six points in the second game and forty-five in the third, Kansas won the tournament, and Gross became a convert. Chamberlain, he decided, was not just much more gifted than Bill Russell, he was the future of basketball, the player who would define the game for the next fifteen years if he remained healthy.

Gross thought that Chamberlain had an astonishing ego for a nineteen-year-old, but it was, after all, commensurate with his talents, and it even served as a sort of survival tool because it enabled Chamberlain to enjoy the stares that he inevitably drew. "My height is getting me an education and all the other things I want," Chamberlain explained to Gross. "It's not too bad having people know me." Gross decided that he liked Chamberlain. The young man was Gross's type of athlete: colorful, controversial, driven, and not just talented but the best at what he did. "I've never seen anything like him," he told his readers.

Indeed, Chamberlain had defied comparison as an athlete almost from the moment of his arrival at Kansas. While more than a few sportswriters considered him ready for the pros, he could not, under the NCAA rules in effect at the time, join the varsity team during his first year at the university, and instead became a member of the freshman squad, which had no formal schedule and played exhibition games. At the beginning of each season, the freshman team took on the varsity squad, a game the varsity team had won every year since it was first played in 1923. Since the freshmen were always egregiously outmatched, the game had attracted little attention on campus in the past, but in the year of Chamberlain's arrival a record 14,000 spectators crowded into the University of Kansas field house to watch it. Among them were several coaches from the Big Seven conference, including Jerry Bush of Nebraska, curious to evaluate the young man who had been the subject of so much hype. The freshmen easily won, and despite being double-teamed, Wilt scored forty-two points. In one spectacular play, he leaped toward the basket and then, while still rising up, twisted himself until he faced away from it, swung the ball one-handed over his head and behind him, and punched it down through the hoop. When he saw the move, Jerry Bush turned to a companion and said, "I feel sick."

After the game, Bush went up to Phog Allen and said he had detected a weakness in Chamberlain.

"And what is that?" Allen asked.

"He doesn't handle the ball so well with his left foot," Bush said.

Allen could not resist the temptation to crow. "Wilt Chamberlain's the greatest basketball player I ever saw," he told reporters. "With him we'll never lose a game. We could win the national championship with Wilt, two sorority girls, and two Phi Beta Kappas." Chamberlain's debut on the freshman squad had actually made headlines around the country, and in the South admiration for his athletic prowess seemed tinged with racial anxiety. The *Daily Eagle* in Enid, Oklahoma, ran an article headlined "Phog Calls Negro 7-Footer 'Today's Greatest Player,' " and reported that "Allen—and 14,000 others—watched in amazement as the big but graceful Negro poured in forty-two points."

Despite the claims made by the black Kansans who'd helped Allen recruit Chamberlain, Kansas turned out to be almost as racially divided as any state in the Deep South, as Chamberlain found out when, the day he arrived, he was refused service in a local diner. "It took me about a week to realize the whole area around Lawrence . . . was infested with segregation," he recalled. Chamberlain informed Allen that he would not play basketball unless, on road trips with the team, he was able to sleep in the same hotels and eat in the same restaurants as the white players, and Allen immediately canceled exhibition games the freshman team had scheduled with Rice, Southern Methodist, Louisiana State, and Texas Christian.

The coach was prepared to do just about anything to placate his new star. Allen had turned seventy the night of Chamberlain's freshman debut, and Chamberlain's brilliant and highly publicized performance had convinced him that the Kansas administrators would now never dare force him into retirement. Although Allen's assistant, Dick Harp, was in charge of the freshman squad, Allen worked personally with Chamberlain. He had him shoot foul shots blindfolded, to develop his intuitive feel for the basket's location. And he presented him with a copy of Helen Keller's autobiography, thinking it would help Chamberlain improve his sense of touch for the ball.

Allen also served as Chamberlain's champion and defender when scandal continued to dog him. Bill Russell, then in his final year at San Francisco, was on the U.S. Olympic basketball team going to the 1956 games in Melbourne, and Chamberlain was virtually assured a slot as well, but he announced he was not going to play, which led to speculation that he had already in some way compromised his amateur status. "Why isn't Chamberlain a candidate for the Olympic team?" Colonel Harry Henshel, a member of the Olympic Basketball Committee, publicly demanded in March. "Is Kansas afraid to let him get around?"

The question flared up again the following month, when J. Suter Kegg, sports editor of the Cumberland, Maryland, *Evening Times,* wrote an article alleging that Chamberlain had once received money to play under an alias for a local semipro team. "He played here under the name of George Marcus in a professional game," Kegg declared. Harry Grayson, sports editor of the wire service NEA, and one of those who had claimed that corruption tainted Chamberlain's college recruitment, picked up the story and gave it national coverage. At the time, Wilt firmly denied the allegation—"I was never there," he stated—but while the charge was never proven, it also never went away, and years later Chamberlain admitted that it was true, he'd played some games in Cumberland and in Quakertown, Pennsylvania, and in a few other cities for expense money and a few extra dollars—so what? He considered the NCAA rules against such games—while the universities were earning huge sums off their amateur stars—utterly hypocritical.

At the end of Chamberlain's freshman year, the university informed Phog Allen that it would not waive the mandatory retirement policy; he'd be required to leave. Chamberlain was surprised. He'd assumed Old Phog, as he called him, was canny enough to extract an extension from the school. The decision left Allen shocked and embittered. After all he had done for the school, it was, he thought, unforgivable, particularly because he knew that as soon as Chamberlain joined the varsity as a sophomore, Kansas would become the most avidly followed college basketball team in the country. And it was. In Chamberlain's second year, on the day of Kansas's first game, against Northwestern, the *Lawrence Journal-World* ran a front-page photo of Wilt dunking. Northwestern's center, Joe Ruklick, who later became Chamberlain's teammate on the Warriors, was convinced the photograph was staged; Wilt must have been standing on a ladder. But Kansas destroyed Northwestern 87–69, with Chamberlain scoring fifty-two points and pulling down thirty-one rebounds—setting new records for Kansas in both categories. "He scored at will," Ruklick recalled, "but I wasn't awed until after the game, when I saw the stat sheet." As the season progressed, opposing teams assigned at least two men to guard Chamberlain, and at times three and even four. Kansas still won. Bill Strannigan, the coach of Iowa State University, felt he had to see Wilt play before his own team took on the Jayhawks, and he traveled to Lawrence to watch a game.

"I'd enjoy the next few weeks a lot more if I hadn't seen him," he told a reporter afterward. "He's the greatest player I've ever seen."

"What can be done about him?" the reporter asked.

"Just be patient and he'll graduate," Strannigan said.

Chamberlain was by then not just the most recognizable person on the Kansas campus, where he worked as a deejay on the college radio station, but also a national celebrity. He was profiled in *Time* and *Newsweek*. Fans wrote the university asking for signed photographs, and the university complied, mailing out copies of a publicity shot stamped with Wilt's signature. When the team traveled, people now stared at Chamberlain not just because he was tall but because they recognized him. But he was not universally accepted, and when the Jayhawks went to Dallas to play in the NCAA regionals after winning the Big Seven championship, Chamberlain was subjected to a storm of racial abuse.

To begin with, Dick Harp, who had replaced Allen as coach, had inherited Allen's promise to Chamberlain that the team would stay together, and because Dallas's hotels were segregated, he could find accommodations only in a motel in Grandview, twenty-six miles away. During the games, the greatest hostility came not from students but from older adults, who booed Chamberlain, screamed "Nigger!," hurled seat cushions, pennies, and cups onto the court, and tore the Kansas banners. Players on the opposing teams also shoved and tripped Chamberlain, and muttered "Nigger" whenever he got close. The next day, the referee Al Lightner acknowledged the racial hostility of Kansas's opponents who, he said, were deliberately roughing up Chamberlain and his teammate Maurice King. "The trouble seemed to be," Lightner said, "that they were dark-skinned." Chamberlain had not responded to the provocation, deciding that the most satisfying course of action would be simply to win, and indeed, Kansas easily took the Midwest regionals, beat San Francisco—which no longer had Russell or K. C. Jones—in the semifinals, and wound up facing off against undefeated North Carolina for the championship.

FRANK MCGUIRE, North Carolina's coach, was one of the many people who had predicted even before Chamberlain put on his varsity jersey that he was going to in some fashion ruin the college game. "I told Phog that he was trying to kill basketball by bringing that kid into school," McGuire had told Jimmy Breslin at the beginning of the season. Going into the championship game, McGuire's team was considered the underdog. The night before, in the semifinals, the Tar Heels had barely beaten Michigan State in triple overtime when Michigan's Johnny Green choked on a pair of critical free throws. But there was also a mystique about the team. It was on a thirty-one-game winning streak, which extended back into the previous season, and the streak had created almost hysterical excitement on the university's campus in Chapel Hill. Students were superstitiously growing beards and making sure that, every day, they took the same number of steps from class to class. One student had become convinced that if he moved his car from its parking spot, he would break the streak, and so he was letting it sit there, accumulating tickets.

Although Chamberlain's team was favored to win, McGuire had watched Kansas play during the NCAA tournament, and he did not consider it invulnerable. Chamberlain, he thought, was spectacular, but the rest of the team was unimpressive. McGuire, the thirteenth child of a New York City cop, was a credentialed member of that city's Irish community, and a network of policemen, firefighters, and dockworkers who were on the streets in every neighborhood had helped him fill the roster at Chapel Hill with tough New York talent. He had strong, fast, experienced players—Tommy Kearns, Joe

Quigg, Lennie Rosenbluth—and they were known for their poise, for making few mistakes and instead forcing their opponents to make them, and then for exploiting those mistakes.

McGuire believed that if his team could control the pace of the game and contain Chamberlain, the rest of the Jayhawks would not be able to score as well as McGuire's own men. Since Chamberlain was so difficult to stop once he got the ball, the only way to hold down his score was to reduce the number of shots he took, and so McGuire wanted his team to focus on preventing Wilt from getting the ball in the first place. In the locker room before the game, he told his players to take only shots they were confident of, shots where their teammates had boxed Chamberlain out, preventing him from getting the rebound. If they had to wait for the entire first half to take a shot, he added, that was fine with him. "We're playing Wilt, not Kansas," McGuire explained to his team. "Just stop him and don't worry about those other guys."

Before the game, in the Kansas Municipal Auditorium, Tommy Kearns displayed North Carolina's distinctive sangfroid when a reporter asked if the Tar Heels felt intimidated by Chamberlain. "We're a chilly club," Kearns said. "We play it chilly all the time. I mean, we just keep cool. Chamberlain is not going to give us the jitters." McGuire decided to have Tommy Kearns, who at five feet nine was the smallest player on the team, face Wilt for the opening jump. McGuire figured Wilt would get the tap no matter what, so he thought he might as well use his tall players to go after the ball. And he knew Wilt would feel like a freak standing in the circle with someone who barely came up to his clavicle. If he could bewilder and embarrass Chamberlain, if he could get him thinking, *Is this coach crazy?,* he might be able to throw him off his game at the outset.

Chamberlain, of course, outjumped Kearns at the tip-off, but just as McGuire hoped, the matchup perplexed him and he missed his first shot. McGuire had two of his biggest players, Joe Quigg and Lennie Rosenbluth, guarding Chamberlain so tightly that he found it hard just to move, and his teammates had trouble getting the ball to him. That left the other Jayhawks open, but they couldn't make their shots, and North Carolina surged to a 19–7 lead. In the second half, however, the Jayhawks found their range and took the lead, lost it but then retook it, and with ten minutes to go were ahead 40–37. At that point, instead of pressing North Carolina, which was tired from its semifinal game the night before, Kansas slowed the pace. Dick Harp wanted the Jayhawks to control the ball, and the Kansas fans were cheering the tactic. But Frank McGuire was secretly elated as well, since by stalling, the Jayhawks were giving the Tar Heels time to rest for a final surge.

With less than two minutes to play, Kansas was still ahead by three, and Chamberlain figured all he and his team had to do was let the clock run out. But by then North Carolina had caught its wind. To turn the ball over, the Tar Heels fouled Chamberlain's teammate Gene Elstun. Elstun missed his free throw and North Carolina rebounded. Quigg quickly scored, and Kearns, who was fouled, made his free throw, tying the game at 46–46 and sending it into overtime. Once the extra period began, both teams, afraid of a turnover and wanting to stall until the final seconds, played so conservatively that each scored only one field goal in the next five minutes, sending the game into double overtime. As the clock started for the second extra period, the tension on the court seemed to immobilize the players. Both sides again stalled until a tussle for the ball between Chamberlain and North Carolina forward Paul Brenna emptied the two benches and sent players from both teams shoving and pushing onto the court. The second overtime ended with no score, and the game went into a third overtime. At that point, both teams broke out of their paralysis, and a flurry of points ensued that ended when, with six seconds left and Kansas ahead 53–52, North Carolina's Joe Quigg was fouled.

McGuire called a time-out. As North Carolina had extended its streak toward the final, fans had been coming up to the coach and giving him nut-megs and rabbits' feet to carry in his pocket, begging him to wear the same sport coat to every game, anything to keep the streak alive, and now it had all come down to this: a pair of foul shots by Joe Quigg. McGuire told Quigg he had missed a one-point foul shot earlier in the game when the team was be-hind by a single point, and now he had a chance to make it up. Quigg was nervous. All he could think about was making those two shots, clinching the title, and going out undefeated. He was glad he had two shots. If he had only one shot, he thought, the pressure would have been even greater. When the time-out was over, Quigg stepped up to the foul line, and while he certainly felt nervous, he looked, as Tommy Kearns had put it, chilly. He dribbled, aimed, made his first and then his second shot, putting North Carolina ahead 54–53 and sending its delirious fans pouring out onto the court.

Now it was Dick Harp's turn to call a time-out. With six seconds on the clock, Kansas still had time to score. As the officials cleared fans off the court, Harp ordered Wilt to move in under the basket, in position for a high pass he could then dunk for the game-winning field goal. As play resumed, Chamberlain's teammate Ron Loneski, standing out of bounds at the far end of the court, wound up to make the inbounds throw, but McGuire had shrewdly assigned the six-nine Quigg to guard him. Loneski heaved the ball. Quigg leaped, got a hand on it, and knocked it to Kearns, who hurled it high into the air as the buzzer sounded, giving the victory to North Carolina, and for the second time the screaming fans stormed onto the court.

Chamberlain, who would go on to play more than one thousand professional and college basketball games in the next sixteen years, would always be haunted by this particular defeat. He'd been double- and triple-teamed throughout the game, and it had inhibited his play so much—he'd scored only six field goals and eleven foul shots for a total of twenty-three points, compared with his season average of thirty—that the frustration practically drove him wild. Also, North Carolina—overall a better team, an undefeated team—had won by only one lousy point. The game, as the sportswriters liked to say, could have gone either way. And it wasn't his fault, he felt. He'd gotten into position under the basket to take the pass and was there waiting when that damned Loneski threw the ball right into Quigg's hands.

But that counted for nothing. In the end there were the champions and then there was everybody else. North Carolina had come into the game being told by Coach McGuire that they were not playing Kansas, they were playing Wilt. And that meant that they had beaten Wilt. Despite all the press coverage, despite the fact that he was voted the tournament's Most Valuable Player, people would say in years to come—Chamberlain would hear it again and again, until it became a kind of nightmarish refrain—that the defeat by North Carolina was the first real sign that he was someone who was not able to deliver the title. That he choked in the clutch. That he was a loser.

7

BY MARCH, when the NCAA tournament was under way, the Celtics had established themselves in first place in the Eastern Division. Russell's December arrival had initially thrown his teammates out of sync, since they had gone through training camp and the opening weeks of the season playing an entirely different type of game, but after a dozen matches with Russell starting, they had adjusted to his presence, and had begun winning regularly. Russell, who'd given up perimeter shooting and now confined himself for the most part to safe inside shots, was providing the Celtics with defense. The team's offense, already strong, had been strengthened even further by the addition of its second rookie, Tommy Heinsohn. Heinsohn, sometimes known as Heinie, was a tough, handsome young guy with blue eyes and a military crew cut. Bob Cousy, who'd adopted Heinsohn as his wingman on the fast break, considered him an awesome natural athlete, a man with speed, power, and an incredible will to win. Heinsohn always played hard, but since he smoked, his wind was bad, and Auerbach typically sent him in for short spells and then rested him. "If you play for me, Tommy, go at top speed," Auerbach had told him during training camp. "If you poop out in four, five, or six minutes, that's all right."

Throughout the season, Heinsohn had done just that. He never paced himself, playing instead at a fever pitch until he was ready to collapse. He loved to shoot. He had a distinctive line-drive shot, the result of learning to play basketball as an eleven-year-old in a gym in Union City, New Jersey, that had an extremely low ceiling and an even lower pipe running across it. Players at the gym had to shoot either over the pipe or under it, and Heinsohn always shot under the pipe, his balls rifling toward the basket with scarcely any trajectory. After joining the NBA, he developed a reputation as such an eager shooter that he became known as Gunner and then as Ack-Ack, for machine gunner. His teammate Jim Loscutoff once kept count during a game, and found that, of the twenty-three times Heinsohn got the ball, he shot twenty-one times, lost the ball once, and passed off only once. Cousy liked to say that Heinsohn never shot unless he had the ball.

As the regular season drew to an end, emotions on the Celtics were high. Auerbach and Walter Brown felt that the team could, for the first time, make it through the playoffs and go all the way to win the championship. But tensions were high, too. When the Celtics lost the last game of the season to the Nats, the team that had eliminated them in the three previous playoffs, Walter Brown rushed into the locker room enraged. "You bunch of chokers!" he shouted. "I'll never come into this dressing room again." But then a few days later, when the Celtics beat the Nats in the first game of the playoffs, Brown returned to the locker room. "I'm sorry," he said. "I'm just a fan, and I was so scared that we were going to lose everything again that I got frustrated. I didn't mean it. I was upset. I apologize."

Tensions existed between players, too, particularly between the two rookies, Russell and Heinsohn. Heinsohn felt that Russell resented him. He thought the reason might date back to 1955 when Heinsohn, playing center for Holy Cross, had developed a reputation on the East Coast much like the one Russell was developing out west. But since the national press was based in the East, Holy Cross received more attention, and East Coast sportswriters had predicted that it would crush San Francisco in the 1955 Holiday Tournament. Instead, Holy Cross had taken a pounding, and Russell seemed to go out of his way to put Heinsohn in his place. It was something Russell still seemed to want to do. Shortly after Russell joined the team, Heinsohn brought a young cousin to Madison Square Garden, where the Celtics were playing in the second half of a doubleheader, and while the first game was under way, he asked Russell to sign an autograph for the kid. Russell refused. "Russ, this is my cousin," Heinsohn said.

"I'm not going to sign," Russell said. "If I sign for him, I've got to sign for everybody, and I want to watch the game."

Despite that slight, Heinsohn had tried to be accommodating. At the beginning of the season it had been Heinsohn's job, as the rookie, to carry the ball bag on trips. Once Russell joined the team in December, Heinsohn had tried to pass the assignment on to him, since Russell at that point was the team's most junior player. But Russell made it clear he was not about to play Stepin Fetchit, carrying ball bags and running out for sodas and sandwiches, as most rookies were required to do. Auerbach let the players sort out such matters themselves, and rather than make a fuss, Heinsohn had ended up carrying the balls for the entire season. But instead of showing any gratitude, or even thawing a little, Russell had remained cool and distant.

Then, during the first round of the playoffs, the NBA announced that it was naming Heinsohn Rookie of the Year. Heinsohn had established himself as a terrific player, a defensive rebounder as well as a gunner, but even so, everyone in the league, including Heinsohn himself, knew that Russell, not Heinsohn, had been the key to the Celtics' first-place finish in the regular season. Russell was not simply dominating all the other tall men in the league—Ed Macauley, Bob Pettit, Johnny "Red" Kerr, Ray Felix. He had in one season, or more like half a season, redefined the sport in a way that had earned him comparisons to Babe Ruth.

The ostensible reason Russell did not receive the award was because he'd joined the team in mid-season and thus did not qualify. But this struck Russell as a flimsy rationale. Russell could not believe that the decision to deny him the award was not motivated by racism. The previous season, Maurice Stokes had become the first black player to be named Rookie of the Year, and it seemed clear to Russell that the owners wanted to assure fans that blacks were not taking over the NBA and so were offering up Tommy Heinsohn, not Bill Russell, as the new face of the league.

The letter to Heinsohn from Commissioner Maurice Podoloff announcing his selection was accompanied by a check for $300. Heinsohn received it during the first round of the playoffs, while sitting in the Celtics dressing room. Russell, whose hook in the dressing room was next to Heinsohn's hook, saw it.

"I think you ought to give me half that check," Russell told Heinsohn.

"Why?" Heinsohn asked.

"Because if I had been here from the beginning of the year," Russell said, "you never would have gotten it."

He wasn't smiling.

THE CELTICS finished off the Nats in three straight games to take the Eastern Division title in a best-of-five series, then sat back to see who emerged victorious in the Western Division face-off between St. Louis and Minneapolis. Cousy and a number of other Celtics hoped they would end up playing the Minneapolis Lakers in the finals. The Lakers were superior to the Hawks in terms of talent, but the Hawks were much more driven. They had desire and determination, and when they beat the Lakers, Cousy and the other Celtics knew the championship series would be tough and hard.

The Hawks were then in their second year in St. Louis, trying hard to win the hearts of a town that seemed to have no love for any team except the Cardinals and hoping to avoid the fate of the Bombers, the basketball team that had folded seven years earlier. Ben Kerner's decision to trade the right to draft Russell for Ed Macauley and Cliff Hagan had paid off for the Hawks. The two players had attracted fans and rounded out a team that also included Bob Pettit, Slater Martin, Chuck Share, Jack McMahon, and Alex Hannum, the player-coach. The first game, played in Boston, underscored Cousy's concern. St. Louis won 125–123 after two overtimes. Cousy had a hot hand that night, scoring twenty-six points, but with three seconds to go in the second overtime, he missed a shot, and spent the rest of the night kicking himself for costing his team the game. The Celtics won the second game walking away, 119–99, then flew to St. Louis for game three.

St. Louis was a brawling city of breweries and German and Slavic immigrants. It had been the site of one of the country's most notorious race riots— the East St. Louis Massacre of 1917—and racial tensions remained high. In fact, those tensions were one more reason Hawks owner Ben Kerner had decided not to draft Russell. The Hawks still had an all-white roster, and when the Celtics played there during the regular season, the crowd pelted the team with eggs and taunted Russell with shouts of "Coon!," "Black nigger!," and "Baboon!" If possible, they despised Auerbach even more. "The hatred between Red Auerbach and St. Louis is a beautiful thing—deep, lasting, and built on mutual disgust," wrote one local columnist, who went on to describe the "rapturous acrimony" between the two. The personal antagonism between Red Auerbach and Ben Kerner added to the hostility between the Celtics and the Hawks. Auerbach had never forgiven Kerner for overruling him on the John Mahnken trade back in 1950 when Auerbach had been coaching the team in its incarnation as the Tri-Cities Blackhawks. Kerner, for his part, considered Auerbach an obnoxious upstart and was irritated by the talk that Auerbach had outsmarted him in the Russell trade.

One reason Kerner and Auerbach disliked each other so intensely was that they were so similar. Kerner was just as obsessed with control as Auerbach, and almost as brash and volatile. At every game, he could be found sitting at half-court next to his mother, the team's most devoted fan, and a group of friends who were referred to by officials as Murderers' Row for the noise they made protesting the calls that went against St. Louis. If the Hawks lost, Kerner was apt to storm into the locker room afterward, his tie askew, throwing chairs and screaming, "You're all stealing from me!" But emotion also carried him away when his players did well. Once when the team was on a winning streak, he called out before a game, "Make it five straight, boys, and I'll buy everybody a new sport coat." They did and he did. "Win tonight," Kerner shouted before the next game, "and you will all get a new pair of slacks." It happened. "Make it seven in a row," he said the next night, "and you get new sweaters." Eventually, the commissioner forbade such incentives, but by then, Bob Pettit figured, the Hawks were the best-dressed team in the league.

Both teams were playing for the championship for the first time—the Hawks had made it into the playoffs only once since Auerbach coached them—and Kiel Auditorium on the night of game three was wilder than any St. Louis crowd the Celtics had ever seen. To get to the court from the dressing room, they had to walk down a passage that cut through the seats, and the fans showered all of them, but particularly Russell, with abuse. Auerbach was determined to show the Hawks and their fans that he and his team did not feel intimidated. He began by complaining about the beat-up balls the Celtics had been given to practice with. Then, as the Celtics were warming up, Bob Sharman started shooting free throws that fell short. He felt that the height of the basket was slightly off, and Bob Cousy agreed.

Auerbach complained to the referees, Sid Borgia and Arnie Heft, that the basket at the Celtics end of the court was not regulation height. Kerner stood nearby watching irritably. "What the hell is going on, Red?" he called out. The officials measured the distance and found it to be exactly ten feet high, which proved to Kerner that Auerbach, as usual, was hoping to throw the officials off balance and insinuate that the Hawks were cheating. "That's bush!" Kerner shouted. "It's just a cheap trick!"

Auerbach's back was to Kerner. Before the sportswriters, the officials, the players on both teams, and thousands of fans, he turned and, operating on the Brooklyn-street theory that you always strike first, smashed Kerner in the mouth with his fist. The blow gave the shocked Kerner a bloody lip and knocked loose a tooth, but before he could respond, his staff pulled him and Auerbach away from each other. "Look at that," he said despite the blood and pointed to his mouth. "Nothing happened." He turned to Auerbach. "You can coach that team of yours from a hotel room!" he yelled. "And on top of that, you can't even punch!"

The fight was over so quickly that many people in the arena were unaware of it, and when reporters surrounded Maurice Podoloff to ask what he intended to do, the commissioner said, "I must ascertain the facts." Auerbach was not thrown out of the game, which had not officially started at the time he hit Kerner, but Podoloff subsequently fined him $300, causing Walter Brown to write a letter to Podoloff complaining that Kerner should also be fined for inciting the incident. "From all I hear," Brown declared, "Auerbach had some provocation."

For all Auerbach's theatrics, the Hawks won game three, and the series remained intensely competitive, with the teams alternating victories and the outcome at times decided by a single basket in the final seconds. By mid-April the series was tied 3–3, and the seventh and final game was scheduled to take place in Boston on a Saturday afternoon, April 13, 1957, before a sellout crowd and a national television audience. The Celtics began arriving at the Garden two hours before game time. The team's locker room, behind the green clubhouse door under the stands, was smaller and drabber than many college locker rooms. In fact, it was not, strictly speaking, a locker room at all, since it had no lockers. What it did have was one toilet, two benches, one shower, and ten hooks. After each game, Walter Randall, the locker-room attendant, washed the players' uniforms at home and before the next game hung them on their proper hooks. After each player arrived, he put on his uniform and hung his street clothes on the hook. If the players tossed towels on the floor, Randall would come down on them hard: *Don't be throwin' no towels around! Clean up after yerselves!*

The locker room also had a hot plate and a coffeepot. Each player had a mug with his team number stenciled on it. Most players had a cup of coffee before the game. With the championship at stake, the dressing room was quieter and more tense than usual. Bill Sharman stretched and brewed a cup of tea. Auerbach smoked a cigar, and Heinsohn smoked a cigarette. Some players ate: a can of corn, a bologna sandwich. Russell vomited. The Celtics were notorious for playing with injuries, for appearing courtside wrapped, bandaged, and patched, and before the game Jack Nichols, one of the bench players, taped every team member who needed it.

Just before it was time to take the floor, Auerbach called the players together. Auerbach did not, as a rule, believe in pep talks, which he thought were more effective on high school and college kids than grown professionals, and so he didn't go in for any rousing oratory. He did point out the size of their playoff bonuses if they won: a total of $18,500 to be split among the team. "Defense and dollars," he said. "Dollars and defense." Russell had already vomited once when it came time for the Celtics to take the floor, but he still felt so nauseated that he told Auerbach he didn't think he could play, and the team left the dressing room without him. Russell sat alone for a few seconds and then, realizing that regardless of how he felt he would never be forgiven and would never forgive himself if he missed even part of what might turn out to be his first championship, he hurried after them.

In the years to come, some of the sportswriters who saw it would decide that the seventh game of the 1957 NBA championship series was one of the greatest athletic events they'd ever seen. Both teams, still financially unstable, were desperate for their first championship. Boston had won two of the three games played in the Garden during the series, and the home-court advantage made the Celtics slightly favored, but both clubs played fast-breaking ball, both were operating at peak intensity, and from the outset, the game was frenzied and high-scoring. Bob Pettit and Tommy Heinsohn, shooting better than anyone else on the court, practically traded baskets, but both Bob Cousy and Bill Sharman had gone cold in game six, and they remained cold during the first half. As a result, the Celtics went into halftime trailing by two points. The dressing room during the break was largely quiet. Then Auerbach told the team to go out and play the way they always played and their superiority would decide it.

In the second half, Cousy and Sharman remained cold, but Auerbach kept them in, feeling he had no choice but to maintain his confidence in his key players and hope they would shoot their way out of their slumps. Heinsohn made the difference, scoring at key moments, rebounding, even passing, tearing tirelessly up and down the court. Russell was also playing magnificently, spinning, running, blocking shots, but in the huddles he excoriated himself for his inability to contain Pettit. "Shut up, Russell, you're doing great," Auerbach told him. In the fourth quarter, the Celtics established a six-point lead, but then the Hawks surged, going up by two with twenty seconds left. Then Russell scored, St. Louis recovered the ball, and Jack Coleman raced down the court on a fast break. It looked as if Coleman was going to put the game away for the Hawks, but Russell, in an astonishing display of athleticism and sheer determination, raced after Coleman, caught up with him, and at the last moment was able to knock aside Coleman's layup. Heinsohn thought it was the most incredible single play he'd ever seen.

When the clock ran out, the game was tied 103–103. In the first overtime the two teams traded baskets, neither able to break out. As the second overtime started, Heinsohn, who had scored thirty-seven points—more than anyone on the team, more than Cousy and Sharman combined—fouled out. Heinsohn didn't want to leave the game and argued hysterically about the call, but by that time, he was almost too exhausted to continue playing. Because of his bad wind, Auerbach normally played Heinsohn for short bursts, but the rookie had proved himself so crucial in this game that Auerbach had kept him in, and now that he was finally going out, he was so drained—and the tension in the Garden was so high—that he walked off the court in tears, sat down on the bench, and wrapped his jacket around his head so the crowd would not see him crying.

With less than four minutes left to play in the second overtime, the Hawks center, Ed Macauley, fouled out. The Hawks had been fouling out right and left, and by then the only players still sitting on the team's bench were Irv Bemoras and Alex Hannum, the player-coach. Hannum was an aging journeyman who'd played all over the league and had been picked up on waivers by Ben Kerner once the regular season started. Hannum had spent most of his time on the bench, however, and when Kerner fired his coach, Red Holzman, midway through the season, Hannum had ended up with the job more or less by default, but then to everyone's surprise had managed to bring the team all the way to the finals. While Hannum was still on the team roster and suited up in his uniform, he'd been devoting himself almost entirely to coaching and had not played in a game in three weeks. In other circumstances, Hannum would have sent in Bemoras. But Irv Bemoras was six-three. Hannum had four inches on him and since, at this point, rebounding was more important than shooting, Hannum put himself into the game.

Boston had established a narrow lead, and as the clock wound down, the team managed to cling to it, largely because Russell was making it difficult for the Hawks to score. It seemed to Ben Kerner, watching from the sidelines, that Russell had retrieved practically every defensive rebound since the fourth quarter began. *How could you possibly win,* he wondered, *if you got only one shot on every possession?* But the Hawks were also making unforced errors. Alex Hannum, rusty after weeks without playing, muffed an easy shot and a few moments later had to turn the ball over when he was called for walking. In the final seconds Boston had a one-point lead and was trying to run out the clock, and when Hannum fouled Jim Loscutoff to force a turnover, Loscutoff made his free throw, bringing the score to 125–123.

Hannum called a time-out. The Hawks had possession, but by then only a single second remained on the clock, which meant they did not have time to dribble the ball the length of the court and set up a play. But Hannum liked to sit around brainstorming improbable game situations and how he'd handle them, and he'd contemplated just such a moment. When Hannum had played for the Rochester Royals, one of his teammates was Bobby Davies, who had such an incredible arm that he could stand at one end of the court and hurl the ball all the way down its length, hitting the backboard at the far end. Since the clock did not start until another player touched the ball, such a throw would be a way of getting the ball downcourt without using up any time, though its success depended of course on the player who was making the inbounds pass actually hitting the backboard.

It was a long shot, but Hannum thought that since the Celtics would be expecting a pass, it was worth a try, and during the time-out he told Pettit to make his way downcourt and keep his eyes on the basket. Hannum himself would make the full-court inbounds pass. Hannum had never practiced this throw, but he had strong shoulders. Still, he was one of the worst shots on the team, and Ed Macauley wondered how he was going to hit the backboard from ninety-four feet out when he had trouble hitting it from fifteen. Standing under Boston's backboard, Hannum reared back and hurled the ball in a line drive to the far end of the court. Auerbach, watching from the sidelines, realized what Hannum was trying to do and thought, *Impossible*. To everyone's surprise, Hannum's included, he actually hit the backboard, but he had thrown the ball so hard that it ricocheted off with too much force, and Pettit did not have complete control over it when he batted it up toward the basket. Still, the ball hit the rim and rolled around and around before, just as the clock ran down, finally falling out.

Russell stood on the court watching. His jersey was soaked, his controversial goatee—the one he'd grown during the season and had promised his teammates they could cut off if the Celtics beat the Hawks—was dripping with sweat. When the ball fell out he instinctively raised his arms in victory. In thirteen months, he had won an NCAA championship, an Olympic gold medal, and now an NBA title. For a man who, four years earlier, had graduated from McClymonds High and applied for a job as a sheet-metal worker because he had no other prospects, nothing would ever compare to such moments of pure unadulterated triumph, when the game was finally over and he stood there alone, the winner.

BY THE END of his sophomore year at Kansas, Chamberlain had grown accustomed to the fact that controversy would be a constant in his life. Off the
court, he continued to be dogged by accusations that he had taken money
under the table to enroll at Kansas. Walter Brown—afraid that if Chamberlain joined the Philadelphia Warriors, they might unseat the championship
team he had just put together with Bill Russell—had demanded that the
NBA investigate Chamberlain's financial arrangement with the university,
and that, if it discovered any impropriety, it should ban him from playing in
the league. "I have no definite proof what might be the figure," he told reporters, "but it is a matter of fact that no one in the NBA can afford to pay
Chamberlain what he gets at Kansas."

The problem, as Brown conceded, was that he had no proof. Neither did anyone else. Chamberlain and the Kansas administrators maintained that all he received from the university was tuition, room and board, and the fifteen dollars a month that he earned by selling programs during the college's football games. But it was obvious to everyone that Wilt's lifestyle required more than fifteen dollars a month. When he first arrived on campus as a freshman, he was driving a two-year-old Buick that he claimed to have paid for with money he'd made from his summer job as a bellhop at Kutsher's Country Club. But then in his sophomore year, he began driving a brand-new Oldsmobile convertible.

To the officials at the NCAA, this was too egregious to ignore. They summoned him to their Kansas City office, where they turned on a tape recorder and interrogated him about his finances. They wanted to know the exact nature of his financial arrangement with Kansas, whether he was compensated for his campus radio show, *Flipping with the Dipper,* and how he had paid for his car. Chamberlain insisted that he'd taken out a loan for the convertible, and had received no illegal payments of any kind from the university or its alumni. The interview lasted four hours. "It was nice talking to you," the chief investigator said when the interview was finished, "but I don't believe a word of it."*

Chamberlain spent part of the summer after his sophomore year traveling around the country testing his skills against other college and professional players. He went up to New York City for school-yard pickup games against people such as Tom "Satch" Sanders and Walter Dukes, and to Indianapolis to play Oscar Robertson. By the end of the summer he figured he'd learned more from these games than he had in that entire year with Coach Harp. He returned to Kansas determined to win the national championship that he'd been denied the previous year. But halfway through the season, when Kansas had won ten straight games and was ranked number one in the nation, Chamberlain was accidentally kneed in the groin during a game with Kansas State.

---

*In 1960, two years after Chamberlain left Kansas, the NCAA issued a report that found that people representing the university's "athletic interests" had put up $1,564 for the car, and it placed the university on a two-year athletic probation. A quarter century later, in 1985, Chamberlain acknowledged that while he was at Kansas three alumni whom he referred to as "godfathers" paid him $4,000 a year in cash.

The injury caused Chamberlain's testicles to swell up, a condition the university delicately referred to as a "glandular infection," and he was sidelined long enough for Kansas to fall out of playoff contention.

By the end of the season, Chamberlain had recovered, and he and his team delivered a 61–44 thrashing to Kansas State as it concluded, but he decided he'd had enough of college basketball. It wasn't just the injury, or the missed opportunity for another crack at the championship. Chamberlain had begun to find the game, at least the way it was played in college, frustrating. He was constantly triple-teamed, with opposing players crowding him so tightly he could barely move, and other teams froze the ball, passing endlessly instead of shooting, just so they could prevent him from scoring. Smaller players ran under him when he jumped, trying to cause him to fall and hurt himself, and at other times they climbed up on his back and just stayed there, clinging to him. He wasn't developing the skills he figured he'd need in the NBA.

Also, Chamberlain figured that he had ten years left as a basketball player. And to deprive himself of being a professional for one of those years just to earn a degree made no sense, because whatever advantage a degree might give him would never offset the financial loss of one of his ten years as basketball player. He had to make his money now, while he was young. And there was his family to consider. His parents were still struggling to raise children on the sixty dollars a week his father, who was now in his late fifties, was making as a handyman and the money his mother brought in as a domestic.

At the end of his junior year, Chamberlain got a call from Abe Saperstein. While Saperstein had failed to sign Chamberlain directly out of high school, he had not abandoned his hopes of hiring him. Saperstein had a minority interest in the Philadelphia Warriors and was well aware that Eddie Gottlieb had drafted Chamberlain. But under NBA rules, if Chamberlain left Kansas at the end of his third year, he would have to wait a year before turning pro, and Saperstein hoped he would play for the Globetrotters during that year. His two stars, Goose Tatum and Marques Haynes, had left to form a rival team, the Harlem Magicians, and the Trotters needed a new player with dazzling skills and a large personality. Once Chamberlain joined the team and got used to the money, Saperstein thought he might be persuaded to stay. And if he did not, he would at least be going to a team in which Saperstein had an interest.

Saperstein offered Chamberlain a base salary of $46,000, but the package also included bonuses based on fan attendance that could bring it up to $65,000. Chamberlain found the terms irresistible, particularly the attendance bonuses. "Very early in my career, I learned to count the house and figure out what the crowd was worth to me," he said later. Haskell Cohen, the publicity man for the NBA who had gotten Chamberlain his job as a bellhop at Kutsher's, did not want him to go to the Globetrotters, thinking it would hurt his game and his reputation, but when Chamberlain told him how much he'd be making, Haskell said, "You might as well go ahead, you're sure never going to get that kind of money in the NBA."

On June 18, 1958, Saperstein held a press conference at Toots Shor's in New York to announce the deal. Chamberlain appeared in a red, white, and blue Globetrotters warm-up suit and, as a reporter for *The New York Times* noted, was "idly palming in each hand a basketball that appeared pea-sized in his monstrous grip." As soon as the event was over, Chamberlain flew to Italy to join the Globetrotters. In Europe, he discovered to his delight that he was treated as an object of exotic fascination, but with none of the racial tension that complicated his popularity in the United States. As soon as he stepped from a hotel, a small crowd would gather and follow him wherever he went. In almost every city, he got requests to make personal appearances and give television interviews. The food was wonderful, and so was the climate, the wine, and the women. He was astonished at how available women were. His fellow Globetrotters did not even have to proposition them. If, during a game, a Trotter saw an attractive woman in the crowd, he invented some pretext to run into the stands, where he slipped her a note with his hotel room number. If he saw a woman on the street, he gave her tickets to the next game, where he passed her the note with the room number. In no time, Chamberlain was emulating the tactic.

Many sportswriters had ridiculed Chamberlain's claim that he was leaving college for the Globetrotters to play more challenging basketball, but in fact he was able to develop his game during his year with the team. Saperstein played him at guard, an entirely new position that allowed him to practice his feints and work on his passing and outside shooting. While Chamberlain had sworn he would not become one of the Globetrotters' clowns, playing guard did allow him the opportunity to move around the court and engage in the sort of theatrical stunts that amazed spectators and sold tickets. In one of the team's favorite plays, he would fall back to mid-court, another Trotter would feed him the ball, and he would then take two of his enormous nine-foot strides, which would carry him into the paint and up into the air toward the hoop for a dunk.

After touring Europe, the Globetrotters returned home and barnstormed around the country. Saperstein calculated that his ticket sales had increased 20 percent as a result of Chamberlain's presence on the team, and he offered Chamberlain a considerable raise to stay on with the Globetrotters. Chamberlain had enjoyed himself immensely that year. It would prove in fact to be the most enjoyable year in his entire basketball career. The Globetrotters' travel schedule was grueling, and they played a total of 205 games a year, which meant sometimes two or even three games a day, but the games themselves were not demanding. Since victory was foreordained, there was no pressure to win, the fans were uniformly adoring, and the team hardly ever practiced. Even so, Chamberlain was looking forward to testing himself in the genuinely competitive game played in the NBA. But he had become adept at playing suitors off each other, and as April approached and his contract with the Globetrotters came to an end, he hinted publicly that he might renew it, since Saperstein was offering him more than he could make in the NBA. The prospect filled Eddie Gottlieb with desperation. He had waited for four years for Chamberlain and was afraid that the Warriors might fold without him.

Gottlieb, known as the Mogul, was a small, overweight, balding man with a deeply creased face and sad eyes offset by a snappy bow tie. Red Smith once described him as "a wonderful little guy about the size and shape of a half-keg of beer." He'd been born in Kiev, Russia, in 1898, but when he was still small his parents migrated to New York, and as a boy he hitched rides on the backs of ice trucks to watch the baseball Giants at the Polo Grounds. His family moved to Philadelphia when he was nine, and he transferred his affections to that city's teams. He was athletic and, despite his small size, he set a scoring record at the Philadelphia School of Pedagogy, but his true talents were intellectual rather than physical. He had an almost photographic memory and later could recall not just the scores of games—all games, baseball and football as well as basketball—but the box office, the size of the crowd, and, if the game was played outdoors, the weather.

Gottlieb had been involved in basketball since 1918, the year he started a team of Jewish players called the South Philadelphia Hebrew Association, or Sphas, which later accepted gentiles and became part of the loose association of professional basketball teams in the twenties. Spectators coming to see the Sphas in the thirties climbed a marble staircase up to the third-floor ballroom of the Broadwood Hotel on Saturday nights and, after buying a ticket (thirty-five cents for women, sixty-five cents for men), sat on plush upholstered seats to watch a game that almost invariably included a fistfight between the Sphas' Chickie Passion and one of the opponents. Gottlieb all but guaranteed a fight. When the game was over, the spectators took to the floor to dance while Gil Fitch, another Sphas player, swapped his basketball uniform for a tuxedo and led the band.

After World War II, what remained of the Sphas became the nucleus for the Philadelphia Warriors, one of the original members of the Basketball Association of America. Gottlieb never married and, unlike a number of the early owners, had no source of income outside his team. He was manager and coach, sold tickets, and even drove the team to exhibition games. He understood the rules, and then, as the game evolved with the arrival of new generations of talent, he understood how they had to be changed. He appreciated ability, he saw how a limited player might fill a narrow but useful role on a team, and he knew how to motivate. Even after he stopped coaching, he would sit on the bench during games, indiscreetly second-guessing the coach he had hired and getting into arguments with the referees that often ended with him tearing off his suit coat and hurling it on the floor.

Gottlieb was notoriously tightfisted. But it was an understandable trait in those uncertain early days and one that helped the Warriors survive when many other franchises folded. Despite doling out taxi money and meal money reluctantly, despite haggling endlessly with his players over contract terms, he was loyal and could be generous, and most of his players not only respected him but came to consider him a lifelong friend. Gottlieb also had a gift for promotion. "He pumped the house and carried tickets in his pocket," recalled Joe Ruklick, who joined the Warriors in 1959. Gottlieb hired local sportswriters such as Herb Goode of the *Philadelphia Record* and Harvey Pollack of the *Bulletin* to handle public relations for his team. He sensed early on what would draw fans to the game. It was not so much violence, though occasional outbreaks of it provided an undeniable thrill. It was not mere victory in itself, which if acquired by the stalling tactics common before the use of the twenty-four-second clock could be nothing more than an exercise in tedium. What would draw fans, he realized, was the excitement provided by high-scoring stars. He signed a string of them, first Jumpin' Joe

Fulks, who in 1949 set a scoring record of sixty-three points in a single game, then Paul Arizin.

Despite Gottlieb's talents, the Warriors franchise for years had such poor attendance that while the league allowed a ten-man roster, he could at times afford to hire only nine players. During one season in the early fifties, the team played 80 percent of its home games on neutral courts such as Raleigh, Providence, and Iowa City, where the guarantee Gottlieb received from local promoters was greater than what he could expect to take in at the gate in Philadelphia. Ever since Chamberlain was in high school, Gottlieb had believed he would be the team's salvation. When Chamberlain returned from his year in Europe with the Globetrotters and began hinting he might be tempted by Saperstein's offer to sign for another year with the team, Gottlieb appealed to the NBA's board of governors. The NBA had a cap of $25,000 on player salaries, and only a few top players such as Bob Cousy and Bob Pettit earned it. Gottlieb persuaded his fellow owners to raise the cap, and offered Chamberlain roughly $27,000, but still Wilt refused to commit. One night that spring, during a doubleheader at Madison Square Garden, sportswriter Irv Goodman asked Gottlieb if Chamberlain was actually going to join the NBA. "What can I tell you," Gottlieb said plaintively. "I'm waiting for him, that's all."

YOU DUMB SCHVARTZEH! *You big schvartzeh sonofabitch!* It was during training camp at the start of Bill Russell's second season and Red Auerbach was yelling at him. Russell hated to practice, and Auerbach felt from time to time that he had to lean on him. He also felt he had to show the rest of the players that no one, not even Bill Russell, was allowed to slack off or got the kid-gloves treatment when Auerbach was around. Before the start of training camp, Auerbach had explained to Russell why from time to time he was going to have to scream at him. "If I can't yell at you, then I can't yell at any-body," he said. "So I'm going to yell like hell tomorrow and throughout the week, but don't pay any attention to it, okay? You *know* you're going to make the team."

Russell agreed. And so when Auerbach screamed *schvartzeh!* he said nothing. Auerbach was not an outright bigot, Russell understood. *Schvartzeh* was simply the word New York Jews had used for decades to refer to blacks. Auerbach was also trying to get the racial issue out in front of everyone, so the Celtics wouldn't feel they all had to tiptoe around a taboo subject. Nothing spoiled the dressing-room atmosphere like a bunch of overly sensitive big jocks. Still, the word had an undertone of contempt, and Russell got a little annoyed when he heard it, as he did over some of Auerbach's other racial assumptions. At the end of the previous season, Auerbach had called Russell to tell him he was thinking of drafting Sam Jones from North Carolina Central.

"Do you think he can go good for us?" Auerbach asked.

"Who the hell is Sam Jones?" Russell asked in reply.

"He's a *schvartzeh* who plays for North Carolina. I thought you'd know him."

In other words, Russell realized, Auerbach assumed because both he and Jones were black that he would have heard of him. Russell wanted to ask Auerbach if he knew every damned Jewish player in the country. Auerbach, despite being known for drafting the first black player in the NBA, was not exactly a model of progressive racial etiquette. But he did eventually realize that while the use of *schvartzeh* may have been socially acceptable on the streets of Brooklyn in the 1930s, Russell and the other black players considered it a borderline slur. "Russell, what do we call you guys?" Auerbach asked one day. "I can use *colored,* or *Negro,* or *African American.* Is it *black* or what?" Russell replied that the preferred word was *black.*

Russell had to put up with far worse language from some of the Celtics fans. "Coon!," "Nigger!," and "Chocolate boy!" were a few of the words shouted at him from the stands of Boston Garden. He would later tell his daughter, Karen, that he never listened to the boos or the insults, because he never listened to the cheers. But the attitude of the Celtics fans was one of many reasons that Russell never developed much affection for the city of Boston, which despite its reputation as a bastion of liberal thinking seemed to Russell to be as racist, in its own way, as any city he'd ever seen. For all the phenomenal success of his rookie year, he'd had trouble finding a job in Boston during the off-season. While he and Bob Cousy were not particularly close, they did enjoy playing golf together, but Cousy, who lived in Worcester, was unable to invite him to the Worcester Country Club. No one at the club had ever come out and said so, nonetheless Cousy knew it was out of the question. And Russell was coolly rebuffed in the first suburb in which he tried to buy a house.

Eventually, Russell and his wife found a handsome but unimposing ranch house in suburban Reading. He could have moved into Roxbury, the black section of Boston, but by then he had a young son, and he wanted his children to go to good schools. The Russells were the first black family to move to Reading, their house was in a largely Irish Catholic neighborhood, and, initially, their relations with their neighbors were stiff. The first year in their new home, it was broken into twice.

But Russell liked the house itself. It was large and comfortable, with a finished basement big enough for an elaborate electric train set. When Russell was growing up, he'd wanted a train set, but his parents could never afford one, and now he acquired a huge one, actually fourteen different sets joined together, with engines, cars, lakes, tunnels, depots, towers, bridges, switches, signals, and crossing gates. He bought a $2,100 hi-fi set and amassed a collection of 1,500 records, leaning toward jazz and protest-folk but including Broadway musicals such as *Kismet* and the soundtrack to the movie *Exodus*. He could afford an expensive car, but since he considered the sight of a black man in a Cadillac to be a racial cliché, he drove a Lincoln Continental. His jersey number was six, and so he ordered a license plate that read CELTICS 6.

The Celtics' first black players from the early fifties, such as Chuck Cooper and Don Barksdale, had moved on by the time Russell arrived, and when he joined the team he was the sole black on the roster. It seemed obvious to him that the NBA had a quota on black players. It was not as if all the owners had sat down and worked out a secret agreement to restrict black players. There was no need to actually discuss it, just as there was no need for the members of the Worcester Country Club to tell Bob Cousy he couldn't invite Bill Russell out to play golf. Everyone knew what the situation was. No team in the league had more than two or at the most three blacks.

In the early fifties, when there were few black players in the NBA, they were almost all forwards and they would be assigned to guard each other, which in effect meant they canceled each other out, leaving the game to be played by the four white players on each team, who often refused to pass the ball to the black players. By the late fifties, blacks were playing all positions and black representation on teams had increased, but a de facto quota system was still in place. What that meant was that when a black tried out for a team, he felt he was competing not only for one of the twelve spots on the team but for one of the two or three black spots, which meant that if he made the team, the owner would drop one of the other black players.

When Sam Jones joined the team in 1957, the Celtics reached what Russell thought of as the outer limit of the quota. Then the following year Auerbach signed K. C. Jones and drafted a fourth black player, Ben Swain of Texas State. "The Celtics will not keep four Negroes," one sportswriter declared. "The crowds won't stand for it, and neither will the owners." Russell confronted Walter Brown, who denied the existence of a quota. "I look for players, black, white, vermillion," he told Russell. "I couldn't care less." Russell didn't believe him. The facts spoke for themselves, and he was not prepared to silently accept indignities at a time when the civil rights movement was quickening its stride. Two years earlier, in 1956, Martin Luther King, Jr., had successfully led the boycott of the bus system in Montgomery, Alabama. He'd been featured on the cover of *Time* the following year, and in the process became, as one historian pointed out, "a permanent fixture of American mass culture." By 1958, the Southern Christian Leadership Conference had voter-registration drives going on in some twelve Southern cities. In June, King became the first Negro leader to formally meet with President Dwight Eisenhower in the White House, though three months later he was arrested in Montgomery on charges of loitering in a courthouse.

Those were the sorts of stories making the headlines in 1958 when the Celtics flew into Charlotte, North Carolina, to play a neutral-court game. Despite the attention King had received, Southern cities remained rigidly segregated, and on the trip down, trainer Buddy LeRoux told Russell and Sam Jones that since the hotel where the rest of the Celtics were staying wouldn't allow them as guests, they would have to stay at a Negro hotel. Russell's fury at this was compounded by the deplorable state of the Negro hotel, but when he complained to Auerbach, the coach tried to minimize the matter. Russell stayed to play the game, but he also decided that from then on he would simply refuse to play in any city if he was forced to sleep in a segregated hotel or eat in a segregated restaurant. After the 1958 playoffs, a promoter scheduled an exhibition tour for the all-star teams. When the teams arrived in Dallas and Russell found out he could not stay at the same hotel as the white players, he spat on the promoter and immediately caught a plane home, forfeiting the exhibition money.

It enraged Russell to think that he was living in a society that simultaneously celebrated his athletic accomplishments and considered him inferior because of race, to realize that not only did a large portion of the population hate him for his skin color but that this hatred inescapably seeped into his own view of himself. In his memoir, *Go Up for Glory,* composed in the free-floating Beat style of the early sixties, he wrote:

> *It stood out, harsh and unyielding, a wall which understanding still cannot penetrate.*
>
> *You are a Negro. You are less.*
>
> *It covered every area. A living, smarting, hurting, smelling, greasy substance which covered you. A morass to fight from.*

And so Russell retreated into himself, refusing to rely on or even to respond to the applause of fans and the friendship of neighbors, considering it transient and insincere, aware that at any time it could be withdrawn and when it was it would probably reveal an undercurrent of racial bigotry that had been there all along. For motivation, for validation, he relied instead solely on his pride, his own sense of self-worth, which was based not on what anybody said about him or to him but on what he had accomplished, not on what he'd been given but on what he'd earned. Because he'd been given nothing.

EDDIE GOTTLIEB'S attorney was a man named Ike Richman, and in the spring of 1959, when Chamberlain had returned from his European tour with the Globetrotters and was still negotiating with Gottlieb over terms for joining the Warriors, Gottlieb brought Richman into the negotiations. One night, Richman, who didn't like to drive, came home and asked his son Michael, a high school senior, to drive him into town. After they parked on Broad Street, a white Cadillac Eldorado pulled up, with Wilt Chamberlain at the wheel. Richman told his son to wait, and got into the Cadillac. When he returned a half hour later, and climbed back into his car, he said, "Mike, I just worked as hard as I ever did in my life."

Richman, who would go on to become Chamberlain's attorney and lifelong friend, had just persuaded him to sign with the Warriors instead of returning to the Globetrotters, who were offering more money than Gottlieb could hope to match. He had clinched the argument by appealing in part to Chamberlain's vanity. The Trotters would always be regarded as entertainers, Richman said. Chamberlain would never be taken seriously as an athlete unless he played in the NBA. On May 30, 1959, Gottlieb and Chamberlain announced his signing at a press conference at the Sheraton Hotel in Philadelphia. Chamberlain looked stylish in a dark-blue suit and a straw boater. Gottlieb told the reporters that he was paying Chamberlain the highest salary ever paid to a player in the NBA. At first Gottlieb refused to discuss the figure, but finally he admitted that he was paying Wilt more than $30,000 and that with additional bonuses based on increased attendance the figure could rise even higher. In fact, he pointed out, he was paying more for Chamberlain's services than he had paid to buy out the other investors and acquire the entire Warriors franchise—all the contracts with the players, the team's NBA charter, and even an old equipment truck—just seven years earlier.

One of the first things Chamberlain did after signing with the Warriors was buy his parents a nine-room house on Cobbs Creek Parkway, a quiet, well-kept neighborhood in southwest Philadelphia. With the money Chamberlain was now earning, his mother was able to stop working as a cleaning woman but his father kept his job as a handyman. Wilt, who continued to live at home, spent the summer in Philadelphia, lifting weights, running cross-country, and playing pickup basketball games on city playgrounds. In August, he drove up to Kutsher's Country Club in the Catskills, where just a few years earlier he had worked as a bellhop, to play in a benefit game for the quadriplegic Maurice Stokes.

In the mid-fifties, when Bill Russell was capturing national attention at San Francisco and Wilt Chamberlain was doing the same at Overbrook High, when Elgin Baylor was playing at Seattle University and Oscar Robertson was leading Crispus Attucks High in Indianapolis, a fifth outstanding black basketball player appeared on the scene. Maurice Stokes joined the Royals in 1955, a year before Bill Russell came to the NBA, and in doing so became basketball's first black superstar. Stokes was six feet seven, which was little more than average height in the league at the time, but he weighed more than 250 pounds, with massive shoulders, and was also unusually graceful and quick for a man of his stature—so quick that he could rebound the ball and then, instead of passing out, take it down the court himself in a fast break. He became Rookie of the Year in 1956, and in his second season, the year Russell joined the Celtics, he was the league's leading rebounder. Faster than anyone who was bigger than him and bigger than anyone who was faster, he was poised to become one of the greatest basketball players ever.

Then, in a game against Minneapolis at the end of his third season, Stokes had his feet kicked out from under him, fell to the floor, and hit his head on the hardwood. It briefly knocked him out, but he regained consciousness within a minute and seemed none the worse for the fall. Three days later, however, in a playoff game in Detroit, he inexplicably felt so weak that he seemed ill, and he played badly. The year before, Lester Harrison had moved the Royals from Rochester to Cincinnati, and as soon as the plane took off on the flight home from Detroit, Stokes began sweating heavily and moaning incoherently, and then he passed out. The captain radioed ahead for an ambulance, which met the team at the Cincinnati airport.

Apparently, the concussion three days earlier in the game against Minneapolis had caused Stokes's head to swell, and then the changing air pressure in the cabin as the airplane took off stimulated an attack of encephalitis. Stokes was in a coma by the time the plane touched down. Early the following morning, surgeons operated on his brain but were unable to reverse the effects of the attack. Afterward, Stokes regained consciousness, but the stroke had seriously damaged his motor nerves, and for the rest of his life he would be virtually unable to move or talk.

Stokes's paralysis stunned the entire league. He was twenty-five at the time, he had been hurt on the last day of the regular season, and, like all players then, he had only a one-year contract, which meant that he was without any income. He also had no medical insurance, no disability insurance, and no pension, and he could not be moved back to his family in Pittsburgh. His medical bills were rapidly exhausting his savings. Stokes's white teammate Jack Twyman came up with the idea of raising money for the injured player by holding a benefit game at Milt Kutsher's Catskills resort, where Stokes, like Chamberlain, had worked as a bellhop.*

Kutsher invited the league's top players. He also invited Wilt Chamberlain, who drove up from Philadelphia in his Eldorado. Chamberlain had known and liked Stokes, but he wanted to play in the game for another rea-

---

*Twyman spent much of the next twelve years of his life looking after and raising money for Stokes, who finally died of a heart attack at the age of thirty-seven.

son as well. His NBA debut was a few short months away. He had played at the college level and on the Globetrotters, but he had never yet taken the court with a full contingent of hardened professional basketball players, and he wondered how he would measure up. All of the players who came up to Kutsher's had of course heard about Chamberlain, and a number of them had seen him play. But while they all expected him to be good, they were surprised by just how good he was. To begin with, he was in better shape than most of them. And many of them were astonished by his moves. At one point he single-handedly broke up a three-man fast break by Bob Cousy, Frank Ramsey, and Guy Sparrow, blocking Ramsey's shot when Cousy passed off to him, and then blocking Sparrow's shot when he retrieved the ball. Cousy thought Chamberlain was better than his own teammate Bill Russell. And Chamberlain, when the game was over, felt pretty good about his performance as well. It was time, he decided, to take on the NBA.

IN THE FALL of 1959, when Red Auerbach was going into his tenth year as coach of the Boston Celtics, Vince Lombardi had just taken over as head coach of the Green Bay Packers. Auerbach and Lombardi would come to be regarded as the two best professional team coaches of mid-century America. Lombardi would become the more famous of the two, but in the end Auerbach's record dwarfed Lombardi's. Whereas Lombardi coached the Green Bay Packers for nine years and during that run produced five championships, Auerbach coached the Celtics for sixteen years and won nine championships, eight of them—from 1959 to 1966—consecutively. Both Lombardi and Auerbach were strong-willed, energetic, and determined. Lombardi, however, was obsessed with playbooks and diagrams. He micromanaged his players' moves, calculating down to the inch the size of the crossover step a guard needed to take before cutting across the backfield to lead a sweep. Auerbach was not a clipboard coach. Complex patterns of *x*'s and *o*'s on the blackboard, flow charts, organization, index cards, briefing books—none of that was for him. And he was not the best technical coach; others were more articulate on the fine points of shooting and passing. But he had an instinctive understanding of the rhythms of the game, and this made him a master at the art of substitution. He could sense, even before the player himself knew it, when a man was beginning to fade, or when the other team had slowed a fraction and would be vulnerable to an injection of energy from the Celtics' deep bench.

In the dressing room, during the time-out huddle, on the practice floor, in training camp, he was an unparalleled motivator. He knew which players reacted to anger or threats, which were too sensitive or proud for criticism, and which were tough enough to endure a rebuke intended to send a message to the entire team. He inspired loyalty, trading only one player in the ten-year period after Russell joined the team, but he was also an unapologetic authoritarian who tolerated no challenge to his control of the team. He kept his distance from his players, who were never allowed to question his decisions. He had phrases he liked to use to cut off dissent: *I'm not running a union here!* or *I hired you, and I can fire you!* or *I may not always be right, but I'm never wrong!*

Auerbach's chief talent lay in his understanding of the nature of the game, of the simplicity that was the key to its beauty, and he recognized the need to avoid unnecessarily complicating it. He saw a basketball team as a machine or system that functioned by the harmonious interaction of its specific parts. Unlike many coaches, he was as a rule unimpressed by mere talent. He coldly but shrewdly evaluated players based on their ability to play a particular role needed by the team at a particular time. He had a gift for sensing potential in an underperforming player, one who would be susceptible to coaching, who showed determination, and who could be molded into the Celtics team. He had no time for troublemakers or gloryhounds—attitude was as important as talent—and when investigating a potential young player, he'd call the coaches, teachers, principals, even the ministers and police chiefs in the kid's hometown, trying to find out less about his ability than about his character. The selection of the player, Auerbach felt, was more important than how he was handled once he arrived. Get the right guys in the beginning and you were all set.

Auerbach served as his own scout, but his time was limited and he was helped by a network of former players and the coaches he knew, people such as Bill Reinhart, Bob Feerick, Freddy Scolari, and Horace "Bones" McKinney. In the previous two years he had added two more unheralded men who rounded out the legendary Celtics roster of the sixties, and it was Bones McKinney—one of Auerbach's old players from the days of the Washington Capitols—who had alerted him to the first of them. Sam Jones was a student at all-black North Carolina Central when McKinney, then the chaplain at Wake Forest University, happened to see him play. Unlike most basketball players, who aim for the rim, Jones ricocheted his shots off the backboard, which gave him a greater variety of angles. Bank shots were as a rule more difficult to hit, but it was said of Jones that he worked the backboard the way a pool shark worked the cushions. McKinney was so impressed that he called Auerbach. "Red," he said, "there's a colored kid down here with the damnedest bank shot you ever saw." Jones's college had played against so few good teams that it was almost impossible for NBA coaches to assess his talent, and he had gone undrafted until Auerbach, picking last, selected him.

The following year, Auerbach signed K. C. Jones, who had been Russell's roommate at the University of San Francisco. The Celtics had drafted K.C. in 1956, the same year Russell and Heinsohn joined the team. But when K.C. graduated, he had gone into the military and did not join the team until 1958. Since K.C. was quiet and relatively small, many in the Boston press initially decided he'd been hired simply to provide a friend in town for his old college roommate Bill Russell, and they derided him as "Russell's little buddy." But Auerbach had recognized both his exceedingly quick hands and his defensive strengths, which he had acquired from San Francisco's coach, Phil Woolpert. K.C. had been about to go to work for the post office when Woolpert had offered him a scholarship, and as the sportswriter C. Michael Curtis noted, "Had he attended a school where race-horse offense was the predominant pattern, it is fair to presume that Jones might have wound up back at that post office."

Though Auerbach had never met Joe McCarthy, the legendary manager of both the New York Yankees and the Boston Red Sox, he had gotten to know

Yankees shortstop Phil Rizzuto while in the navy during the war, and Rizzuto had told him how McCarthy ran his teams. As a coach Auerbach emulated McCarthy's champion-molding principles. One of McCarthy's rules was that champions should play the part of champions—"You're a Yankee," McCarthy would tell players. "Act like one"—and he required the Yankees to wear coats and ties when traveling. Auerbach, too, insisted that while traveling together as a team, his players wear jackets and ties and refrain from drinking liquor. Beer was acceptable, but he did not like to see his players sitting at bars with cocktail glasses in front of them. Anyone thus caught was fined. But at the same time, Auerbach was not a stickler for rules. While the Celtics had a curfew for road trips, he made it clear that he considered his players adults; he would not sneak around hotels checking up on them, and instead he made it a point to stay in his room.

For all Vince Lombardi's meticulous planning, his players liked to joke that once the game started he was the most useless person on the sidelines. Auerbach, by contrast, came to life most truly during games. He was such a forceful presence that it was as if he functioned as a member of the team, as responsible as any one of his defensive players for controlling the score. Auerbach believed that if he, together with the crowd, could make the officials hesitate on just a couple of crucial judgment calls against his team, he could create two to four points for the Celtics as surely as if he'd put the ball through the basket, and this could provide the winning margin in a close game. Auerbach also believed that the referees reflexively, even unconsciously, favored the weaker teams the Celtics played against, and he felt, or convinced himself, that he had to compensate for their inclination. At the same time, Auerbach used what he called "strategic" technical fouls and ejections, shrilly contesting calls to stir up the crowd in a lackluster game or having himself thrown out to inspire his team with his sacrifice. He once estimated that the Celtics won 80 to 90 percent of the games from which he was ejected.

And so Auerbach perfected the art of courtside intimidation as no coach before or since has ever done. During the course of his career, he was fined more often than any other coach in the NBA. By the time of his retirement, the fines totaled more than $17,000. He was fined for calling referee Arnie Heft "stupid and incompetent." He was fined for giving referee Richie Powers the choke sign. He was fined for calling referees Norm Drucker and Mendy Rudolph "a couple of chokers." He was suspended for actually shoving referee Joe Gushue. In a game against the Lakers, referee Richie Powers became so upset with Auerbach that he threw his whistle at him and announced that he was quitting. "I won't go for a league where they can vilify you like this," he said.

Auerbach's attack on Kerner during the 1957 playoffs was not the only time he erupted in actual violence. He once punched Philadelphia Warriors coach Neil Johnston when Johnston interrupted an argument he was having with the timekeeper. During a game against the Royals, Auerbach attacked a Cincinnati fan, a gas-station attendant named Edward Finke, who in addition to showering him with abuse, spat on him and, according to one account, kicked him in the shins. Auerbach went into the stands after him, and a brawl ensued. After the game, Finke pressed charges, claiming Auerbach had broken his glasses and knocked out a couple of teeth. Auerbach was arrested at his hotel, but Finke later dropped the charges, and out of gratitude Auerbach subsequently left tickets at the box office for Finke when the Celtics were in Cincinnati.

Many Boston sportswriters still disliked Auerbach, but Colonel Dave Egan of the *Record* remained a fan until his death, at age fifty-seven, in 1958. Egan particularly admired Auerbach's courtside tirades. "He guarantees the integrity of the sport," Egan once wrote in defense of Auerbach's behavior. "He stands outspokenly for his men. He fights for them, as he goes around the country playing wide-open, spectator-appealing, aggressive basketball." Auerbach had also won the admiration and support of Milton Gross of the *New York Post*. "No coach is so violently disliked by the other coaches in the NBA," Gross reported in an apt summation of the prevailing view of Auerbach. "No coach has been slapped so consistently with fines so large by Maurice Podoloff. No coach has cast himself as such a general nuisance to the league's head man. None beefs more with referees, tangles with spectators or ignores propriety more by shouting instructions louder from a seat in the stands after he has been banished from the floor. And none is more appreciated by his players than Auerbach."

Auerbach had spent almost a decade assembling his team. What set it apart was that each of the men he had brought to the Celtics had a defined role, and each of them understood what it was, excelled at it, and accepted the limitations that accompanied it. No other team in the league had so many men who were so capable at executing their specific assignments. Cousy led the fast break and set the play in motion; Russell controlled the backboard; Heinsohn shot and, if Russell was out of position, rebounded; Sharman and Sam Jones scored; K. C. Jones played defense; Loscutoff provided muscle; Frank Ramsey came off the bench to lead the rally. In 1976 Jeff Greenfield was to write a book making the argument—one that had been heard for years in Boston saloons—that given the record they would eventually set, the Celtics of this era were not just the greatest basketball team ever assembled, but the best in the history of professional team sports or, as Greenfield put it, "The World's Greatest Team."

Be that as it may, none of the Celtics, including Russell, was a dominant player who carried the team in the way that, a few years later, Oscar Robertson would carry the Royals, or Kareem Abdul-Jabbar would carry the Milwaukee Bucks, or Magic Johnson the Lakers, or Michael Jordan the Bulls. And in the fall of 1959, the attention of the basketball world was focused on Wilt Chamberlain, the man expected to become the greatest franchise player of all time. "He will dominate the game," Irv Goodman wrote in *Sport* as the season got under way. "He will be the mighty drawing card that will jack up the NBA to full status as a major league. He will save the weaker franchises. He will rush league expansion. He will raise players' salaries. He will force changes in the rules which may well alter the very character of the game. For a professional sport that has come close but hasn't quite made it yet, he will be Babe Ruth."

CHAMBERLAIN'S DEBUT took place on October 24, 1959, at Madison Square Garden in New York. It was a Saturday night, and 15,000 fans turned out to watch him lead the Warriors to a 118–109 victory over the Knicks. The final score underrepresented the magnitude of the defeat for the Knicks. They were stunned by how devastating Chamberlain was. By the time the game was over, he had scored forty-three points and pulled down twenty-eight rebounds. He completely shut down the Knicks offense, stifling anyone who drove to the basket and consigning the New York players to perimeter shots. And when the shots missed, Chamberlain raked in the rebound and even before his feet touched the ground had rifled the ball out to a teammate to set up the fast break. The *Times* called his performance "both beautiful and frightening," and the *Herald-Tribune* declared it "the finest debut in league history." "The Age of Wilt has arrived," Jack Kiser wrote in the *Philadelphia Daily News*. "The NBA will never be the same again."

So many people wanted to be able to say they had met Chamberlain on the night of his NBA debut that, after the game, a huge crowd gathered outside Madison Square Garden on the corner of Forty-ninth Street and Eighth Avenue, spilling into the street and blocking traffic. When Chamberlain finally appeared, he happily spent half an hour shaking hands and signing autographs. In the days to come, crowds lined up at arenas throughout the league to watch the new phenomenon. Haskell Cohen, director of publicity for the NBA, estimated that attendance league-wide was up 23 percent over the previous year, and he attributed 19 percent of that increase directly to Chamberlain. In fact, ticket sales at other arenas that hosted the Warriors surged so much when Philadelphia came to town that Eddie Gottlieb asked the other franchise owners to change the NBA rules to allow the visiting team to receive a cut of the home team's gate. Gottlieb argued that since the crowds were coming to see Chamberlain, and since he was the one paying Chamberlain's astronomical salary, he should be able to share in the windfall profits his star was creating for the other owners. The owners, who had already changed league rules once at Gottlieb's request because of Chamberlain—to allow Gottlieb to draft him while he was still in high school—refused.

As the season got under way, the rest of the teams in the NBA quickly discovered that it was almost impossible to contain Chamberlain. He scored fifty-eight points in a second game against the Knicks and another fifty-eight against the Detroit Pistons. Other teams started telling jokes such as: How do you defend against Chamberlain? Lock the door of the dressing room, and if that doesn't work, use an ax. There were other players in the league as tall or almost as tall as Chamberlain, among them Ray Felix, Walter Dukes, and Clyde Lovellette. But Chamberlain *seemed* taller. That was because none of the other men had Chamberlain's athletic ability. Indeed, until then, the NBA's tall men had been considered relatively graceless and unathletic. The less charitable sportswriters bluntly referred to them as "goons." Chamberlain was not without his limitations as a basketball player. He was said to have hard hands, big cinderblock-like mitts that made it difficult for him to receive a vigorously thrown pass or allow the ball to roll gracefully off his fingers into the basket. And his strength was said to deprive him of finesse, which was why his outside shots often lacked the arc to drop in all-net.

But unlike the other tall men, Chamberlain had the grace and stamina of the track-and-field star that he was. In fact, the presumption that his athletic accomplishments were due to his height infuriated him, and he sometimes wished he were six inches shorter just so his talents could get the respect they deserved. His body was capable of what were essentially superhuman feats. On the track field, he could clear six-ten in the high jump and put a sixteen-pound shot fifty-five feet. He ran a quarter mile in forty-seven seconds. His stride on the run was nine feet. He could easily play an entire forty-eight-minute basketball game without ever being relieved, and in fact preferred to play the whole game because he lost his rhythm and his muscles stiffened up if he sat on the bench.

Chamberlain had been rail-thin when he went to Kansas, but had started lifting weights at the recommendation of some of the members of the track team, and now, while he still had a thirty-inch waist, he weighed 240 pounds and could shoulder-press 400 pounds. *Sports Illustrated* once called him "probably the greatest athletic construction ever formed of flesh and blood." He sweated off eight to ten pounds during every game, and to restore his strength, he needed to consume some 6,000 calories a day—twice the intake of the average man. Every day, he ate two large meals and one huge one—the huge meal consisting of, for example, a tall glass of juice, three soft-boiled eggs, a two-pound T-bone steak, vegetables, salad, six pieces of bread, two desserts, and a quart and a half of milk.

With his height, his strength, and his athleticism, Chamberlain was able to score and rebound virtually at will, and so, partly out of frustration and partly as a deliberate tactic, his opponents began to challenge him physically. This was more than simply the veteran players putting the question to a rookie in the league's ritual hazing. Chamberlain was pulled, shoved, elbowed, grabbed, tripped, held, jabbed, and jostled like no player before him. The abuse he took astonished his teammates and even his opponents. Tommy Heinsohn decided he would never have wanted to trade places with Chamberlain, because the poor guy was subjected to an unprecedented amount of manhandling.

There was little downside to the tactics. If a player was called for fouling Chamberlain, it only meant that Chamberlain got a free throw, and his foul shooting was so bad that he was embarrassed to go to the foul line. But often, the fouls were not even called. The referees for the most part were of average height. Like most men that size, they found Chamberlain physically intimidating, and since many fouls were judgment calls, they tended to favor the smaller men playing against Wilt, either because the fouls against Wilt seemed less significant given his size or because they identified with the smaller players. After all, Chamberlain was so tall that he needed only to walk up to the basket, catch a pass thrown high enough so that none of the defenders could reach it, then dunk. It didn't seem fair. "If we let Wilt stand under the basket, he'll ruin the game," one official privately complained.

The harassment infuriated Chamberlain, who regarded it as a failure in officiating. He felt that his coach, Neil Johnston, was not doing enough to protest the referees' double standards, and that encouraged them to overlook all but the most egregious fouls against him. Johnston, however, felt that it was up to Chamberlain himself to make it clear to his opponents that he would not tolerate rough treatment. "They're getting away with murder," Johnston told an acquaintance. "It would help if he would bop a few." Joe Ruklick, Chamberlain's white backup, felt there was clearly an element of racism in the harassment. Even some of Chamberlain's own white teammates referred to him as a "nigger" behind his back. They seemed to Ruklick to regard Wilt as a freak of nature who would be gone sooner or later, at which point they could return to playing basketball the way it had been played before.

Since Chamberlain did nothing about the harassment, opposing players pushed him further and further, waiting to see where he would draw the line. Then, with the season less than two weeks old, Philadelphia played St. Louis, and Clyde Lovellette, the Hawks center, proved how dangerous it had been for Chamberlain to fail to retaliate immediately. Lovellette, by reputation one of the dirtiest players in the league, was a massive man who wore cowboy hats, had a gun collection, and took pistols with him on the road. He was popular with his teammates; John Havlicek, his friend and roommate when Lovellette later joined the Celtics, regarded him as a thirty-three-year-old juvenile delinquent. But opponents hated taking the court against him. He rarely used his fists; instead he knocked players down with an elbow to the face, with a knee to the groin, or by sticking out his foot to trip them, usually apologizing and pretending it was an accident, only to do it again.

In the locker room before the game between the Warriors and the Hawks, Lovellette and some of his teammates discussed their plans for Chamberlain. "Clyde said he was going to get Wilt," recalled Cal Ramsey, a black player who had joined the team that year. Ramsey, concerned for Chamberlain's safety, went up to Wilt before the start of the game. "Be careful," Ramsey said. "They're out to get you." The warning did no good. During the game, Wilt was running up the court when Lovellette came running toward him from the opposite direction and, as they passed, let fly an elbow at Chamberlain's face. The blow, heightened by the momentum of the two big men hurtling toward each other, landed on Chamberlain's chin and drove his jaw upward. Two of his lower front teeth were knocked back and punctured the roof of his mouth. "It really killed him," Ramsey recalled.

The next day, an infection set in, and Wilt's face became so swollen that he had difficulty both eating and sleeping that night. The Warriors, however, needed to leave for Detroit for a game against the Pistons, and Chamberlain was unable to get to a doctor. Philadelphia was in second place, trailing Boston, and coach Neil Johnston was afraid of falling too far behind, so that night he started Chamberlain, who wore a large mask to protect his face. He played the entire game, despite the fact that his head hurt and was swelling up. Afterward, unable to eat solid food, he consumed quantities of orange juice and 7-Up.

The next night, in New York, Chamberlain was hit in the mouth again, this time by Willie Naulls. The team physician, Dr. Si Ball, realized Chamberlain had blood poisoning so acute that Ball was surprised that he had been able to remain on his feet. Furthermore, the infection in his mouth had become so bad that he needed immediate treatment, and an ambulance took him to the hospital. Dental surgery was performed, and by the end of the procedure he had lost a total of four teeth, and was out for three games.

Ike Gellis, sports editor of the *New York Post,* had befriended Chamberlain early in the season, and like Johnston he encouraged Chamberlain to fight back against players such as Lovellette. Gellis told Chamberlain the story of how, when Nat "Sweetwater" Clifton had first joined the Knicks, he had been pushed around by white players until one day he coldcocked Bob Harris of the Celtics. The intimidation stopped. But Chamberlain, for all his size, had never been a rough player, as Blinky Brown had noticed when he was teaching Wilt to play basketball at the Haddington Recreational Center. The idea of resorting to violence as a calculated solution to violence simply puzzled him. "If I punch someone in the face, what does that prove?" Chamberlain asked Gellis.

It seemed to Gellis that on some level Chamberlain simply didn't understand what the NBA was all about. The fact of the matter was that, although basketball was officially a noncontact sport, players were expected to both inflict and endure an enormous amount of pain. In the middle of Chamberlain's rookie year, *Sport* magazine surveyed all eighty of the league's players and found that, in a given week, thirty-three of them—a little short of 50 percent—were nursing injuries or ailments of one sort or another. To begin with, many were sick. The constant travel weakened the resistance of the players, who were always coming down with colds and the flu, and more often than not these illnesses spread through the team. In addition, players suffered from sprained ankles, pulled ligaments, strained tendons, hairline kneecap fractures, muscle strains, charley horses, blisters, bruises, and infected feet. Many of these injuries occurred in fights for the ball, or blocks made against a driving player, or scuffles for position under the boards, and many of them were inflicted intentionally by players such as Clyde Lovellette.

Players were trained to view their own injuries with Spartan disdain. Because the teams were so small, every player had a function, and the coaches could rarely afford to take an injured man off the active roster. And even if the coaches were willing to let a player sit out a game, the player worried about what it might do to his career. "There were less than a hundred players in the league back then, which meant every one of them was good," recalled Al Domenico, the first trainer hired by the Philadelphia 76ers. "No one wanted to miss a game, because if you did the person who replaced you might turn out to be better than you were and you'd lose your spot." So virtually all of them continued to play. "There are days when the NBA looks like a dance marathon of the twenties," Steve Gelman wrote in the article in *Sport,* which was titled "Walking Wounded Everywhere."

THE TEAM Chamberlain had joined had finished in last place in the Eastern Division the year before. The Warriors were not without talent. Forward Paul Arizin had one of the best jump shots in the league. In the backcourt there was Guy Rogers, a fast-moving ball handler, and Tom Gola, whose strength was defense. But neither Gola nor Rogers was a particularly effective scorer, and the Warriors bench was weak. Once Chamberlain joined the team, however, the Warriors had become contenders, and they spent the season chasing the Celtics for the lead in the Eastern Division. Twice they came within two games, but each time the Celtics pulled ahead, and Boston finished the regular season ten games in front. But the performance of the Warriors *as a team* seemed almost beside the point. Chamberlain was an act unto himself. By the end of the season, he had run up a total of 2,707 points, exceeding by more than 600 points the record set by Bob Pettit, and pulled down a total of 1,941 rebounds, exceeding the record of 1,612 set by Russell. The New York Metropolitan Basketball Writers Association voted him Rookie of the Year and Most Valuable Player—making him the first player ever to receive both awards at once.

The only player in the league who had given Chamberlain any trouble was Bill Russell. Russell did not completely shut Chamberlain down—Wilt was always going to get his points—but he was able to contain him to the degree that Boston was the only club in the league that did not feel it necessary to double-team Chamberlain, which meant the other four Celtics were free to concentrate on the rest of the Warriors, who were simply no match for them man-to-man. When Philadelphia beat Syracuse in round one of the playoffs and faced Boston for the Eastern Division crown, the entire nation was riveted by the prospect of Chamberlain and Russell battling each other in a title series that had an almost ideological character, pitting as it did individual genius against team effort. Would Chamberlain rise to the occasion and singlehandedly score enough to take the series, or would Russell and his fellow Celtics, working together, be able to contain the greatest individual athlete the sport had produced? "Suddenly, housewives and college coeds who generally avoid athletic events with a passion are taking sides in this battle between the giants," *Sport* magazine observed that spring. "The names of Russell and Chamberlain have given new life to the game, perhaps even to the world of sport."

The games were played back-to-back in a grueling schedule designed to pack as many of them as possible into weekend television slots. Halftime was also cut to six minutes to enable the games to finish at the designated hour. The league seemed unprepared for the spotlight, with hysterical fans packed into seats directly above the benches heaping abuse on the opposing teams, with eggs and garbage splattering on the courts, and with Auerbach and Gottlieb screaming at the referees and exchanging insults and bickering in the press about the officiating. So many sportswriters used the word *bush* to describe the atmosphere that Mrs. Maurice Podoloff asked one of them, "What do they mean by the term *bush* I keep reading?"

Everyone expected the series to be rough. Back during the regular season, in a game against the Hawks, Chamberlain had finally snapped. Feeling that he was being guarded too closely by Bob Pettit, he let fly with an elbow to Pettit's face, and the Hawks forward had to leave the game to receive two stitches. But this had done little to dissuade Chamberlain's opponents, who still felt that if they were not going to let him run away with the game, they had little choice but to foul him. And Boston was known as one of the most physically aggressive teams in the league. Jungle Jim Loscutoff was the team's official enforcer, and it had earned him such hatred from the fans of rival teams that women had run out of the stands during halftime and attacked him with their purses and umbrellas. But Auerbach also gave Tommy Heinsohn assignments involving physical confrontation. Heinsohn was utterly fearless. Growing up a German American in Jersey City during World War II, he had been taunted as being a Nazi by the neighborhood's kids until one day when his father, who worked for the National Biscuit Company, rounded them all up and had him fight them one by one. On the basketball court, Heinsohn showed such little hesitation in using his elbows or hands that to players on other teams it seemed as if he simply did not care if he hurt someone.

Boston won game one, but Chamberlain proved himself a force at both ends of the court. And so, during game two in Philadelphia, Auerbach told Heinsohn to stand in Chamberlain's way whenever the Warriors scored, thereby preventing Chamberlain from getting back to defend his basket while Russell rushed down to take an open shot. The first time Heinsohn did this, Chamberlain was astonished that an opponent would actually try to hamper him from moving when he didn't even have the ball. But, to Chamberlain's amazement, Heinsohn did it again and again, cutting in front of him each time the Warriors scored. The guy was blocking him blind.

"You do that again and I'll knock you on your ass," Chamberlain warned.

"Bring your lunch," Heinsohn replied.

The two men ended up elbowing each other under the basket—the area sometimes referred to as "the butcher shop"—on almost every possession. Chamberlain thought he was being fouled, but none of the referees saw any hands used and nothing was called. After one particularly sharp exchange, Chamberlain lost his temper and shoved Heinsohn, who fell and slid twenty feet across the floor. Chamberlain went after him, fists clenched, arms flailing. The crowd roared, and players from both the Celtics and the Warriors charged onto the court. In the melee, Chamberlain struck out with his fists for the first time in his career, swinging a roundhouse right at Heinsohn, but missing Heinsohn's chin by inches and landing the punch squarely on the head of his own teammate Tom Gola. "Believe it or not, the Stilt's punches are even less accurate than his free-throw shooting," Celtics radio announcer Johnny Most told his listeners. "He just decked his own teammate!"

By halftime, Chamberlain's knuckles and hand had swollen up painfully. The team doctor packed the hand in ice and Chamberlain kept playing, but he scored only nine points during the rest of the game. After the virtual riot on the arena floor, both teams turned sloppy, missing passes and acting hesitant on defense, but the Warriors pulled ahead to win, tying the series. The following day, when the third game was to be played in Boston, Chamberlain could barely move his fingers. He played so badly that he managed to score only twelve points, and Neil Johnston took him out in the third quarter. When the game was over, he went to Massachusetts General Hospital. X-rays showed that while none of the bones in his hand had been broken, the joints on the second and third fingers were severely bruised. Chamberlain's hand continued to hamper his play during the fourth game, which the Warriors lost, but then, with the series at 3–1 and the championship on the line, he pulled himself together for the fifth game, in the Garden, and delivered an incredible performance. Although his hand was far from healed, he scored fifty points, a record for an opponent in the Garden, and led the team to a startling 128–107 victory before a crowd of Celtics fans stunned to silence.

The commanding win put the series at 3–2 and made the Warriors feel they could take it. "They have momentum now," the Celtics' Frank Ramsey told Leonard Koppett of the *New York Post,* who wrote, "The Boston-Philadelphia series now reaches the hysteria-level anticipated ever since Wilt Chamberlain came into the NBA last fall." The intensity brought out the best in both teams in the sixth game, played two days later in Philadelphia. Chamberlain and Russell effectively neutralized each other, the shooters on both teams found their range, and with eleven seconds left, the score stood tied 117–117. Then Philadelphia's Guy Rogers, who with thirty-one points was the game's leading scorer, missed two free throws, and Boston recovered the ball. Bill Sharman took a jump shot and missed, but then Tommy Heinsohn leaped up for the ball. He had jumped short, but as he fell back he was able to swat the ball with his fingertips, and it popped up and into the basket for the winning points just as the buzzer sounded.

Chamberlain was stunned. In the locker room, dripping with sweat, he sat down on the bench exhausted and embittered, his taped hand throbbing. Ike Gellis came over to talk to him. Chamberlain was the most spectacular basketball player Gellis had ever seen. The number of records Chamberlain had broken in his rookie year, Gellis thought, was in itself an astonishing record. Wilt had taken more shots, scored more points, gotten more rebounds, taken more free throws, and played more minutes than anyone else in the history of the game. Gellis, however, knew that none of the accolades had made Chamberlain happy. He had left Kansas in part because he was frustrated with the way his opponents played him, but he had found the NBA even more frustrating than college. He had complained all season about the officials' double standards, the way he was double- and triple-teamed in defiance of the man-to-man rule, and most of all about the violence, hinting that if the situation didn't improve he might just quit playing. Like all sportswriters, Gellis was aware of Chamberlain's frustrations, and he wondered if now, with this bitter defeat, Chamberlain might actually go ahead and leave the NBA.

"Is it true, Wilt?" Gellis asked. "Are you going to leave?"

Chamberlain nodded. "This is my last game," he said. "This is it."

Gellis asked him why he was quitting.

"If I come back next year and score less points than I did this year, I may have to punch eight or nine guys in the face," Chamberlain said. "I may lose my poise. I don't want to. The pressure is too great."

Gellis asked him what he intended to do.

"Hibernate."

11

BY THE SUMMER of 1960, the eight teams in the National Basketball Association had stabilized, although many of them remained financially troubled. While no one realized it at the time, the league was about to embark on the first leg of the expansion that by the end of the century would result in a total—quite literally unimaginable in 1960 even to the game's most enthusiastic supporters—of thirty teams. Two factors were now in place that made the growth of the league possible. The first was television. In 1950, when Red Auerbach initially joined the Celtics, only three million Americans owned televisions, and the first coast-to-coast broadcast—Harry Truman speaking to the Japanese Peace Treaty Conference in San Francisco—would not come for another year. By 1960, the number of American families with televisions had risen to forty million, or 88 percent of the population. In the basketball season that had just ended, executives at NBC, anticipating the excitement that Chamberlain's debut and the rivalry with Russell would bring, had doubled its coverage of the league, featuring games on both Saturday and Sunday afternoons. There was no doubt that, if the competition was exciting enough, the national television audience for sports programming was vast. Slightly more than a year earlier, the first nationally televised NFL championship game, between the Baltimore Colts and the New York Giants, had drawn viewers in 10.8 million homes. That 1958 game, which Tex Maule, the football columnist for *Sports Illustrated,* called "the best football game ever played," amply rewarded those who tuned in to watch, going into a sudden-death overtime but also causing agonizing suspense among the television audience when, as Johnny Unitas was leading the Colts on their final drive to victory, a power cable in the stadium came loose and for two and a half minutes television sets across the country were filled with static, the reception being restored just in time for them to watch Alan "The Horse" Ameche carry the ball across the Giants' goal line.

The second factor that would facilitate the growth of professional basketball was commercial jet travel. Even in the late fifties, many NBA teams traveled by train and bus. But at the end of 1958, the first commercial jet route, from New York to Miami, went into operation. Jet routes spread quickly across the country, and within five years the number of passenger miles on jets would exceed passenger miles on trains by a ratio of three to one. The advent of television and commercial jet travel would make possible one of the greatest franchises in basketball history, a third team that would play a central role in the struggle for league dominance in the sixties, and that would become crucial to the final phase of the rivalry between Bill Russell and Wilt Chamberlain. In 1960, it was one more financially troubled franchise. But the team was about to acquire a new home, and that would be followed by new stars, and then a new owner. Everything about it in fact would change except its name, which made absolutely no sense in the city to which it relocated. But the name, when coupled with that of the new hometown, would have such a pleasingly alliterative quality that everyone quickly forgot how inappropriate it was, and in no time at all it became impossible to imagine the Los Angeles Lakers in any other city, with any other name.

• • •

During the winter of the 1959–60 season, Chamberlain and the Warriors had played the Minneapolis Lakers in a neutral-court game in Los Angeles's Sports Arena. The game was a milestone, not for its outcome or on-court feats but because it was the first professional basketball game played in Los Angeles. To Bob Short, the owner of the Lakers, what was most remarkable about it was that 10,202 fans attended. Two baseball teams, the Brooklyn Dodgers and the New York Giants, had moved to California with great success in the fifties, but despite the fact that the state had a strong college basketball program, had two major cities, and was prosperous and rapidly growing, it did not have a professional basketball team.

Short knew he needed to try to do something different with the Lakers. Minneapolis had dominated the NBA in the late forties and early fifties, winning the championship five times in six years. But its big, lumbering center, George Mikan, retired in 1954, and the advent of the twenty-four-second clock gave the advantage to faster, nimbler teams such as the Celtics. The Lakers went into a tailspin. Mikan tried to make a comeback in the 1955–56 season, but he was unable to adapt to the rapidly evolving game, averaging only ten points a game, and he appeared, in the words of one sportswriter, "an overweight ghost." Halfway through the season, frustrated and embarrassed, Mikan quit again, this time for good.

The Lakers struggled for a few years, with attendance steadily dwindling. In the 1957–58 season, they won only nineteen games out of seventy-two, and lost $38,000. Bob Short, a snappily dressed man with large ears and a gregarious manner, ran a Midwest trucking business and was the head of a group of Minneapolis investors who had acquired the team for $250,000 in 1957, more out of civic pride than any intense love for or knowledge of basketball. He and his partners realized they had three options: fold the franchise, sell it, or revitalize it. They could find no buyers, and if they folded the team they would lose their investment, so even though Short knew it was what he called a lousy risk, he decided to try to revive it. The Lakers had flourished with a star, center George Mikan, and it was obvious to all that if the team was to survive, it needed another star.

Since Minneapolis had finished with the worst team record in 1958, it had first choice in the college draft.* Short briefly considered Archie Dees of

_____

*The draft was changed to a lottery in 1985 and subsequently modified several times.

Indiana, but then John Kundla, the Lakers coach, scouted Elgin Baylor, the astonishingly athletic and acrobatic forward at Seattle University. "By far the best player," Kundla wrote in his report.. "Could we use him!" Baylor was eligible, since his entering class graduated that spring, but he was a transfer student at Seattle, with one more year to go before earning his degree, and under the encouragement of his coach, John Castellani, who maintained he was looking out for his player's interest but who also hoped to get one more year of college play out of him, Baylor had announced that he was going to complete his studies.

Short, undaunted, told Baylor that if he moved to Minneapolis, the Lakers would see to it that he completed his degree at St. Thomas College. Baylor came from Washington, D.C., where his father was a custodian in a public high school. A family friend named Curtis Jackson served as his adviser, and, mustering the same reasoning that Wilt Chamberlain had used to decide to drop out of college, Jackson pointed out that right now Baylor might well be playing the best basketball of his career, that he could command one of the top salaries in the league, and that it made no economic sense to turn down that money, especially since he could complete his education in Minnesota. Persuaded, Baylor signed with the Lakers for $20,000, only slightly less than the $22,500 Bill Russell was then earning. "If he had turned me down," Short said later, "the club would have gone bankrupt."

Baylor, who had led his college team to a number-two rank in the NCAA that spring, was six-five and weighed only 225 pounds, but he had fearsome strength and was so quick that he could bounce a ball off an opponent's head, then spin around him and go to the hoop before the man had recovered. He could jump higher than Joe Fulks, who had set the league's scoring record in 1949, or Bill Russell, and he stayed in the air so long that one sportswriter wrote, "He never broke the law of gravity, but he's awfully slow about obeying it."

Like Russell, Baylor was a serious student of basketball, with an analytic approach to the game; he thoughtfully evaluated his own moves and their shortcomings, and he developed mental files on everyone he played with and against. His one idiosyncrasy was a tic that he'd developed in high school, an involuntary jerk of his head toward his shoulders when he became nervous. The press had harped on it after his Madison Square Garden debut in the 1957 National Invitational Tournament, and Baylor consulted a neurologist, who told him that since it only occurred during moments of stress like games, he had nothing to worry about. It was later diagnosed as a form of ataxia. While Baylor simply ignored the tic, his Laker teammates would kid him that he was the only man in the league with a built-in head fake, and in fact, it often did throw his defender out of position.

But what really set Baylor apart was the fact that he was the most inventive player the game of basketball had yet produced. He used reverse English, spins, and the aforementioned head fakes. He dribbled going backward almost as fast as going forward. He would jump, and then, while seeming to hang suspended, he could make several moves—a pump, a body fake, and then an off-balance shot. He ricocheted the ball off the backboard and then dashed across the lane to rebound his own shot. He rebounded, passed out, and then raced down the court on the fast break to catch the return pass.

In the opening seconds of Baylor's first game, on October 22, 1958, the Lakers center, Jim Krebs, tipped the opening jump ball toward him, and he swung down the court, swept passed Cincinnati's Jack Twyman guarding the basket, and dropped in his first two points as a pro. Bob Short leaned over to the Lakers coach, John Kundla, and held up his hand, his thumb and forefinger forming a circle. After Baylor's arrival, the Lakers sold out some games in the drafty old Minneapolis Auditorium and Bob Short optimistically raised ticket prices from $2.50 to $4.50. Baylor quickly became an indispensable franchise player. He was intelligent and congenial, neither haughty nor self-aggrandizing. With sportswriters and fans he tended to be reserved and serious to the point of formality, an impression enhanced by the expensive tailored suits and English shoes he took to wearing after he joined the NBA. But in the locker room, among his teammates, he was a joking prankster, forever bumming cigarettes, who talked so much he had earned the nickname "Motormouth."

Baylor also had the distinction of becoming—some months before Bill Russell walked away from that exhibition game in Dallas—the first black basketball player to boycott a game. He had already established himself as the league's third-highest scorer when the Lakers arrived in Charleston, West Virginia, to play a neutral-court game against the Royals. Once they reached their hotel, Vern Mikkelsen, one of the veterans, went to the desk to register the team.

"You can stay, but the colored fellows can't stay here," the clerk said.

"We have reservations for the whole team," Mikkelsen said.

"Then take the team somewhere else," the clerk told him.

When Baylor tried to intercede, the clerk utterly ignored him, which enraged Baylor, and then his teammate Rod Hundley, who came from Charleston, got involved, telling the clerk that Baylor was wealthier and more successful and famous than he, the clerk, would ever be, but the clerk refused to bend the policy. Hundley called two other hotels but was told they too did not accommodate Negroes, so the entire team then checked into a Negro hotel called Edna's Retirement Hotel. Baylor could tell that some of his white teammates were not exactly delighted to be staying at Edna's Retirement Hotel, but the team did support him, so he was committed to playing the game that night.

Later that afternoon, however, Baylor and two black teammates, Alexander "Boo" Ellis and Ed Fleming, went out to find something to eat and discovered that the only place that would serve them was the concession at the Greyhound bus station. Baylor had grown up with segregation in Washington, D.C.; his family had lived next to two public parks where black children were not allowed to play. He'd had no choice then but to accept the situation. Now, however, he had a choice—he could boycott a town that refused to regard him as equal to its white citizens—and at that point Baylor decided he was not going to play basketball in Charleston, West Virginia.

In the locker room, while the rest of the Lakers suited up, Baylor stayed in his street clothes. "When you gonna dress?" Hundley asked. Baylor explained that he was refusing to play in a town where he could not be served in a restaurant. The Lakers were in second place at the time, and a couple of the players, afraid that Baylor's decision could affect their chance to get into the playoffs and earn playoff bonuses, asked him to reconsider, but the coach, John Kundla, told him, "Hey, it's your decision."

Hundley asked Baylor to play as a personal favor. Since he was from Charleston, Hundley explained, he would know a lot of people in the audience who were coming to the game either to see their native son or to watch Baylor himself. "Elj, you've got to accept some things down here," Hundley said, "and besides, this is a kind of homecoming for me, and I'd like it to be a special night."

"I'm not an animal," Baylor said. "I'm a human being and I want to be treated like one."

Hundley, for the first time, truly comprehended that what he was asking Baylor to endure was not simply a minor inconvenience but an assault on his essential dignity. "Elj," Hundley said, "Don't play."

While Baylor sat in the dressing room, the Lakers lost. It was, reporters noted, the first sit-down strike by a Negro in basketball or baseball. Commissioner Podoloff initially threatened to fine Baylor for breaking his contract, which required him to play, but backed off after the publicity Baylor received, which in the North was so favorable that when the team returned to Minneapolis, attendance tripled. The game in Charleston also served as a reminder to everyone on the Lakers, particularly to those who had taken issue with his decision not to play, that Baylor was not just an important member of the team, he was the player who was single-handedly transforming the Lakers into winners. "Never before had a major sport franchise depended so much on the individual effort of one player," the sportswriter Murray Olderman observed during Baylor's rookie year. By the end of that first year, Baylor had become so indispensable to the Lakers that when coach John Kundla left for the University of Minnesota, Short hired John Castellani, Baylor's coach at Seattle, as his replacement. And when Baylor was called up for military service and sent to San Antonio for basic training, Short shipped the entire team down to Texas and conducted training camp on the army base to which Baylor had been assigned.

The army, more than happy to cooperate, gave the team a barracks, and Baylor practiced with the Lakers at night when his military duties were over. The army allowed Baylor to fulfill his obligation piecemeal, and he rejoined the team for the first game of the regular season, scoring fifty-two points. Then, on November 8, 1959, one night after the first Russell-Chamberlain confrontation, the Lakers played Boston, and Baylor scored sixty-four points, breaking the record of sixty-three set by Joe Fulks in 1949. While the game was under way, Red Auerbach saw that Baylor was closing in on the record, and in the final minutes he ordered four Celtics to guard him, yelling from the sidelines not to let Baylor shoot, but in the confusion caused by the Boston players swarming over Baylor, one of them fouled him and he broke the record by tossing in a free throw.

For all Baylor's accomplishments, the Lakers' attendance again dwindled, this time so drastically that Short's other investors wanted to pull out, and to avoid seeing the team fold, Short and his partner, Frank Ryan, bought them out for what then seemed like a grand sum, $85,000. Now they had to decide what they were going to do with their investment. The Lakers didn't even have their own arena and were moving from venue to venue. Minneapolis was also about to acquire a major-league baseball franchise, and Short had seen what happened just to the south in 1955, when the Boston

Braves moved to Milwaukee and effectively crushed fan interest in Ben Kerner's Hawks. Meanwhile, the migration of teams in the NBA's Western Division had continued—the Royals moving from Rochester to Cincinnati, the Pistons from Fort Wayne to Detroit—as franchises abandoned the smaller cities associated with the league's origins for larger metropolises with more fans and bigger arenas. After seeing the turnout for the game between the Warriors and the Lakers in the Sports Arena, Short decided to relocate his team to Los Angeles.

He proposed the move at the 1960 meeting of NBA franchise owners. At the time, no team was farther west than St. Louis, and the other owners, concerned about the cost of flying their teams to and from California, initially voted against Short's idea. Short, however, countered by offering to pay the difference between what any team spent to fly to Minneapolis and what it would spend to fly to Los Angeles. The owners voted again, and this time all of them approved the move except Ned Irish of the Knicks, who hoped that if the Lakers remained in Minneapolis their money problems would become so serious that Short would have no choice but to sell him Elgin Baylor.

SHORT HAD TOLD none of his players about his plans. Baylor found out about them by reading the newspapers, but while he liked Minneapolis, the prospect of moving appealed to him, if only because of California's weather. It had been snowing when the team left Minneapolis for that neutral-court game in Los Angeles, and when the Lakers arrived it was so warm that Baylor couldn't wear the clothes he'd packed and had to go out and buy some sport shirts. Short also made a second decision that summer that would prove to be crucial to the fortunes of the Lakers in the decade ahead, and it came during the college draft. The draft was unusually rich that year. Cincinnati, which had the first pick, chose Oscar Robertson of the University of Cincinnati. The two other top players were Darrall Imhoff, a promising center from California, and Jerry West, a nimble outside shooter from West Virginia. The Lakers, who had the second pick, already had two tall men, Jim Krebs and Ray Felix, and so Short selected Jerry West, who had hoped to play for the Knicks.

West was thin, undersized, and boyish looking in comparison to many of the pros, but he had a deadly line-drive jump shot and was an aggressive defender. And while he stood only six-two, he had such an incredible reach that he and Wilt Chamberlain, who was nine inches taller, wore shirts with the same sleeve length. "He has arms so long he could drive a car from the back seat," Jim Murray of the *Los Angeles Times* once wrote. His long arms and his quick reflexes enabled him, while guarding an opponent dribbling in front of him, to snake out a hand and steal the ball from the man, who had thought he was a safe distance away.

Short had continued to be unhappy with the Lakers' coaching, and not long after signing West, he hired Fred Schaus, West's coach at West Virginia. As the season got under way, West hoped to be made a starter, the way Oscar Robertson, Elgin Baylor, Wilt Chamberlain, and Bill Russell had all immediately become starters, and since Schaus had gotten the job largely because of his connection to West, sportswriters assumed he would start him right away. But Schaus, who had played professional basketball himself, for Fort Wayne and New York, felt West needed gradual exposure to the professional level of the game. Rookies brought into the NBA with high expectations for immediate results often were not given the time to adjust to the rougher, deeper level of play, and it wreaked havoc with their confidence. Schaus believed that because West was intensely self-critical, he would be particularly vulnerable to this problem. Also, West needed to master his new position. He had played forward at West Virginia, but at six-two he simply lacked the stature to succeed in the position in the NBA, and Schaus had recast him as a guard.

As the season progressed, however, it became clear to everyone following the Lakers that West was an extraordinary basketball player. Even though he was only coming off the bench, he was outscoring starters such as Hot Rod Hundley three to two. He was also demonstrating to the rest of the league a defensive ferocity uncommon in a shooting guard, and he radiated an energy level, a joy in the game, and a competitive ferocity that raised the play of all his teammates. Everyone on the Lakers looked sharper, moved faster, worked harder, and acted bolder when West was on the floor.

Schaus finally started him for the first time in the middle of the season, but such opportunities came intermittently, and West looked for a chance to prove he could be a key player. Then, toward the end of the season, the Warriors came out to Los Angeles for a game against the Lakers. West arrived at the arena suffering from a cold and expecting not to play, but Baylor was out with the flu, and so even though West was sick, Schaus started him. He played the entire game, cold and all, scoring thirty-eight points and getting fifteen rebounds and carrying Los Angeles to a 126–116 victory over Philadelphia, one of only two times the Lakers beat Chamberlain and the Warriors the entire season.

The Lakers made it to the Western Division playoffs, where they faced the Hawks. Hollywood celebrities such as Dean Martin, Peter Falk, and Jim Garner had become fans of the team, regularly appearing in courtside seats, but the crowds had followed more slowly, and interest in the playoffs was presumed to be so low that no radio station was willing to broadcast them. So Bob Short bought time at KNX and hired Chick Hearn, one of the station's announcers, to call the play-by-play. The Hawks were favored to win easily, but the Lakers fought them to a 3–3 tie in an exciting series that captured the public's attention. KNX's broadcast of game seven had the highest rating on the local spectrum. The Hawks ultimately won, but the Lakers, with their two stars, Elgin Baylor and Jerry West, had succeeded in establishing themselves as a genuine presence in the city. They began thinking about the next season. The Dodgers had won a championship the year after moving to Los Angeles, and the Lakers saw no reason why they could not do the same.

DURING THE SUMMER following his announcement that he was retiring after his first season in the NBA, Chamberlain went back to Europe to tour with Abe Saperstein and the Globetrotters. "He loved Saperstein," recalled his attorney Sy Goldberg. "It was against NBA rules for a player to play for another team, but Wilt did what he wanted. Eddie Gottlieb wasn't going to tell him what to do." Owners around the league thought Chamberlain's decision to quit was, as Danny Biasone of the Syracuse Nationals said, spoiled and immature. Sportswriters called him a crybaby, a quitter, and an ingrate. He was derided by players ranging from Dolph Schayes to Bob Cousy, who went around telling people he hoped Chamberlain *would* quit, then the rest of them could get back to playing real basketball.

And so, unsurprisingly, by the time Chamberlain returned from Europe he had changed his mind, and when Gottlieb raised his salary to $65,000 a year he decided to continue playing in the NBA. The fact was, he loved competition and the glory that came with achievement, and the NBA was the only place to get it. But by reconsidering, he made his original decision to quit seem empty and disingenuous. Some people around the league simply dismissed him as a petulant attention-seeker who couldn't be taken at his word. Even people inclined to have sympathy toward Chamberlain began to think he was someone who did not know what he wanted, or how to get it.

Chamberlain's second year in the NBA turned out to be more frustrating than his first, and the problems began almost immediately with his coach. In the late fifties, the Warriors had been coached by Al Cervi, an abrasive, snarling man with a chronic ulcer. When the Warriors finished in the cellar in the 1958–59 season, Gottlieb replaced Cervi with Neil Johnston, the team's lanky and jut-jawed center, who had been sidelined by a knee injury the previous year. But Johnston had distinct shortcomings as a coach. "He never seemed to get over the fact that he wasn't still playing," recalled Joe Ruklick. For all of Al Cervi's distemper, he knew how to run a ball club, and Johnston, an amiable but quiet fellow, lacked any air of command. The players had been his friends, and once he became coach they continued to be his friends.

But Johnston's biggest problem was the disadvantage he found himself at when dealing with Chamberlain. To begin with, Chamberlain had no respect for Johnston as a player. During that benefit game at Kutsher's Country Club in the summer of 1959, Chamberlain had beaten Johnston badly, and Chamberlain believed he had nothing to learn from Johnston, who had become coach, Chamberlain felt, only because of Eddie Gottlieb's sentimental loyalty to an athlete whose injured knee had ended his career. So Wilt ignored Johnston's instructions to shoot hook shots and set screens and instead continued to favor his fadeaway jumper, even though it thrust him away from the basket and out of position for the rebound. When Johnston fined Chamberlain for disrespectful comments, Chamberlain simply appealed to Gottlieb, who overruled Johnston, which diminished the coach's authority over all the players.

By the start of Chamberlain's second season, they were openly feuding. In an early game against St. Louis, Johnston accused Chamberlain of not guarding Clyde Lovellette—the man who'd knocked out Chamberlain's two teeth the previous season—closely enough.

"I'm trying to rebound and cover my man, too," Chamberlain protested. "You never tell Arizin or Gola or anyone else they have to cover their man more closely."

"They're not making sixty-five thousand a year like you are," Johnston said.

Chamberlain, who felt Johnston had no right to bring up his salary, particularly in front of the rest of the players, erupted, declaring that he was the one running the team, and the two men almost came to blows. After that, Chamberlain refused to play until Gottlieb interceded. "From then on, Neil and Wilt never spoke," recalled Ruklick. Chamberlain also began skipping the team's occasional practices. This enraged Johnston, who had a maxim he liked to cite: "Every player should be treated exactly the same—except on payday." But Gottlieb backed up Chamberlain, who maintained that since he played so much during games, what he needed between them was rest not practice. "Chamberlain's view was—do you want me for the game or do you want me for practice?" recalled his teammate Paul Arizin.

Some of the Warriors, particularly shooters such as Tom Gola, resented the way the team's game had been reconfigured around Chamberlain, who seemed to Gola to be more interested in scoring than winning. Wilt would get his forty points and his team would still lose. Chamberlain, always inordinately sensitive, picked up on the resentment of his teammates and fell into a funk, swearing at Johnston, ignoring the other Warriors, complaining about the officiating, and refusing on one occasion to play the second half of a game. His mood infected the entire team. The players who resented Chamberlain became surly and uncooperative. Sometimes during games, some of them refused to pass the ball to him if he was open under the basket, even if he was signaling for it. Johnston, for his part, had been stripped of all authority, and the players cruelly joked that his only job now was to reimburse them for their cab fares on road trips.

The strained atmosphere in the dressing room was primarily responsible for a slump the Warriors fell into shortly after the season began, but the team's disappointing performance was also due to the fact that Chamberlain's foul shooting, always a weakness, had become truly atrocious, falling below 40 percent at one point. In a game against Syracuse, which the Warriors lost by one point, Chamberlain took twenty-seven free throws and made only nine. Opponents started baiting Chamberlain during games, telling him they were going to foul him just for the fun of watching him blow his free throws. When he went to the line, the other players started chanting that he was *going to miss, going to miss, going to miss.* The fans of opposing teams hooted as he set up, and if he actually made a shot they'd break into derisive applause.

Chamberlain blamed the problem variously on his arthritic knees, his height, his strength, his big hands, the English on his shot, and the illegal stickum that rubbed off players' hands onto the ball. But he had also developed an inhibiting anxiety about free throws. *Don't let it bother you, don't let it bother you,* he told himself as he lined up a shot, knowing all the while that simply by telling himself not to let it bother him he was allowing it to do just that. Eddie Gottlieb was so exasperated that in the middle of the season he hired a free-throw tutor for Wilt named Cy Kaselman, who in the twenties had played for Gottlieb's team, the Sphas. In his heyday he'd been arguably the greatest foul shooter in professional basketball. His intuitive sense of the basket was so strong that he could actually hit free throws wearing a blindfold. Kaselman had Chamberlain dispense with his overhand foul shot altogether and instead start shooting free throws underhanded. It was a graceless, ungainly shot, triggering its share of jeers from the fans, but Chamberlain was able to concentrate on making the basket rather than worrying about missing it, and his statistics began to improve slightly.

As the season drew to an end, the Warriors were still in second place in the East, but they looked listless and disorganized, and the Celtics had surged far ahead. On one occasion, Eddie Gottlieb barged into the locker room and yelled, "You're not a team! I could get ten guys off the street and they'd play together better than you guys!" Nothing helped. Syracuse knocked Philadelphia out in the preliminary round of the playoffs, and Chamberlain's second year in the NBA came to a demoralizing end. Once the season was over, Gottlieb knew either Chamberlain or Johnston had to go, and he also knew it wasn't going to be Chamberlain. He had no choice but to get rid of Johnston, who immediately went public with his view of the Warriors. Chamberlain was impossible, he told the local sportswriters. No one could coach a team when one player had so many privileges that he could act as if he were in charge. There was going to have to be a big change in Wilt Chamberlain, and in all the Warriors, he maintained, before the team could win the championship.

Chamberlain, for his part, was convinced Johnston had been the problem.

He wanted a coach who would stand up to him and stand up for him, like Red Auerbach. In fact, Chamberlain wished Auerbach were his coach. If Auerbach had been his coach, he felt, he'd have already won the championship, and the fact that Auerbach was coaching Russell rather than himself made him angry at Auerbach. Once, watching Auerbach charge onto the court to protest a call against the Celtics—arguing with a vehemence Neil Johnston never mustered—Chamberlain approached him and said, "That's enough out of you." Russell immediately materialized and told Chamberlain, "If you're going after Red, you've got to go through me." On the Celtics, Chamberlain saw, the coach defended his players and the players protected the coach.

Auerbach, who had stood between the two men looking at them during their face-off, had followed Chamberlain closely throughout the season, and he agreed with Neil Johnston's analysis of the Warriors' problems. Auerbach felt that Gottlieb spoiled Wilt something fierce. A lot of times Wilt didn't even travel with his teammates. He was out of control. Auerbach doubted that he himself would have been able to coach Wilt. Maybe if he'd gotten him straight out of college. But Wilt quit school, spent that year with the Globetrotters, tasted the big money and the stardom, and he began thinking he was more important than his coach or his teammates. Gotty, afraid of losing his big draw, let him get away with it. Chamberlain had become convinced that people came to games in order to see him and that, therefore, the point of every game was to give him an opportunity to play the star. There was a certain box-office logic to this thinking, but it made Chamberlain uncoachable, in Auerbach's view, and as long as he was uncoachable, any team he played on would never become a real winner.

IN THE SUMMER of 1961, Eddie Gottlieb called Frank McGuire, the basketball coach at the University of North Carolina, and asked him to take over as coach of the Philadelphia Warriors. At first, McGuire was not sure that he wanted a job in the NBA. The Knicks had tried to hire him on three separate occasions, and each time he had turned them down, even though New York was his hometown. He was a revered icon in North Carolina, where he had developed five all-Americans and had won two conference titles and a national championship when his team defeated Chamberlain and the Kansas

Jayhawks in 1957. "The best public relations man we've ever had in North Carolina," Governor Luther Hodges once called him. The university had appointed him an honorary Doctor of Humane Letters, and he had a house with a pool, three children, and one grandchild. Why give all that up for the headaches and uncertainty of the NBA?

McGuire talked about the offer with other coaches, and some of them said it would be a mistake. The money was better, but the job security was a lot worse, and, as everyone knew, college coaches often failed to make successful transitions to the pros. On top of the difficulties every pro coach faced, McGuire would be dealing with Wilt Chamberlain, the man who'd just gotten his own coach fired after refusing to defer to Johnston's authority. If McGuire took the job and could not bring Wilt under control, his experience would be just as disastrous as Neil Johnston's had been. But Chamberlain had fascinated McGuire ever since the Tar Heels had beaten Chamberlain and the Jayhawks in that 1957 NCAA championship game, which was the highlight of McGuire's career. Chamberlain was quite simply the greatest player of the game McGuire had ever seen. And McGuire's friend Joe Lapchick, who had made a successful transition from college to the NBA, told him that Wilt Chamberlain was an irresistible coaching opportunity, a great but frustrated athlete in need of the right coach to unleash the full range of his potential.

By then, McGuire had been at North Carolina for nine years. Two Tar Heels players had recently been implicated in a bribery scheme, and though the scandal had not touched McGuire personally, it had cast a cloud on the entire team, and administration officials had decided the time had come to de-emphasize the school's basketball program. It seemed to McGuire like a propitious moment to take on a new challenge. The Knicks were still pursuing him, but he thought the true test, and the best avenue to championship glory, lay in coaching Wilt Chamberlain.

McGuire's reputation was so great that, when he decided to accept Gottlieb's offer, it was seen as a coup not just for the Warriors but for the entire NBA. Ray Cave, a writer for *Sports Illustrated,* declared that "never before has the NBA gotten a coach who was as famous, esteemed, and skilled at handling athletes as Frank McGuire." Cave thought McGuire might actually lead a wholesale transformation of the league. "His eventual effect may be to measurably change the character of professional basketball from the brawling, hustling, cigar-in-the-mouth and eye-on-the-till game it has been for decades to the major league sport it longs and deserves to be."

• • •

Frank McGuire was a forceful, dignified man who was also charming and politically shrewd. He had grown up in New York's Greenwich Village in the twenties, worked as a stevedore, and played basketball in the American League. He had a blunt Irish face, spoke with a brogue, and attended mass regularly, but he was also a stylish man in a masculine, mid-century way. His drink of choice was a J&B Mist. The Barbers of America once ranked him one of the country's ten best-groomed men. He was always freshly shaven, his white shirts starched, his silk ties crisply knotted, his suit jacket buttoned. At North Carolina, McGuire was known for his meticulous, even exhaustive preparation. He had movies taken of every game. He kept files on all his team's opponents. Before any game, the relevant file came out and McGuire gave his team a two-hour blackboard briefing. During games, a student assistant stayed close to McGuire, taking down his observations about the opponents, and those notes also ended up in the files.

McGuire prepared for his first meeting with Chamberlain just as thoroughly. He watched films of Chamberlain. He filled a file folder full of reports on Chamberlain, and he spent hundreds of dollars calling players, sportswriters, and coaches such as Dick Harp at the University of Kansas, who told him Chamberlain responded to leadership by someone he respected. McGuire figured Wilt was still a kid in a lot of ways, and if he was unable to control Chamberlain, it was going to be his own fault, not Chamberlain's. The key to the relationship, he thought, was to respect Chamberlain and ensure that Chamberlain respected him. It had to be reciprocal. He would also need to get the rest of the players to accept the fact that Wilt was a unique athlete who, by the nature of things, was going to be accorded special status and special treatment.

McGuire met Chamberlain for the first time at the Coco Inn, near the Warriors training camp in Hershey, Pennsylvania. He told Chamberlain that he was supposed to be tough to coach, but that that was probably because Wilt had never had a coach who treated him like a man. McGuire pointed out that he, McGuire, had always been a winner and said that if Chamberlain listened to him and they worked together, it would be possible to beat Boston. Chamberlain wanted to believe McGuire, but he thought Boston was unbeatable. It simply had too many good players. McGuire said it was true that Boston was better than Philadelphia when Chamberlain was scoring thirty-seven or thirty-eight points a game. But if he scored fifty points a game, McGuire said, the Warriors could beat Boston.

"Fifty?" Chamberlain protested. "Nobody can average fifty a game in this league."

McGuire told Chamberlain he could do it. The other players wouldn't be happy, he said, and he, McGuire, was going to have to put up with a lot of bitching, but that was his problem. He would have to convince them that the only way they could win was with Chamberlain shooting constantly. In McGuire's view, Chamberlain wasn't being selfish in taking so many shots. He just had the highest shooting percentage on the team. It made more sense to have your 50-percent shooter taking the shot than it did your 40-percent shooter, which meant that if one of Wilt's teammates with a poorer shooting percentage did not pass to Wilt, that man was not acting in the team's interest. "I have two goals," McGuire told Chamberlain. "I hope we win the championship. And I hope you break every record in the book."

AT NORTH CAROLINA, the basketball team traveled in style, and when Eddie Gottlieb sent the Warriors on the road to play a series of exhibition games before the season began, McGuire could not believe how small the budget was. To begin with, the team set off without a trainer. When McGuire asked who was going to tape the players' ankles, Gottlieb suggested he pay the home team's trainer two dollars to do the job. McGuire, who had no assistant, also had to call for taxis and make restaurant reservations himself, checking to ensure that the places would seat his black players. The team stayed in dreary hotels, and at night after games they washed their own uniforms in the sinks in their rooms. At one point, after playing one game in North Carolina and then flying to Oregon the next day for another game that night, McGuire grew so frazzled and so disgusted by the team's poor amenities that he called Gottlieb to quit. Gottlieb talked him out of leaving, but in return the coach was able to secure improved treatment for the team, booking his players into a better class of hotels and ending Gottlieb's pennysaving requirement that they ride five in a cab to the arena.

McGuire set out to redesign the Warriors offense. He moved Tom Gola from the backcourt to the front, brought in rookie Tom Meschery, and assigned second-year man Al Attles to the backcourt. The team had two simple tactics. After rebounding, they could feed the ball to Paul Arizin on the fast break and he could take a jump shot. But if the other team was in place, the Warriors had a variety of plays all with the same end: setting up and working the ball in to Wilt. McGuire had a mantra: *Feed Wilt.* Some of the Warriors were less than enthusiastic about being reduced to mere supporting roles, and a number of them had genuine financial concerns, since salaries in the NBA were typically pegged to statistics. They felt that if their statistics declined, this could diminish their reputations and Eddie Gottlieb might want to reduce their pay. "If my scoring average goes down, will you sit alongside me when I go to talk contract next year?" Guy Rogers asked McGuire.

"You bet your ass I will," McGuire said.

The coach also charmed Chamberlain, taking him out to dinner, getting him the best room in the hotel, checking on him before going to bed. "Frank was a more soothing coach than Neil Johnston," recalled Paul Arizin. "Wilt took to Frank's style." As a result, McGuire succeeded in persuading Chamberlain to change his game. Chamberlain was used to roaming around the court looking for an open spot to shoot his jumper. McGuire urged him to move into the low post near the basket, where he could take passes from his teammates, dunk, and make rebounds. McGuire also asked Chamberlain to appear at practice but made it clear that he would not have to work hard and could save his legs for the games. Finally, McGuire told him not to worry about his foul shooting. "Wilt," he joked, "if you hit all your free throws we'd never lose. It would be too easy, and it wouldn't be any fun."

With McGuire's new system in place, Chamberlain set off on an extraordinary scoring tear once the regular season got under way. He was averaging close to forty-seven shots and fifty points per game. And, because of overtimes, he was playing an average of forty-eight and a half minutes per game even though regulation play lasted only forty-eight minutes. Chamberlain was not the only player in the NBA shooting phenomenally in the 1961–62 season. Ten years earlier, only three players—George Mikan, Ed Macauley, and Alex Groza—had averaged more than twenty points a game. By December 1961, a total of eleven players were averaging more than twenty points a game, among them Oscar Robertson and Jack Twyman of the Royals, Bob Pettit of the Hawks, Tom Heinsohn of the Celtics, and Elgin Baylor of the Lakers. The best shooters in the league were racking up fifty- and sixty-point games, and to them, the nights when they scored only twenty points were actually embarrassing.

While Chamberlain led the league in scoring, Baylor was close behind him in second place. Early in the season, in a game against the Knicks, Baylor had set a league record for the most points scored in a single game, seventy-one, breaking the previous record of sixty-four points, which he himself had set a year ago. Then, on December 8, 1961, the Lakers faced the Warriors in Los Angeles in what became an explosive shooting duel between Baylor and Chamberlain. By the end of regulation play, with the score tied at 109–109, Chamberlain had scored fifty-three points and Baylor forty-seven. That in itself was a record; never before had the two top players in a game combined to score one hundred points. Then, in triple overtime, Chamberlain scored another twenty-five and Baylor another sixteen. With baskets by Jerry West, the Lakers ended up winning, but what made the news was Wilt's seventy-eight points, another single-game scoring record, though the statisticians qualified the achievement with an asterisk noting that it had been accomplished with three overtime periods whereas Baylor's seventy-one points had all been scored in regulation play. "Some day soon Chamberlain is going to score a hundred," McGuire told reporters after the game. "He'll do it even if five men guard him."

A month later, in a game against the Chicago Packers, an expansion franchise, Chamberlain ran up seventy-three points during regulation play, unequivocally taking the title for the single highest-scoring game. To everyone who followed the sport, basketball was undergoing a startling transformation. Traditionalists such as John McPhee, a writer for *The New Yorker,* found the change deplorable. "The game seemed to me to have lost its balance, as players became taller and more powerful, and scores increased until it was rare when a professional team hit less than a hundred points, win or lose," he wrote. "It impressed me as a glut of scoring, with few patterns of attack and almost no defense anymore. The players, in a sense, had gotten better than the game, and the game had become uninteresting. Moreover, it attracted exhibitionists who seemed to be more intent on amazing a crowd with aimless prestidigitation than with advancing their team by giving a sound performance."

By contrast, the *New York Post*'s Milton Gross was fascinated by the developments. Professional basketball, it seemed to him, was inhabited by a new race of men, who were not just larger but also faster and more powerful and more beautiful to watch than any players in the history of the game. "Basketball, professional basketball in particular, not only has come of age, but has reached its atomic, most explosive stage," he wrote in the middle of the season. "Individual skills have been perfected, scores are hovering in a special stratosphere. But still, the big show, the *really* big show, is yet to come."

The really big show Gross was referring to was the theoretical outer limit of scoring. As the records for individual single-game scores continued to climb, Gross began to wonder how far they could go. Eighty seemed easily within reach, and if eighty, why not ninety, and if ninety, why not, as McGuire had predicted for Chamberlain in December, one hundred points? When the Lakers were in New York to play the Knicks, Gross dropped by Baylor's room at the Hotel Manhattan and put the question to him. Baylor, one of the game's most astute analysts, thought it was inevitable that one day, and one day soon, somebody was going to score one hundred points in a game. There was no inevitable ceiling on scoring, he explained. The main reason it had increased was that so many players had perfected the jump shot. Just a few years earlier, the standard shot had been the two-handed set shot, which was easily blocked. But the jump shot was almost indefensible if a player's teammate set even the slightest screen. It was a quick shot, and the top players had become incredibly accurate with it, so the number of points they scored really depended on the number of times their teammates fed them the ball.

During a game, Baylor himself never thought about the number of points he was scoring. He considered it meaningless. He wanted to win, and if he set a record in a game but his team lost, he'd have felt that he'd accomplished nothing. Baylor thought that if anyone was going to break one hundred points it would be Chamberlain. He didn't think he himself could do it—even if he set his mind to it—because he didn't have Chamberlain's height, which enabled Wilt to pull down twenty-eight or twenty-nine rebounds a game. Wilt could score forty points alone from offensive rebounds and tip-ins and another fifty with his jump shot if he was hitting it consistently. On a night when he was that active, Baylor explained, he would be fouled more than normal, and if he made his foul shots, he could reach or exceed one hundred points. The key would be his foul shooting, which had always been Chamberlain's big weakness. "On a hot night," Baylor told Gross, "Wilt could make it."

ON MARCH 2, 1962, near the end of the regular season, the Warriors arrived in Hershey, Pennsylvania, for a neutral-court game against the Knicks. The Warriors, with only five games left to play, had secured second place in the Eastern Division, behind the Celtics, and their playoff berth was set. The Knicks, on the other hand, were in last place, and so neither team had reason to exert itself that night. The game was seen as so unimportant that none of the New York papers had deigned to send reporters along to watch it. Harvey Pollack, the public relations man for the Warriors, was covering the game for *The Philadelphia Inquirer* and the Associated Press. He was also assigned to keep the statistics, and he had brought his son along to take down a record of the play-by-play action.

The arena in Hershey was dark and dank, with overlapping rafters. The air outside smelled perpetually of chocolate. Only 4,124 people bought tickets for the event, which was a doubleheader. In the first game, the Globetrotters played a team made up of professional football players, and since the Trotters all knew Chamberlain, a number of them stayed on after their game was over to watch the professional match. In the years to come, when the game would achieve legendary status, Chamberlain would say that he was exhausted that day. Averaging fifty points a game was exhausting work. Also, he would say, he had been up all the previous night entertaining a lady friend in the Manhattan apartment where he now lived, then catching the train to Philadelphia, and sleeping only a few minutes on the team bus to Hershey.

Still, he was feeling relaxed and lucky. In the dressing room before the game, McGuire showed him a couple of New York newspapers predicting that the Knicks would outplay the Warriors. "Let's run 'em tonight, Wilt," McGuire said. In February, Chamberlain had cut a record album of rock and blues tunes called *By the River.* It was eminently forgettable, if not downright embarrassing, but Chamberlain had gotten a kick out of making it. Now, as the Warriors took the floor to warm up, Dave "the Zink" Zinkoff, the public address announcer for the Warriors who had come along to call the game, began playing it over the loudspeakers, and the music added to Chamberlain's nonchalant, lighthearted mood.

Phil Jordon, the Knicks starting center, was ill with the flu. His backup was Darrall Imhoff, then in his second year. "You're all I've got tonight,"

Eddie Donovan, the Knicks' coach, told Imhoff before the game. "Try not to foul out." Chamberlain started scoring furiously at the very outset of the game, and Imhoff, unable to stop him from driving to the basket, resorted to fouling him, which sent Wilt to the free-throw line. *Don't let it bother you,* Chamberlain usually told himself as he prepared to shoot his free throw, and then more often than not proceeded to choke. But on this night in Hershey, Pennsylvania, under absolutely no pressure in a sparsely attended game in which nothing was at stake, Chamberlain astonished himself by hitting his first nine foul shots in a row. If he kept it up, he thought, he might set some sort of foul-shooting record.

By the end of the first quarter, the Warriors were leading 42–26. Chamberlain had scored twenty-three of those points. As the second quarter got under way, Chamberlain continued to score, and Imhoff, unable to contain him, had no choice but to keep fouling him. It seemed to Imhoff that one reason Chamberlain was scoring so easily was that the hoops in the Hershey arena were as soft as garbage cans; a ball hitting them from any angle tended to drop in. Frustrated, Imhoff turned to Willie Smith, one of the officials, and asked, "Why don't you just give him one hundred points and we'll all go home?"

Imhoff soon had his fifth foul called and was replaced by Cleveland Buckner, who was thinner and shorter than Imhoff and had even less hope of containing Wilt. Chamberlain proceeded to rip off another eighteen points, bringing his total at the half to forty-one. In the locker room, the Warriors still thought of the game as nothing more than yet another of Wilt's high-scoring nights. But in the third quarter, even with three Knicks collapsing back to guard him, he continued to dunk and to sink jumpers and one-handed set shots. By the end of the third quarter he had run up another twenty-eight points, and then, with ten minutes and ten seconds left to play in the game, he pulled down a rebound and shoved it through the basket, bringing his total to seventy-five. He had broken his own record for most points scored in a single game, and he still had the bulk of the fourth quarter to play.

At that point, everyone in the building sensed the possibility of something historic taking place. Since it was a neutral-court game, the crowd had no rooting interest in either team, but now many of the spectators left their seats and moved down to stand along the sidelines. Every time Chamberlain scored, cheering erupted, and if one of the other Warriors took a shot, the fans booed. Each time Philadelphia got the ball, they chanted, *Give it to Wilt!* Soon, Chamberlain abandoned his defensive role altogether to concentrate on scoring, and stayed down by the Knicks' basket. As a result, the Knicks, though trailing the Warriors, were running up a score that in any other game would have been impressive. Cleveland Buckner, the backup to the backup center Imhoff, was on the way to scoring his all-time career high of thirty-three points.

Chamberlain's friend and teammate Al Attles had hit his last eight straight field goals, but with five minutes to play, he sacrificed an easy shot to pass high to Chamberlain, who jammed through another dunk, bringing his score to eighty-nine. Knicks coach Eddie Donovan called a time-out. If Chamberlain did rack up a hundred points, the members of the losing team would forever be branded as goats—it was just the sort of nugget obituary writers loved—and Donovan was determined that he and his team were going to avoid that fate. "There's no way that big S.O.B.'s going to get a hundred against us," he said in the huddle. Donovan ordered the Knicks to slow the game and to start fouling the rest of the Warriors. He figured that by sending Wilt's teammates to the line he could keep the ball out of Wilt's hands and set up the Knicks for rebounds.

At first it looked like Donovan's strategy might work. By fouling the other Warriors, the Knicks kept the ball away from Chamberlain for the next two minutes. Then McGuire called over three Philadelphia substitutes, York Larese, Ted Luckenbill, and Joe Ruklick, and told them to get in the game and retaliate by fouling the Knicks whenever New York got the ball. The final minutes of the game seemed strange to all the players. It was an ironic reversal of typical basketball strategy, thought Chamberlain's teammate Paul Arizin. The losing team, instead of trying to speed up the game to increase scoring opportunities, was freezing the ball, and the winning team, instead of stalling to maintain its lead, was fouling in an effort to turn over the ball.

A number of the Knicks, such as Richie Guerin, had become angry about the way the Warriors were playing. The game back in November when Elgin Baylor had scored seventy-one points had been a real game, with the points scored during the normal flow of the action. This game, it seemed to Guerin, was not a real game. The Warriors had clearly decided that their goal was for Wilt to score one hundred points, and instead of playing a normal game, all they were doing was feeding him the ball. He was taking a shot, or more, on virtually every single possession, while the other Warriors hardly took any shots at all. Guerin became so disgusted with the spectacle that he wanted no part of it and intentionally fouled out.

To counter the Knicks' foul strategy, the Warriors started inbounding the ball directly to Chamberlain, who was standing up near the basket in the forecourt. With two minutes left, Chamberlain got the ball and was promptly fouled. He made first one free throw. "Ninety!" Dave Zinkoff called out. And then another. "Ninety-one!" He was entitled to a penalty shot as well, and he made that, too. "Ninety-two!" He followed it, when the Warriors got the ball back, with a long jump shot. "Ninety-four!" And then another jumper. "Ninety-six!" With one minute and nineteen seconds left on the clock, Larese tossed a pass up toward the backboard and Chamberlain leaped up, caught it, and drove it through the net. "Ninety-eight!"

Chamberlain, wild now that the magic number was just one field goal away, stayed under the basket to harass the inbounds passer. "He's going for one hundred, sit back and relax," Zinkoff told the crowd. Chamberlain succeeded in actually stealing the inbounds pass and went up for a jump shot that missed. The Knicks got the rebound and, determined to keep the ball away from Chamberlain, brought it slowly down the court, but the shot clock forced them to shoot, and when they missed, the Warriors brought the ball back up-court with less than a minute to play. Wilt shot, missed, rebounded, and missed again. Ted Luckenbill got the rebound and passed out to Joe Ruklick, who lofted a high pass over the heads of the Knicks toward the basket. Chamberlain once again leaped up, caught the pass, and, with forty-six seconds left, dropped the ball through the hoop. "One hundred!" Zinkoff screamed.

The fans surged onto the court, running toward Wilt, slapping at his hands, clapping him on the back, pulling his jersey. Forty-six seconds remained on the clock, but the officials at first were unable to clear the floor. There was too much pandemonium, and in any event, somewhere back in the third quarter the game had ceased to become a contest between two teams and had turned instead into a one-man carnival feat. Willie Smith, the official, gave the game ball to Harvey Pollack. "This ball is a relic," Smith said. "Get it out of here." Pollack gave it to Jeff Millman, the Warriors equipment manager, and he placed it in Wilt's duffel bag in the dressing room. Pollack gave Smith a new ball. The officials cleared the floor. The Knicks had the ball, but Chamberlain, who wanted to keep his score at an even one hundred, simply stood at mid-court, and New York scored twice before the game finally ended.*

*Some players, and Frank McGuire, recalled that the final seconds of the game were never actually played out, but both Pollack and Ruklick vividly remember the final seconds.

Hysterical kids were climbing up Chamberlain's legs, hanging from his arms and jersey. His teammates swarmed around him along with the fans, and even a few of the Knicks, reluctantly acknowledging the accomplishment, came over and shook his hand. The Warriors headed down to the locker room, which was no bigger than one you'd find in a high school, with a single long wooden bench for all the players. The Warriors passed around the game ball, everyone signing it except Harvey Pollack, who was busy phoning in the box scores to the Associated Press.* No photographers had been assigned to cover the game, but a sports editor, listening to it on the radio, had realized in the second half that it was significant enough to warrant a picture, and shortly before the end of the game, a photographer did appear. Pollack scribbled the figure 100 on a sheet of paper, Chamberlain held it up, and a photograph was taken.

But Chamberlain seemed strangely quiet. The fact of the matter was that he was embarrassed. He had been given the stat sheet, and it showed that, while he had scored one hundred points, he had taken sixty-three shots. That worked out to one every forty seconds. In the second half, it had been more like one every twenty seconds. He knew that any ball hog who took upwards of sixty shots in a school-yard pickup game would never be asked to play again.

"I never thought I'd take sixty shots in a game," Chamberlain said to his teammate Al Attles.

"But you made thirty-six," Attles said. "That's better than fifty percent."

"But Al," Chamberlain went on, "sixty-three shots, Al?" He shook his head in disbelief.

It was an amazing accomplishment, one never again repeated in professional basketball. Chamberlain had run up thirty-one points in the final quarter alone. He'd made thirty-six field goals for a total of seventy-two points. What accounted for the difference in his overall score that evening was his free throws. If he'd hit his usual percentage of foul shots, he would have

---

*Accounts vary as to the fate of the game ball. After Chamberlain's death in 1999, a man named Kerry Ryman claimed that as a kid he had been at the game and had stolen the ball, and he sold it for $550,000 through Leland's Auction in New York. When Pollack gave interviews disputing Ryman's story, the buyer canceled his purchase. According to Pollack, the ball simply disappeared.

ended the game with a score in the mid-eighties. But, with nothing at stake in an unimportant game in a small-town arena, the pressure had been off and he was able to make twenty-eight of thirty-two free throws. Despite Chamberlain's reputation as a terrible free-throw shooter, those twenty-eight points set an NBA record for the most made free throws in a single game—a record that remains unbroken.

GOING INTO the 1962 playoffs, Bill Russell felt wrung out. That season the Celtics had lost Gene Conley, their backup center, to the new Chicago franchise in an expansion draft, and Russell, without a substitute to spell him, had been playing far longer than he was accustomed to doing. But his team was even more dependent on him than ever. In January, he had twisted his ankle driving to the basket in a game against the Lakers, and the Celtics did not win again until he returned to the lineup after sitting out four games.

Despite Chamberlain's stunning scoring average, Boston finished the regular season eleven games ahead of Philadelphia, and Russell was voted the Most Valuable Player. The award gave Russell some satisfaction because he felt that the only statistics of any significance at all were the numbers of wins and losses. Chamberlain had Russell beat in every category but one, victories, and that, Russell felt, was because for all of Chamberlain's unsurpassed athletic talent, the man at heart did not understand how to play the game. Basketball was a team game, and every single person on the team—and most important the star of the team—had to recognize that. Every man, even a 30-percent shooter, had to feel respected and valued by his teammates, particularly by the star, had to feel that if he was in a position to take his best shot, his teammates were going to feed him the ball. If the star did not have the brains to look after his teammates, they were going to leave him in the lurch, and the only person Russell saw Chamberlain looking after was Chamberlain.

The Celtics rested while the Warriors dispatched the Nats in the first round of the playoffs, and when the teams faced each other for the Eastern Division finals, they seemed more evenly matched than in any year since Chamberlain had joined the league. Boston had won eight of the twelve games the two teams had played against each other during the regular season, but by the end of the season the Warriors had perfected McGuire's system, and they took four of the last six games. Earlier in the season, *Life* magazine described the Russell-Chamberlain rivalry as "the fiercest private war in sports today." Both men were now experienced professionals, but both were still at their physical peak, and both were accustomed to dominating the court when they played, except against each other. Typically, Chamberlain outscored and outrebounded Russell, but Russell held Chamberlain's scoring well below his average. One reason for Russell's success against Chamberlain was his uncanny ability to anticipate Chamberlain's moves. "All season Russell has known just which way Wilt was going to turn," Frank McGuire complained to an acquaintance as the playoffs began. But under McGuire's direction, Chamberlain was now playing out of the pivot at the top of the key. As a result, reporters were writing about a "new" Wilt Chamberlain—"Warriors' Wilt to Display New Style Against Celtics" was a headline in *The Philadelphia Inquirer* before the series began—and McGuire was hoping that, since Chamberlain had more options in the pivot, Russell might be forced to play him more conservatively, which in turn could free up Chamberlain to shoot.

Once the series began, Chamberlain was able to score more frequently. In fact, the Warriors' five starters—Chamberlain, Paul Arizin, Guy Rogers, Tom Meschery, and Tom Gola, who was playing with a sprained back—

outscored the Celtics' five starters—Russell, Bob Cousy, Tom Heinsohn, Sam Jones, and Satch Sanders. But this advantage was offset by the fact that Boston's top three relievers—Frank Ramsey, K. C. Jones, and Jim Loscutoff—outscored their Philadelphia counterparts—Al Attles, Ed Conlin, York Larese—by an even greater margin. The two teams split the first four games, and the inability of either of them to draw ahead frustrated both, leading to an increase of tension on the court that erupted in game five, in the Garden.

During the fourth quarter, in a sloppily played game with the Celtics enjoying a solid twenty-five-point lead, Chamberlain collided with Sam Jones, and after some angry words, Chamberlain took after him. Jones had no intention of tangling with a man Chamberlain's size, so to protect himself he picked up a photographer's stool from the baseline and threatened Chamberlain with it. As fans screamed and police ran onto the court, Carl Braun, a veteran formerly of the Knicks whom Auerbach had signed for one season, rushed in to help Jones. At that point, Chamberlain's friend Guy Rogers stepped in and, thinking Braun was about to hit him, punched Braun in the mouth. Before Braun could retaliate—he later had to have two stitches—a Boston policeman grabbed his arms, and Braun wanted to say, *What are you doing? You're our cop, not theirs. Let go of me so I can get him.*

Seeing Braun struck, his fellow Celtic Jim Loscutoff moved furiously toward Rogers, who, like Sam Jones, picked up a photographer's stool to defend himself. At that point some two hundred fans, with piercing war cries, stormed onto the court to join the fight but were driven back by a phalanx of a dozen policemen led by Lieutenant Michael O'Malley of Station 1. "There would have been more," Bud Collins wrote in the *Herald,* "if Jaguar Jim Loscutoff could have got at Rogers, if Bob Cousy had reached Ted Luckenbill, if Wilt Chamberlain and Sam Jones, the latter brandishing a stool, could have fulfilled their frowns and curses. However, pacifists on both teams, ushers and club officials strong-armed the would-be fighters and cooled them out." As Frank Dolson noted in the *Inquirer,* "The brawl had its comic overtones."

When the police finally restored order, Boston won the game. Back in Philadelphia, the Warriors took game six, and the series came down to a seventh and final game in the Garden. It was an exciting but emotionally draining game for the Boston fans as well as for all the players, because the Celtics, who were eleven-point favorites, repeatedly established substantial leads only to have the Warriors catch up and overtake them. In the second quarter the two teams swapped the lead five times. In the fourth quarter the game was again tied, but then Frank Ramsey came off the bench for the Celtics and Boston built up a ten-point lead. The Warriors, however, whittled it down again. Russell, who had suffered from insomnia ever since the series began, was feeling exhausted but had done a spectacular job of containing Chamberlain for much of the night. In that final effort, however, Chamberlain scored seven of his twenty-two points. With a minute and a half remaining, Boston was ahead 107–102, but Chamberlain hit two foul shots and made a three-point play to tie the game with sixteen seconds left.

The Celtics worked the ball down the court. They had no game plan, no set play in mind; the idea was simply to look for the man with the good shot. K. C. Jones went up for an outside jumper, but at the last instant decided it was a mistake—pressure baskets were not his strong suit—and he twisted in the air and passed off to Sam Jones, standing fifteen feet from the basket. Sam Jones had now been with the Celtics for five years, but had become a starter only this season, when Bill Sharman retired. A quiet, self-effacing man who rarely smiled, Sam also never became rattled. Because he was bigger than most guards, he could often jump over his defender when taking an outside shot, and that, together with his nerveless manner, had turned him into the Celtics' clutch shooter.

When Sam got the pass from K.C., he did not know exactly how much time remained on the clock, but he knew there was less than twenty seconds. Time was almost out and he was open and everyone on the Celtics bench was screaming, *Go!* The club rule was that when the bench was shouting like that, the man with the ball was supposed to take the shot, so Jones jumped up and let go with a one-hander. The shot felt off, and as he released the ball he wriggled his shoulders, creating a little body English that he hoped would spin the ball into the basket. As it arched through the air, there was a huge gasp in the arena from the simultaneous intake of almost 14,000 breaths, but then it dropped through cleanly, and on the court the *swish* of the snapping net was drowned out by an enormous roar.

When the ball fell in, three seconds remained on the clock. The Warriors immediately called a time-out, but once the clock actually stopped, only one second remained. On the sidelines, Frank McGuire was enraged. He was convinced the timekeeper, a Celtics employee, had let two crucial seconds run down, and he demanded that referee Rich Powers restore them to the clock. Powers refused. The Warriors tried an inbounds pass to Chamberlain, who was under the basket, but Russell deflected the ball to Sam Jones, and when the final second expired the score stood at 109–107.*

McGuire was so infuriated over the lost seconds, which he blamed on the biased referees, that he slammed his fist through the door of the officials' dressing room. A little while later, Bud Collins of the *Herald* found him sitting in the visitors' dressing room.

"Who beat you?" Collins asked. "Jones? Russell? Cousy?"

"The referees," McGuire said bitterly. "Did you ever see such homers?"

Chamberlain, however, was elated. The seventh game could have gone either way, and he felt it proved that McGuire had been right when, at the beginning of the season, the coach had argued that Boston was not invincible. "You remember, at the beginning of the season, when you said we could beat Boston and I said we couldn't?" Chamberlain asked McGuire after the game. "Well, you were right, and I was wrong. We *can* beat them—and next year, we will!"

THE LAKERS had already clinched the Western Division, beating the Pistons in six games, and Jerry West had flown into Boston to watch the final game between the Celtics and the Warriors. He thought it was the single greatest basketball game he had ever seen, an opinion supported by the sportswriters, one of whom called Boston's victory "the hardest earned and most exciting in the Celtics' glorious history," while another declared, "If it were baseball, Sam [Jones] couldn't be more of a hero with a homer in the bottom half of the ninth and the score tied in the seventh game of the World Series."

Both teams had been playing at their peak, West thought, but what it came down to was that Boston could prevent the Warriors from doing what they did best—scoring—while the Warriors could not prevent the Celtics from doing what they did best—defending. The Celtics were not nearly as good a team offensively as the Warriors, but they were so superior defensively that they were better overall, and ended up with the higher score. The Lakers were an offensive team—West and Baylor together scored an average

---

*Auerbach would admit years later that a "malfunction" in the clock caused it to jump forward in the final seconds of each quarter.

of seventy points a game that season—and West wondered how well the Celtics would be able to contain them when the finals began two days later.

West was one of the new breed of players who made professional basketball a game increasingly played "off the floor," in the air around the baskets. As that had happened, scoring had increased and consequently so had the amount of physical contact from defenders trying to prevent it. To avoid interrupting the flow of the game, however, owners, coaches, and players all pressured the officials to interpret the rules on contact liberally. Some people actually argued that a degree of physical contact should be allowed in order to counter the excessive scoring. As a result, referees often ignored fouls as the game was getting under way and also tended to overlook the least egregious of them if they were unintentional or did not affect the outcome of the play.

While this unofficial policy gave players more flexibility in defending the basket, particularly against the increasing number of big men, it also made the game more dangerous. And no athlete seemed to expose himself to physical injury more than West. Now at the end of his second season, West was one of the smaller, lighter players in the league, a stripling compared to, say, Chamberlain, who was ten inches taller and seventy pounds heavier. But he had become the third-leading scorer in the league, after Chamberlain and Baylor, because unlike most light guards—who confined themselves to bringing the ball upcourt, passing off, and shooting from the perimeter—he drove for the basket and rebounded against men several inches taller and dozens of pounds heavier than he was.

And he paid a price for it with constant injuries. West had already had his nose broken four times on the basketball court by then, and it was permanently crooked, but most of his injuries were to his feet and legs. In one grim stretch that season, he sprained his right ankle in a rebound rumble, and was still hobbling when he sprained it again a week later, a sprain so excruciating that when he was resting his foot up on a chair at home and his wife accidentally brushed against it, the pain made him shout out. Two days later, playing with his ankle taped, he injured it a third time stealing a pass. Three days later, in Syracuse, he limped off the court after falling on his right hand and left foot. Then the next night he twisted his right ankle once again, this time so badly he was almost sobbing with pain.

Arnold Hano, a writer for *Sport* magazine, was afraid West was going to literally destroy his body. Whenever Hano watched West play, he did so with a sense of impending disaster, fighting the temptation to cover his eyes with his hands as West drove in against some rock-like monster such as Clyde Lovellette, who weighed 240, and came crashing down on the hardwood. And every time West went down on the court, his coach Fred Schaus either turned white or buried his head in his hands. But both Hano and Schaus knew that the injuries West suffered were the direct result of his unparalleled desire to win, and that because of it the Lakers were, for the first time since the days of George Mikan, contending for the championship.

Jerry West was a pale man with hooded blue eyes whose wide cheekbones, flat head, and narrow chin made his face appear triangular. His features, together with his long arms and thin legs, gave the impression that he was composed of lines and angles. He had a high-pitched reedy voice—his teammates on the Lakers called him Tweety Bird—cracked his knuckles, and spoke in an Appalachian accent so thick that his Olympic coach, Pete Newell, once irritably told him to speak English. Awkward off the court, West was the embodiment of physical grace once the game began. Despite his modest height, when he jumped up to the backboard, he could reach his hand sixteen inches above the rim of the basket. But what set him apart was his determination, which was arguably unmatched in the league. West was brooding and introspective, a loner, even something of a hermit, someone who was intensely self-critical but also extremely sensitive to criticism from others. He was born a good player and had made himself a great one, practicing endlessly, constantly dissatisfied with himself and always striving to improve his game. A natural shooter who decided while still a teenager that shooting was overrated, that the world of basketball was full of players who thought the game consisted of nothing more than putting the ball through the hoop, he willed himself to become a ferocious defender, someone who could pressure, harry, steal balls, and anticipate his man.

West came from the tiny hamlet of Cheylan, south of Charleston in central West Virginia, but since the family's mail came through the post office in nearby Cabin Creek, many people assumed that was his hometown. His father worked as an electrician in a coal mine. He was inordinately shy as a child, and basketball attracted him not because it was a team sport but because he could practice it in solitude, shooting baskets hour after hour on an outdoor hoop in a neighbor's dirt yard. He also listened on the radio to the basketball games played by the West Virginia University Mountaineers, though reception in Cheylan was so poor that he could follow the team only sporadically. By the time West joined the basketball team at East Bank High School, he had already developed his line-drive jump shot. He led his team to its first state championship, and the school's students were so proud of the victory that, as a joke, they proposed changing the school's name to West Bank High.

Out of state loyalty and a devotion to the Mountaineers nurtured by those radio broadcasts that wafted unevenly up into the hollows, West never intended to go anywhere but WVU. Many of the team's players came, like West, from tiny hill towns, and the people in coal country followed its fortunes with revival-tent enthusiasm, driving in caravans across the state and through mountain snowstorms to watch it play. Elmer David Bruner, a convict on West Virginia's death row, was such a passionate Mountaineers fan that he once offered to donate one of his eyeballs to Bucky Bolyard, a teammate of West's who was almost completely blind in one eye. Bolyard, who had a shooting accuracy higher than 50 percent with his one good eye, turned him down. When West became a freshman at West Virginia, it was Bolyard who nicknamed him "the hick from Cabin Creek"—*the heeick fr'm Cab'n Creeik.* At the time, Hot Rod Hundley was the varsity team's reigning star and the state's first real basketball hero, leading West Virginia to three straight Southern Conference titles. Hundley was the polar opposite of West in temperament, a flashy, hard-drinking, gregarious prankster—the son of a pool shark—who treated basketball more as an entertainment than a sport. He passed the ball behind his back and between his legs. He shot free throws with his back to the rim or from his knees. He liked to spin the ball on his finger and punch it toward the basket. The crowds loved Hundley's antics, but it pained the coach, Fred Schaus, to think that with Hundley the Mountaineers were known more as hijinksing hillbillies than serious basketball players.

Hundley was a senior when West was a freshman, and since freshmen were then prohibited from joining the varsity, the two did not play on the same college team, and many West Virginians speculated that if they had, the Mountaineers would have won a national title. In West's sophomore year, when he became part of the varsity squad, Hundley was drafted by the Lakers, and West followed his career intently. Despite Hundley's exceptional talent—many regarded him as a better ball handler than West—he failed to distinguish himself in the NBA, and West decided it was because Hundley treated the game as a lark. Hundley didn't particularly care about winning, liked to head out on the town after a game then sleep late, and never attended voluntary practice sessions. Talent without the requisite drive, West realized, simply did not take you very far.

Fred Schaus, the Mountaineers coach, was a big burly man with a warm sympathetic manner that appealed to the painfully shy West. Schaus was also an ardent believer in team spirit and team pride as motivating forces. Wanting his team to look cleaner and sharper than other teams, he insisted that all his players shave their armpits, and while West thought the policy was strange, he complied. Many college coaches played with a rigid system, penalizing their players for improvisation even if they succeeded in scoring, but Schaus emphasized a free-floating, high-scoring game, grounding his players in the fundamentals and then setting them free to follow their instincts on the court. West's fast, jump-shooting style was perfectly adapted to this approach, and in his junior year West Virginia went all the way to the NCAA finals. While they lost the championship by one point to California, West was voted the tournament's Most Valuable Player.

What made West so extraordinary was that he played much better against good teams (averaging thirty points in close games) than against poor ones (twenty-two points in easy games). Indeed, fourteen of the Mountaineers' twenty-nine wins in West's senior year were the result of second-half rallies he had inspired. West was named to the 1960 U.S. Olympic team, along with future NBA stars Oscar Robertson, Darrall Imhoff, Walter Bellamy, and Jerry Lucas.* The team went undefeated in Rome, and when West returned to East Bank with his gold medal, the townspeople, in his honor, did actually rename it "West Bank" for a day.

The year West joined the Lakers, the team was considered talented but uneven. Baylor was brilliant—strong, driving, almost unstoppable—and he played up front with the tough, defensively aggressive Rudy LaRusso. But the Lakers were weak at center, where Ray Felix alternated with Jim Krebs. Neither was able to contain the league's great centers, and the Lakers backcourt alternated Bob Leonard, Rod Hundley, and Frank Selvy, all of whom

---

*The pool for the Olympic team was so deep that among those who failed to make it and then went on to great pro careers were John Havlicek, Larry Siegfried, Satch Sanders, and Tom Meschery.

had been great college players but lacked the talent or the motivation to achieve true distinction as pros. In West's second season, the team's profile improved considerably once West beat out Hundley for a starting position. Coach Schaus began using Hundley more and more as the equivalent of a house jester, bringing him into the game only when the Lakers had a comfortable twenty-point lead and allowing him to entertain the crowd with his antics. Hundley came to hate the role—his wife found it embarrassing as well—but it was what the fans wanted to see and what paid for his expensive Malibu house. Unwilling earlier in his life to take his considerable talent seriously, he now had no choice but to play the clown.

With Baylor at forward, driving into the lane, and West at guard, drilling his jump shot from the perimeter, the two men developed their formidable one-from-the-inside-one-from-the-outside double threat. But then the Communist regime in East Germany erected the Berlin Wall, and in response President John F. Kennedy called up units of the National Guard and the Army Reserve. Among those ordered to report for duty was Baylor, whose National Guard unit was sent to Fort Lewis, Washington. Baylor was able to play when he got occasional weekend passes, but he missed many games, and in his absence, West became the Lakers' primary shooter. With each game, his confidence improved and his scores began to climb, and in midseason in his second year he began a great scoring run, hitting sixty-three points in January against New York—a record for a guard—and running up subsequent tallies of fifty, forty-five, and forty-six.

West also emerged as the team leader, someone who both inspired the other players and carried them all at critical moments. Many of basketball's shooters, while desperate for the ball during most of a game, wanted to avoid it in the final seconds if the game was on the line. No one wanted to be responsible for a defeat by shooting and missing. West, however, almost perversely *did* want the ball when there were ten seconds left on the clock and the Lakers were down by one. And more often than not, he could make the shot. Many perfectionists are troubled by self-doubt, but West had an almost preternatural poise when the pressure was the most intense. It was a remarkable trait. West had concentration, determination, discipline, and singleness of purpose, but his poise was arguably the greatest of his mental assets. Chick Hearn, whom Bob Short had hired to call all the Lakers games for the radio, was trying to build fan interest in Los Angeles by creating stars. West was one of Hearn's potential stars, and the broadcaster came up with, and used over and over, the nickname that would stay with West throughout his career. Hearn called him "Mr. Clutch."

THE ARMY had released Baylor for the playoffs, and in the first two games of the final series, which were played in Boston, the teams seemed evenly matched, each winning once before flying to Los Angeles for the second two games. It was the first time a basketball championship game had been played in Los Angeles, and 15,000 fans packed into the L.A. Sports Arena, a spanking new building on the campus of the University of Southern California where escalators ferried spectators up to the stands, a fan made the flag flutter when "The Star-Spangled Banner" was played, and an automatic attendance counter posted the crowd size on the scoreboard.

The third game was tight and wild through all four quarters, the two teams swapping the lead with almost every basket. With a minute to go, Boston was up by four points, but West scored with a jump shot and then, when the Celtics missed a shot, dropped in another jumper to tie the game. There were three seconds left. The Celtics, who had possession, called timeout to set up their final play. Sam Jones took the ball out, and West figured it would go to Bob Cousy, their playmaker. Just as Jones was throwing in the ball, West darted in front of Cousy, intercepted the ball, and tore down the court dribbling. Afraid at any moment he would hear the sound of the buzzer, he pulled up and released, and the ball swished through the net at the very instant the buzzer went off. West had scored his team's last six points in the final minute of the game and hit the winning basket at the bell. It was, he decided lying in bed that night, the ultimate trophy moment.

The two teams continued to trade victories, however, and at the end of six games, they were tied 3–3. Game seven was to be played in Boston, but the Celtics' traditional home-court advantage had not prevailed during the series; the Lakers had won two of the three games played so far in the Garden, and victory certainly seemed within their grasp. They had the superior shooters in West and Baylor, who had scored a playoff record of sixty-one points in game five. The problem was that neither Jim Krebs nor Ray Felix, the Lakers' alternating centers, could compete with Russell. And so, while Baylor and West shot marvelously, the Celtics, with Russell outrebounding Krebs and Felix, had been able to keep pace.

The day after the sixth game, more than 10,000 fans swamped the Garden demanding tickets, which were sold out by 11:00 a.m. Both the Celtics and the Lakers, drained from the long round of playoffs, felt the pressure, and the result was an exciting but error-prone and physically punishing game. West found it hard to find his rhythm, and Baylor, so hot earlier in the series, went cold, missing almost three out of every four shots. Russell, summoning his final reserves of energy, played ferociously, blocking shots, intimidating Krebs and Felix, even scoring thirty-five points. But neither team was able to establish a commanding lead, and with thirty seconds left, Boston was ahead 100–98, when Frank Selvy, who filled out the Lakers backcourt with West, found himself standing under the basket.

Selvy was the oldest player on the team. His teammates called him Pops and Rivers, as in "Ol' Man River." He had been considered a player of great promise when he was drafted, a reputation largely based on the fact that, while at Furman University, he had scored one hundred points in a single game. Selvy could shoot but not quickly, and was also a poor ball handler, and over the years he'd been signed and then let go by a series of NBA coaches who'd been impressed by his statistics but disillusioned by his actual on-court performance. But Lakers coach Fred Schaus thought Selvy was a good complement to West. He was slow, but he *could* shoot—his two-handed perimeter shot was known as the "Furman flea-flicker"—and since the aggressive West tended to draw defenders, that often let Selvy open.

Now, in the seventh game, standing under the basket with thirty seconds left, Selvy was able to tip in a missed shot by West, tying the game. Boston's Frank Ramsey got the ball and tried for one final shot but missed, and with five seconds left, the Lakers called a time-out. Schaus, shouting to make himself heard above the noise of the crowd, told Selvy to make the inbounds pass to Hundley, who would then pass either to West or back to Selvy if West was covered. When the play began, Hundley received the ball. K. C. Jones was all over West, so Hundley, after considering for an instant whether he should shoot the ball himself, passed back to Selvy, who was only eight feet from the basket and in the open. Selvy rose for a jumper and released.

All the men on both teams stood watching. The Celtics had expected Baylor or West to take the last shot. West himself had wanted to take the shot, he felt he had proved in game three that he could make the clutch point, and he was sure he could do it again. But Selvy had a hot hand and had been open, standing in a spot where he made the shot eight times out of ten, the time was running down, and instead of waiting for West to try to break free, he had gone for it. As the ball arched through the air, it seemed in a perfect trajectory to drop through the hoop. Russell, watching from the paint, felt his heart seize up. Auerbach, standing by the Celtics bench, thought it was all over. The ball hit one side of the rim, then the other, rattled and teetered, and finally fell out. *I missed it,* Selvy thought. *I missed it, I missed it. It was there for me and I missed it, and all that work is wasted.* Russell leaped for the rebound, grabbed the ball with both hands and, while still up in the air, brought it protectively into his stomach, then landed, elbows flared, daring anyone to try to take it from him. The buzzer sounded and regulation play ended in a tie.

During the break before overtime, Russell sat on a stool, winded and overheated. One of the Celtics poured a bucket of cold water over him, and that seemed to revive him. Since Heinsohn, Sanders, and Loscutoff had all fouled out, the Celtics were at a distinct disadvantage. No sooner had the overtime period begun than Frank Ramsey fouled Baylor and was out of the game. Other than Russell, the Celtics had no big players left. They would have to depend on the little guys.

Auerbach turned to Gene Guarilia, a reserve forward who hardly ever played. Night after night, Guarilia suited up and sat on the bench. The call from Auerbach came so infrequently that he sat through each game with the expectation that he would not be called, that he'd return to the locker room with a uniform so dry he could hang it up unwashed and wear it for the next game. And when he did get sent in, it was usually because Boston was ahead by twenty points in the last half of the fourth quarter and, with the game in the bag and spectators already filing out, Auerbach wanted to rest his starters. Now, all of a sudden, it was overtime in the seventh game of the finals, the championship was at stake, he was going in absolutely cold, to be pitted against Elgin Baylor, and the thousands of Garden fans, not to mention the national television audience, were staring at him wondering if he would rise to the occasion. But Auerbach had sent Guarilia into one of the games in the series against Philadelphia when it had gone into overtime and he'd run out of players. The unexpected order had completely shaken Guarilia up at the time. He'd made up his mind he would never allow himself to get so rattled again, and he'd spent the entire game steeling himself for just this eventuality.

Guarilia trotted onto the court. Baylor scored two points, and then the Celtics had the ball. Cousy shot and missed. Russell was trapped outside the key, unable to go for the rebound, but Guarilia, on the far side of the court, managed to slip around Baylor, and came up with the ball. Russell came charging in and Guarilia passed it to him. He rose up, clutching the ball with both hands so no one could tear it from his grasp, and dunked it. The crowd roared.

Guarilia was so keyed up, and Baylor by now so tired, that the Celtics bench player was able to keep the league's second-highest scorer off balance. By pressing Baylor, Guarilia forced him to make a poor shot that banged off the rim. Russell got the rebound and, setting the Celtics' fast break in motion, fired the ball to K. C. Jones, who tore down the court, then passed across the key to Sam Jones. Rudy LaRusso was the only Laker who'd made it back to defend the basket, and when Jones went up for a layup, LaRusso fouled him but the ball went in. Sam made his free throw to put Boston up by three points. In the short time remaining, the Lakers were unable to close the gap, and suddenly it was over and the Celtics were again the champions.

In the Celtics locker room after the game, reporters swarmed around Guarilia for the first time in anyone's memory. One went looking for Russell and found him far from the commotion, leaning against the wall, tears running down his cheeks. The tension had been so high and now that it was over the relief was so great that the proudest, most intimidating man in basketball was actually crying. After a minute, Russell got ahold of himself. "Well," he said, "I'm glad that's over."

The Lakers dressing room was quiet. As the players walked by on their way to the shower, Frank Selvy sat on the bench in his bare feet, smoking a cigarette. He'd made the two points that brought the Lakers from behind to tie the game, but he took no consolation in that, because he'd missed the shot that would have won it. One of his teammates, trying to cheer him up, said, "Hell, think of the shots we all missed."

"Yeah," Selvy said, "but I missed the big one."

THE CELTICS' victory in the 1962 finals was the team's fifth championship in six years. The club had won every year since Russell joined except for 1958, when he injured his left ankle during the playoffs, and the Celtics were now in a league with the New York Yankees, who won the World Series five times·between 1949 and 1953, and the Montreal Canadiens, who took home the Stanley Cup five times between 1956 and 1960. Sportswriters now commonly spoke of the "Celtic dynasty" and the "Celtic mystique" and "Celtic pride." The Celtics home quarters, however, were hardly commensurate with their dynastic status. Unlike the Lakers, who had a flashy new arena complete with escalators and an automatic gate counter, the Celtics continued to play in the aging Boston Garden. "The Celtics conjure up the picture of a Rolls-Royce on a garbage scow," Bob Hoobing once wrote in the *Herald*.

The arena itself was a dank and drafty place. It had no air-conditioning and perpetually smelled of cigar smoke, beer, and popcorn. It had been designed, in 1928, for ice hockey, boxing, and indoor track, so the small seats were ranged in steeply banked rows that made the crowd feel closer to the action, unlike newer arenas where the seats were set farther back. John Kiley played the organ; Weldon Haire was the public address announcer. There were no mascots, no dancing cheerleaders, no rock music blaring from the loudspeakers during time-outs. The atmosphere was informal. A columnist for *The New York Times* once described the fans as members of the sociological subset known as Corner Boys. They had names like Whitey, Lefty, and Spike, and during the warm-ups before games they would gather along the sidelines of the court and banter with the players.

Like the team, the arena had acquired an aura, and to many people it was inextricably associated with the Garden's distinctive parquet floor. The floor had been constructed of Tennessee oak by the DiNatale family in the Boston suburb of Brookline in 1946, and the parquet pattern had been chosen because, due to a wood shortage at the end of World War II, long boards were considerably more expensive than short pieces. There were 264 panels, each five feet square and one and a quarter inches thick, and they were held in place by 956 bolts that all had to be removed every time a hockey game was played and then replaced before each basketball game. The "bull gang," a crew of sixty workers, was able to accomplish the job in forty minutes.

Dolph Schayes of the Syracuse Nationals believed that playing in Boston Garden was worth at least ten points to the Celtics. It was true that both players and referees were affected by the crowds, but privately, the Celtics admitted that there was another reason for their home-court advantage, and it was literally the home court. The arena was built over North Station, and through the years the vibrations caused by the trains rumbling in and out had created cracks in the cement subflooring, and that in turn resulted in an uneven floor. When the parquet squares were laid down on top of the cement, some fit snugly, others had hollow spots and ridges beneath them. There were gaps between some of the squares, and the bull gang simply screwed the parquet into place with no system for applying uniform torque. As a result there were innumerable loose screws and dead spots in the floor, places where a bounced ball would sag as if it had suddenly been punctured. From their years of playing in the Garden, all of the Celtics carried in their minds a road map of the floor's dead spots. They knew what places to avoid, and just as important, what places to maneuver a dribbling opponent toward. If an unsuspecting out-of-towner hit a dead spot, he could lose control of the ball or overcompensate coming off the dead spot and have the ball bounce right out of his hands.

Over the years, visiting coaches and players also complained about conditions in the visitors' dressing room, and while the Celtics front office always dismissed the complaints, most of them were valid and could be traced to Walter Randall, the Celtics equipment manager. Randall was an irascible, mischievous man who liked to call the players by their numbers. "Hey, Fifteen!" he'd yell at Heinsohn. He had a master key, and during games he'd use it to slip into the visitors' dressing room to replace dry towels with wet ones, open the windows in cold weather and lock them closed when it was warm, and shut off the hot-water valve. "Johnny, I got those bastards good tonight," he'd tell Johnny Most, the team's radio announcer.

For all the aura the team had acquired, its ticket sales remained flat, and some years there were unsold seats even during playoff games. The Celtics were not nearly as profitable as Walter Brown's hockey team, the Bruins, which was not nearly as successful, and so Brown saw to it that the Celtics were always a frugal operation. Auerbach himself negotiated directly with the players about their contracts. And in fact, these sessions usually were not negotiations at all. Auerbach assessed each player and told him what he was worth based on his contribution to the team. Auerbach hated it when players tried to squeeze him for better terms by bringing up their statistics in the previous season. He'd tell them to leave the stats at home. Auerbach thought there was nothing more misleading than statistics. A player could argue that he averaged twenty points a game in the previous season, but the figure was meaningless unless Auerbach knew how many of them were scored against good teams and how many against crummy teams, how many were garbage points, when the game had been decided, and how many were clutch points, when the game hung in the balance. Auerbach measured a player's worth only by the extent to which the man contributed to victory. He was only going to become interested in statistics when they measured intestinal fortitude, coming through in the clutch.

With salaries that for the most part were strictly middle-class, most of the

Celtics had off-season jobs. Heinsohn, one of the highest-paid Celtics, sold insurance in the Worcester office of State Mutual of America, and he made more money doing that than he did playing basketball. Gene Guarilia played guitar in a nightclub orchestra. Bob Cousy ran a basketball camp in New Hampshire. Auerbach still handled some accounts for CelluCraft, the plastics company, and had invested in a Chinese restaurant in Brookline.

But come September, the players who did not live in and around Boston began drifting back to the city. Rookies such as John Havlicek, who'd just graduated from Ohio State and had been picked by Auerbach in the 1962 draft, were put up at the Hotel Lenox. Veterans took up quarters they often shared with other players up in the old Sherry Biltmore. Training camp was held at the Babson Institute, fifteen miles outside Boston in the town of Wellesley. There were no curfews, no supervised diets. To Havlicek, accustomed to university training camps where players were force-fed steaks and pancakes and where lights were turned out at ten o'clock, the freedom Auerbach granted the players was surprising.

Nonetheless, the Celtics training camp was notorious as the most grueling in the league. For the Celtics to play the kind of fast-breaking game Auerbach favored, they needed to be able to run up and down the court without tiring for forty-eight minutes. Many players in the NBA hated training camp and preferred to play themselves into shape once the season began, but Auerbach liked the Celtics to start the season in peak form, beat a few out-of-shape teams, and establish an early lead. When he was in the navy during the war, he had been responsible for physical fitness on the base, and as a basketball coach he had always retained the military emphasis on conditioning. The veterans almost invariably gained weight during the off-season— Russell could put on twenty or thirty pounds, becoming, in his own words, one fat center—and so training camp consisted of drills, running, scrimmaging, more running, calisthenics such as jumping jacks and push-ups, and yet more running. To anyone not in superlative shape, Tom Heinsohn thought, it was torture pure and simple.

Auerbach rode all the players. *Are you shitting me?* he'd yell. *That's false hustle!* One of his tasks was to grind down the egos of the rookies. *You're nothing but a nothing!* he'd shout at them. But he would also go after the veterans, forcing players who'd been injured the season before to dive after balls to prove to him, and to themselves, that they were not playing scared. Always wary of the dangers of overcoaching, Auerbach passed out no notebooks or playbooks. The Celtics had seven basic plays, each with a few variations, and during training camp he concentrated on one play a day. Auerbach also held hardly any meetings. But on the first day of camp, before the training even began, he always called the players together and gave a variation of what he called his standard speech:

Gentlemen, you are the world champions. You've heard the accolades all summer long. You've had a good time. And now everybody's out to knock your jocks off. So, is this the year we get lazy? Is this the year we start feeling content? Because if you want to let them get you, just try living off last year's reputation. What we have to do is meet them head-on and say, "You're damned right we're the world champions, and if you want this title you're going to have to take it from us!"

ONCE THE 1962 PLAYOFFS were over, Chamberlain and a friend of his

from the Globetrotters named Wee Willie Gardner flew to Europe. They stopped first in London, where Chamberlain took command of a custommade, heather-colored Bentley Continental he had ordered in New York a year and a half earlier. Then they went on to Paris, and drove the Bentley down to the Riviera. While they were in Cannes, Chamberlain received a call from a friend in Philadelphia telling him that Eddie Gottlieb was selling the Warriors to a group of investors in San Francisco. Chamberlain called Gottlieb, who confirmed the news.

Gottlieb had been coach, manager, and part owner of the Warriors since 1946, the year the team was founded as a charter member of the Basketball Association of America. His initial investment in the Warriors was $2,500, and people liked to say he borrowed $2,800 of it. In 1951, he'd bought the team outright from his partners for $25,000. Now, eleven years later, the San Francisco investors were offering him $850,000 for it. And on top of that they wanted to pay him $35,000 to move out to San Francisco for one year to oversee the transition and manage the team.

The deal was contingent on Chamberlain coming with the team, and while Chamberlain liked Gottlieb, at first he refused. It was not because of any particular affection for the city of Philadelphia. Chamberlain had friends and family there, but he felt that compared to New York, where he now had an apartment, the restaurants and nightlife were second-rate. The year before, in fact, prior to Frank McGuire becoming coach, Chamberlain had told Gottlieb he would be happy to be traded to a city with more action. But then he and McGuire had their great run, and Chamberlain was now looking forward to playing for the Warriors for another season only because he thought he and McGuire could take the championship from the Celtics.

When Chamberlain learned that McGuire would not accompany the Warriors to San Francisco—he had a son with cerebral palsy who was under treatment by doctors on the East Coast—he saw no reason to go himself and told Gottlieb he might just stay on in France. Gottlieb made numerous expensive transatlantic calls, selling Chamberlain on San Francisco and increasing the financial inducements, until finally he offered his star $85,000 a year for three years if he came west. Chamberlain agreed. He had the Bentley shipped back to the United States and at the end of the summer drove it cross-country to San Francisco.

The investors acquiring the Warriors for San Francisco, led by business executives Matty Simmons, Len Mogul, and Franklin Mieuli, hoped to duplicate the success Bob Short had enjoyed by moving the Lakers to Los Angeles. It seemed like a promising idea. San Francisco was a thriving, vibrant city full of sports fans who passionately rooted for the football club, the 49ers, and who had welcomed the Giants when the baseball team moved there from New York in 1958. Additionally, Bill Russell's two national championships at the University of San Francisco had created an enthusiasm in the city for basketball. The team, which would continue to be called the Warriors, would play at the Cow Palace, which had a capacity of 14,000, and the Lakers in Los Angeles would provide them with a natural rival that would boost the local rooting interest.

But the World Series that fall was between the New York Yankees and the San Francisco Giants. The games had been postponed because of rain, which extended the series until it overlapped with the NBA's exhibition season, and as the Warriors prepared for their debut the San Francisco sports pages were devoted not to Wilt Chamberlain but to Willie Mays and Juan Marichal. To make matters worse, on the night of the Warriors' first game, the Gene Fullmer–Dick Tiger middleweight championship fight was being held in Candlestick Park, and only some 5,000 people came out to watch San Francisco's new basketball team.

The Warriors started the season strongly, routing Detroit 140–113 in their maiden appearance in the Cow Palace. They remained in first place for almost two weeks, until the Lakers trounced them 127–115 in a game in which Chamberlain scored seventy-two points—a number that, one year ago, would have represented a record for a single game total. From then on, the Warriors steadily declined, losing eleven games in a row in one stretch, until they wound up in last place. And the team's investors had miscalculated San Francisco's interest in basketball. An average of 4,000 fans were showing up at each game, meaning the stands were more than two-thirds empty, and a third of those tickets sold were special one-dollar admissions. What the local memories of Bill Russell's glory years at USF really translated into was not enthusiasm for Wilt Chamberlain and the Warriors but nostalgia for Bill Russell. The high point in attendance for the Warriors came when the Celtics first played in San Francisco, and many of the fans cheered for the Boston team.

One reason for the Warriors' poor performance was turnover on the roster. Paul Arizin had retired, Tom Meschery broke his wrist in the season opener, and Tom Gola decided he disliked San Francisco and asked to be traded to an East Coast team. Of the regular starters who had almost beaten the Celtics the previous year, only Al Attles, Guy Rogers, and Chamberlain were still with the team. The club had seven new members. But the Warriors also suffered from weak coaching. Bob Feerick, the coach Eddie Gottlieb had hired, had been the highly regarded and successful coach at the University of Santa Clara. But Feerick lacked the shrewdness and force of personality needed to run an NBA club, and by the middle of the season, Gottlieb was regretting his choice.

Staying at the Mark Hopkins Hotel, Gottlieb was in touch with his associate Mike Ianarella, who'd sold tickets for the Warriors in Philadelphia and who sent Gottlieb newspaper clips so he could monitor the progress of the Phillies and the Eagles. Gottlieb complained in one of his regular letters to Ianarella that Feerick did not "know the 'score.' " The coach did not discipline the players and seemed to have no idea what it took to run a professional basketball team. He was "just a nice guy and they always finish last," Gottlieb wrote. "His ideas on the game are 'ass' backwards." Gottlieb missed Frank McGuire. The Warriors' erstwhile coach had contacted Gottlieb to get his help landing the coaching job with the Nationals—a job that ended up going to Nats player Dolph Schayes—and Gottlieb grumpily wondered why, if McGuire still wanted to be a pro coach, he hadn't stayed with the Warriors, where he could have prevented the problems the team was now having with

Feerick. "Frank McGuire must have taken the signing of Schayes badly, as he still felt he might get that job," Gottlieb mused in another letter to Ianarella. "Well, that's the way things go. He passed up the best job when it was offered."

AS A WAY of paying tribute to Lakers owner Bob Short and the success of the Lakers' move to the West Coast, the NBA decided to hold the 1963 all-star game in Los Angeles. The day of the game, Short hosted a lunch at the Coconut Grove in the Ambassador Hotel, and some 1,000 people paid fifteen dollars a ticket to sit in the same room with the best players in the league. To commemorate the event, Short had a program printed with a self-congratulatory cover depicting a globe rendered as a basketball and over it the line "Basketball Capital of the World." Chick Hearn, who called the Lakers games, was the emcee, cracking jokes and bantering as he invited players and coaches to the podium to say a few words. The tone was light, all pleasantries and encomiums, and when it was Fred Schaus's turn to take the podium, the Lakers coach spoke in breezy but gracious generalities about the honor of coaching the Western Division all-stars and the excitement he felt about the upcoming game. Red Auerbach, who was coaching the Eastern all-stars, followed Schaus to the podium.

After thirteen years as coach of the Celtics, Auerbach's sideline theatrics had long ago turned him into a coach the fans of other teams loved to hate. Each new episode only added to his aura of despicability. In fact, Ben Kerner, the owner of the St. Louis Hawks, believed that Auerbach was so successful at inciting fans that he was one of the few coaches in the history of any sport who actually sold tickets. Hawks fans came to the game just for the sake of jeering Boston's coach. Auerbach himself claimed that one of the franchise owners once actually encouraged him to act up, promising to pay whatever fines he incurred. *Red, give 'em a little show tonight. It's good for the gate.*

Over the years, Auerbach had been pelted with rotten tomatoes, spitballs, paper hatchets, snowballs, beer cans, rolled-up programs, purses, peanuts, and lit cigars. But eggs were by far the favored projectile of the era's NBA fans. St. Louis fans held contests during which people in different parts of the arena took turns trying to hit him with eggs. During the 1957 championship series against the St. Louis Hawks, one egg struck Auerbach squarely in the head and splattered on Tommy Heinsohn, who said, "Red, I'm not standing near you anymore." But Auerbach thrived on such confrontation. The boos of the opposing fans were a bracing stimulant. Appreciation discombobulated him. Appearing on *The Regis Philbin Show,* he appeared taken aback when the studio audience started clapping. "How come the people applauded?" he asked. "It makes me feel uneasy."

As time passed, Auerbach came to take such pleasure in defying conventions, thwarting rules, and generally sticking it to whoever crossed him that doing so became second nature. And on the day of the all-star lunch, he was feeling particularly irritated. He disliked playing in the Lakers' fancy new arena, which he considered antiseptic and cold. One of the Lakers fans, a season-ticket holder, had a seat right behind the visitors' bench and always brought a bullhorn, which he used to rail at Auerbach. *Hiya, Red, you're nothing but a bum!* The fan was entitled to express his views, but Auerbach felt that using a bullhorn was going too far. When he complained to the general manager, however, nothing was done, and that had made him annoyed with the entire club.

On this day, Auerbach was also furious with the Lakers coach, Fred Schaus, and with the local reporters, who in Auerbach's view carried Schaus's water for him. Auerbach had an abiding dislike for the Los Angeles sportswriters, particularly Sid Ziff of the *Los Angeles Times* and Ziff's fellow torpedo man, Jim Murray. Both *Times*men had argued that Auerbach was overrated and that it was Bill Russell who deserved all the credit for the Celtics' success. They had also attacked him as unsportsmanlike. "He could sit there like a mummy and his team would do just as well," Ziff once declared. Murray on one occasion compared him to "a bleeding shark," and on another he had said, "A top sergeant with corns has a better outlook on life." Now, on the very day of the all-star luncheon, a column appeared that Ziff had written calling Auerbach "a ham actor" and suggesting he was a coward. "He'll deliberately try to bait the crowd," Ziff said in that morning's paper. "Then he'll scream for police protection when the fans start throwing things at him." Ziff also quoted Fred Schaus complaining at length about Auerbach's courtside behavior and saying, "I don't think he'll ever win a sportsmanship award but he's won a lot of championships."

While Auerbach was all too happy to criticize officials in the press, he tried to avoid attacking his fellow coaches, and he felt none of them had ever taken as cheap and low a shot as Schaus had just done in the *Los Angeles Times*. It stung, too. After all, Auerbach felt that his approach to his job was no different from that of any coach or athlete in any sport where winners were paid more than losers. They all played every angle they could find and bent or interpreted the rules to their advantage. And so, as he approached the podium during the all-star lunch, Auerbach was angry at the city of Los Angeles, at its fans and its sportswriters and at the management and, most especially, at the coach of its NBA franchise, and he had made up his mind to share his feelings.

"I suppose you people expect me to make some more nice chitchat like Schaus," he told the crowd. Auerbach had decided he was not going to single out Schaus for attack, but he did express his scorn for everyone associated with the Lakers, and he ridiculed the team's record. "You're a bunch of bushers," he said. "That goes for the club, the fans, and all the writers." He held up his copy of the program, with its cover line "Basketball Capital of the World." "I come here today, and I see this—it's ridiculous!" he shouted. "What do you people think this is? Win a couple of championships first, then talk about being the basketball capital of the world. Right now, the basketball capital is Boston. And it's gonna stay in Boston for a long time!"

THE WESTERN DIVISION had won the all-star game the two previous years and—with a lineup that now featured Wilt Chamberlain, Elgin Baylor, and Jerry West—it was favored to win again. But Auerbach had certainly succeeded in baiting Fred Schaus that afternoon at the lunch, and that may have contributed to the fact that Schaus's West Coast all-stars lost to Auerbach's East Coast team. With Russell controlling the rebounds, the East took the lead in the first quarter and never relinquished it. Russell was helped considerably by Bob Cousy. While Cousy scored only eight points, he and his backcourt partner, Oscar Robertson, had set the pace of the game from the outset. "Cousy and Big O passed the West dizzy," was how one sportswriter put it.

Cousy was thirty-four by then and had played professional basketball for thirteen years. He felt that physically he was capable of a couple more years in the NBA. His legs were holding out. But the game was no longer the joy it had once been. The travel, particularly because the schedule now included regular flights all the way out to California, was exhausting. It was hard to work up the motivation needed to play eighty games at the level the sport required. And for more than a year now, he'd felt that the pressure of competition had worn him down.

The Cooz, as he was known, loved pressure, he had always felt he needed it, that without it he became edgy and irritable and distracted. Before games he would sit by himself in his hotel room visualizing his opponent as a hated antagonist who had to be treated with no mercy. He played at such a level of intensity that in contrast to many players, who found themselves keyed up after games, he was so drained he had to fight to avoid passing out altogether. But the pressure he had thrived on had exacted a price. He suffered from nightmares and sleepwalking and had a tic in his right eye and a constantly twitching nerve under his left arm. William Flynn, the director of athletics at Boston College, had offered him the job of basketball coach, and he had decided to take it.

Cousy, who was also known as "Mr. Basketball," was the most popular Celtic among Boston fans and one of the most popular players in the league. He had published his autobiography, *Basketball Is My Life,* at the age of twenty-nine, and it had gone through three printings. He was the personification of the underdog, the one player every tough little Boston Southie wanted to become, the small white fellow with the dazzling moves who could run rings around all the bigger lumbering players. Arenas around the league held Bob Cousy days to honor him, and on March 17, 1963—St. Patrick's Day—a capacity crowd filled the Boston Garden for a formal farewell ceremony.

Cliff Sundberg, writing the next day in the *Herald,* said, "Not since that memorable day when Babe Ruth limped to the microphone in Yankee Stadium on Lou Gehrig Day to say his farewell have we been so emotionally spent." President John Kennedy sent a telegram praising Cousy's "rare skill and competitive daring." Walter Brown paid tribute to Cousy's loyalty and character. "I'm the guy who didn't want Bob Cousy in the first place," he told the crowd. "What a genius!" Auerbach declared Cousy was the quintessence of the sport. When Cousy himself walked up to the microphone, the applause was thunderous, and when it subsided he tried to talk but became so choked up he could say nothing. The cheering continued and now Cousy's eyes welled up, and his twelve-year-old daughter, Marie Colette, crossed the floor to pass him a handkerchief. As Cousy dabbed at his eyes, the noise abated. For a moment, the huge, damp, echoing, malodorous arena was silent, and then a single voice, high up in the balcony, rang out:

"We love ya, Cooz!"

It was Joseph Dillon, a thirty-two-year-old city worker, and that did it. Everyone in the Garden surged to their feet, roaring and stamping, the applause ferocious, and Cousy was now so overwhelmed he started sobbing outright, and the players and the people in the stands were sobbing as well, a flood of unabashed Irish sentimentality for the little guy, for one of their own, for the way things used to be, for the farewell we must one day always bid our heroes.

"We love ya, Cooz!"

"We love ya!"

BUT COUSY was playing out the season, which the Celtics finished in first place in the Eastern Division. They felt indomitable. Although Chamberlain led the league in scoring and rebounding, the Warriors had finished the season in second-to-last place in the West. In the playoffs, the Celtics faced the Cincinnati Royals, who, with Oscar Robertson, proved tougher than expected, and overconfidence almost undid Boston. "The long reign of the Boston Celtics as NBA champions may be ending," ran the AP lead after Cincinnati took a 2–1 lead in the series. But while the series came down to seven games, in the end the Royals could not prevail, and once again the championship would be decided between the Celtics and the Lakers.

To the Celtics, the Lakers seemed like a relatively easy conquest in comparison to the Royals. They had a weaker team than the year before because Jerry West had pulled a hamstring while diving for the ball and had missed twenty-four games, almost the final third of the season. By the time the finals began, he had recovered enough to play, but he was not in peak form, and the Lakers lost the first two games. They took game three but not game four, and with a 3–1 lead, victory seemed certain for the Celtics. But the Lakers rallied once more, beating Boston by seven points at the Garden, and Cousy, who had fouled out for the second time in the series, blamed himself for the loss.

Game six was in Los Angeles. The Celtics now flew in a chartered plane on shorter trips, but for longer journeys they still traveled commercially and—

since Walter Brown considered first-class a luxury—squeezed into coach-class seats for the trip to the West Coast. When in Los Angeles, the team usu-ally stayed at the Sheraton West, but the hotel had been taken over by the Milwaukee Braves, who were scheduled to play the Dodgers, and the Celtics were forced to put up at the Olympian Motel. Cousy used to room with Bill Sharman, but he liked isolation in the hours before a game, and so once Shar-man retired he started taking a room of his own. The night before the game, he ran a hot bath and lay in the water visualizing the moves of Frank Selvy and Dick Barnett, the two Lakers he would most likely be guarding. The ef-fort worked him into a hostile lather against the men, but while this state of mind would help motivate him in the game tomorrow, it did not exactly in-duce sleep, and when he turned off the lights he lay in bed feeling the metro-nomic pulsing twitch of his eye tic.

The next morning, some of the Boston sportswriters were playing hearts out by the motel pool, but Cousy stayed in his room. The game, if the Celtics won it, would be the last of his professional career, and all he could think of was Frank Selvy. Selvy's job was to bring the ball up the court and pass off to Baylor and West, but he had a jumper he could hit 90 percent of the time if Cousy gave him enough room. And if Selvy got the ball to Baylor often enough, Baylor could score sixty or more points. Any number of things could go wrong if Cousy didn't keep the pressure on Selvy, which meant running. He did not want to repeat the disastrous experience of the previous game, when he'd lost his focus and concentration, and by the time the Celtics were scheduled to leave for the arena, he was churning with agitation and anxiety.

At the arena, Cousy headed for the back of the dressing room. In Los An-geles, celebrities liked to drop by the dressing room, and Auerbach took them around and introduced them to the players—a ritual Cousy disliked, since all he wanted to do was focus on the game. One of the celebrities who came by that night was Johnny Mathis, who had gone to high school with Bill Russell in Oakland, and the two men sat around joking about the old days. Frank Ramsey was also sitting in the back, brooding. The locker boy brought Ramsey a hot towel, and he wrapped it around his knee. Ramsey—too short to play in the frontcourt on most teams and too slow to be a guard—was one of the talented but limited players who had flourished on the team Auerbach had designed. For eight years as the sixth man, he had been as es-sential to the Celtics as any starter, but he had hurt his knee so seriously the previous season that he'd had to wear an elastic brace around his entire leg, from the ankle to the hip, which chafed his skin raw. Limping when he ran, he was virtually useless to the team during last year's playoffs, and had wanted to retire. Auerbach had talked him into returning, but his leg still bothered him, and Ramsey, who had once been one of the most gregarious and fun-loving people in the dressing room, had turned dark and withdrawn.

Cousy changed into his uniform, which took all of five minutes, then Tommy Heinsohn joined him and Ramsey in the back. Cousy was as close to Heinsohn as he was to anyone on the team. The two lived near each other in Worcester and carpooled in to the Garden and out to the airport. While Cousy liked Heinsohn, he felt that Heinsohn's undeniable talent was undercut by a lack of personal discipline. For example, Heinsohn smoked two packs of cigarettes a day for years, and it hurt his wind. Cousy had always been after Heinsohn to quit, and finally, toward the end of this season, he had, and was now playing better than he'd ever played. Cousy told Heinsohn and Ramsey they needed to win tonight and put away the series. Heinsohn said they couldn't allow the series to go to a seventh game. Ramsey agreed. Anything could happen in a seventh game.

Then Cousy went to the toilet to urinate. It was a trip he made with increasing frequency before a big game, as all the world now knew, because he'd been on the Mike Wallace show a while back and when Wallace asked him how he coped with the pressure of the playoffs, he'd said without thinking, "Well, I go to the toilet much more often." Finally, twenty minutes before the Celtics were to take the floor, the celebrities cleared out, Russell hurried into the bathroom to throw up, and Auerbach summoned his players, who pulled up chairs and sat in a semicircle around him. "Has everyone gone to the head?" Auerbach asked. "Has everyone been taped? Has everyone taken care of all their problems so we can get this meeting started?"

The players would have considered a pep talk an unprofessional embarrassment—except maybe at halftime when they were behind in a close game—and Auerbach focused instead on each player's assignment. Heinsohn needed to box out Rudy LaRusso. Russell needed to double-team Baylor when he was bulling in on Satch Sanders. Everyone needed to pressure Gene Wiley and LeRoy Ellis, the Lakers' two rookie centers. Cousy, as team captain, then spoke up. The key to winning, he said, was to run and to keep running, to avoid at all costs sitting on any lead they did acquire. And then it was time to take the floor. "Okay," Auerbach said. "This is for all the marbles."

. . .

A record of 15,521 fans turned out for the game. The Sports Arena had the greatest number of seats—and the most expensive tickets—in the league, but it couldn't fit everyone, and another 6,000 had to be turned away. The Los Angeles fans were more sedate and prosperous than the typical East Coast fan, and most of the men sitting quietly in the cushioned seats wore jackets and ties. "You don't have fans here, you've got spectators," Nats coach Alex Hannum once told Fred Schaus. Doris Day was there, directly across from the Celtics bench, drinking soda and eating popcorn. Pat Boone was there as well, wearing a yellow shirt and red pants and looking virtuous and mild.

Despite the fear that had gripped him back in the motel, once the game started, Cousy felt himself shooting with a nice loose wrist, shooting so smoothly he scarcely felt the ball leave his hands, as if instead of popping out of his grip it simply evaporated. Cousy was the playmaker—he brought the ball down, called the play, and then set it in motion, if all went well, with some moves that threw the defense out of position. As a rule Cousy himself shot only to get the respect of the man guarding him, to keep him honest, but now he was feeling so good about his shooting that he was banging away at the rim like a gunner, and he had to tell himself to calm down, to stay focused on his assignment.

The Lakers could not contain Boston, and trailed at the half by fourteen points. In the locker room during the break, the statistician brought in the sheet with the Celtics' first-half stats, which Auerbach always checked in order to see who was in foul trouble. The sheet showed that the Celtics had shot 55 percent in the first half. It was a startling figure. The players sensed victory, and Cousy had to keep reminding them that they couldn't afford to sit on the lead, that they had to keep running. The Lakers, by contrast, wanted to slow the pace, and in the second half they finally succeeded in doing so, shutting down the Celtics' fast break by rebounding aggressively against Bill Russell, who was so fatigued from the endless playoff games that his legs had gone numb. The game slowed so much that Cousy even found himself walking up the court at one point, and all the while the Lakers chipped away at Boston's lead. In a time-out Cousy lashed out at his team-mates. *We've got to run. Nobody's moving out there. Nobody!*

Just after the start of the fourth quarter, with West bringing the ball up the court, Cousy backed up to cover Dick Barnett. When Barnett cut, Cousy tried to cut with him, but his ankle gave way, and he collapsed on the floor in agony. Jim Loscutoff and Buddy LeRoux, the Celtics trainer, helped him limp to the bench, where Dr. Ernie Vanderweghe examined him and decided that even though the ankle now felt numb, he had a bad sprain. Vanderweghe told Cousy that while he had not broken anything, he was out for the night.

Cousy's injury seemed to give the Lakers the break they needed, because once he went out they began playing with a new lift. As soon as he sat down, the Lakers scored two consecutive baskets, reducing Boston's lead to seven. Three more minutes passed, and the Celtics' lead shrank to one point. Cousy asked LeRoux if it would be possible to freeze his ankle. The trainer warned Cousy that he could hurt himself, but Cousy insisted. He was afraid that if he did not go in and the Celtics lost, his ankle would become so tender by the following day that he might not be able to play at all if the series had to go to a seventh game, and that could make the difference between winning and losing.

Finally, LeRoux sprayed Cousy's ankle with a numbing spray and bound it as tightly as he could. Cousy tested the ankle and decided it could accept his weight. With four minutes left on the clock, Cousy signaled to Auerbach that he wanted to go back in the game.

"How does it feel?" Auerbach asked.

"I think I can go," Cousy said.

Cousy's return immediately restored the confidence and rhythm of the Celtics. Satch Sanders, who rarely shot, threw the ball up just to unload it when Baylor started pressing him, and it went in. But Baylor and Barnett were shooting well, too, and with thirty seconds left, the Lakers were behind by just one point. Then a pair of foul shots by Heinsohn, a jump ball that went Boston's way, and two more foul shots by Heinsohn put the Celtics solidly ahead, and although Baylor managed one last dunk, everyone knew the game was over.

Cousy got the inbounds pass as the final seconds ran out, and he finished his career not just as a champion but as the man in possession of the ball. He had been limping when he first returned to the game, but now he had forgotten about his ankle altogether. He took a few long strides to build momentum, then hurled the ball high into the rafters. The fans looked upward to follow its arc, but Cousy turned and, without watching to see where it would land, trotted off the court for the last time.

The next day, both the Boston press and national sportswriters abandoned irony and their fixation with process and instead wrote about Cousy's last game the way Grantland Rice, the sports poet of the thirties, might have done, as if composing odes to a storied warrior retiring in all his glory from the battlefield. "With a farewell performance of supreme virtuosity, Cooz, the Magnificent, had led his Boston Celtics to the fifth straight championship," the normally reserved Arthur Daley wrote in *The New York Times*. "Thus did the Celtic captain complete his playing days on the triumphant note he deserved, still a champion among champions."

AT THE END of the Warriors' first year in San Francisco, the team not only finished in second-to-last place, it had lost $1 million, and the investors who had acquired it were frustrated and disappointed. Eddie Gottlieb, who agreed to stay on for an additional season as general manager because the team was doing so badly, accepted the fact that Bob Feerick lacked the temperament to coach professional athletes and began looking for a replacement. At the top of his list was Alex Hannum. That year, the Syracuse Nationals had moved to Philadelphia and become the 76ers, but Hannum, their coach, decided not to accompany the team. He and his wife were both from the West and they missed it, and so he chose to return to his hometown, Los Angeles, to become a building contractor.

Hannum was unquestionably one of the best coaches in the NBA. Under his guidance the Nats had regularly made it into the playoffs. He had enjoyed the distinction of coaching the St. Louis Hawks when they came within two points of beating the Celtics in the 1957 finals and then when they did beat them in 1958. Gottlieb had known Hannum for years, and respected him as both athlete and coach. In the summer of 1963, Gottlieb flew down to Los Angeles and asked Hannum to take over Feerick's job. The offer intrigued Hannum. He had of course heard all the stories about how impossible Chamberlain was to coach, but he thought that the critics overlooked a single significant fact: all of Chamberlain's coaches had lacked professional experience. Dick Harp at Kansas had been an assistant coach when he took over the Jayhawks in Chamberlain's sophomore year. Neil Johnston, Chamberlain's first coach on the Warriors, was a former player who had never coached before. Bob Feerick came from a college, and so had Frank McGuire, the one coach who'd had any success with him.

Chamberlain, Hannum thought, had never worked with a seasoned NBA coach, one who had handled professional players for years and who knew how to motivate them, how to earn their respect, and how to respect them for the grown men they were. Much less had Chamberlain ever worked with a coach who had taken a team not just to the playoffs but to a championship. There were only two such men around in the league—Auerbach and Hannum himself. So Hannum thought he was the right man for the job, but he had followed the travails of the Warriors in San Francisco and had become convinced that Chamberlain was out of control, playing for his own statistical glory rather than for the good of the team, as if he were being paid by the point. If the Warriors were going to make it to the playoffs, Chamberlain would need to change his game, to share some of the scoring and the playing time, and Hannum was not sure if that was possible.

"Does Chamberlain demand to play the full forty-eight minutes of every game?" he asked Gottlieb.

"Absolutely not," Gottlieb replied.

"Is Chamberlain going after points to insure his high salary?"

"Absolutely not." Gottlieb explained that while Chamberlain was entitled to a bonus, it was based on the performance of the team, not on his own statistics.

"Okay, you've got yourself a coach," Hannum said.

• • •

Alex Hannum had been a big, tough basketball player, and he remained intense, enthusiastic, loud, and aggressive, a beer-drinking brawler who could be so stubborn that he was known as Old Iron Head. He was tall, at six-seven, and big, at 230 pounds, barrel-chested, muscular, with piercing blue eyes and a strong jaw. He kept his receding hair in a sharp crew cut that made him look like a drill sergeant, and in fact he was also sometimes called "the Sarge" in honor of his wartime service in the army. Hannum was the first to admit he had never been anything more than a journeyman player. He'd averaged six points per game, shooting one for three from the field, and had rarely started. Still, he loved it like nothing else, both the sport itself and the league camaraderie. There were only eight teams back in the days when he was playing, which meant that if there was a doubleheader at Madison Square Garden, half the NBA was in town, and after the games they'd all go out beer drinking, like a company of soldiers on the town with Saturday-night passes, prowling for action, ready to mix it up with anyone who crossed their path.

Hannum had started playing professional ball in 1948, first for the Oshkosh All-Stars of the National League, then for Anderson, Syracuse, Baltimore, Rochester, Milwaukee, Fort Wayne, and St. Louis. In 1954, after Les Harrison had dropped him from the Rochester Royals, he'd been called by Ben Kerner, who'd acquired the rights to him for $500 and who wanted him to play for the Milwaukee Hawks, as his team was at the time designated. Since the season was by then almost halfway over, Kerner said all he could offer Hannum was a day rate of forty dollars. When Hannum reached the team, the man he was replacing handed him a bag containing his uniform. Hannum asked if it was clean. No, the man said, and told Hannum he would have to clean it himself. At the end of the season, Kerner dropped Hannum, and Fred Zollner of the Fort Wayne Pistons picked him up but then put him on waivers. Kerner, who had in the meantime moved the Hawks to St. Louis, picked him up again, this time for nothing.

Kerner was known for getting rid of coaches on practically an annual basis, and midway through that season, he fired Red Holzman and made Slater Martin, Hannum's roommate, the player-coach. But Martin was more interested in playing than coaching, and since Hannum spent most of his time on the bench, he had Hannum making substitutions and calling time-outs, and once, on a trip out of town when Kerner was not around, Martin turned everything over to Hannum. "What the hell," Martin said. "We're on the road. Who'll know who's coaching?" Pretty soon, Hannum had taken over the job full-time, and discovered he was a natural at it. He knew the levels of the game, had a sense for what a given critical moment required, and understood how to motivate and direct players. He had a young, talented team, and they'd managed to get themselves into the playoffs and then to the 1957 finals where, despite the fact that they were the underdogs, they had taken the Celtics to seven games—the last being the one in which, with two seconds left, Hannum threw the ball the length of the court and off the far backboard to Bob Pettit. The following year, when Russell was sidelined with an injury, the Hawks had actually beaten the Celtics. Even with Chamberlain in the league, no one else had done so since.

When Hannum arrived for training camp in Santa Cruz, California, he held a scrimmage between the veterans and the rookies trying out for the team. Chamberlain had not yet arrived, and to Hannum's astonishment, the rookies—raw college kids, most of whom wouldn't even make the cut—beat the veterans. The Warriors, he thought, had become so completely dependent on Chamberlain it was as if they had forgotten how to play the game. Chamberlain reached the camp two days late. He was a good forty pounds over his playing weight, and in a bad frame of mind. He had not been pleased to hear that Hannum would be his new coach. When Hannum coached the Nationals, he was always baiting Chamberlain from the sidelines, and he had urged Dolph Schayes, his top player, to harass Chamberlain on the court. Chamberlain knew that Hannum and Schayes had simply been trying to rattle him, to undermine his game, but even so the taunting seemed to him to involve a meanness of spirit that was demoralizing and unsportsmanlike. Also, Chamberlain did not like what he'd heard about Hannum's plans to change his style of play and get him to score less. During his best season with the Warriors, when Frank McGuire had coached the team, they had won 80 percent of the games in which he scored at least fifty points. If he scored less, it seemed clear to Chamberlain, they were less likely to win.

Hannum knew he and Schayes had made Chamberlain's life miserable on some nights. But as far as he was concerned, that was Chamberlain's fault. Despite his size—"You don't raise your eyes to him," one sportswriter noted that year, "you tilt back your head."—Chamberlain allowed opponents to push him around. Hannum felt Wilt needed to become more aggressive. He was also determined that Chamberlain play a complete game. In the previous year, without the influence of Frank McGuire, Chamberlain had reverted to his old habit of favoring his fadeaway jump shot. Hannum wanted him to move into the basket, where he could shoot or feed off and be in position for the rebound. There was no point, it seemed to him, in having a seven-foot athlete on the team if the man wasn't going to rebound.

But Chamberlain made it clear that he did not like to be told what to do. He complained to reporters about Hannum's strategy, and Hannum insisted to the same men that Chamberlain was going to have to change. The tension built until one night in Vancouver, British Columbia, shortly before the opening game of the regular season, Hannum and Chamberlain got into a violent locker-room argument and avoided coming to blows only when the other players intervened. Hannum, deciding a showdown was necessary, ordered the other players out, then took off his jacket.

"You've been fighting me as a coach all the way," Hannum said. "Now fight me as a man."

Chamberlain glared at Hannum for a long moment and then folded, saying, "Aw, I can't fight you, Alex."

Hannum felt that his approach was vindicated when, in the opening game of the season, against Baltimore, the Warriors won easily although Wilt scored only twenty-three points. In the second game, against St. Louis, the Warriors won again with Wilt scoring only twenty-two. As the team continued to win, sportswriters began talking about the "new Chamberlain" and the "new Warriors." One article was headlined, "The Fight to Remodel Wilt Chamberlain."

This emphasis irritated Chamberlain, suggesting as it did that he had previously been an immature and selfish player who was responsible for the failures of his teams. Despite grudgingly yielding to Hannum's authority, he still resented the coach, and complained about him to Guy Rogers, one of his closest friends on the team. But Rogers thought Hannum's strategy was obviously paying off. Rogers wanted to see the Warriors win, and it vexed him that Chamberlain seemed willing to put his own pride ahead of the best interests of the team. "You've got to bow down, Wilt," Rogers told Chamberlain. "Admit it, cat, that we're a much better club with you feeding us part of the time and then getting back to protect our basket."

BY THE FALL of 1963, Bill Russell was no longer the stiff, awkward, over-grown postadolescent he'd been when he first joined the Celtics. The six championships, the years of playing night after night to crowds of thousands of people who either cheered him or booed him, the national television exposure, the second-guessing and criticism from sportswriters, who also sought out his opinions on everything from politics to music—all of it had given him an imposing, even lordly presence. Russell was of course aware of his presence, and in fact took a great deal of satisfaction in it, doing whatever he could to heighten its effect. He had grown back his goatee, which he'd agreed to cut after his first championship season, and he wore tailored three-piece suits, white shirts with cuff links, and narrow black ties.

Russell had what Tom Heinsohn once called "a neurotic need to win," but that was not to be confused with any need for anyone's approval. In the locker room, with his teammates, Russell talked and joked and laughed his shrill, cackling laugh, but on the court and out in public he was cold and self-contained. People who pestered him or asked foolish or obvious questions were treated to the Russell Glower—an icily contemptuous stare accompanied by a long silence. He refused to sign autographs and usually ignored the people, whether kids or old ladies, who asked for them. Tim Horgan of the *Herald* considered Russell the most selfish, surly, and uncooperative athlete he'd ever met. Russell did have his admirers, but one of the central ironies of his career is that while he was the key to the Celtics dynasty, he was also one of the reasons the team was not, during those years, a bigger draw in Boston.

At this point in his life, Russell had become determined to seize every opportunity he could find to protest racial inequity. The previous spring, the Celtics had gone to Lexington, Kentucky, to play an exhibition game with the Hawks. It was a symbolically important game because it would be the first time the stands at the University of Kentucky were to be integrated. Until then, black fans could sit only in the less desirable upper tiers. Before the game, however, Satch Sanders and Sam Jones were refused service by the manager at the hotel lunch counter, who told them they could eat there with the rest of the team but not by themselves. Sanders and Jones decided to boycott the game, and as soon as Russell heard about the incident, he told Auerbach he was leaving. The black players on the Hawks also decided to boycott the match, and as a result the first game played before an integrated audience at the University of Kentucky was played by two all-white teams.

That same year, the town of Reading finally felt good enough about its celebrated local hero to hold a testimonial benefit in his honor. Russell, who welcomed the acknowledgment after years in which he felt he'd been slighted by neighbors and harassed by the cops, took the microphone at the testimonial and joked, "I thought the only people who knew me in this town were the police." A month later, however, word got out in Reading that Russell was planning to move to a more affluent neighborhood, and the people who lived there circulated a petition to dissuade the seller from proceeding. When that failed, a group of the neighbors joined forces and tried to buy the house to prevent Russell from buying it. It infuriated Russell that while his neighbors were happy to celebrate him as a great athlete, they still refused to accept him as a human equal. And then, in the summer, Russell took his children down to visit his grandfather in Louisiana. He was the winner of five world championships, but although he was driving a nice car and had plenty of cash, from Virginia to Louisiana he could not find a place where he and his children could eat and sleep. And the worst part was that he had no idea how to explain it to them.

Like other black Americans of the time, Russell thought he might feel more at home in Africa. After touring Liberia twice during the off-season, he and a friend, Clarence Holder, together paid a reported $100,000 for 200,000 acres of land on which they built a rubber plantation that eventually employed more than one hundred laborers at a rate of fifty cents a day. Since it took rubber trees ten years to mature, their intent was to plant a new crop every year for the next ten years, at which point the plantation would be self-sustaining, able to produce an annual harvest of rubber. Holder actually went so far as to become a Liberian citizen, and Russell began thinking that when he retired, he might move there himself.

By the summer of 1963, the civil rights movement and the segregationist backlash had reached a crisis in the South. That spring, police had set dogs on black demonstrators in Birmingham, Alabama, and Greenwood, Mississippi. Martin Luther King, Jr., had been jailed in Birmingham and had written his famous "Letter from Birmingham Jail," repudiating white ministers who were urging patience and caution on civil rights leaders. The black demonstrators, while not sufficiently patient for the white clerics, had nonetheless been following King's creed of nonviolence, and Bill Russell had been tempted to join them, except he was certain that if a white man spit on him, he was not going to remain nonviolent.

In June, Alabama governor George Wallace promised to prevent integration "by standing in the schoolhouse door," and President John Kennedy gave a televised address announcing plans for federal civil rights legislation. On the very night of Kennedy's speech, NAACP field director Medgar Evers was shot and killed while walking from his car to his house in Jackson, Mississippi. After Evers's murder, Jackson was, as its mayor, Allen Thompson, told President Kennedy, an "explosive situation," and to help defuse matters, Evers's brother, Charlie, called Bill Russell and invited him to come to the city and hold basketball clinics. Two days later, Russell flew to Jackson, where armed white men were openly displaying their weapons to activists and outsiders—including Russell himself—and for the next three days conducted the first interracial basketball clinics ever held in the Jackson Auditorium. Russell also attended the historic march on Washington that August and was present when King gave his "I have a dream" speech, a moment of apparent racial promise that was violently undercut less than three weeks later with the bombing of the Sixteenth Street Baptist Church in Birmingham, Alabama, which killed four young black girls.

Russell's experiences that summer, and the country's overall racial tumult, had made him increasingly angry and radical. More than ever, basketball seemed a trivial occupation unworthy of a black American male at a time of such crisis, when black men, women, and even children were being taunted, arrested, beaten, and killed simply because they were black. "I consider playing professional basketball as marking time, the most shallow thing in the world," he told Gilbert Rogin of *Sports Illustrated* that fall. He was more interested in discussing the country's racism. "The Muslims say . . . the white man is evil. I wonder about that in the sense that I wonder whether all men are evil. I dislike most white people because they are people. As opposed to dislike, I like most black people because I am black."

Frank Ramsey, a Kentuckian and the white player with whom Russell was perhaps the closest, read the article shortly after it appeared, and was sitting in the locker room when Russell walked in. "Hey Russell, I'm white," Ramsey said. "You hate me?"

The two men looked at each other for a moment. "I was misquoted, Frank," Russell said.

Ramsey let the matter go. But no one actually believed that Russell had been misquoted. If there were any doubts, Russell made similar points in a second interview that fall, with Ed Linn of *The Saturday Evening Post,* who described him sitting at home in Reading with his three young children and wife, Rose, while she discussed her work for the Boston chapter of the NAACP and her near arrest during a sit-in over de facto segregation in the city's schools. She said a local politician had told her that he liked black musicians because "all darkies have rhythm." "Isn't that sweet," Russell interjected with a sarcastic laugh. "Those darkies, they sure do cheer things up nights around the plantation."

Russell also gave vent to his bitterness about racism in the NBA and his disdain for Celtics fans. "I'm of the opinion that most of the teams in this league have a quota," he told Linn. "In order for any sport to be really successful, two or three of the top guys have to be white. Most sports, even these days, are looking for the White Hope. . . . The first thing we [as Negroes in sport] have to get rid of is the idea that this is a popularity contest. I don't work for acceptance. It doesn't make any difference to me whether the fans like me or not. . . . What I'm resentful of, you know, is when they say you owe the public this and you owe the public that. You owe the public the same thing it owes you. Nothing! . . . I refuse to smile and be nice to the kiddies."

No prominent black athlete had made such controversial, provocative, and blatantly hostile statements in public before, neither Jackie Robinson, nor Willie Mays, nor Jim Brown, nor Muhammad Ali, who in the fall of 1963 still called himself Cassius Clay and was known more for his egotistical boasting; he had recently released a record of his poems and monologues, which included the line "I'm so great, I impress even myself." Since Russell's middle name was Felton, some sportswriters began referring to him as Felton X. The Russell family received so many threatening letters at their Reading home that Russell notified the FBI, and years later, when he requested his FBI file after Congress passed the Freedom of Information Act, he found that he was described as "an arrogant Negro who won't sign autographs for white children."

When the Russells returned from a three-day road trip, they found that their house had been vandalized. The furniture had been overturned and destroyed, and the felt on the pool table ripped up. Russell's trophy case had been broken into, and the trophies themselves beaten and disfigured. The walls were spray-painted with the word NIGGA. Russell was enraged, his wife shocked, his children terrified. He called the police, who came and catalogued the destruction, and then when they left and the Russells had restored some order to the house and were preparing to go to sleep, Russell and his wife pulled back the sheets of their bed to discover that the intruders had defecated in it.

ON JANUARY 13, 1964, the biggest storm of the winter swept across the Northeast, dumping twelve inches of snow from New York to Boston. Gale-force winds of fifty miles an hour created drifts five feet deep. The NBA all-star game was to be held in Boston on January 14, with most of the players planning to arrive the day before for a pregame party thrown by Walter Brown at the Sheraton Plaza. But flights into New England from all over the country were canceled, and twenty-six of the players scheduled for the game, including Elgin Baylor, Jerry West, Oscar Robertson, and Wilt Chamberlain, were stranded elsewhere. The weather cleared by the following morning, and throughout the day players and owners straggled into the city.

The all-star game was one of the regular occasions when all the owners gathered together, and they were eager to meet at the luncheon arranged the afternoon before the game. The league was changing rapidly. Teams had relocated, the Syracuse Nationals moving to Philadelphia and becoming the 76ers and the Chicago Zephyrs relocating to Baltimore and becoming the Bullets. Franchises that were worth less than a hundred thousand dollars a few years ago were now selling for upwards of a million, and the owners were no longer regarded as bush-league hustlers but as successful executives in the increasingly lucrative business of sport.

While the owners were meeting, Tommy Heinsohn, who had become the head of the NBA Players Association, was trying to get the all-stars together to discuss a possible boycott of the game that night. The association had been started back in 1953 by Bob Cousy in an effort to limit excessive fines, reduce the number of exhibition games, and ease the demanding schedule that often had a team traveling to one city and playing a game and then traveling to a second city all in the same day. Cousy had polled the other teams back in the early fifties and all were in favor of a union except for the Fort Wayne Pistons, who were afraid that their owner, Fred Zollner, an archetypal industrialist with a virulent hatred of organized labor, might actually fold his team if it tried to unionize. At the 1955 all-star game in New York, Cousy had tried to persuade Zollner that a union would be good for the entire league, but the owner refused to consider it. "I've never had a union in my shops and I won't have a union in my ball club," he told Cousy.

Eventually, Cousy was able to form an association in which the Pistons declined to participate. For years, the NBA's board of governors ignored it, trying to accommodate the players' grievances without acknowledging the association, but finally, in 1957, the board agreed to meet with it once a year and to make a handful of minor concessions, such as guaranteeing players seven dollars a day in expense money while on the road. The players themselves were only slightly more enthusiastic about the association. Cousy had written every player in the league to ask for dues, but two-thirds of them simply ignored the letters. Cousy became frustrated, and in 1958 he asked Heinsohn, who had a degree in economics, to take over as president. Heinsohn had a reputation as a clowning prankster—Leigh Montville of *The Boston Globe* once described him as "the kid forever in the back of the room, making funny noises while the teacher is declining Latin words on the blackboard"—but he took his new responsibilities seriously, holding organizational meetings with all of the teams when they came to Boston and venturing into their dressing rooms before games to demand twenty-five dollars from players who'd avoided paying their dues.

The association remained weak compared with the baseball players' union, but Heinsohn had managed to extract a few more concessions from the owners, such as a minimum salary for rookies of $7,500 and agreements on playoff schedules. On other matters he was less successful. The players had asked the NBA to require all teams to have full-time, traveling trainers, primarily to treat injuries, but the owners had refused, arguing that teams could not afford the additional $30,000, including transportation, it would add to team budgets. They wanted to continue to hire trainers part-time, on a game-by-game basis, to come in and tape up the players of both teams, then sit on the sidelines in case of injuries.

For years, Heinsohn had also been pressing the owners about a pension plan for the players. The association wanted the owners to contribute $500 a year for each player, which would be matched by $500 from the player himself. As they had done when Cousy tried to form the players' association, the owners simply stalled. Two months before the all-star game, when the board of governors gathered at the Hotel Roosevelt in New York, Heinsohn and some of the other representatives—including Oscar Robertson, Bob Pettit, and Jerry West—flew in at their own expense to discuss the pension issue with the board, but the owners refused to see them. "We sat cooling our heels in the lobby the whole afternoon," Heinsohn recalled.

At that point, Heinsohn told the other players it was time to give the owners an ultimatum. He suggested that if the owners had not agreed to a pension plan by the time of the all-star game, the players should refuse to play. Heinsohn knew Walter Brown would be upset by a boycott, and felt that out of loyalty he had to warn him of the possibility. A few weeks before the game he told the owner the players might not play. Brown did not understand why the players had become so confrontational. "I don't even have a pension," he told Heinsohn. "Why do you guys need one?"

When Walter Kennedy, who'd replaced Maurice Podoloff as commissioner, arrived in Boston for the all-star game, he learned about the possibility of a strike. He met with Heinsohn to explain that there had been a misunderstanding and that the owners would vote on the pension plan by the summer. Larry Fleisher, a young graduate of Harvard Law School working with the players, suspected that this was yet another stall tactic. He thought that with all the owners assembled in one place, the time to force them to act was now.

He persuaded Heinsohn that the players needed to be prepared to go on strike, that only by threatening the cancellation of a nationally televised game could they force the owners to address the issue. Heinsohn had scheduled a meeting of all the players at 3:00 p.m. to discuss their course of action, but because of the snowstorm some of them were still arriving. When each player reached the Garden, Heinsohn had him sign a statement declaring that none of the players would take the court and play the game until the owners officially agreed to move forward with the pension. If the whole thing backfired, Heinsohn didn't want the other players trying to put the blame for it all on him.

By five o'clock, Oscar Robertson, Bob Pettit, and Elgin Baylor had all finally arrived. The three were strong backers of the association. Robertson was particularly outspoken about how he was willing to lead a revolt by the players next season if the owners continued to be uncooperative. Shortly before six o'clock, Heinsohn, Fleisher, Pettit, Bill Russell, and Lenny Wilkins of the St. Louis Hawks went to see Walter Kennedy in his room at the Sheraton. Kennedy, getting ready for a dinner engagement, was wearing a dressing gown. Heinsohn told him that before the all-star game could take place, all the owners needed to meet with the twenty players who'd come to Boston and sign a paper promising to put into effect the pension plan. Kennedy agreed to call all the owners individually, and they unanimously refused to meet. They would not be ordered around by their employees, and when the players left the hotel, a walkout seemed imminent.

The idea of a strike instigated by his own player made Walter Brown wild with fury. He told Auerbach that he might call off the game himself, forfeiting the $30,000 he'd spent on promotion. He also said he might fire Heinsohn, Russell, and Sam Jones, the three Celtics who'd been named to the all-star team, and try to persuade the board of governors to banish the seventeen other players if they participated in a boycott. Auerbach had maintained a position of neutrality about the association, but he felt that Heinsohn was betraying Brown, who was one of the pension plan's biggest advocates, and he sought him out in the hallways of the Garden.

"You can't do this to your own boss," Auerbach said.

"I'm sorry, Red," Heinsohn said. "I'm the players' representative and I have no choice."

"Don't show me how much guts you got, you idiot," Auerbach told him. "I know how much guts you've got. Think about what you're doing to Walter."

Heinsohn refused to reconsider. Thirty minutes before the game, he invited the players on the Western Division team to join the Eastern players in the Celtics locker room. He told them that all together they were the best and most powerful players in the league. If they could not stand up now for the poorer, weaker players, they never would. The players took a vote. It was 11–9 against a boycott. They took a second vote and this time it was 11–9 in favor of one.* Heinsohn went out to deliver the verdict to Walter Brown.

The minutes continued to tick down as the players sat nervously in the locker room. Heinsohn had stationed a security guard outside the door with instructions to forbid anyone from entering without permission, and the guard now came in to say that Bob Short, the owner of the Lakers, was outside demanding that Jerry West and Elgin Baylor come out and talk to him. "You go tell Bob Short to fuck himself," Baylor said.

The guard returned to the corridor. A few moments later, the players heard a noise through the wall. Short had barged into the trainer's room next door, and he now began ranting about the betrayal by the players. All of the players, including Baylor and West, could hear him, and Short knew it. "If any of my players are in on this, they're through!" he shouted. "Finished for life!"

Baylor and West said nothing.

At that point, Walter Kennedy went down to the locker room to try to persuade the players to go ahead with the game. Kennedy's biggest concern was the detrimental effect a delayed game might have on the league's chances of landing a new television contract. In 1962, NBC had canceled its contract with the NBA after an eight-year run, its executives complaining that all the high-scoring games, and the interminable interruptions that occurred when coaches quarreled with officials, had driven away the audience. Since then, its games had been carried by a syndication service, and one of Kennedy's most important goals was to secure a new network contract. Kennedy was hoping to use the all-star game—with West, Baylor, and Chamberlain playing for the Western Division against Russell, Robertson, and Jerry Lucas on the East team—to showcase the league's stars and attract network interest. But if the NBA proved so unreliable that it could not even have a major event like the all-star game take place on schedule, executives from all the networks would be extremely leery of making any commitment to the league.

---

*Russell voted for the boycott. Chamberlain, who didn't think a showdown was necessary, voted against it.

Kennedy was accompanied by Haskell Cohen, the NBA's publicity director, who foresaw a public relations nightmare if the players refused to take the floor. "You can't do this," he kept saying. "You can't do this." Kennedy warned the players that if they refused to play the game, they would ruin pro basketball, in Boston and across the country. By now, fans had filled the Garden. It was well past the time the players should have taken the floor to warm up, but none of them appeared. Down in the locker room, Kennedy finally yielded, telling Heinsohn that if they all went out and played the game as scheduled, he would personally guarantee that the owners would produce an acceptable pension plan.

It was just fifteen minutes before tip-off time when Heinsohn asked Kennedy to leave so they could vote again. A number of the players, particularly Oscar Robertson, felt frustrated. If it had just been a question of disappointing the fans in the Garden, they would have voted to boycott the game despite Kennedy's promise, which seemed like just another stalling tactic, but because the game was to be televised nationally, they risked turning the nationwide audience against them if they called it off so abruptly, and they reluctantly decided to play. With five minutes remaining before tip-off time, Bob Pettit went out to tell Kennedy that the game was on, and twenty minutes later the players took the court.

Even though catastrophe had been averted, Walter Brown was still furious. He had always been loyal to his players, and he expected loyalty in return. But something seemed to be changing. The old ways, the old loyalties, the old relationships—the days when an owner could ask the players to take a pay cut if he'd had a bad year and would spontaneously give them a bonus if he'd had a good one—they were all disappearing, replaced by a new kind of self-centered assertiveness, an ingratitude and hostility that did not conform to Brown's idea of sportsmanlike conduct. Just a couple months earlier, Bill Russell had given that one interview saying he considered basketball the most shallow thing in the world and then that second interview declaring that he owed the public nothing. This gratuitous slap at the Celtics fans upset Brown, particularly because, Brown felt, Russell did owe the public something. After all, the fans paid his salary. And they did more than that. Brown himself had given Russell permission to make an appeal to fans at the Garden to contribute to a cancer fund Russell was endorsing, and the fans had responded. If nothing else, Russell owed them for that.

And now Heinsohn—one of Brown's own players—was the individual who had been responsible for leading this revolt and disrupting the start of the all-star game. Brown had always had a particularly warm relationship with Heinsohn, and he made it clear at every opportunity how much he valued him as a ballplayer. Just a month earlier, at a basketball luncheon, Brown had taken the microphone to single out Heinsohn for praise, saying, "Whenever we win a big game and the situation is properly analyzed, it turns out that Tom Heinsohn's play was a big factor." When Brown learned Heinsohn was working in insurance in the off-season, he had asked Heinsohn to help him with his estate planning, and as a result Heinsohn was privy to such intimate details as the number of shares in the Celtics that Brown intended to bequeath to Red Auerbach—something even Auerbach himself didn't know. That was how much Brown had trusted Heinsohn. On top of everything else, Brown had always supported the players association and had even paid Heinsohn's travel expenses to attend league meetings as the players' representative. And Heinsohn had repaid him by embarrassing him in front of the other owners—who'd think he was unable to control his own men—and delaying a nationally televised game at a time when the league was desperate for a network contract.

The more Brown brooded about Heinsohn's disloyalty, as he saw it, the more it upset him. A couple of days after the all-star game, Brown was still angry, and finally, when he ran into the *Herald*'s Joe Looney before the start of a Bruins game, he gave vent to his feelings. "Tom Heinsohn is the number one heel in my long association in sports," Brown said when Looney asked him how he felt about his player. Looney, who knew he had the lead for his column the next day, asked Brown if he wanted to trade Heinsohn. "No, I wouldn't trade him," the owner said, "but if I had a team in Honolulu, I'd ship him there."

Heinsohn had a great deal of affection for Brown, and he was deeply pained when he read the article. Auerbach did not want to see open warfare break out between Heinsohn and Brown, and he arranged for the two to get together and hopefully make amends. When Heinsohn arrived at Brown's office in the Garden, he was surprised to find, crowded in among the stuffed brown bears that Bruins fans sent the owner, a group of photographers and reporters. Brown had turned the meeting into a public ceremony of submission on Heinsohn's part. Once the photographs were taken and the reporters were ushered out, Heinsohn tried to explain to Brown that this was not personal, that he knew Brown had always been fair to him and all the Celtics, and had at times even gone out on a limb for him. If all the owners were as fair as Brown, Heinsohn said, none of this would have happened. But as it was, he went on, he was the president of the players association and had an obligation to act in the best interests of the group. Brown, sitting with his chin in his hand looking glumly at his desk, said nothing during the entire twenty-five-minute conversation. He was still furious. "Tom Heinsohn told me nothing I didn't already know," he said to reporters afterward. "I'm burned up and I'm sore about it. It was a fine way for one of my players to treat me."

BOB SHORT, the owner of the Lakers, was furious at Elgin Baylor for participating in the near boycott the night of the all-star game, and Baylor was angry at Short for thinking he could intimidate him. But unlike Walter Brown and Tommy Heinsohn, Short and Baylor quickly put the events of that night behind them. Short needed Baylor too much, and Baylor felt he owed the owner for the good that life had brought his way. Short was paying him $50,000 a year—money that had enabled Baylor to buy the apartment building he and his wife and son lived in off Wilshire Boulevard. Short had also advised him on other investments that would ensure that when he retired he did not, like some former NBA players, end up driving a taxi to make a living.

Baylor knew he had at most a few more years left as a basketball player, and in fact he was now worried that his career might even be cut short. In training camp that fall, he had begun to feel pain in his knees. At first he thought it might be caused by the slab floor of the training camp's basketball court, but the pain continued into the regular season and then his legs simply stopped performing, even when he was injected with painkillers. He couldn't turn the corner on the man defending him. The spring that enabled him to make his hanging jump shot was gone. His shooting touch abandoned him.

At first, none of the Lakers trainers or doctors seemed to know what was wrong. Someone told Baylor it was tendinitis. Someone else said the problem was psychological, but Baylor knew damned well that was untrue; he had never lost his confidence in himself. But the speed with which his game collapsed startled everyone who followed the team. "It's sad to speak of Elg in the past tense," Jim Murray wrote in the *Los Angeles Times*. "The average athlete sets like the sun. Baylor dropped like a rock."

Some seven doctors examined Baylor. They eventually decided that he was suffering from calcium deposits in his knees. The years of running and even more of jumping, they believed, had led to numerous minute tears in the ligaments and muscles of both knees. The body's own healing process created scabs on these tears. When the tears healed and the scabs came loose, they turned into small grains of free-floating calcium that grated against the knee joint every time it moved. Despite Baylor's obvious problems, coach Fred Schaus continued to play him, and Tom Heinsohn, as head of the players association, questioned whether the Lakers management was allowing Baylor to destroy his legs game by game, for the sake of the gate. "The Lakers are ruining Baylor," he declared. "He can't do anything and he shouldn't be out there."

Schaus was infuriated by the accusation of mistreatment. The doctors had in fact told Baylor that continuing to play basketball might actually help his knees by breaking up the deposits. "What about the claim you're 'ruining' the player?" a reporter asked him in the middle of the season.

"Listen," Schaus replied. "Do you think Bob Short would let me jeopardize a quarter-of-a-million-dollar ballplayer? Don't you think we have solid medical opinion that exercise is more liable to help his legs than to hurt them? The trouble with the Celtics and some of these other teams that are squawking so loud is that they have too many self-appointed orthopedic specialists on their squads. None of them know a piece of calcium from a watermelon—yet they can stand around and insult my intelligence and people listen to them."

Bob Short was torn between a fear that Baylor might suffer a lasting injury and a fear that if he took Baylor off the playing roster for a long period of rest, the result could be a dramatic, even fatal, slump at the box office. In 1960, before moving to Los Angeles, the Lakers had run up losses of $100,000. Now, four years later, they had become the first club in the NBA to gross more than $1 million, in large part due to Elgin Baylor. Fans specifically came to see him. When he was on military duty and playing sporadically, they called the box office before games to ask if he would be appearing. The Lakers front office had run figures calculating Baylor's ability to sell tickets, and they determined that in games when he did not play, the Lakers drew an average of 2,000 fewer fans. That amounted to approximately $6,000 per game, or $200,000 over the course of a season.

Finally, the Lakers arranged for Baylor to be examined by Dr. Robert Kerlan, the team physician for the Los Angeles Dodgers who had treated Sandy Koufax. Kerlan determined that the calcium deposits were located in the quadriceps group of muscles and tendons above the knee—a condition more common in football than in basketball. He decided against surgery; the harm that might be caused by cutting into Baylor's knees would more than offset any potential benefit that would come from scraping out the calcium. Instead, he recommended continued injections of painkillers, exercise therapy, and the use of a peripheral vasculator, which applied air pressure to reduce swelling. Kerlan did not discourage Baylor from playing, and as the season progressed, Baylor remained on the active roster, but his drive had lost its power, and even his depth perception seemed off. In one game against the Hawks, he did not score a field goal for the first thirteen minutes. "Take a vacation, bum!" one Lakers fan yelled. "Do us all a favor!"

THE WARRIORS had started the season unevenly, but they improved as the months passed, taking second place in the Western Division in January and first place in February. Alex Hannum had retooled the team, drilled it incessantly, pushed and pushed. He called his style of basketball "muscle and hustle." The Warriors were not a fast club, the fast break was not a part of their repertoire. They jogged down the court. Chamberlain moved into the low post to the left of the basket, took the pass from Guy Rogers, then paused, raising the ball above his head with one upstretched hand. When he judged the moment right, he drove forward for the dunk or, if the opponents fell back to cover him and freed up one of the other Warriors, he passed to the open man. His scoring average fell by almost 20 percent, but his teammates more than made up for it. With the team in first place, he stopped sulking, and the atmosphere in the dressing room improved remarkably. Hannum even had Chamberlain coach one game when he was ejected after disputing a call, and the Warriors won, surprising Chamberlain by their willingness to accept his authority. "I told them what I thought would work," Chamberlain said afterward, "and I got their cooperation."

With the team such an apparent success, Guy Rogers and Al Attles began to urge Chamberlain to acknowledge to all his teammates that Alex Hannum had been right in their dispute and that he, Wilt Chamberlain, had been wrong. Admitting he'd been mistaken was something Chamberlain was almost constitutionally incapable of doing. But Rogers and Attles persisted, and finally, in mid-March, during halftime of a game with Philadelphia that if the Warriors won would give them the Western Division title, Chamberlain made his concession speech in the dressing room.

"I want to tell you that I made a mistake, a bad one," he began. He said he had not at first appreciated the fact that Alex Hannum knew how to win games in the NBA. But Hannum did know, and winning was what the Warriors had been doing, particularly toward the end of the season, when they had not just won but won emphatically, decisively, when they had crushed their opponents, taking the Pistons by fourteen, the Lakers by sixteen, the Bullets by twenty-three. Chamberlain ended by saying that Hannum was the best coach he'd ever seen and he was willing to do whatever Hannum asked of him. His teammates applauded, and then they went out and beat the 76ers, locking up a division title for the first time in Chamberlain's career.

San Francisco bested St. Louis in the Western Division playoffs while Boston again took the Eastern Division, and so for the first time Chamberlain faced Russell for the championship. In the usual formulation of the rivalry, Chamberlain was described as the ultimate scoring machine and Russell as the ultimate defender. But Chamberlain was now scoring less, and some of Russell's teammates, such as John Havlicek, thought the traditional formulation underacknowledged Russell's offensive strengths. Russell did not shoot much, but his passing was superb. The entire Celtics offense was built around Russell's passing. What made it stand out was his instinctive awareness of where, at any given moment, every single player on both teams was to be found. It was a rare skill in a big center, since most of them usually thought about nothing but themselves and the ball.

Havlicek loved to watch Russell and Chamberlain go at each other one-on-one. Chamberlain was bigger and more athletic, but Russell outhustled him. Russell liked to get downcourt first and box out Chamberlain's favorite low-post position. Russell was also quicker than Chamberlain in the paint and could jump practically from a standing position, whereas Chamberlain had to bend down and thrust himself up into his jump. Since Russell was three or so inches shorter than Chamberlain, nothing seemed to give Russell more pleasure than blocking Chamberlain's shot. Havlicek had watched during one game as Russell blocked one of Chamberlain's shots. Chamberlain recovered the ball and drove in for a second shot, and again Russell blocked it. Chamberlain again recovered and started in for his third shot, but at that moment Russell stepped back. "Go ahead and take it," Russell said. Havlicek watched as Chamberlain dunked the ball and then turned to follow Russell up the court. It was a masterful psychological ploy, Havlicek thought. Russell had let Chamberlain have his two points, but he had also created the impression that Chamberlain could score only when he, Russell, was willing to let him do so.

That sort of psychological fencing had become a central part of the relationship between Russell and Chamberlain. Despite all the attention paid to their rivalry, they had become friendly off the court. In defiance of Auerbach's ban on consorting with the players of other teams, whom he wanted the Celtics to treat as enemies, Russell socialized with Chamberlain from time to time. When the Warriors were in Boston, he periodically invited Chamberlain to eat at his house in Reading, and if Russell was in Chamberlain's hometown, Wilt would take him out for dinner.

Some sportswriters were convinced that, even in this seemingly friendly gesture, Russell was seeking some psychological advantage. After all, Russell was considered the shrewdest and most manipulative player in the league. He prided himself on his ability to identify and then exploit an opponent's weakness, and he had developed a virtual arsenal of psychological ploys: feigning illness or exhaustion, unexpectedly complimenting an opponent, baiting a rookie, pretending to charge a ball handler. He once wrote a cover story for *Sports Illustrated* called "How I Psych Them," and some players were convinced that befriending Wilt was one more such tactic, a subtle attempt to soften by some small fraction Chamberlain's ferocity as he drove into the basket against him.

Throughout the season, Russell had followed Chamberlain's changing game—and read all the articles about the "new Wilt"—with some bemusement. Russell himself had never changed his game. He knew Chamberlain was always going to outscore him, sometimes by a margin of two-to-one or even three-to-one, but Russell never let himself get distracted by that, never tried to compete with Chamberlain on Chamberlain's terms. Similarly, he knew he was a poor outside shooter, and he never gave in to the temptation to try to hit from the perimeter. What Russell always tried to do was focus on the role he needed to play if his team was to win.

It seemed to Russell that Chamberlain, by changing his game as often as he did, didn't know what it was he wanted to accomplish in his career. Chamberlain wanted to win, but he seemed just as interested, and maybe even more interested, in statistical glory, press attention, and the bragging rights that came with his huge salary—in being known as the best, though Russell did wonder from time to time if Chamberlain put such an emphasis on these other accomplishments because he didn't have the championships to brag about. Russell's game, on the other hand, remained fundamentally the same throughout his career because his goal remained the same: *to win*.

But going into the finals in 1964, Russell was even more tired than he had been at this point the previous year. His hamstrings had become strained so often that he loosened them up with a heating pad before each game. His Achilles tendon bothered him constantly. His knees, which had troubled him since college, had gotten so bad that the trainer had to rub them down before each game. He hated the travel more than ever, but when he returned home he felt like he had nothing to say to his wife, Rose. The civil rights protests in the South were inspiring, but the violence they'd incited—the German shepherds loosed on young black demonstrators, the beatings, the murders, the bombings—were terrifying. He didn't feel safe in his own home. He also was suffering from insomnia and felt like he was on the verge of a nervous breakdown, and so, a few days before the series began, he announced he was thinking of retiring.

The sportswriters were soon speculating that Russell's complaints of exhaustion amounted to nothing more than another attempt to psych out the opposition, and one that succeeded, because Russell played magnificent defense in the first game, holding Chamberlain to a mere two points through the second and third quarters, and the Celtics won by fourteen. In the second game, the defensive battle intensified, as both Russell and K. C. Jones worked to force Chamberlain out of his position. They pushed and elbowed him from behind, their hands always on his back, and blocked him out with their legs and hips. As teams around the league began imitating the Celtics' emphasis on aggressive defense, the level of contact had increased, and Hannum had pushed Chamberlain to respond more vigorously to physical challenges. It frustrated the coach. Hannum would watch Wilt go up for a dunk and then, when a defender put his hand up to stop the ball, pull back because he was afraid he might hurt the man. "You know," Hannum told Chamberlain, "maybe if you came down once and maybe broke somebody's finger, people wouldn't be so anxious to try to stop you like that anymore." But Chamberlain, for the most part, could not bring himself to inflict pain, not out of fear but as if he thought it would be unfair—or make him look ridiculous—to actually tussle with someone smaller.

Now, however, in the third quarter of game two, Red Auerbach started yelling at Chamberlain from the sidelines, and Chamberlain, already agitated by the Celtics' physical tactics, rushed over to confront him. A distance of four feet separated the two men, and Russell tried to push them apart. "Get back, Red, you're about six inches too close," he told Auerbach. Russell put a hand on Chamberlain's arm, and Chamberlain knocked it away. Russell and Chamberlain had never gotten rough with each other, but Russell, who considered Chamberlain probably the strongest man alive, had never seen him so angry, and he thought they were now, for the first time, actually going to come to blows.

Chamberlain backed off but remained agitated. Then, near the end of the game, with the Celtics safely ahead, Auerbach decided to rest Russell and sent in Clyde Lovellette, the player who had elbowed Chamberlain in the mouth in his rookie year, knocking out two teeth. Auerbach had acquired him from the Hawks the year before. Known as "The Great White Whale," Lovellette by now weighed upwards of 290 pounds, much of it around his waist. He liked to play the cut-up and, deciding to get a rise out of the Boston fans in the final minutes of the game, began bumping and tripping Chamberlain and pulling at his pants. All of that added to Chamberlain's agitation. With twenty-five seconds left, when Chamberlain caught the ball in the pivot, Lovellette threw an elbow at him. Chamberlain, finally losing it, turned and punched Lovellette in the jaw, dropping him to his knees.

The Boston players swarmed off the bench and onto the court, and that brought out the Warriors, requiring the police to separate the two teams. Auerbach was screaming, "I want Wilt out of the game!" Officials Norm Drucker and Earl Strom had seen the exchange, and they both felt Chamberlain had clearly been provoked. Also, with only twenty-five seconds left and the game no longer in doubt, they simply wanted to get it over, so they only called a technical. Meanwhile, Lovellette was woozily climbing to his feet.

"Clyde, take the eight count, don't get up!" one of the Warriors yelled.

"Red," Strom said, "get this stiff out of here so we can finish the game."

But Auerbach continued to argue that Chamberlain should be ejected, and finally Chamberlain himself had had enough. "Red, if you don't shut up, I'm going to put you down there with Clyde," he said.

"Wilt's right cross was about the best scoring effort by the Warriors," Joe Looney wrote in the *Herald*. If nothing else, it epitomized the brutal defensive warfare that defined the series and created an extensive casualties list. By game five, with San Francisco down 3–1, Tom Meschery had dislocated a thumb, Guy Rogers had twisted his ankle, and Chamberlain's hand was bleeding after he gouged it on a basket rim. On the Celtics, Russell's knees were killing him and Tommy Heinsohn was playing with a white bandage over one eye. The series came to an end when, with Boston up by two in the final seconds, Heinsohn tossed a left-handed hook shot over Chamberlain's head, hoping that if it missed, Russell could tip it in. The ball bounced off the rim, but Russell jumped up past Chamberlain, grabbed it with both hands, and emphatically shoved it into the basket just as the buzzer sounded.

At the Celtics' breakup dinner the next day, Walter Brown paid tribute to Frank Ramsey, Jim Loscutoff, and Clyde Lovellette, who were all retiring. And then he turned to Tommy Heinsohn. Brown had not spoken a word to Heinsohn since mid-January, when Heinsohn had come to his office to try to clear the air after the averted strike at the all-star game. He had ignored Heinsohn when he went into the dressing room. If Heinsohn sat down to watch the opening game of a doubleheader in the row of seats reserved for the team, Brown got up and left. After beating the Warriors for the championship—capping a year in which Heinsohn thought he'd played the best basketball of his career—Brown had come into the dressing room and congratulated everyone on the team, all the way down to the ball boys, except Heinsohn.

But the owners were finally putting together a pension package, and with the season over, Brown had decided the moment was ripe for a public reconciliation. At the breakup dinner, he made no mention of the strike or their disagreement, but he thanked Heinsohn for his effort that year, for his hard work on the court, and for his contribution to the team's success. "I would like to say a kind word, for a change, about Tom Heinsohn," he said. "I never saw a horse, a dog, or a man put out as much for us as Tom Heinsohn did this season."

But Heinsohn's biggest contribution that year was not to the Celtics but to the players association. By persuading the other players to stand up to the owners on the day of the all-star game back in January, he had made the association viable. Within a decade, the NBA Players Association became the most powerful such organization in professional sports, and it negotiated an end to the reserve clause, which potentially bound a player to one team for the duration of his career, leading to free agency.

ROONE ARLEDGE, the vice president of sports at ABC, had been closely following the rivalry between Russell and Chamberlain. He realized that it even attracted viewers who did not find either man particularly sympathetic; the rivalry made each of them seem involved in a mythic contest greater than himself. Arledge was also aware that professional basketball was proving increasingly popular. During the previous season, overall attendance at NBA games had risen by 20 percent. And then there was the simple fact that, in Arledge's mind, basketball made for great television. It was both intimate and dramatic, both beautiful and violent. It had constant motion, which meant the viewer's eye was always engaged, and involved continuous decisions by all ten players, which meant there was always something for the commentators to discuss. It was stocked with theatrical personalities. And unlike baseball, it had a field of play small enough for a single camera to capture all the action in a crucial overview shot.

Since 1961, when he launched *ABC's Wide World of Sports,* the ambitious young Arledge had been on a controversial mission to make sports coverage more intimate, human, and entertaining. He put cameras on risers and in helicopters and Jeeps, and created a "creepie-peepie" roaming mini-camera for close-up reaction shots. "We will utilize every production technique that has been learned in producing variety shows, in covering political conventions, in shooting travel and adventure series to heighten the viewer's feeling of actually sitting in the stand," he wrote in an early memo.

The NFL and the major golf tournaments already had television contracts with NBC and CBS, and with ABC the perennially third-ranked network, Arledge had had to start small. He first used his techniques on track meets and soccer matches, cliff diving and barrel jumping on ice skates. But by 1964, the program had established itself, and Arledge, with ABC still locked out of the NFL, saw in the NBA an opportunity for a scrappy but growing network to ally itself with a scrappy but growing professional sport. That summer, he negotiated a deal with Walter Kennedy, for three years at $650,000 a year, that would allow *ABC's Wide World of Sports* to broadcast an NBA game every Sunday afternoon. "ABC Sports gained a franchise that, thanks to the amazing rivalry of Wilt Chamberlain and Bill Russell, was about to take off," he later recalled.

Arledge planned to install cameras throughout the arenas and to produce sixty-second mini-biographies of players that would allow the fans to connect to them as individuals. He also wanted to explain the game's strategy to the viewers, to allow them to understand that basketball had an intellectual dimension as well as a physical one. To do this he hired Bob Cousy, one of the most famous names in the game, without even meeting him. When they did meet, Arledge was surprised to find out that Cousy spoke with a French accent and, like many French speakers, substituted *w*'s for *r*'s. Instead of saying "Roone," Cousy said "Woone." Arledge told Chris Schenkel, who would be calling the games with Cousy, to have Cousy spend time repeating, as quickly as possible, "Russell and Robertson rebound rapidly."

ON LABOR DAY, Walter Brown was with his family at his summer home on Cape Cod when he suffered a massive coronary. His family rushed him to Cape Cod Hospital, but he died that night at the age of fifty-nine. Brown was one of the most popular and well-known figures in Boston, a big, generous, hot-tempered, forgiving man admired for his charity work as well as his sports teams; he allowed groups such as the Jimmy Fund free use of the Boston Garden to hold benefits. While his first love was hockey, his greatest accomplishment was the creation of the Celtics. "The Celtics—the very name implies basketball supremacy around the world—stand as the most towering monument to a man who thought he had dedicated his life to hockey," wrote Jerry Nason in *The Boston Globe*.

Tributes arrived from basketball players, hockey players, Olympic Committee members, Boston mayor John Collins, and Senator Edward Kennedy. His funeral, despite the rain that day, was one of the largest ever seen in Boston. Cardinal Cushing eulogized him as "the personification of personal integrity" before an overflow crowd at St. Ignatius Church in Chestnut Hill. After the funeral, Brown's wife, Marjorie, gave Red Auerbach her husband's St. Christopher's medal. She told him she hoped it would bring the team good luck in the coming season. In memory of Brown, the Celtics had small black patches sewn into the shoulder straps of their basketball jerseys, and Auerbach promised to reporters that the team would win the championship that season as a way of honoring its late owner.

UNLIKE THE YEAR BEFORE, when he'd loafed off and arrived at training camp weighing more than three hundred pounds, Chamberlain in the summer of 1964 was determined to remain in shape during the off-season. He spent part of the summer in Europe with the Globetrotters, but he still had his apartment in New York, and from time to time showed up at outdoor courts in Harlem for pickup games that, once word sped through the neighborhood, drew up to 1,000 spectators. As the summer wore on, however, Chamberlain began to be bothered by recurrent stomach and chest pains. He initially suspected his diet was the cause. He ate hot dogs constantly, as many as four or six at a time, and he decided to eliminate them from his diet, but the stomach pains continued to plague him.

In late September, back in San Francisco, Chamberlain was paged at the airport just as the Warriors were about to board a plane to fly to an exhibition game. It was the team physician, Dr. Dudley Fournier, who had given him his routine physical the previous week. Fournier asked Chamberlain to come immediately to St. Mary's Hospital, and when Chamberlain arrived, the doctor said his electrocardiogram indicated he had a heart problem. Chamberlain described the stomach pains, and Fournier said they might be connected. He ordered Chamberlain hospitalized for a complete physical examination.

The specialists at St. Mary's were unable to explain either the stomach pains or the heart irregularity. Several days passed, then a week, then a second week, without any diagnosis. When Dick Friendlich, a sports reporter for the *San Francisco Chronicle,* visited him in the hospital, Chamberlain told him he had three types of doctors: Dr. Good News, Dr. Bad News, and Dr. No News. "Dr. Good News comes in," Chamberlain said, "and he says, 'Don't worry, Wilt, you'll be skiing next week.' Then Dr. Bad News comes in and he says, 'Wilt, you might as well make up your mind, you're going to be here for a while.' Then Dr. No News comes in. He just shakes his head and says nothing."

Chamberlain's mysterious medical condition made headlines across the country. One widely published report claimed that he was a "heart patient." A rumor expanding on this notion speculated that because Chamberlain was so big, with so many more miles of blood vessels than the average man, his heart had given out trying to keep his massive body supplied with blood. All the speculation further dismayed Chamberlain, who was fielding constant phone calls from reporters. "The only heart attack will be the one my mother gets when she reads a story like that," he told one San Francisco sportswriter who called to inquire about the latest rumor.

After three weeks in the hospital, with the San Francisco doctors still unable to diagnose his condition, Chamberlain called Dr. Stanley Lorber, a Philadelphia gastroenterologist who had treated him before. Lorber told Chamberlain that he'd always had an irregular EKG, that it was common among black athletes, and that white doctors unfamiliar with the condition frequently misdiagnosed it. Chamberlain decided to check out of St. Mary's and fly to Philadelphia. Before he left, a small crowd of reporters and television camera crews gathered in the hospital's conference room to talk to him and Dr. Fournier. The team physician admitted that he and the other doctors had been unable to find any signs of a tumor, ulcer, or gallbladder problem that might explain Chamberlain's stomach pains. "It's a little strange," he said.

Chamberlain, who had lost weight, was weak, irritable, and depressed, with no sign of the humor he had shown when he'd first entered the hospital.

"How long will it take you to get into shape once you've been given permission to play?" a reporter asked.

"I have no idea," he said.

Alex Hannum and Franklin Mieuli, who had become chairman of the Warriors board, were genuinely concerned about their star. Chamberlain, Mieuli thought, complained about a lot of things but not about pain. For a man who put up with such physical punishment during games to stay in a hospital for three weeks, he had to be in serious pain. But Mieuli also fretted about the impact of Chamberlain's illness on the team's finances. Sick or well, Chamberlain had to be paid. His huge salary absorbed a good portion of the team's earnings, and if the illness turned out to be debilitating, the team could face serious financial problems.

For his part, Hannum worried about the team's lineup. By the time Chamberlain checked out of St. Mary's, the opening game of the season was a little more than a week away. Chamberlain had provided the Warriors with thirty-seven points a game the previous season and now was on the injured-reserve list for some indeterminate period of time. During the exhibition games, Hannum had used Nate Thurmond at center. Thurmond, who was six-eleven and in his second year as a pro, had actually played center at Bowling Green, but Hannum had recast him as a forward after drafting him since the Warriors already had Chamberlain. Thurmond couldn't score like Wilt, but he had defensive potential, and if the Warriors could maintain the low-scoring game Hannum had developed the previous season, he might succeed at the job.

In Philadelphia, Dr. Lorber had Chamberlain check into Temple University Hospital. After a week of tests, he and his associates determined that what Chamberlain was actually suffering from was pancreatitis, an inflammation of the pancreas caused by a malfunction of the parathyroid glands which had resulted in the stomach pains. It was this double-blind between the presenting symptoms and the actual cause of the condition that had bewildered the doctors in San Francisco. Dr. Lorber placed Wilt on a special diet and prescribed medication, but decided that he was essentially healthy and could rejoin the Warriors.

Even before leaving the hospital, Chamberlain started working out, but he flew back to San Francisco in a terrible mood. After his four-week stay in two different hospitals, he was thirty-five pounds underweight and his muscle tone had deteriorated. He had missed training camp and the exhibition games, and he felt weak. He was irritated at the San Francisco doctors who had failed to diagnose his condition, and he was irritated at the Warriors management for failing to find a doctor who could make the diagnosis.

Chamberlain was greeted at the airport by Franklin Mieuli. Eddie Gottlieb had returned to Philadelphia to live, where he became the league's schedule maker, and Mieuli was now taking an active role in the running of the team. Mieuli, a flashy young entrepreneur who wore a beard and drove a motorcycle, had first made his fortune in billboard advertising and was one of the original investors in the San Francisco 49ers. When the Warriors had won the divisional title the previous season, Chamberlain suggested to Mieuli that he give the players diamond stickpins instead of the traditional rings. Mieuli had ignored the suggestion then, but now, at the airport, he presented Chamberlain with a diamond stickpin. Chamberlain—who felt that Mieuli, instead of helping him when he was in the hospital, had left him on his own, and as a result Chamberlain was now going to have to start the season late and in poor condition—looked at the stickpin and said, "What's this piece of shit?"

Mieuli was shocked and humiliated. He had never particularly liked Chamberlain, whom he considered ungracious and uncooperative. The idea of a professional basketball team in San Francisco had once seemed like a stroke of brilliance to Mieuli, but the Warriors, now in their third year, were still not drawing fans, and the investors were losing money despite the fact that the team had won the Western title, had gone all the way to the finals, and had the most famous player in the league. Chamberlain was aware of the team's financial straits, but he seemed not to care and dismissed requests by Bob Dean, the Warriors publicist, to promote the team by making appearances. And now he had personally insulted Mieuli himself. At that moment, Alex Hannum later decided, Wilt Chamberlain was finished with the Warriors.

CHAMBERLAIN, dressed in an Italian silk suit, sat on the bench for the Warriors' opening game in San Francisco, which they lost to Los Angeles. In addition to Chamberlain, a number of the other Warriors were ill or injured. Tom Meschery had a broken hand and a sore ankle. Gary Phillips was recovering from an ankle operation. Guy Rogers came down with the flu. Al Attles had been playing with an excruciating charley horse. "At times," Stu Herman wrote in the *Chronicle,* "the Warriors look like out-clinic patients at St. Mary's hospital."

Most of the hurt Warriors were playing, but not well, and by the time Chamberlain was eligible to be taken off the injured-reserve list, the team's record was a dismal 1–4. Hannum felt so dejected and helpless that he would have been happy if the team had been able to win two games out of five. But still, it was early in the season, and the coach and the sportswriters thought that once Chamberlain rejoined the team, it would return to its division-winning form. "Look Out, NBA! Wilt Is Back" was the headline in the *Chronicle* at the end of October, just before Chamberlain's season debut.

Although Wilt had not yet fully recovered, Hannum started him immediately and worked him hard. He played thirty-three minutes and scored sixteen points in his first game, but his moves were tentative and his legs looked shaky. Chamberlain, however, was nothing if not a physical phenomenon, and he managed to get back into shape extraordinarily quickly. In his second game, he played a full forty-eight minutes and scored thirty-seven points, and he scored fifty or more points six times in his first six weeks. But even with Chamberlain in the lineup, the Warriors weren't winning. "Wilt's 53 Not Enough; Warriors Bow" ran a mid-November headline. A week later another headline declared "63 for Wilt but Warriors Still Lose."

One problem was that with Wilt out for so much of the beginning of the season, the team had adjusted to playing with Nate Thurmond at center. The young Thurmond was promising; Hannum went around saying he wouldn't trade him for any other center in the league. And unlike the moody, withdrawn Chamberlain, Thurmond was outgoing, buoyant, and eager to do anything that publicity director Bob Dean asked. He liked to talk to the sportswriters, to whom he described himself as a "playboy bachelor," and he was a figure on the North Beach nightclub circuit, dancing the frug, the twist, and the Watusi at his favorite spot, the Playpen, and throwing around mid-sixties slang like "dig," "cat," and "baby."

But Thurmond was also an extremely talented and serious basketball player, popular with his teammates, versatile, agile, long-armed, better at defense than Chamberlain in the view of some sportswriters, and better at offense than Russell. He was, however, only in his second year, and he still had a lot to learn. He often started a game excitedly keyed up, burned too much energy in the first half, and ran out of gas in the stretch. And he lacked Chamberlain's inimitable scoring ability. Still, the team had drilled with him and adjusted to him, and now with Chamberlain back, they had to readjust, and Thurmond wound up back at forward, the position he'd played in his rookie year. It threw everybody off.

Another troublesome fact was that the other teams had responded to Hannum's slow-paced offense by speeding up their own game. What worked against San Francisco, opposing coaches had discovered, was the fast break. The Warriors, with their injuries, their ragged defense, and their unrehearsed offense, could neither contain it nor counter it. There were other problems as well. Dick Friendlich, who covered the team for the *Chronicle,* recognized two trends: the Warriors would play fantastically for three quarters and then fold in the fourth; and while they had won every game on the road so far in the season, they had not won a single game at home.

One of the ironies of Chamberlain's career was that, as Eddie Gottlieb had first learned six years ago, Chamberlain was a bigger draw for the fans of the teams he played against than he was for his own team's fans. The novelty of seeing him brought out other opposing fans, as did the pleasure of rooting against a player whose size and dominance made him easy to hate. Chamberlain had taken to comparing himself to Goliath and was fond of saying that nobody rooted for Goliath. While the crowds who arrived to boo Chamberlain on the road seemed to fire up the Warriors, the quiet, sparsely filled stands in San Francisco had a depressing effect. The team, Friendlich decided, had acquired that rare and paradoxical stigma in sports: the home-court jinx.

With the Warriors sinking to last place, everyone on the team felt demoralized and frustrated, but no one's mood was bleaker than Chamberlain's. Racial tension had invaded San Francisco, that haven of liberal secularism, the previous summer when the Republicans held their national convention at the Cow Palace and nominated Barry Goldwater. All but a handful of black delegates had been excluded from participating, and those who did were shoved, spit on, and cursed. Jackie Robinson, attending as an observer, said, "I now believe I know how it felt to be a Jew in Hitler's Germany." Then in November, California voters approved Proposition 14, repealing the California Fair Housing Act, which the legislature had created the preceding year to prohibit racial discrimination in selling or renting residential dwellings. Overall, the measure was approved by the voters by a margin of two to one, and it even passed in San Francisco. Chamberlain enjoyed life in San Francisco, where he had taken up sailing and waterskiing and ate out at smart restaurants such as the Blue Fox and La Bourgogne, and where, from his apartment in Pacific Heights, he could see the bay and watch the fog envelop the Golden Gate Bridge. But he took the passage of the proposition as a personal insult. It was as if his neighbors had stood up and declared that they did not want people like him living in Pacific Heights and they reserved the right to refuse to allow him to do so.

Chamberlain's mood turned absolutely poisonous on December 4, in a game against the Celtics in which once again violence broke out. Physical contact, and its consequences, was by now an even bigger issue in the NBA than it had been the previous season. Just three days earlier, the Warriors' Wayne Hightower had broken his nose while diving for a free ball. Bob Pettit of the Hawks suffered fractures of the lumbar transverse processes on his back that month after colliding with Laker Rudy LaRusso. The same week, Arlen Bockhorn of the Royals was knocked down by Gus Johnson of the Baltimore Bullets and had to be sent to the hospital for a knee operation; it looked like he might never play again.

Some people, including Bob Feerick, who had moved over to become general manager of the Warriors, took the position that players in the NBA had simply become bigger. That development, together with the new emphasis on defense and the full-court press, had produced a more physical game, which, as a matter of course, led to more injuries. But others felt that play in the NBA had become dangerously rough, that players were pushing the envelope and officials were letting them get away with it. Ben Kerner, owner of the Hawks, demanded a meeting with Commissioner Walter Kennedy to investigate the league's officiating standards. Afterward, he told reporters that the state of play in the NBA was the roughest he had seen in his eighteen years in professional ball. Oscar Robertson also thought that loose officiating had led to a dangerous environment, but he felt the Celtics were primarily responsible for creating a physical game that other teams had been forced to imitate. "Boston plays all over you," he told an acquaintance. "But all the teams are doing it now. The guys pick you up high. You make a move, they grab and hold you. But they do it because they can get away with it."

When the Celtics had visited the Warriors a month earlier, they had handed the team a devastating 110–84 defeat. But the December 4 game at first looked to be the Warriors' best so far that season. They took a quick lead and steadily widened it until late in the second quarter they were ahead by an astounding thirty points. Even though the first half was not yet over, Red Auerbach realized the cause was hopeless. Instead of wearing down his top players trying to come back from that far behind, he decided to rest them, and began sending in replacements.

One of the first was John Thompson, a rookie who stood six-ten and weighed 230 pounds (and who later became well known as coach at George-town). Muscled and aggressive, but very green, Thompson was charged up, determined to seize this opportunity to prove himself. Trying to tear a rebound out of Chamberlain's hands under the San Francisco basket, Thompson swung an elbow wildly. It struck Chamberlain square in the face, shattering his nose. Wilt was rushed to the hospital—his third hospital stay in four months—and underwent surgery. In the week it took him to recuperate, his mood became so ugly—with his swollen, throbbing nose, his team in the cellar, the people in his city denying him the right to live where he chose—that he decided to do some-thing different, something defiant. He grew a goatee.

When Chamberlain returned, he had to protect his nose by wearing a plastic mask. The mask, together with his new goatee, gave him a frighten-ing, savage appearance. Wayne Hightower, who'd broken his nose that same week as Wilt, was also wearing a mask, and the press naturally had a field day with them. There were references to the "masked Warriors," to the "grotesque masks," and to how the players looked "like something on the Late, Late Show" and "out of central casting for a Hollywood horror movie." Even Hannum called them his "wild spacemen."

Chamberlain didn't think it was funny. The masks were uncomfortable and they interfered with breathing and peripheral vision. Chamberlain was also worried that opposing players might think they could take advantage of the fact that he and Hightower had facial injuries—or try to compound them. In a game in mid-December, he felt that Bob Boozer of the Knicks had swung an elbow at Hightower while coming down after a rebound. He turned on Boozer, who had played with him at Kansas and considered him a friend, and Boozer backed off while his teammate Len Chappell rushed onto the court and grabbed Chamberlain's arms from behind. "Let me go!" Chamberlain shouted, and he broke Chappell's grip by jerking his elbows away. In the locker room after the game, a reporter asked Boozer what had happened. "Poor Wilt," Boozer said. "He used to be a happy guy, and easygoing. Now he's tense and irritable and real aggravated."

RED AUERBACH had no apologies for the way the Celtics played against Chamberlain, and he felt no sympathy for the man. "I've heard enough about his troubles," he told an acquaintance. "I'd like to be so healthy!" Indeed, Auerbach himself, while not injured, felt extremely worn out. His workload, particularly since Walter Brown died, was enormous. He was coach and general manager and scout. He traveled with the team, looked after travel arrangements, conducted practices, was on the bench at every game, attended meetings of the board of governors, and negotiated contracts with players, radio stations, and the directors of the Garden. "It's questionable how much longer Auerbach can go on," Bill McSweeney observed in the *Boston Record*. "He doesn't eat. He doesn't sleep. And he takes the losses much harder than his players."

McSweeney was wrong about Auerbach not eating. He ate constantly, but his diet was atrocious. He drank Coca-Cola and ate cream puffs or doughnuts or hot dogs for breakfast. For lunch he liked deli meat: salami or corned beef. Throughout the day he drank upwards of ten Cokes and snacked constantly on nuts: pistachios, Indian nuts, almonds, walnuts, sunflower seeds, pumpkin seeds. Auerbach could be disciplined about food. The day of a game, he'd have a light sandwich around two, then eat nothing until the game was over. The slight hunger, he felt, gave him an edge. It was an idea he got from Ted Williams, who once told Auerbach that he liked to go into a game just a little bit hungry. Once the game was over, Auerbach ate Chinese, a habit he got into because the food—always steamed, no fried dishes—could be digested easily and he could hit the sack. He favored lobster in meat sauce, steamed fish in wine sauce, chicken wings in oyster sauce. He rarely drank liquor, maybe a single cocktail at a party, and made a point of touching nothing—no beer, no wine, certainly no booze—on a game day. He didn't want a player or referee smelling booze on his breath and putting around the word that his courtside behavior was influenced by alcohol.

Cigars were Auerbach's one notorious vice. It was a habit he'd picked up in the navy. Most days, he lit his first one after breakfast, and while he claimed to smoke only seven or eight a day, his players felt he smoked ten times that number. He smoked in his office, he smoked in his car, he smoked in the dressing room, he smoked during practice, and he smoked on the bench, at the end of the game, once he was confident the Celtics had put it away. Other coaches hated the arrogance of this particular gesture, as did some of the Celtics themselves, since it enraged the fans rooting against them and ratcheted up the intensity of the opponents. It also provided other teams' fans a moment of gleeful triumph when the Celtics, as even the best teams regularly did, lost a game. "Hey, Red, where's the cigar, skinhead?" they shouted when that happened. Once, Commissioner Podoloff actually wrote him to request that he stop smoking cigars during games. It made the entire league seem shady, carnivalesque—in a word, bush. Auerbach pointed out to Podoloff that other coaches such as Joe Lapchick of the Knicks smoked cigarettes on the bench and said that as long as they were allowed to do so he would smoke cigars.

By 1964, in his eighteenth year as a coach, Auerbach's cigars were not just a smelly indulgence but a key component of his identity—of his ongoing disregard for and defiance of the world at large—and he acted as if he had a prerogative to smoke them whenever and wherever he wished. In the middle of the season, Irv Goodman, a writer for *Sport* magazine, accompanied Auerbach on a flight from New York to Boston after the Celtics had lost to the Knicks. Against flight regulations, Auerbach lit up a cigar, and a stewardess walking down the aisle noticed it.

"You'll have to put out that cigar," she told Auerbach.

"Honey," he said, "that sign doesn't say no smoking cigars."

"Sorry, but for the comfort of all passengers, we don't permit cigar smoking."

"So why don't you ask the passengers if my cigar smoking bothers them?"

"I'm sorry, sir, but I'm afraid I'll have to insist."

"Don't be afraid, honey, and don't insist."

Eventually, the stewardess just gave up.

THE DAY AFTER the Warriors returned from the game in New York during which Chamberlain and Bob Boozer almost came to blows, the *Los Angeles Times* reported that the Lakers had offered the Warriors $500,000 for Wilt Chamberlain. Frank Mieuli, who had accompanied the team on the road trip, scoffed at the report, but while the $500,000 figure was exaggerated, it was true that the Lakers management had been in discussions with Mieuli about a possible trade.

The fact of the matter was that, less than three months into the season, Mieuli had become desperate to get rid of Chamberlain. His main concern was money. Chamberlain was making $85,000 a year, an astronomical sum at the time. When the team had drawn big crowds during its run at the championship the previous year, the additional revenue Chamberlain had been able to generate for the club had more than offset the cost of paying for him to play. But now, with the team in last place, attendance had slumped down below even what it had been during the team's first year in San Francisco. Some nights barely a thousand people bothered to show up, giving the Warriors the worst attendance figures in the league. As a result, almost one-third of the team's gate revenue was going to pay Chamberlain's salary. Chamberlain was still a big draw on the road, but the NBA stipulated that all gate revenue went to the home team, so Mieuli got nothing from his star player's out-of-town appeal.

By December, gate revenue at home in San Francisco was suffering so badly that Mieuli had actually been unable to pay Chamberlain on time—there were the salaries of all the other players to consider as well as front-office costs—and Chamberlain had begun hassling him about the money. The Warriors were in such poor financial condition that some of the investors had talked of moving the team to Oakland, where it might find a more hospitable fan base, or of cashing out of their investments altogether. But Mieuli pointed out that the San Francisco 49ers—Mieuli's first sports investment—had endured a long climb to their eventual popularity, and he convinced his partners to be patient. After all, the value of NBA franchises was continuing to rise—the Baltimore team had been sold that very month for $1.1 million—and Mieuli had no doubt that, over the long term, the Warriors were a good investment.

Mieuli believed that if he traded Chamberlain, he could reduce overhead enough for the team to survive until it developed a fan base, and he had begun talking to the other team owners. With the exception of Boston, every team in the league was theoretically interested. But many of them had reservations. Wilt was difficult, demanding, and expensive. He could so overshadow the team's other players that he'd end up alienating them, and the team could fall apart. And he had proved both in Philadelphia and in San Francisco that once the novelty wore off, he was no guarantee at the gate.

But the other owners also knew that it was not necessarily Chamberlain's fault that the Warriors were unable to draw a crowd in San Francisco. If a team with some marketing savvy and a big arena acquired Chamberlain and he re-energized it, and if the city had a true passion for basketball and showed up to watch, and if the major media turned it all into a national story, Chamberlain could generate an additional $300,000 a year at the gate. So Ned Irish of the perennially losing Knicks, Ike Richman of the Philadelphia 76ers, Ben Kerner of the Hawks, and Lou Mohs, the general manager of the Lakers, were all in discussions with Mieuli about acquiring Chamberlain. Mieuli hoped to keep the discussions secret, but on Christmas Eve, Kerner told reporters that he had been in trade talks for Chamberlain, that Chamberlain was available and almost certainly would be traded, but that the deal involved such a large amount of money that he had dropped out. Even though his arena in St. Louis had 9,000 seats and the Hawks had the highest attendance in the league in the early sixties, it lacked the seating capacity to draw the size crowd that could justify Chamberlain's salary.

By that point, Mieuli had already received one solid offer for Chamberlain. Earlier in the month, during a road trip by the Warriors that took them back to Philadelphia, Ike Richman, one of the principal owners of the 76ers and a personal friend of Chamberlain's, made a formal bid for him on the condition that Mieuli accept or reject it by January 13, the day of the all-star game, which also functioned as the mid-season break. The 76ers at that point were in second place, but their aging center, thirty-two-year-old Johnny Kerr, had begun to fade. Richman felt that to make the playoffs, his team required a new center, and if he couldn't get Chamberlain he needed the time to find someone else before Kerr collapsed altogether and the team fell out of playoff contention.

Richman was a gregarious, balding man who wore thick-framed black glasses and smoked enormous cigars. A well-connected attorney, he counted Eddie Gottlieb among his clients, and through Gottlieb he had begun to represent Chamberlain. It was Richman who had been instrumental in persuading Chamberlain back in 1959—during that nighttime meeting in Chamberlain's Eldorado—to join the NBA rather than return to the Globetrotters. Richman had helped Gottlieb arrange the sale of the Warriors, but he had at the same time always felt that Philadelphia deserved and would support another pro team. After all, there were solid college basketball programs at La Salle, Temple, Penn, St. Joseph's, and Villanova that drew as many as 15,000 spectators to the doubleheaders in their annual post-Christmas tournaments. The city also had its tradition of professional basketball dating back to Gottlieb's Sphas in the twenties. And so, in 1963, when Gottlieb, then working for the Warriors in San Francisco, had told Richman that Danny Biasone wanted to sell the Syracuse Nationals, Richman decided to try to buy the team.

The Nats were at that time the last team in the league still playing in one of the small cities that had nurtured professional basketball in its early days. They averaged only about 4,500 fans at home games, some 2,000 less than needed to make a profit. Tickets cost five dollars apiece, and the gate was the team's only source of revenue. At the same time, with two teams on the West Coast and teams flying to games instead of taking the train, as the Nats had done just a few years earlier, travel had become much more expensive. Danny Biasone accepted the fact that an NBA franchise in Syracuse, New York, was no longer a viable financial proposition.

Although Richman was a successful attorney, he did not have the upwards of half a million dollars it would take to purchase the Nats, so he brought in Irv Kosloff, who had founded the Roosevelt Paper Company, a successful supplier of printing paper for magazines. Kosloff and Richman paid Danny Biasone between $500,000 and $600,000 for the franchise he'd bought for $6,000 seventeen years earlier. Since the name Nationals sounded dated and evoked an old rival, their first order of business was to rename the team. As a publicity gimmick, they held a contest, and among the more than four thousand entries were nine proposals to call the team the 76ers. Richman liked the name. It had a snappy ring. It spoke to the city's identity, and because the recently completed Schuylkill Expressway had just been named Interstate 76, it even seemed propitious.

The front office that Richman set up was, by today's standards, an astonishingly small operation. It was housed in the office that Eddie Gottlieb had rented when he was running the Warriors, one carved out of a former VIP parking garage in the Sheraton Hotel at Eighteenth Street and John F. Kennedy Boulevard. Ike Richman served as the general manager, Mike Ianarelli sold tickets, the trainer, Al Domenico, made travel arrangements, and Richman's son Michael, then a college student, handled payroll. Eddie Gottlieb had returned from San Francisco, and from five o'clock until seven he and announcer Dave Zinkoff could usually be found holding court in the tiny office with other old-timers from the early days of basketball.

The renamed team had stumbled through its first season, losing more than half its games and falling to Cincinnati in the 1964 playoffs, but initially its most serious problem was attendance. Richman estimated that the 76ers' core of loyal fans stood at only 1,000. One of the most publicized games of the year—Wilt Chamberlain's return with the Warriors to play the team that had replaced them—drew only 5,800 fans. In fact, local turnout was so dismal that sportswriters estimated the new team cost its owners as much as $50,000 that first year. There were so few fans at some games, and the rows of seats were so empty, that the smack of the bouncing ball, the sneakers slapping on the hardwood court, and the occasional smattering of applause all had a hollow, echoing sound. Spectators in the upper reaches of the stands could hear the point guard calling out the plays. "Plenty of times it was so deserted you could sit anywhere you wanted," recalled Michael Richman.

One reason for the poor attendance was that, because of the fierce rivalry that had existed between the Syracuse Nationals and the Philadelphia Warriors, the city's basketball fans had for years regarded Dolph Schayes, Hal Greer, Larry Costello, and the other Nats with virulent hatred. They were the players the fans had jeered, screamed at, pelted with garbage, and attacked, and the idea of now rooting for them, Ike Richman acknowledged, needed to be accepted over time. Richman was also convinced that another reason for poor attendance was that the city's two biggest newspapers, the *Daily News* and the *Inquirer,* were ignoring the team. "It was a blackout," recalled Michael Richman. "All they printed was box scores."

Indeed, after each game, since no paper deigned to send a reporter to cover them, the 76ers publicity director, Harvey Pollack, and trainer Al Domenico would go into the locker room and call the papers and give them the box scores. The publisher Walter Annenberg owned both the *Daily News* and the *Inquirer,* but when Richman called to try to find out the reason for the blackout, Annenberg refused to see him. Richman never was able to get to the bottom of the blackout. Annenberg may have been punishing him for trying to hire one of Annenberg's employees, as Richman sometimes speculated, or for helping to sell the Warriors, which had angered Philadelphia's fans, or he may not have considered the struggling team newsworthy.

In any event, as the 76ers began their second season, Richman realized that the key to the team's success would be to bring in a certifiable star, one who would draw fans and whom the working press would find it impossible to ignore. And it was that same fall that he and Kosloff heard the rumors that Wilt Chamberlain, the biggest star in the game, a hometown boy and someone who just happened to be a friend of Richman's, was on the market.

Unable all season to develop any momentum, the Warriors went into a truly dreadful tailspin in January, losing eleven straight games—going three weeks without a win—and bringing their record to 10–34. The system Alex Hannum had put together for the Warriors the previous season had long since collapsed. Chamberlain, in his bad mood, had abandoned the habits of teamwork Hannum had inculcated, and the "new Wilt Chamberlain" of a year ago had been replaced by the "old Wilt Chamberlain," who ignored his teammates and shot whenever he had the ball. He continued to post high scores, but as had happened in Philadelphia, his scoring streak had the perverse effect of undermining his teammates, who lost their heart for the game. "He can do one thing well—score," Jim Murray wrote in the *Los Angeles Times*. "He turns his own team into a congress of butlers whose principal function is to get the ball in to him under a basket. Their skills atrophy, their desires wane. Crack players like Willie Naulls get on the Warriors and they start dropping notes out of the window or in bottles which they cast adrift. They contain one word, 'help.' "

On top of that, the unending trade rumors distracted the team. Since the Warriors management discussed nothing with the players, they were forced to try to act as if the rumors did not exist, but that was difficult. The most recent rumor had it that a deal would be made by January 13, the day of the all-star game, and they all knew that in a short time they would be playing on a radically reconfigured team. It was hard, under those circumstances, to work up any motivation, and Hannum felt as anxious as his players. Nate Thurmond was particularly frustrated, not just by the team's performance but also by the fact that, after stepping in at center and playing admirably when Wilt was sick, he was now once again relegated to forward. In fact, Thurmond was so discouraged that he told Hannum he wanted to be traded. Hannum thought that between Chamberlain and Thurmond, the Warriors had the best and the third-best centers in the league, but what that meant, strangely enough, was that the team had too much talent, at least in a given area. With Wilt playing almost forty-eight minutes a game, Thurmond could either sit on the bench or play forward, and he didn't want to do either.

As the all-star game and mid-season break approached, Hannum felt the Warriors had three options. One was to stand pat, keeping both Chamberlain and Thurmond, but that made no sense with so much money going out and so little coming in. Either Chamberlain or Thurmond should go. The question was whether the Warriors should trade Thurmond for a top-notch shooter and hope that once the team's injuries healed, they could recover their fire and bring home a championship this year, jump-starting ticket sales for the following year. Otherwise, the Warriors could accept the fact that Chamberlain was simply not drawing a large enough gate to justify his salary, trade him, and rebuild the team around Thurmond, who was earning approximately $13,000, less than one-quarter of Chamberlain's salary. That was the financially prudent move, but it meant accepting as well that it would be a few years before the Warriors became championship contenders.

Hannum personally felt the team should not trade Chamberlain, who was, after all, the leading scorer in the history of the game and the man who had gotten the team to the finals the year before. But the decision was not his to make. It was up to Franklin Mieuli, the man Chamberlain had publicly insulted at the beginning of the season.

THE WEEK the all-star game was to be held, Martin Luther King, Jr., who had received the Nobel Peace Prize the previous month, had returned to Selma, Alabama, to lead a voter-registration drive. He urged the city's blacks to act on the federal civil rights legislation passed the previous year by applying for whites-only jobs and trying to register in Selma's white hotels and eat in its white restaurants. The issue of race was embroiling major-league sports as well. In baseball, some teams, such as the St. Louis Cardinals, had embraced integration, but their opponents in the World Series that fall, the New York Yankees of Mantle and Maris, still refused to sign more than the single black player on their roster, Elston Howard, fearing that white fans might turn against the team. "I don't want you sneaking around down any back alleys and signing any niggers," Yankees president George Weiss had told his scouts. And during the same week in which the NBA's all-star game was to take place, black players on the American Football League's all-star team had voted to boycott the game, after arriving in New Orleans, where it was scheduled to take place, and encountering cab drivers who refused to serve them, nightclub owners who denied them entry, and white hotel guests who insulted them.

Professional basketball, by contrast, was so far ahead of other major-league sports on the matter of accommodating black athletes that the issue was almost moot. The NBA was now dominated by black stars, and while white players such as Jerry West and John Havlicek and Bob Pettit remained sentimental favorites, white fans now largely accepted and rooted for the league's pace-setting black players. And for weeks they had talked of little except an impending Chamberlain trade, the teams in contention for him, and how it would affect the playoffs.

On January 12, 1965, the day before the all-star game, Ike Richman flew into St. Louis, where it was to be held. That night he went to see Chamberlain at the Hotel Chase and told his friend and occasional client that he hoped to acquire him. "Are you sure you're doing the right thing?" Chamberlain asked. Chamberlain was once again considering retiring at the end of the season. Dr. Lorber, after diagnosing his pancreatitis, had advised him to take a few months off to recuperate. Chamberlain had been entitled to do that, and under his contract with the Warriors, Mieuli would still have had to pay his salary. But he had felt that the Warriors needed him, and so he had returned to the team, only to endure a miserable losing season, a broken nose, and weeks of reading that Mieuli intended to trade him, without Mieuli himself once showing him the courtesy of coming to discuss any of the plans with him. Chamberlain had other interests—he'd invested in restaurants, apartment buildings and real estate, and trotting horses—and by now he was so fed up that he was not sure what he was going to do once the season was over. He told Richman he was worried that if he did decide to quit, the 76ers would have spent a lot of money or traded away good players simply to acquire his services for three months. "Don't do it, Ike," Chamberlain said. "You'll be making a mistake."

Richman was not concerned. He had seen Chamberlain in these moods before and had heard Chamberlain make the same threats before. Three times, to be precise: while at Kansas, then after his rookie year, and then when the Warriors moved to San Francisco. Chamberlain always worked himself out of the moods, and he always signed up again. Richman was confident that, at the end of the summer, when it came time to talk about a contract, they could work things out because, as much as he complained about it, for Chamberlain nothing in life could compare to playing professional basketball. All Chamberlain needed, Richman thought, was a good year and some enthusiastic fans, and he'd be back. Philadelphia was thirsting for a sports hero, he told Chamberlain. The Eagles had had a losing season. Going into the last week of the baseball season, the Phillies had been out in front of the Eastern Division by six and a half games, the National League pennant within their grasp, but then they tanked. If Chamberlain fired up the 76ers, as Richman fully expected him to do, they'd have every sports fan in the city cheering them on.

Franklin Mieuli hoped he could get a better deal than the one Ike Richman had offered him in December, but he had already decided that if he could not do that, he would go ahead and trade Chamberlain to Philadelphia. "I'm not leaving St. Louis until I get rid of that son of a bitch," Mieuli told Alex Hannum on the flight in from San Francisco. "He'll be traded before I go home."

When Mieuli arrived in St. Louis, Richman repeated his standing offer. Mieuli reacted noncommittally and then spent the rest of the day negotiating with other owners. The Lakers' Bob Short made a cash offer of upwards of $200,000, but Mieuli also wanted players, and Short refused to part with any of his stars, afraid that if he did, the fans would turn against the team. In any case, Mieuli preferred to trade Chamberlain to an Eastern Division team, where he would not stand in the way of the Warriors' advancing in the play-offs. He had hoped Ned Irish of the Knicks would top the standing offer from Ike Richman, but Irish turned out to be more interested in acquiring Nate Thurmond, and by the end of the day, Mieuli had still failed to nail down a deal.

Speculation about a trade completely eclipsed the all-star game itself, and that evening, once it was over, the players, owners, officials, and sportswriters all trooped over to Stan Musial's restaurant for a postgame celebration, where the negotiations continued. As the midnight deadline approached, Richman still had not heard back from Mieuli. He became convinced that the Warriors were trading Chamberlain to another team, and he prepared to leave the restaurant. Then, at two minutes before midnight, Mieuli stopped him on the staircase and said, "You've got a deal."

One of the referees, Joe Gushue, was on the way to the bathroom and overheard the conversation. He rushed back to his table. "Chamberlain's been traded!" he shouted. "Wilt's been traded to Philadelphia!" Word spread throughout the restaurant, and Chamberlain heard about it only when a reporter came over to ask what he thought. Mieuli and Richman had planned to hold an official press conference the following day to announce the deal, but the reporters were hectoring them for statements—they wouldn't let Richman leave the restaurant without one—and so the two men stood up in the middle of the dining room and made the announcement then and there.

In exchange for Chamberlain, Philadelphia was giving San Francisco three players: Lee Shaffer, Paul Neumann, and Connie Dierking. There was some logic to these choices. All three had played for Hannum when he was coaching the Nats, and he thought he could fit them into his system. Dierking, a center, could serve as a backup for Nate Thurmond. Neumann was a solid guard and Shaffer a big forward who Hannum thought had all-star potential. Even so, compared to Chamberlain they were an undistinguished group. In the previous year, Chamberlain had scored more points and gotten more rebounds than the three of them put together. On top of that, Dierking had an injury and had recently been suffering from fainting spells, and Shaffer, who had hurt his knee the previous season, was a holdout, working for a trucking firm in North Carolina because the 76ers had turned down his demand for a 25-percent salary increase.

Mieuli also received a cash payment from Philadelphia. The figure was never officially released, but the Warriors front office dropped hints that it was upwards of $300,000. However, owners who had acquired Chamberlain in the past had inflated his salary for the publicity value. Other sources put the figure closer to $50,000—and much of it, Chamberlain would later maintain, went to pay his back salary.

After the news about the trade broke that night, Wilt locked himself in his hotel room and refused to answer the phone. He was irritated because, although the deal had been announced, no one had as yet deigned to inform him officially about it. The one reporter he did talk to was his friend Milton Gross, who was also in St. Louis.

"What would it take for Ike to persuade you to play for the 76ers beyond this year?" Gross asked.

"More than he can offer," Chamberlain said. "I got to play for them for the rest of this season because my contract says so, but that's up at the end of the year and I'm through."

Gross had his doubts about that, but he kept them to himself. Gross also doubted that the 76ers had paid much if any money for Chamberlain. They would have been foolish to do so if he was going to leave at the end of the season. Also, if big money had changed hands, Chamberlain would have wanted a considerable portion of it in exchange for an agreement to play the following season. Richman, Gross believed, had picked up Chamberlain cheap, but would have to cough up a huge sum to get him to come back. But Gross, and many of his colleagues, were pretty sure that he would. "At mid-point, the pro-basketball season has a familiar look," Frank Deford wrote in *Sports Illustrated* after the trade. "The Celtics are running away from the rest of the league; the East won the all-star game, and Wilt Chamberlain is threatening to quit."

Most sportswriters felt that the trade, purely in terms of talent exchanged, was an insult to Chamberlain. Writing in *Sport* magazine, Leonard Shecter called it "one of the weirdest deals in the history of professional sports." Jim Murray of the *Los Angeles Times* said, "The San Francisco Warriors did everything but list him in the Yellow Pages. It was a situation unique in sport. Man O'War was being dropped in a claimer. Jim Brown was going to be dealt off for a fifth-round draft choice. Babe Ruth was being put up for two relief pitchers and an old scorebook."

But for Franklin Mieuli, Chamberlain had become more a burden than an asset. Mieuli was happy to have the 76ers take Chamberlain simply to see them assume the financial responsibility of paying his enormous salary for the rest of the season. By making the deal now, the Warriors could depreciate Wilt's value for income-tax purposes. Without attracting a single new fan, Mieuli would see his team's revenues shoot up some 25 percent.

IKE RICHMAN realized he needed to restore Chamberlain's enthusiasm for basketball, and he set out to make his new player feel welcome and appreciated back in his hometown. When Chamberlain arrived in Philadelphia, Richman made sure that he was greeted at the airport by reporters, photographers, and camera crews. He invited Chamberlain to stay with him and his family in their sprawling house in the affluent suburb of Elkins Park, and even lent Chamberlain his Cadillac. "Don't let any of the neighbors see you, Wilt," Richman joked. "I don't want them to know we've integrated Elkins Park."

Because a bowling tournament was taking place in Convention Hall, Chamberlain's first game with the 76ers had long before been scheduled to be held in the Arena, a small alternative forum in West Philadelphia considered more than adequate for a typical 76ers game since, at the time, the team was drawing fewer than 4,000 fans per game. But hours before the game began, spectators were lining up outside the Arena and the traffic on Market Street was completely backed up.

The small arena sold a record number of tickets. "My sales went up four hundred percent," ticket manager Mike Ianarella told an acquaintance. "I am selling tickets to guys who haven't been here since 1961." Richman wanted a big crowd, and for days in advance he'd had kids out on the streets giving away free tickets. Once the seats were full, the manager closed the entrances and fans still waiting outside charged the gates trying to get in. The fans sitting in the stands held signs saying BIG WILT IS BACK! and ANOTHER DIPPER DUNK. Down in the dressing room, the 76ers could feel the crowd's enthusiasm. One of the players had brought a record player, and he put on a forty-five-rpm single. It was Chamberlain singing, *"By the river . . . 'Neath a shady tree . . . Just my baby . . . Just my baby and me."* As the music played, Chamberlain, dressed only in plaid undershorts, demonstrated a new dance craze, the jerk.

So many spectators were trying to get to their seats that the start of the game had to be delayed. When the crowd had finally settled, the players were introduced one by one. "And now," announcer Dave Zinkoff boomed over the public address system, "Philadelphia's own Wilt Chamberlain!" Chamberlain stepped onto the court and into the glow of the spotlight. The crowd roared and roared, and then people began climbing to their feet, and soon everyone in the arena was standing cheering as Chamberlain turned around acknowledging the applause—a full-throated standing ovation that went on for thirty seconds. He'd never seen a crowd react to him, or to anyone, this way before. Finally, Zinkoff had to cut off the applause. "Ladies and gentlemen," he said, "there are two more ballplayers."

Coincidentally, their opponents that night were the Warriors, and before stepping out of the spotlight Chamberlain looked over at Alex Hannum. The two men remained friends despite the trade, and when Chamberlain smiled, Hannum smiled back in a proprietary fashion. The Warriors were then on a thirteen-game losing streak, and Chamberlain, who was still wearing his plastic mask—"as ferocious as something out of *Dr. Strangelove*," the *Bulletin*'s Sandy Grady commented—tied them up under the boards, freeing his teammates Hal Greer and Larry Costello to score. When Chamberlain rebounded, he fired the ball out for fast breaks. Every time he scored, and particularly when he dunked, the crowd roared again.

Once they had beaten the Warriors, the 76ers set out on an East Coast road trip that included a match with the Celtics, who were then enjoying a sixteen-game winning streak. If the Celtics beat the 76ers, they would tie the NBA record of seventeen straight victories, but Chamberlain played brilliantly against Russell, who took fifteen shots without making a single one, and Philadelphia won. After the road trip, the Celtics came down to play the 76ers again, this time in Convention Hall. The stands were crammed with over 10,000 fans, more than double the number who usually showed up, and Chamberlain again outplayed Russell, scoring and rebounding but also creating opportunities for his teammates. The 76ers handed Boston another defeat, which made them the only team that year to beat the Celtics twice in a row.

THE TWO GAMES against the Celtics were part of a nine-out-of-eleven streak the 76ers went on once Chamberlain joined the team, a dramatic turnaround considering that until then they had been winning only about half their games. Instead of the limelight-seeking ball hog some of the 76ers expected, Chamberlain proved to be a true team player. He passed out from under the basket, protected his teammates on defense, and allowed Hal Greer and Larry Costello to rack up solid shooting scores. Still, some of the players found it difficult to accommodate him. Greer, the team leader, had trouble adjusting to both the attention focused on Chamberlain and the consequent neglect of the rest of the players, and to the fact that Chamberlain, by playing in the middle under the basket, clogged up the lane and prevented Greer from driving. But the primary conflict that soon emerged was between Chamberlain and the team's coach, Dolph Schayes.

One reason Chamberlain had been reluctant to return to Philadelphia was Schayes. Schayes was a big, dark-eyed, easygoing Jewish guy from the Bronx known around the NBA for his signature gesture as a player: pumping his fist victoriously in the air as he ran down the court after making a basket. Before becoming a coach in 1963, he had been the Nats' star, leading the team into the playoffs every year for fourteen years. Schayes had played against Chamberlain for four years, and he had found it a horrifying experience. With the encouragement of Alex Hannum, who was then coach of the Nats, Schayes had tried to throw Chamberlain off his stride. Schayes would make fun of Chamberlain by leaning against him like he was a lamppost. He pulled at his shirt and his shorts and tried to trip him up. And then at the end of Chamberlain's rookie year, when the new star had written an article in *Look* complaining about precisely that sort of behavior and threatening to quit the NBA, Schayes, like a lot of people in the NBA, had been annoyed by Wilt's self-pitying tone, and he'd responded by writing a mocking article in *Sport* calling him a lazy, immature, stubborn, pampered crybaby.

Schayes now felt somewhat chagrined to have aired those opinions. While it was at times tempting to sound off about other players, it was a small league and the comments often came back to haunt you. And Schayes knew that Chamberlain was morbidly sensitive to criticism. It surprised people that a man so large and strong and accomplished, and with such a dominant personality, could be so sensitive, but that was Wilt. He never forgot a slight, and Schayes knew Wilt had never forgotten Schayes's tongue-in-cheek comments.

While Schayes had tried to be lighthearted in that article, the truth was, he'd always felt that Chamberlain was egotistical and that he insisted on dominating every team and every coach he played for. Wilt refused to abide by the rules imposed on the other players, which inevitably led to dissension, and on all his teams his teammates forgot how to work the ball themselves. Chamberlain was always the king, Schayes thought, and his teammates were always the serfs and pawns. That had changed somewhat when Hannum joined the Warriors, but even so, Chamberlain always seemed to Schayes to be fighting the temptation to take over. Schayes had also always thought Chamberlain was not worth his enormous salary. How much talent did it take to work your way in close to the basket and then dunk the ball? In fact, Schayes didn't even consider it real basketball.

This was not the most ideal baggage to be bringing to a coach-player relationship, but Schayes hoped they could put the past behind them, and, keeping his private views to himself, he officially welcomed Chamberlain to the team and declared himself capable of handling his temperamental new player. But privately, he worried that he would become one more coach who tangled with Chamberlain and lost, particularly given the ill will that Chamberlain harbored toward him. "Why did this have to happen to me?" he asked an acquaintance.

Schayes would later decide that becoming a coach was the worst decision he ever made. But he'd done so at the end of the 1962–63 season, when he'd played badly all year, had had an operation on a troublesome knee, and began to think his career as a player was over. In 1963, when the team was sold to Kosloff and Richman and moved to Philadelphia, Alex Hannum had quit as coach and returned to California. Frank McGuire had been interested in the job, but since everyone on the team knew and liked Schayes, and since he had been one of the league's best players, Richman offered it to him.

While the older players considered Schayes a pal, the younger ones tended to treat him dismissively, and after joining the team, Chamberlain was unable to develop any respect for him. Schayes seemed unable to communicate his thoughts on strategy, and above all he seemed to Chamberlain to be in over his head. He was simply not tough enough. He was a decent, generous, soft-spoken, well-dressed man who was kind to children but was being eaten alive by hard-boiled NBA veterans. Still, just as Schayes had professed his admiration for Chamberlain ever since he'd joined the team, Chamberlain for the time being kept his feelings about his coach to himself.

Then, toward the end of the season, Chamberlain was approached by Bob Ottum, an editor for *Sports Illustrated*. It had been a tumultuous year for Chamberlain, even by his own unusually high standards in that department, and Ottum hoped he would want to get a few things off his chest about his pancreatitis, Mieuli's decision to trade him, his triumphant return to Philadelphia, and his possible retirement. Ottum told Chamberlain that the two of them could talk and then he, Ottum, would write a piece in Chamberlain's own words and Chamberlain could read it and sign it.

Chamberlain, who could never resist the opportunity to ventilate his opinions, liked the idea. Ottum, the quintessential nebbishy little-white-guy sportswriter—his chin was level with Chamberlain's elbow—began spending time with the athlete. He accompanied him on the train from New York down to Philadelphia for practice and games. They spent evenings in nightclubs, Chamberlain drinking orange juice and Ottum ordering screwdrivers, and in Chamberlain's apartment on Central Park West. Ottum found Chamberlain fascinating. He wore imported silk shirts but carried his money in a brown envelope. He spoke in a bebop vocabulary but was capable of sudden displays of erudition. He also ate in amazing quantities. On their first trip down to Philadelphia he consumed a dozen sweet rolls and a barbecued chicken and drank two cartons of milk and a container of orange juice. Ottum found himself eating more when he was around Chamberlain, and by the time he'd finished interviewing him he'd put on six pounds, which was a lot for a little white guy who weighed only 130 to begin with.

AFTER THAT GREAT eleven-game run when Chamberlain first joined the 76ers, Greer and Costello were injured, then Chamberlain's pancreatitis flared up, and Philadelphia lost hope of catching the Celtics. In one game at the end of the season, Chamberlain's pain became so unbearable that he had to stop playing. His internist, Dr. Lorber, was unable to diagnose the problem, and Ike Richman suggested he see a hypnotist. By this time, every player and fan in the country was familiar with Chamberlain's pancreas troubles, and jokes about it were common. Before the playoffs began, Cincinnati coach Jack McMahon, whose team was facing the 76ers in the first round, was telling reporters that his players might try hitting Wilt in the pancreas only no one knew where in the hell Wilt's pancreas was.

At the outset of the playoffs, the 76ers, who finished the regular season in third place in the East, were considered the weakest team to make it in, but Oscar Robertson had a strained tendon in his left foot, and Philadelphia beat the Royals three games out of four. In the locker room afterward, some of the jubilant players shouted, "Bring on the Celtics!" The Philadelphia fans, after ignoring the 76ers the previous year, were just as keyed up. Their football and baseball teams had disappointed them, but Chamberlain, back in his hometown, looked to have a chance to take the 76ers all the way to the championship, and the spectators who filled Philadelphia's Convention Hall were in a raucous mood.

Red Auerbach liked to call Convention Hall "a snakepit," and all the Celtics hated playing there, no one more than John Havlicek. The balconies extended practically out over the court, which created an incredible level of noise and a claustrophobic atmosphere and made it easy for the fans to hurl garbage onto the floor: flashlight batteries, the half-quart containers of orange drink they sold there, all kinds of weird stuff. In one game, when Havlicek was lining up a free throw, a rock-like object smashed into the backboard. It turned out to be a raw potato. What kind of fan, Havlicek wondered, brought a raw potato to a basketball game? The Philadelphia fans particularly hated Auerbach. Once, one of them tried to choke him by jerking on his necktie, and during the playoffs Auerbach got into a scuffle with another one of the 76ers fans, a guy who always sat near the visitors' bench. Russell and other players were convinced the heckler was a management plant, put there by Philadelphia for the specific purpose of harassing the team. Auerbach would have paid ten bucks just to punch him in the mouth.

The series was rough as well. The players fed off their fans, and each team won its first two home-court games, Boston using the full-court press on defense, the 76ers countering with long clothesline passes. Dolph Schayes thought Chamberlain was playing the best basketball of his career, and Russell felt exhausted trying to keep up with him, but the sense of camaraderie and purpose that the fans and Chamberlain's inspiring play instilled in the 76ers collapsed after game four, when the next *Sports Illustrated* hit the stands. The cover line read "My Life in a Bush League." In the cover photograph, Chamberlain, his goatee divided into a mustache and a separate chin tuft, glared up at the camera, which was placed above a basketball hoop, in a photograph with a curious pink background. Inside, he was pictured strumming moodily on an electric guitar. "Oh, man, this is going to be better than psychiatry," Chamberlain declared in the first sentence of the article, which was headlined, in the style of the New Journalism just then coming into vogue, I'M PUNCHY FROM BASKETBALL, BABY, AND TIRED OF BEING A VILLAIN.

The article was written entirely in the first person, and in it Chamberlain complained about biased officials, ignorant owners, and incompetent coaches. "Frankly, I doubt if Mieuli knows very much about basketball. But he wants to speak up about it, and now that he is an owner, now he can. Oh, man!" He described Dolph Schayes as "soft-hearted" and suffering from a "woolly look." "Schayes is so tender-hearted that someone sitting on the bench can look over at him with those big wet eyes and he'll put them into the game—even if the man replaced is having a big night."

The other 76ers were appalled by the article, not just because Chamberlain attacked Schayes, whom many of them considered a friend, but because he had chosen to do so in an article appearing in the middle of the playoffs. Ike Richman was also puzzled and disturbed. Since Richman was both Chamberlain's attorney and part owner of the 76ers, the article put him in a delicate position. He gamely tried to shift the controversy onto the magazine and had the front office issue a statement by Chamberlain declaring that *Sports Illustrated* "interjected many unauthorized thoughts into my story without my consent." Chamberlain also insisted that the editors had promised him the piece would not come out until the season was over. He even threatened to take legal action against the magazine, but no one believed he was the aggrieved party. Commissioner Kennedy was so mortified that he fined Chamberlain. Gordon Forbes of *The Philadelphia Inquirer* wrote, "It appeared that Wilt had stuffed one in the wrong basket."

Schayes, for his part, refused to even read the article. He knew it would only upset and distract him. He had just seen *Séance on a Wet Afternoon,* this great British movie starring Kim Stanley about a crazed medium, and he decided that, like the characters in the film holding the séances, he needed to empty his mind of everything unrelated to the purpose at hand, which was winning the series against Boston. And so he dismissed Chamberlain's article when reporters asked him about it and did not raise it in team meetings, but as Chamberlain sat slouching in his seat while the coach talked, the other players could only wonder what Wilt had been thinking. The article was embarrassing; the spectators would watch them jumping off the bench and taking orders from the coach whom their star center had essentially declared to be a fool. It fouled the atmosphere in the locker room, particularly when combined with the fact that Chamberlain flew by himself up to Boston for game five instead of traveling with the team and then skipped the practice session everyone else was required to attend.

Most of the 76ers were too upset about the article to respond to reporters asking for comment. Chet Walker felt that a lot of what Wilt had said had a certain legitimacy, but still his timing was terrible, and it did not exactly endear him to the rest of the team. Several players, including Johnny Kerr, Larry Costello, and Hal Greer, denounced Wilt and his article to reporters, which only exacerbated tensions and spread a feeling that no team carrying baggage like this could prevail in the playoffs. Angry, depressed, confused, and disunited, the 76ers lost game five, but then, as if to show their faith in Dolph Schayes, they rallied to take game six, tying the series, then prepared for the trip up to Boston for the seventh and final game. It was held on April 17, 1965, and was a game that would, justifiably, become one of the most famous in basketball history.

The Celtics had by then won seven championships in the preceding eight years, and three times the final series had gone to seven games, which had led to the saying *The Celtics always win the seventh game*. That ominous legend, and Boston's well-known home-court advantage—it won four out of five home-court games—had succeeded in intimidating some of the 76ers, who had lost eleven straight games to Boston in the Garden. As game seven approached, a reporter asked Schayes why his team seemed to do badly in that arena. "Pressure! Pressure!" Schayes barked. "Some of our younger players still haven't gotten over the fear of the Boston floor. They see how tough it is for us up there, and in their minds it becomes even tougher. But it's only a floor, ninety-four feet by fifty feet, just like ours, and we can win there."

Schayes had put his finger on it. *The fear of the Boston floor.* It was always there, and the Celtics and their fans—or so everyone on the 76ers was convinced—resorted to all manner of tactics to heighten it. What this meant was that while the Celtics hated playing in Convention Hall, the 76ers positively loathed playing in the Garden. "You never knew what you were going to get," recalled their trainer, Al Domenico. "It was tough to get out alive." The team would arrive at the visitors' dressing room to find the heat not working or else turned up so high it felt to Domenico like it was 110 degrees. He'd run around to find an engineer to turn it down, but the guy would say the Garden's old furnaces couldn't be adjusted, and so in the end their only choice was to open the windows and let in the snow or rain. The pipes groaned and rattled so loudly the players could hardly hear each other talk. Rats and roaches scuttled along the corridors. There was that damned parquet floor with all the dead spots that the Celtics had memorized. Before the game, the Garden's floor crews loosened the screws to the baskets so the ball would simply drop into Russell's hands for the rebound.* Sam Jones climbed up on a ladder and used a piece of soap to mark the spot on the board he needed to hit to make his angled jumper. The fans arrived with eggs, oranges, lightbulbs, anything they could get their hands on. They were blood-crazed, those Celtics fans. After one game, the 76ers got into their bus out in the parking lot when it was suddenly surrounded by upwards of three hundred shouting Celtics fans, who began rocking the bus back and forth, trying to overturn it. The bus driver

---

*In Philadelphia the floor crews tightened the baskets so the ball would bounce hard and Chamberlain could jump for the rebound.

seemed uncertain about what to do, so Domenico shouted, "Run 'em over, for Chrissake! Let's get out of here!"

A light rain was falling when the 76ers arrived in Boston after taking the Eastern Airlines flight from Philadelphia. The streets were filled with dirty slush. The cab drivers, who recognized them, always ragged them on the trip into the city. *Russell rules the boards. Havlicek'll run you dizzy. Satch is gonna shut down Walker. Even Chamberlain now sez you got a bush-league coach.* The pedestrians who saw the 76ers outside the hotel jeered. And once they'd changed into their uniforms in the Garden's cold, clammy, filthy dressing room and jogged up the concrete ramp that led to the court, the fans in the steeply banked seats pelted them with coins and toilet paper and rotten eggs. Chet Walker felt like Daniel heading into the lion's den.

In the pregame huddle, after they'd warmed up, the 76ers assured one another that they were not going to allow the Celtics and their fans to intimidate them, that they were not going to succumb to the fear of the Boston floor, that they had one final chance, now, to show the world that they were capable of playing basketball in Boston Garden, ending the jinx, and taking the game away from the home team. Then they broke huddle, and the starters walked onto the parquet floor, toward the tip-off circle where Chamberlain would face Russell.

Red Auerbach had a saying: *The guys who finish the game are more important than the guys who start it.* He'd repeated it any number of times this past season to John Havlicek, who was now in his third year with the team. Havlicek rarely started, but more and more often he found Auerbach sending him into the game at crucial moments. He had become one of the closers, and now, with five seconds left in the seventh game of the 1965 Eastern Division finals with Philadelphia, he was on the floor, waiting for Bill Russell to throw in the ball.

Havlicek was another one of Auerbach's discoveries. Auerbach, forced to draft last because the Celtics were perennial champions and prevented by the flat box office from spending large sums to trade for players, had continued to search for overlooked college players to fill the holes in his roster left by retiring veterans. In 1961, he had discovered Satch Sanders, a shy, self-conscious NYU forward who found the NBA so intimidating that he'd decided to go to work for the Tuck Tape Company until Auerbach talked him into trying out for the Celtics. The year Cousy retired, he'd come across Havlicek, the son of a Czech grocery-store owner from a small town in Ohio. At Ohio State—where teammates gave him the nickname Hondo, after a John Wayne movie, because they couldn't pronounce Havlicek—he was a low-scoring defender completely overshadowed by the university's reigning star, Jerry Lucas. The broadcaster Curt Gowdy, however, had noticed his drive, and he told Auerbach, "There's this guy Havlicek who runs around like he's got a motor up his ass."

While Havlicek was passed over by all the other teams in the draft, Auerbach always had an eye out for what he called "our type of kid," and sensed that he was teachable. Some of the Boston sportswriters thought Auerbach was wasting the pick. "Have you ever seen Havlicek?" asked Cliff Keane of the *Globe*. "A strong breeze could knock him to the ground." The rookie did not exactly exude virile glamour. He wore horn-rimmed glasses off the court, and had jug ears, narrow, squinting eyes, and a crew cut that emphasized the blockiness of his head. He was so shy and awkward that Russell sometimes called him Country Boy. But Russell, who'd been shy and awkward himself as a young man, saw resemblances in Havlicek—they both had games that depended primarily on hard work rather than flash—and he had befriended the rookie, helping him buy a stereo and going out of his way to praise him to the Boston reporters.

At Ohio State, the team's game had revolved around feeding the ball to Jerry Lucas, and Auerbach initially saw Havlicek—and Havlicek saw himself—as a defensive player. But then he surprised everyone with his ability to score, a capacity for sudden hot streaks that bumped his scoring average up into double digits. This had less to do with an innate shooting eye than with the fact that, because he was always on the move—the Celtics man in motion, as he came to be known—he was open more than the other players. Auerbach's rule for all players was *If you've got the shot, take it,* and the coach began to urge his rookie to shoot more often.

Frank Ramsey, who was nearing the end of his career, also took Havlicek under his wing. He taught him defensive tricks, like how to draw fouls. Since Havlicek was not a starting player, Ramsey encouraged him to sit on the bench near Auerbach without wearing his warm-up clothes, radiating an eagerness to get into the game. Havlicek would work up a head of adrenaline waiting to be sent in, growing itchier and itchier, and Auerbach, aware of it, would sometimes keep him out just a little longer, holding him back like a racehorse, and then send him charging in totally revved up. Havliçek began to think of himself as Ramsey's successor in the role of the sixth man, the one who could come in off the bench to energize the game, the money player taking the big shot and making the key play.

The guys who finish the game are more important than the guys who start it. It was true. And now, with five seconds left in the final game against Philadelphia, Havlicek was standing at Boston's end of the court facing Bill Russell, who was under the basket, waiting for the official to give him the ball. It had been a fierce, relentless game. The Celtics, typically, had surged to an early lead, but the 76ers had come back to overtake them and were a point up at the half. The two teams stayed close in the second half, but with one minute to play, Boston had found itself up by three points. The Celtics tried to run down the shot clock, but no one was open when time expired, and once the 76ers took over, Chamberlain, who'd scored their last four points and was having a stupendous game, quickly scored again. His field goal reduced Boston's lead to one point, but now only five seconds remained on the clock, and it was the Celtics' ball. All Russell had to do was throw it into one of his quickest players—Sam Jones or Havlicek—who only needed to avoid being fouled while he dribbled out those final seconds.

Russell stepped behind the line to make the inbounds pass. The referee handed him the ball under the basket. Chet Walker, who was guarding Russell, took up a position, hands raised, right in front of him. Russell hoisted the ball over his head and looked for an open man.

Just above Russell was one of the backboard guy wires. At the time, the backboards at Boston Garden were stabilized by guy wires. An upper pair of cables ran from the board up toward the ceiling, while a lower pair ran out toward the box-seat sections. Players had always worried about the possibility of the ball hitting one of the lower wires on an inbounds pass from under the board, but it had never happened.

Now, however, with five seconds left in the game, Russell was concentrating so intently on the deployment of the players on the court that he forgot about the guy wires. He leaped up to throw the ball in over Walker's raised hands, and when he let go, it hit one of the wires and bounced back off the court. Earl Strom, the referee, decided that what Russell had done was equivalent to throwing the ball out of bounds. He blew his whistle and called a turnover.

Pandemonium erupted. The Boston bench flooded onto the court, and practically every single person in the building—players, coaches, fans—was screaming something. Russell was stunned. Those damn guy wires—another attempt by Garden management to save money—weren't even supposed to be there. He dropped to one knee, pounding the floor with his fist in frustration, and shouting, "Oh my God, oh my God, it's their ball!"

Auerbach ran up to Earl Strom, hysterically arguing that Chet Walker had been guarding Russell so closely that Walker had stepped out of bounds, forcing Russell to hit the guy wire. Strom was a tough official. He'd had everything from eggs to scotch bottles thrown at him by angry fans and was, in fact, officiating the game with his hand in a cast because he had broken his thumb in a fight with a fan a few nights earlier in Baltimore. Strom also had a core belief—*the players decide the game*—and he was not about to change the course of a playoff final because of some minor, ambiguous infraction. He ignored Auerbach. Russell, like Auerbach, started arguing that it should be Boston's ball because Walker had been out of bounds, but Strom refused to budge. Meanwhile, Johnny Most, the Celtics broadcaster, was in a frenzy, screaming into his microphone, "He hit the wire! He hit the wire! By God, he hit the wire!"

Dolph Schayes immediately called a time-out. The noise was deafening, every fan in the building chanting *Defense! Defense! Defense!* In the huddle, the 76ers, who could hardly hear one another, were compounding the noise by shouting their suggestions for the crucial play. "Hold it!" Schayes yelled. "Let me talk." Schayes's face was rigid with the tension. The 76ers, who were behind by only one point, would take possession at Boston's end of the court. They had five seconds, time enough to execute one play, score two points, take the lead, and win the title. But it had to be the right play. Some of the 76ers were urging that the ball be given to Chamberlain. It was a natural call, but Schayes thought that the Celtics, who were huddling around Auerbach, would assume the pass would go to Chamberlain, and he would in all likelihood be heavily guarded. Also, Chamberlain himself did not want the ball. Some of the players wondered if he was afraid of taking the clutch shot. But he pointed out that if he got the ball, he'd immediately be fouled. He'd go to the foul line—where his problems were legendary—under enormous pressure, and if he missed, Russell would in all likelihood get the rebound for Boston and that would be the game.

Schayes decided he needed a counterintuitive play. He told Greer to make the inbounds pass to Chet Walker, while Johnny Kerr set a screen. But Walker, instead of shooting, would fire the ball back to Greer, who was to duck behind the screen Kerr set. Greer, who was the best outside shot on the team, would take the last shot while Chamberlain took up a position under the basket to guide the ball in if necessary. The team had used the play almost a hundred times during the year, and it seemed to everyone like a good plan. "Let's make the play work for Hal," Schayes said.

Meanwhile, the Celtics were gathered in a semicircle around Auerbach. Since Elgin Baylor was injured, the Lakers, who had won the Western Division, posed no real threat in the finals. This Eastern Division title match was in effect the championship. All the Celtics knew that, with five seconds left, the 76ers had plenty of time to get off a shot before the buzzer rang. Russell was starting to feel sick at the thought of what his error could cost his team. "I blew it," he told his teammates. "Somebody bail me out. I don't want to be wearing these horns."

Auerbach seemed at a loss. The series had been a particularly grueling one for him. He'd been suffering from asthma and chest congestion ever since it began. That fan had attacked him in Philadelphia, and even the public address announcer down there, the Zink, had been mocking him, urging the crowd to light up cigars after the 76ers' wins. He was exhausted and out of ideas. "So what do we do now?" he asked. No answers were forthcoming from any of his players. Unable to think of anything better to say, Auerbach told the team, "Play defense but don't foul." And, he added, "Watch Wilt, of course."

Hal Greer took the ball out of bounds for the 76ers, and Russell assumed a position just behind Chamberlain. Russell was certain that Greer would pass it in to one of his teammates, who would either feed it to Chamberlain for a dunk or pass the ball back to Greer, who would have moved into position for a set shot.

Philadelphia's Chet Walker, standing near the pivot, held up his hands for the ball for the pass from Greer. Neither Greer nor Walker was paying attention to John Havlicek, who was standing off to Walker's side. The inbounds passer had five seconds to throw the ball in, and when the referee gave it to Greer, Havlicek started counting down the seconds in his head. He had been facing Walker, but when he was at one-thousand-four, he looked back at Greer. Havlicek could tell from the way Greer had set up that he was going to make a soft, high pass. That surprised him; he expected a low hard throw to Chamberlain. Greer lobbed the ball at Walker, thinking to keep it from the Celtics with height rather than speed. A moment before the ball left Greer's hands, Havlicek took two steps and leaped high into the air, raising his hands in the hope that he could somehow deflect the ball.

The pass was slightly short. The ball hit Havlicek's arm and bounced into the hands of Sam Jones, who started dribbling upcourt as the final seconds ran down, and the buzzer sounded and the thundering, roaring crowd poured onto the floor in utter delirium, shoving and trampling players, tearing at Havlicek's jersey, ripping the shoulder straps to pieces and giving him rope burns on his collarbone, pushing Auerbach onto people's shoulders and then pulling him off and forcing him up onto other people's shoulders.

Announcer Johnny Most had completely lost his head. Most, who chain-smoked English Oval cigarettes throughout his broadcasts—they contributed to his gravelly rasp—was such an emotional announcer that he was said to have three voices. Voice One was his normal voice and Voice Two his excited mode. Voice Three was the voice that overtook him at the sight of wildly thrilling, game-altering plays, and he was now in full-throated Voice Three mode. *"Havlicek stole the ball!"* he screamed over and over. *"It's all over! . . . It's all over! . . . Havlicek stole the ball! . . . Johnny Havlicek stole the ball!"*

The 76ers were stunned, none of them more than Chamberlain. Four times in the last six years, Chamberlain and his team had made it either to the divisional finals or to the championship series, only to be defeated by the Celtics, more often than not in games just like this one, games that could have gone either way. There seemed to be no justice in it. As the 76ers made their way stonily through the celebrating Celtics fans and off the court, some of the spectators, recognizing Chamberlain's astonishing performance throughout the series, clapped him on the back.

"You were great, Wilt," one said.

"Simply great," another added.

Chamberlain nodded slightly, but he did not smile.

A Boston Garden work crew took down the guy wires two days after the game in which Havlicek stole the ball. They were never used again. Even without the wires as a reminder, the moment embedded itself in the city's consciousness. Schoolboys on street corners, imitating Johnny Most's rasp, repeated the announcer's phrase endlessly. *Havlicek stole the ball!* Later that year, Most put out a record of his broadcasts during the highlights of memorable Celtics games. Not only did the record include Most's hysterical outburst during the final seconds of game seven of the Eastern Division playoffs, it was actually titled *Havlicek Stole the Ball!* The moment became so iconic, so central to Celtics mythology, that it acquired an almost religious significance. A few years later a woman at a party showed Havlicek a brooch that contained, as if it were some sort of saint's relic, a piece of the material from the jersey that the fans had torn from his back that night.

In the years to come, Havlicek would emerge as the second most important player on the team after Russell, a position emphasized when he replaced Russell as captain. If Russell was the heart of the team, as Milton Gross once put it, Havlicek was the motor. In the years to come, sportswriters such as Gross would consider Havlicek the best all-around basketball player in the league, not the most beautiful shooter or the quickest on his feet, but unparalleled in his combination of raw power, inspirational play, and sheer stamina. But that was in the years to come. What sealed Havlicek's reputation in Boston and established him as Cousy's successor to the title of hometown favorite in 1965, was that one hoarse, hysterically shouted, irresistibly imitated phrase: *Havlicek stole the ball!*

IN MID-WINTER, in a game in Cleveland, Elgin Baylor had fallen on his left knee. The hardwood playing surface of the Cleveland court was supported by a cement foundation, and the fall gave Baylor's knee a painful jolt. Then he banged it a second time a few days later in a collision with another player. Baylor, accustomed to painful knees, took no particular notice of these blows when they occurred, but then in Los Angeles in April, during the Lakers' first game in the Western Division finals, against Baltimore, Baylor went up for a twisting shot and lost his balance. When he crashed to the floor, a loud bone-crack could be heard across the court. With thousands of people watching, Baylor rose and tried to take a step, but the moment he put weight on his foot he fell to the floor again, writhing in pain.

The trainer, Frank O'Neill, helped Baylor up, but to O'Neill's disbelief, Baylor made it by himself to the dressing room. Dr. Robert Kerlan, the team physician, had him taken to the hospital. X-rays showed his kneecap had actually split in two. Kerlan decided that Baylor had probably first cracked it on the cement subflooring in that game in Cleveland. Early the next day, in an operation at Daniel Freeman Hospital in Inglewood, Kerlan removed the broken fragment of the kneecap—the top eighth of it—rounded off the remaining section of the patella, drilled tiny holes, to which he attached the torn ligaments, and scraped out the calcium. He then placed Baylor's entire leg, from hip to ankle, in a plaster cast.

The following day, Kerlan gave Baylor the piece of calcium he had removed. It was the size of a quarter and had jagged edges. Kerlan explained that it had been floating around in Baylor's knee, which was why the pain would come and go. Baylor's knee seemed so badly and permanently damaged that Kerlan was almost certain Baylor would never again be the outstanding player he had once been. Kerlan believed that if Baylor was lucky, he might be able to play for another two or three years, most likely in some supporting role, but Kerlan was fairly pessimistic about the athlete's chances of a real recovery. Even after rehabilitation, he thought, Baylor might end up with a permanent limp.

Lying in his hospital bed, Baylor tried to remain optimistic, tried to summon his self-confidence and take it a day at a time. But newspaper articles were predicting the end of his career, and he had to face the fact that he might never play again. Lou Mohs, the Lakers general manager, talked to five other doctors who had operated on broken kneecaps, and they all told him that the chances for Baylor's complete recovery were one in a hundred.

Without Baylor, the Lakers seemed to stand almost no chance in the playoffs, and the responsibility for carrying the team fell on Jerry West. West had broken his nose during the regular season, but otherwise had escaped serious injury. Unlike most other seasons in his career, when some sort of injury benched him for at least a short spell, he had played all seventy-four regular-season games, and had amassed more playing time—3,066 minutes—than anyone else on the team.

Now, through sheer determination and force of will, West almost single-handedly carried his team through the Western Division finals with Baltimore. In the six games it took for the Lakers to win the series, he scored 277 points, an average of 46 points a game. It was a playoff record. Dan Hafner of the *Los Angeles Times* thought it was a particularly amazing feat because someone was hanging on him while he took most of his shots. "They used to say that pound-for-pound and inch-for-inch he was the best in the game," he wrote. "Right now the experts are beginning to believe he is the best, period."

Normally, it would never have occurred to West to take that many shots. Baylor wouldn't have put up with it, for one thing. But Baylor's injury had provided West with a unique opportunity—or challenge—and he felt he had risen to it. At the same time, the intensity of effort had exhausted him. Between the games, he'd scarcely been able to move, and once the series was over, he felt utterly drained.

For the third time in four years, the Lakers faced Boston in the finals. By now Fred Schaus, the Lakers coach, had become obsessed with beating Auerbach. The grudge he bore was so personal that he tended to think of the matchup not as the Lakers against the Celtics but as Schaus against Auerbach. It seemed unjust to Schaus that Auerbach had collected so many championship trophies, especially because Boston had won more than a few of them not by decisively outplaying the other team but because the other team blew a point or two in the final seconds.

But that was not the reason Schaus despised Auerbach. Boston's coach, Schaus thought, had perfected the art of baiting officials. Auerbach knew just how far to push it to intimidate them without getting thrown out of the game. And that, Schaus felt, brought out the worst in other coaches, who had to start beefing every call if they didn't want to cede the advantage to Auerbach. Red's behavior dragged the whole league down. What particularly irritated Schaus was that he knew everything Auerbach did was calculated. When Auerbach was screaming on the sidelines, it wasn't because he was momentarily frustrated, it was because he wanted to make the officials hesitate. And since Auerbach wasn't actually losing his temper at all, he got away with twice as much as any other coach. Schaus could become so irritated and distracted by thoughts of Auerbach that in talks with his team before games with the Celtics, he often found himself bitching about the Boston coach instead of discussing strategy.

Elgin Baylor accompanied his team to Boston for the first game of the finals wearing his cast and hobbling on crutches. There were injuries among the Celtics as well. Heinsohn had an arch injury that required he wear a sponge taped to the bottom of his foot, and doctors had drained John Havlicek's knee—he'd torn the cartilage in it the previous summer during an exhibition tour in Africa—for the seventh time that season. Both Heinsohn and Havlicek were playing, however, and Boston won the first game by a thirty-two-point margin. The teams split the next two games, but in game four, West went cold, missing twenty-one out of twenty-four shots, and the Lakers lost by thirteen.

In game five, back in the Garden, West accidentally jammed a finger into Bill Russell's eye, and Russell collapsed to the floor in pain. Boston trainer Buddy LeRoux examined him. Russell's vision was blurry, and the eye was becoming bloodshot from a hemorrhage. But, as Auerbach liked to say, during the playoffs there were no such things as injuries, and Russell insisted on going back into the game. When he did, the Celtics surged. By the end of the third quarter, they had pushed their lead to sixteen, and at that point they went on a run, ringing up twenty consecutive points while holding the Lakers scoreless, Russell rebounding their missed shots and firing the ball to his fast-breaking guards. The crowd was wild over it. Auerbach, who had lit up one of his monogrammed cigars early in the period, turned around, pulled out a big handful of them, and threw them into the stands.

It was Tommy Heinsohn's final game. He had played in the first half, but Auerbach had taken him out in the third quarter, and as the Celtics' incredible surge began, he was sitting on the bench. He had told Auerbach that he had been offered a good job training recruits at the insurance company where he'd been working summers, and, worn down after nine years as a Celtic, he was pretty sure he would take it. A couple of fans in section 88 were holding up a banner that read, DON'T LEAVE US, HEINIE, and in the fourth quarter other fans started shouting, *"We want Heinsohn! We want Heinsohn!"* But Auerbach felt the momentum of the men on the court was too strong for him to risk interrupting it for the sake of a sentimental gesture to Heinsohn. In any event, Heinsohn had done his job, helping put the team solidly in the lead. Auerbach didn't care what the fans thought. He kept Heinsohn out until the final minute, when he turned to him and said, "Do you want to go in?"

Since it was probably his last game, Heinsohn had desperately wanted to go back in ever since Auerbach had taken him out. He had also not entirely made up his mind to quit. Although he had said he probably would, he'd continued to cling to the idea that he was necessary to the team, that they couldn't win without him, but he now realized that that was obviously a fantasy. He had scored only six points but the Celtics were ahead by thirty-six.

They didn't need him. And to go in at the last moment, in a token gesture—like a second-stringer trotting sheepishly onto the court once the game was safely in hand—would have been humiliating. The whole thing hurt Heinsohn's pride. He had been a clutch player in so many of the team's great championship games, but he'd never been truly appreciated, scoring thirty-five or more points or nailing crucial free throws in the final seconds only to end up with one line of ink at the tail end of the next day's game story. And now, unlike Cousy, who'd closed out his career with a series of Bob Cousy Days and ended his last game with the ball in his hands, here Heinsohn was sitting on the bench. Auerbach hadn't even told him to go in, he'd asked, as if he was doing Heinsohn a favor. "No, I don't want to go in," he said to Auerbach.

When it was all over, the Celtics had won 129–96, a devastating thirty-three point margin. Fred Schaus was amazed at the way the Celtics had kept coming on against his Lakers in the fourth quarter. The Celtics had now won seven straight world championships, and Schaus was forced to accept the cold, hard fact that they had no equal in the league. No one was ever going to beat Auerbach, Schaus thought, and that was a bitter thing to accept because any sense of justice required that the man be taken down a peg.

The Celtics dressing room was thronged with shouting players and excited sportswriters. Auerbach's team had, following the Celtics tradition, thrown him into the shower, and he was soaking, his tie was off, and his white shirt was unbuttoned. "I just wish Walter Brown was here to see this team," he told the reporters, and that reminded him of something. Without telling anyone, he had carried Brown's St. Christopher's medal—the one Brown's wife, Marjorie, had given him after Brown's death last September—with him throughout the playoffs. He'd put it in his pocket that morning, as he had every day, but in the excitement of the game he'd forgotten about it until now. "You want to know a secret?" he asked the reporters. He pulled the medal out and held it up in his hand. "Here's our good-luck charm."

AFTER WALTER BROWN'S DEATH, Marjorie Brown and the Celtics minority owner Lou Pieri had held onto the team through the 1964–65 season. But Pieri had always been a silent partner who had no interest in assuming Brown's role in running the team, and Walter Brown's estate owed the federal government so much in estate taxes that it was hard for Marjorie to see how she could afford to keep the team. And so, in the summer of 1965, she and Pieri sold the Boston Celtics to the Ruppert Knickerbocker Brewery, based in New York.

Auerbach's inclination at the time was to retire as coach. Brown had bequeathed him 11.6 percent of the stock of the Celtics, and when the team was sold he made more than $300,000, so he could consider himself a prosperous man. More important, his workload in the year since Brown's death had taken its toll. Toward the end of the 1965 season, he happened to see a photograph of himself in a newspaper, balding and gray, his face bloated, his eyes haggard, a dead cigar butt in his mouth, and he thought, *My God, do I look that bad?* More significant, he felt old. His inner fire—the competitive instinct, the naked desire to dominate—was flagging, and he became afraid that if he didn't feel motivated, he'd be unable to motivate his players. The truth was, in the past season, he had not been getting himself pumped for games the way he needed to.

John Waldron, a former Fordham football player who was the president of Ruppert Knickerbocker, convinced Auerbach to remain on as coach for one more year while a successor was found. At first, Auerbach kept quiet about the decision, but then he decided that it would motivate the Celtics' opponents—and therefore the Celtics themselves—if everyone knew. Before the season began, he told the Boston sportswriters that he would step down the following spring. "I'm announcing it now so no one can ever say I quit while I was ahead," he explained. "I'm telling everyone right now—Los Angeles, Philadelphia, everyone—that this will be my last season. You've got one more shot at Auerbach!"

The challenge succeeded, as Auerbach intended, in provoking the fans, players, coaches, and owners of every other team in the league, all of whom wanted nothing more than to see his last year in the league become one of ignominious defeat for the Celtics. "They want them to lose because they detest Auerbach," *The Saturday Evening Post* observed. "Auerbach has predicted he would depart a champion and they want him to go out a loser." In every game the Celtics played, it seemed, the fans went out of their way to bait Auerbach. In Cincinnati, when the Royals had a solid lead, hundreds of fans lit up cigars and, in the final seconds of the game, a woman in maroon stretch pants and a white angora sweater skipped from the seats and stood in front of Auerbach, sucking on a mammoth cigar, then blew the smoke right into his face. Auerbach snatched the cigar from her mouth and scattered her with ashes.

No fans were more virulent in their detestation of Auerbach than those of Boston's great rival, Philadelphia. With the 76ers well ahead in one game, not only did hundreds of fans light mocking cigars, but they pelted Auerbach with peanut bags and empty beer cans, and as the game ended one fan ran down to the Celtics bench and threw a lit cigar in Auerbach's face. Auerbach complained to the local reporters—"What a bush town!"—and a few days later, the guilty fan wrote the *Philadelphia Bulletin* to confess to hurling the cigar, but he added, "It did not hit him. That so-called smudge he showed on his fat head was probably from his dirty hands." Shortly thereafter, when Auerbach appeared at a sportswriters' banquet in Philadelphia, he was greeted by persistent boos. "Do me a favor and shut up, will ya?" he said when he took the microphone. "The only time I've ever heard you people quiet was during 'The Star-Spangled Banner.' "

ON DECEMBER 3, 1965, Ike Richman was in the Boston Garden, sitting at the press table next to the 76ers bench, watching his team play the Celtics. Richman loved nothing in his life so much as being part owner and front man for the 76ers; unlike most owners, he even accompanied the team on routine road trips. And he was feeling good, vindicated in his decision to acquire Chamberlain, who, as Richman had predicted, had decided to return to the team instead of retiring when Richman offered him a three-year contract at $100,000 a year.*

Despite the strains between Chamberlain and Schayes, the 76ers had come within two points of beating Boston in the playoffs the previous season. This season, with the team just a game or two out of first place in the Eastern Division, they were looking even better. Chamberlain and Schayes hardly spoke, but the rest of the team ignored that matter and it no longer affected anyone's performance. Two new players, rookie Billy Cunningham and Wally Jones from Baltimore, gave the 76ers mobility and speed to complement the strength of Chamberlain and the big forwards, Luke Jackson and Chet Walker. The team appeared to have a solid shot at the championship, Convention Hall was drawing record numbers of fans, and *The Philadelphia Inquirer,* which used to condescend only to publish the 76ers' box scores, now had a reporter, Gordon Forbes, regularly covering the team.

Richman liked having the reporters around, and he was always available for a quote or a joke. He had once been part owner of a summer resort in the Poconos, South Mountain Manor, where Joey Bishop and other comedians

*Bill Russell countered this by demanding, and receiving, a contract for $100,001 a year.

performed, and he loved kidding around with them; Richman's partner, Irv Kosloff, always thought that Richman himself could have become a stand-up comic if he had so chosen. Richman liked to set up gags for the sportswriters and his team, playing each group against the other, making everyone aware it was all for laughs. The previous year, after a game in which the 76ers had been badly beaten by the Royals, Richman had kept the reporters outside the dressing room while he talked to his team. "Can't you give me a good game once in a while?" he asked loudly. "I'm not kidding you, any more of this stuff and I'm going to shuffle the deck!" He ducked outside and with a grin asked the reporters, "You guys got all that?"

At breakfast on the morning of December 3, Richman had told Schayes and the team's trainer, Al Domenico, that he wasn't feeling well, but when they suggested he return to Philadelphia, he insisted on coming to the game. Richman had wanted to play basketball back when he was a student at Philadelphia's Southern High School, but at five-seven he lacked the height and any compensating talent, and he had instead become Southern High's biggest rooter, a presence at every game, making loud jokes, urging on his team, jeering at the opponents, berating officials. He considered that to be his role with the 76ers as well, and this night in Boston he was behaving the way he always did at his team's games, yelling nonstop at the officials: *Havlicek was traveling! Russell touched the ball! Cunningham was fouled!* Yelling at his own players, too: *Handsup, handsup . . . lotsa hands, lotsa hands—get those handsup!*

Suddenly, five minutes into the game with the score tied 13–13, Richman made a choking noise and slumped over onto the shoulder of Al Bianchi, the player sitting at the end of the bench. Bianchi caught him, held him in his arms and then, realizing he was unconscious, lowered him to the floor. Dolph Schayes saw that his boss was down and shouted for a doctor. Auerbach and Celtics trainer Buddy LeRoux ran from the other end of the court and helped carry Richman behind the 76ers bench. The players crowded around while Al Domenico felt his pulse, tore open his shirt, and began pounding on his chest.

Dr. John Doherty, the Celtics team physician, hurried from his seat and quickly checked Richman's vital signs. There was no heartbeat, no pulse, no blood pressure. Doherty placed an oxygen mask over Richman's face and gave him an injection of adrenaline, but the vital signs remained flat. The Philadelphia players watched in stunned silence as medics arrived, lifted Richman onto a stretcher, and carried him off the court.

Domenico accompanied Richman to the hospital, where he was officially declared dead. He was only fifty-two. The trainer called Richman's wife, Clare. She had been watching the game on television at their home in Philadelphia and had seen her husband collapse beside the court but had no idea what had happened. It fell to Domenico to inform her that he had died. "Tell the team, 'Win this game for Ike, win it for him,' " she said.

When Domenico returned to the Garden, it was halftime and the 76ers were sitting in the locker room in a state of distracted worry, waiting for word. The players all liked Richman, who was generous as well as enthusiastic; both Chamberlain and Wally Jones had lived for a while with him and his family on Heather Road in Elkins Park when they needed a place to stay. Domenico told them Richman had had a heart attack; the doctors figured he was dead by the time he hit the floor. The players and Schayes discussed whether or not they should call off the game. To go back out and finish it as if nothing had happened seemed unthinkable. But Domenico told the team that Richman's wife had asked them to win in memory of her husband. Domenico also told them that Richman would have wanted them to play on, that they could honor him best by playing, and by winning.

At the end of halftime, the players returned to the floor and halfheartedly took some warm-up shots. No one felt like playing. What they had all just witnessed—the death of their boss—was too shocking and upsetting. On top of that, the 76ers had continued their losing streak at the Garden and now, at nineteen straight games, the jinx had acquired almost mystical proportions.

Then the second half started and a strange thing happened. The Philadelphia players developed an unexpected momentum. It was as if by playing— and playing well, playing hard, *lotsa hands*—they could work through or give expression to the grief they were feeling. And as their momentum developed, they went on a scoring spree, racking up basket after basket and ending the game ahead by sixteen points. It was the first time the Celtics had lost a home game since the previous March, and it was the first time in the three-year history of the 76ers that they had beaten Boston in the Garden. For the 76ers, it suddenly began to seem that, this season, anything might be possible.

THAT FALL Howard Cosell interviewed Wilt Chamberlain, and there was one particular subject that Cosell wanted to explore. He was just beginning to develop his reputation as a distinctively sardonic and opinionated broadcaster. He had by then been appearing for a year on *ABC's Wide World of Sports,* but he had started in radio, and he continued to provide a syndicated broadcast for ABC Radio. At the start of his career, he had witnessed the influx of black athletes into major-league sports and had anticipated, as he once put it, the "whole new set of smoldering problems that would emerge." But Cosell had gone into sports broadcasting wanting to move it away from the rip-and-read wire-service summations of games and toward all of the issues that surrounded the actual competition: personality conflicts, strategy, political intrigue, money and ambition, racial tensions. While he appeared at times to have contentious relationships with black athletes such as Muhammad Ali and Wilt Chamberlain, he was actually sympathetic toward them; his forceful questions were merely designed to elicit the most provocative and newsworthy answers. That fall, in his interview with Chamberlain, he asked, "Bluntly put to you, a Negro player, are we reaching the point . . . where perhaps there are too many Negro players in the National Basketball Association for box-office appeal?"

"I definitely think that probably we have," Chamberlain replied. "I think that [there] has been sort of like a stagnant box-office attraction due to the fact that we are somewhat overpopulated with . . . first-class and star Negro players."

It was certainly true that the number of black players had dramatically increased. In the 1955–56 season, the league had eighty players but only six were black, and Maurice Stokes was the sole black all-star. Ten years later, at the start of the 1965–66 season, forty-seven of the ninety-nine players were black. More important, thirty-one of the forty-five starters were black, as were fourteen of the twenty all-stars, which meant that not only were blacks more prevalent, they were dominating the game.

But in fact, the NBA's box office was not stagnant during this period. Overall, ticket sales had grown by 50 percent since 1960, an annual increase of 10 percent—equivalent to the rate at which attendance was growing in professional football, and double the growth rate for baseball. If anything, the rate of growth for basketball seemed to be increasing. Ticket sales the previous year were up 12 percent from the year before. And in the first month of the 1965–66 season, they were up 30 percent.

Nonetheless, the issue of race in the NBA, long confined to bitter asides by players such as Russell, had now become a subject of open debate, as Cosell's interview with Chamberlain indicated. John Devaney began preparing an article for *Sport* magazine to appear in mid-winter that would be titled "Pro Basketball's Hidden Fear: Too Many Negroes in the NBA? It's the Great Concern Among the Owners, But Is It Justified?" Devaney found that, while owners would rather win with a team featuring blacks than lose with a white team, they recognized that it was white players who were the true crowd-pleasers among the fans, almost all of whom were white, and they did what they could to emphasize the presence of whites on their teams. Sometimes they started a game with several white players, but by the end of the first quarter shifted to an all-black lineup. To balance their black starters, they signed white bench players, which meant that once black players aged or slowed, they were more likely to be dropped than turned into substitutes. Roone Arledge had been pleasantly surprised the year before, when the seventeen NBA games he paid $650,000 for ABC to broadcast had attracted 20 percent of the viewing audience, but some producers felt that with white stars the programs would have done considerably better. "I'm only being realistic," one broadcaster told Devaney, "when I say that if a white center were to come along to challenge Chamberlain or Russell, the ratings for those games would jump at least fifty percent."

These tensions remained unresolved. If anything, it seemed clear that they would intensify since the college players of the day who seemed most likely to form the new crop of NBA superstars—Lew Alcindor of UCLA (later to become Kareem Abdul-Jabbar), Louisville's Westley Unseld, Michigan's Cazzie Russell—were uniformly black. Black basketball players were now in the strange position of feeling that they had become the dominant force in a league that was not entirely happy with their presence, and this fostered a more militant outlook.

While overall attendance throughout the league was growing, it varied from city to city, and in his interview with Cosell, Chamberlain pointed out that box-office receipts for the Celtics, despite their unparalleled string of championships, had been more or less flat for the last five years. In 1960, when the team had white stars such as Bob Cousy and Bill Sharman playing alongside Russell, average game attendance had been 7,448. In 1965, by which time Cousy and Sharman had been replaced in the backcourt by black players Sam Jones and K. C. Jones, average attendance was only 8,779—meaning ticket sales had grown by less than 5 percent a year. Chamberlain asked Cosell why a team with a record like the Celtics' did not draw a capacity crowd every night whereas the Bruins, who had finished in last place for the last five years, virtually filled the house whenever they played.

"Are you saying to me," Cosell asked, "that one of the reasons hockey plays to ninety-four percent attendance capacity is because it is all white?"

"I definitely believe that," Chamberlain said.

It was true that fewer than 10,000 fans showed up for the average Celtics game. The team's racial composition may have been a factor, but another factor was that, in the mid-sixties, basketball in Boston still lacked the tradition of the city's baseball and hockey teams. The middling attendance also reflected less a dislike of basketball or the Celtics than it did frustration with the curious architecture of the Boston Garden. The Garden had been designed as a hockey arena. When the basketball court was set up, almost half its seats wound up beyond the two ends of the court, and many had partially obstructed views. In fact, the view of the basketball court was excellent from only 7,500 seats. Any time attendance rose above that, it indicated that the game was such a strong draw that some fans were prepared to put up with bad seats to watch it.

The presence of black players had certainly not driven away white fans, as owners once feared they might. The previous year, Tommy Heinsohn had been injured for much of the season, and in his place Auerbach had often started Willie Naulls, the veteran black player he had signed in 1963. That meant the team was sometimes starting five blacks: Naulls, Russell, Satch Sanders, and Sam and K. C. Jones, referred to collectively by fans as the Jones boys. Although it was a historic moment—the first time any franchise in the NBA had started an all-black team—the development caused muttering among some fans but provoked no public outcry or even much formal acknowledgment.

In fact, some people tried to hold the Celtics up as a model of integration in a city increasingly divided along racial lines. Back in April, an advisory committee to the state's secretary of education had released a report detailing racial imbalance in the city's schools—sixteen of them were 96 percent black and received a disproportionately small amount of funding—but

Louise Day Hicks, chairwoman of the School Committee, had rejected the report and refused to consider remedies such as busing, a position that had led to a strike by black students. "The [Celtics team] offers a lesson in human relations in the midst of the school imbalance controversy," Bob Hoobing wrote in the *Herald*. "No group ever exposed the racial bigots so quickly and decisively. The writer vividly recalls a conversation last year in which one citizen said: 'The Celtics wouldn't dare put five Negroes on the court at the same time. Nobody would come to see 'em.' " Hoobing added, "Not one customer has yet been heard calculating the ratio of skin color on the squad before buying his ticket."

THE CELTICS had named no replacement for Auerbach when he announced his retirement plans, and speculation began immediately about who would succeed him. The decision was essentially Auerbach's, and it was an extremely vexing one. The team, while aging, was still a perfectly tuned machine. Whenever a player retired, Auerbach always managed to find a new player—often a player discarded by some other club, such as Willie Naulls—whom he was able to integrate into the team without ever changing its fundamental character. Any new coach, hired from outside the team, would bring his own values and experiences with him, and even if he insisted that his job was simply to carry on the Celtics tradition, he could not help but tinker with the machine, and that could destroy its exquisite calibration. Also, the team's best players—with the exception of the relatively young Havlicek—were all experienced, and were even by now somewhat weather-beaten veterans who knew each other so intimately that their on-court interaction was reflexive and almost unthinking. They might get prickly if a stranger started ordering them around.

Particularly Russell. When Auerbach thought about it, he could not imagine anyone else in the league coaching Russell. Or, to put it another way, he could not imagine Russell allowing himself to be coached—to be ordered around, to be criticized and second-guessed—by anyone else. Auerbach himself had been able to do it because he'd been working with Russell since Russell was a twenty-two-year-old rookie. But Russell was now thirty-one. He had won seven championships. He was proud, independent, testy, and acutely sensitive to criticism. No stranger coming in out of the cold could possibly have the authority to tell Russell what to do, and that meant the new coach would have to come from the ranks of former Celtics.

Auerbach thought Frank Ramsey, who'd retired in 1964, would make a good coach. Ramsey had not been the best player on the team, but the truly good coaches, like Alex Hannum and like Auerbach himself, were rarely the top players. Instead they were often the journeymen, whose supporting roles gave them an appreciation for the function of all positions and required them to get along with all types of players. Auerbach called Ramsey, who'd returned to his hometown of Madisonville, Kentucky, and become a prosperous businessman, running, among other interests, three nursing homes. Ramsey was willing to take over the team on an interim basis, until Auerbach found a permanent replacement, but he felt that his various businesses were too lucrative for him to give them up, even to coach a championship basketball team.

Next, Auerbach talked to Bob Cousy about the job, but Cousy seemed to Auerbach to have his hands full coaching Boston College, which played only twenty-six games a season, and Auerbach wondered if he'd be up to the demands of an eighty-game schedule. Cousy, for his part, said he thought it would be a bad idea for him to try to coach his former teammates. He also feared that the pressure of coaching a pro team, without the relief provided by actually playing, might be too intense. College was bad enough; at one point when he'd started coaching Boston College, his anxiety had caused his large intestine literally to twist itself into knots.

Tommy Heinsohn, despite his reputation as the team clown, had a forceful personality, a bright mind, and leadership qualities—as he had demonstrated in bringing the players together to stand up to the owners in the threatened walkout in 1964—and Auerbach considered him as a possible replacement. But he told Auerbach he didn't think he could handle Russell. Heinsohn in fact didn't think anybody could handle Russell. He was too proud and too moody, and he was acutely aware of how indispensable he was. It seemed inconceivable to Heinsohn that Russell would allow some former teammate, much less a stranger, to tell him what to do. "Why don't you make Russell the coach?" Heinsohn told Auerbach. "He's got so much damn pride he'll handle himself."

Russell was an obvious possibility. But, as Auerbach knew, Russell had always said he would never want to coach. Sitting on the bench or pacing up and down the sidelines yelling at his team while unable to play himself seemed impossibly frustrating. If he was playing at the same time he was coaching, however, that wouldn't be a problem. There was also the question of whether Russell could be effective as a coach, if he was capable of critiquing all the other players and planning strategy at the same time that he was playing himself. And what if his own performance was subpar? Who was going to call him on it?

Still, with none of Auerbach's other possibilities panning out, Russell led the list simply by default. Auerbach didn't broach the matter directly with him until March, when the Celtics were in Detroit to play the Pistons. Before the game, he invited Russell to his hotel room and said, "How would you like the job?"

"What job?" Russell asked.

"My coaching job," Auerbach said.

"You putting me on?" Russell asked.

"No, I'm serious," Auerbach said. "I think you can handle it."

"Let me think about it," Russell said.

AFTER THE OPERATION on his broken kneecap during the previous year's playoffs, Elgin Baylor had spent six weeks getting about on crutches in his hip-to-ankle cast. Once his physician, Dr. Kerlan, removed the cast, the knee felt sore and stiff, and was difficult to bend. Kerlan at first confined Baylor to walking, then started him riding a bicycle and jogging laps around a track. From there he went on to running up and down bleacher stairs, then Kerlan attached weights to his ankle and had him do leg lifts. But the stiffness and soreness seemed, if anything, worse.

Baylor was determined to play professional basketball again, but there was so little progress with his knee during the summer that he began to realize that he might not have a future in the game. He started talking with his wife, Ruby, about the possibilities of life after the NBA, the different career paths that might be available to him. He kept saying *just in case,* and he kept up with Kerlan's program of workouts and physical therapy, but he was having trouble sleeping, and it was clear to his wife how worried he had become.

When the Lakers training camp opened in September, Baylor still had not recovered. Nor was he ready to play when the season officially began. From time to time, coach Schaus injected him into scrimmages during practices, but only for brief intervals before taking him out. Baylor, Schaus thought, looked pathetic, so stiff-legged he was practically hobbling. Baylor was tight-lipped about his condition, and no one on the team knew what he was really going through, but Schaus was as close to him as anyone, and Schaus had a strong sense of how demoralized Baylor felt. Schaus himself had more or less given up hope. The situation seemed to him almost tragic. Baylor was desperate to play again, but he was also holding back, afraid that his body might not allow him to do the one thing he most wanted to do, afraid as well that if he pushed too hard, his knee might shatter into pieces, and he'd never even play golf again, much less basketball.

Finally, Baylor insisted Schaus play him in an actual game. Dr. Kerlan gave his approval, and before the game Baylor was given an extra dose of Novocain. His performance was dismal. He could still shoot, but he was erratic, and on defense he was tentative and slow, moving with that awkward hobble he'd developed. It was clear he had completely lost confidence in himself, and Schaus used him only sporadically. After games, the trainer wrapped his left knee in ice. Baylor had been favoring that knee, the bad knee, and that put an extra strain on his right knee. During a game in November, he made a sudden off-balance move and ended up straining the ligaments in it. Schaus put him on the injured-reserve list, and Dr. Kerlan now decided that his entire right leg should be encased in a hip-to-ankle cast, just as his left had been six months earlier.

Baylor was sidelined for a month. When he returned his self-confidence was, if anything, worse than before. Schaus, thinking a subpar Baylor was better than no Baylor, put him into a game against San Francisco, but then he regretted it. The Warriors' new shooting star, Rick Barry, began dancing rings around the hobbling Baylor, scoring practically at will and rendering Baylor virtually useless on offense. Much as he knew it would hurt Baylor's self-confidence, Schaus pulled him out of the game after only seven minutes.

At that point, Baylor realized he could either give up or simply develop some patience and wait for his knees to improve. After all, he told himself, he'd had only five months of rest and rehabilitation before going to training camp. Maybe he had come back too soon. Weeks passed. Baylor tested his knees every day without pushing them, but it was not until the middle of the season that they seemed like they might support him. He was still tentative on the court, however. Dr. Kerlan suspected that his problem might be psychological and urged him to go all out. And so in a game in January, Baylor truly pushed himself, running, even jumping, and when he found his knees supported him, he ran harder and jumped higher. The knees held up. He could play.

Baylor knew his body was never going to be what it had been six years earlier, that he no longer had the sheer physical ability of his younger, faster opponents such as Barry, but he had his years of experience. If he concentrated, undistracted now by worries about his knees, he could outthink his younger rivals, playing them tight, throwing them off-balance with unexpected moves, even going for rebounds. He began to readjust his game, and in February, he led the Lakers to a victory over Cincinnati, scoring twenty-nine points and pulling in twenty-one rebounds. It was a victory worthy of Baylor's heyday, and he felt jubilant. "The old pro with the aching legs wound up the big man," the *Los Angeles Times* declared the next day. One magazine headline celebrated "The Elgin Baylor Miracle."

BEATING THE CELTICS in Boston Garden had been a pivotal moment for the 76ers. The Celtics, after that home-court defeat, lost their aura of invincibility, and began to seem more like just another basketball team, talented but aging, with most of their starting players now in their thirties, and undeniably vulnerable. Boston had ended the previous season twenty-two games ahead of Philadelphia, but now, as the 1965–66 season progressed, the two teams traded the lead. The Celtics enjoyed a slight advantage for most of the winter, then the 76ers won a pair of back-to-back encounters with the Celtics in early March and took a one-game lead. The Celtics wanted to win the regular season and rest for two weeks while the second- and third-place teams fought the opening round of the playoffs. They did the best they could, winning all six of their remaining regular-season games, but the 76ers won all of their remaining games as well, and ended the season with that same narrow one-game lead.

It was the first time in ten years that Boston had failed to finish the season in first place in the Eastern Division, and the Celtics' Sam Jones thought Billy Cunningham, the 76ers rookie forward, was the reason. Cunningham had what was rare in a rookie: a complete game. He drove, passed, jumped, and rebounded, and when he didn't have the ball, he moved instead of standing around like so many rookies did, waiting to be told what to do. Cunningham, who was the son of a New York City fireman and had been re-cruited by Frank McGuire to play for North Carolina, also had an appealing cockiness that had made him an immediate hit with the Philadelphia fans.

Boston beat Cincinnati in the qualifying round, and as the Celtics pre-pared to face the 76ers in the Eastern Division finals, Red Auerbach felt that the team's biggest challenge was Cunningham. He had been punishing against Boston throughout the season, scoring but creating even more trou-ble by rebounding. Auerbach figured Cunningham's one weakness was his lack of playoff experience. He'd never been there, and nothing prepared a rookie for it—the back-to-back games against the same team, the packed houses, the tension mounting with each successive match. Before the series started, Auerbach directed the Celtics to concentrate all the intensity of their defense on Cunningham, even if that meant neglecting the other 76ers. "Maybe if we press the kid and upset him," Auerbach said, "Schayes will do us a favor and sit him down."

In the first game, when Cunningham came in off the bench, the Celtics bore in on him, pressing, pressing. Cunningham became disconcerted, missed seven straight baskets, and heard a new and disturbing sound: the fans booing him. In the second game, the Celtics continued pressing him, and he made only one shot in nine attempts, a performance so dismal that Schayes benched him for the entire third game. Cunningham went from feel-ing confused to feeling dismayed to feeling mortified. It was the worst cold streak in his career. Even with the Celtics pressing him, he was getting open now and then and taking shots, but the ball simply would not go through the hoop, and he had no idea why. All he could do was keep plugging away at it, if he got a chance to play.

In Schayes's mind, Cunningham was simply a rookie who had lost his game, a not uncommon experience in an untested young man in the pressure of the playoffs, and he didn't count him out altogether. Philadelphia man-aged to take the third game, and in the fourth game, Schayes, ever hopeful, sent in Cunningham yet again. Pressed by Boston, he promptly missed five out of six baskets. Schayes took him out and Philadelphia lost. In the fifth game, with Boston up 3–1 and the series at stake, Schayes sent in Cunning-ham once more. But the Celtics, still following Auerbach's instructions, again focused their defensive energy on him, and he made only one out of seven shots before Schayes ordered him back out.

With Cunningham sitting on the bench the model of dejection, shaking his head and looking at the floor, Boston won. If, as the sportswriters had been saying, it was Cunningham who had made the difference for the 76ers during the regular season, he had failed to make a difference in the playoffs, and he couldn't help but feel that the team's loss was his responsibility. The series had been one long nightmare for Cunningham, it seemed to Joe McGinniss of the *Philadelphia Bulletin,* and now the nightmare was over.

AS THE REGULAR SEASON had ended and the playoffs had begun, Red

Auerbach had kept talking to Bill Russell about the prospect of replacing him as coach of the Celtics. He stressed the fact that none of the men he'd talked to wanted the job, in part because the notion of coaching Russell himself was so daunting. The point was clear: if no one was willing to become Russell's coach, Russell would need to become his own coach.

Russell still wouldn't commit, so Auerbach asked him if he'd be willing to be coached by Alex Hannum, who'd just been fired as coach of the Warriors. Russell at first accepted the idea, then changed his mind, deciding he did not after all want an outsider coming in, and just as the final series with the Lakers was about to begin, he told Auerbach he'd take the job. He'd decided he could do it, and he liked the idea of proving to the world that he could, especially since that meant sticking it to all those fans—in Boston and elsewhere—who'd shouted racial slurs when he took the court.

Auerbach and Russell held a press conference announcing the decision the day after the first game with the Lakers. Reporters from Los Angeles and New York as well as Boston attended, and the lobby of the Hotel Lenox was strewn with the television equipment of fourteen different camera crews. Asked why he took the job, Russell said, "Being something of a nut, I thought it might be fun." Auerbach explained that, although he himself was going to take the position of general manager and run the team's front office, Russell would be making all the coaching decisions. "I'm not going to sit anywhere near him," he said. "I'm not going to be near the bench in practice or at games." But that was next year, he went on. The Celtics still had the finals in front of them and were looking forward to their next game against the Lakers. "We are leaving for L.A. on TWA at nine o'clock."

"In the morning?" Russell asked.

"You ain't coaching yet, baby," Auerbach said.

When Auerbach was named coach sixteen years earlier, *The Boston Globe* had carried the story on the inside pages, surrounded by racing results and local high school sports scores. But the editors of *The New York Times* considered Russell's hiring so momentous that they ran their article about it on the front page, next to stories on bombing strikes near Hanoi, proposed peace talks between the United States and Vietnam, and the Ford Motor Company's recall of thirty thousand vehicles for safety defects. Milton Gross saw Russell's appointment as a milestone, and in his laconic, hard-boiled prose he celebrated it as such. "Once he had contended in a national magazine article that the NBA had a quota system, unwritten, unspoken, but real," he wrote in the *Post*. "Now here he is the first Negro to coach a big league team. He will not be the last."

The next day, Russell took Gross in his white Mercedes convertible out to lunch at Slade's, the restaurant Russell owned in the Roxbury section of Boston. When Gross asked Russell if he considered himself a racial pioneer in a league with Jackie Robinson, Russell resisted the social significance of his appointment. "I wasn't offered the job because I am a Negro," he said. "I was offered it because Red figured I could handle it."

THE FINALS BETWEEN the Lakers and the Celtics was another tough, high-scoring series that went to the seventh game, which was played on April 28, 1966, and was Auerbach's last game as coach of the Boston Celtics. He slept well the night before, but he woke up that morning thinking, *This is the day.* The Celtics had never lost a seventh game in any playoff series, but still Auerbach had to keep reminding himself that anything could happen in any given match. At one o'clock, he ate a corned-beef sandwich and drank a Coke, but ten minutes later he threw up. That did not particularly bother him. He wanted to be hungry going into the game, hungry and focused and on edge.

Before the game, the Celtics dressing room was particularly quiet. Auerbach felt that there was little to say. In any event, he'd been suffering from strep throat for days, and so, instead of opting for an inspirational speech, he discussed strategy. Lakers rookie Gail Goodrich was capable of dangerous bursts of scoring if guarded carelessly, he said, and he warned Sam Jones to play him close.

"You hear me good?" Auerbach asked.

"I hear," Jones said.

"You stay in that kid's jock."

Auerbach then pointed out that so far the team had won $30,000 in play-off money and that if it won tonight it would take home another $28,000. That was a lot of money, Auerbach said, and it was worth pouring out their hearts and their guts for forty-eight minutes. Then, on a final note, he added that there was one more reason to win. If they did, they wouldn't have to spend their summer explaining to everyone they met why they had lost.

Even though Elgin Baylor's knees had healed, he was not the player he once was, and the Lakers had come to rely even more on Jerry West. But now, in the final game against Boston, West suddenly went cold, hitting only two out of nine shots in the first half. Baylor was even worse, going one for nine, and Gail Goodrich, with Sam Jones all over him, could not make up the difference. By the third quarter, Boston was up by nineteen points, and as the second half wound down Los Angeles was able to do little more than chip away at the lead. It was as if the Lakers by then had surrendered to the idea of the Celtics mystique, as if they actually believed it was impossible for them, or for any team, to beat the Celtics in the seventh game of a championship series.

With a minute left, Boston was ten points ahead. Massachusetts governor John Volpe, who was sitting courtside near Auerbach, assumed the game's conclusion was foregone, and he leaned over and lit Auerbach's cigar for him. The fans, similarly assuming the game was over, surged out of their seats and down onto the court, where a few of them started climbing the basket supports. The referees had to halt the game and clear the parquet, but instead of returning to their seats, the fans stood along the perimeter of the court, waiting to rush onto it.

When play resumed, one of the Celtics slipped on some orange soda a fan had spilled on the floor, the team's defense was thrown off, and Jerry West immediately scored. Within seconds he stole the ball from Russell, scored again, and suddenly the Lakers were down by only six. Russell had expected them to surge at some point during the game, and now, with less than a minute to play, it was happening. Los Angeles got the ball again on an offensive foul and quickly scored a third time. Then Sam Jones, unnerved by the sudden Lakers surge, allowed a pass to slip through his hands and bounce out of bounds, giving control of the ball back to Los Angeles. Their center,

Leroy Ellis, promptly scored on a jump shot, and with four seconds left, the Lakers trailed by only two.

Auerbach sat frozen on the bench. The cigar—*the victory cigar*—smoldered between his fingertips. People had often wondered if Auerbach wasn't jinxing a game by lighting up prematurely, before it had actually ended. Auerbach always claimed that it had happened only once, in the early days, in a game against Providence; with ten seconds left and his team ahead by three, he had lit up, only to see a Providence player fouled while scoring and then make the foul shot to send the game into overtime. Now, with the Lakers down by two and four seconds left to play in the seventh game of a championship series, in what was his last game as coach of the greatest dynasty in sports history, Auerbach wondered if he had, once again, lit up prematurely. Would he go out looking like a goat?

Boston had the ball. With four seconds left, the Lakers would try to foul, hoping to send a Celtic to the line, where Los Angeles could rebound a missed point and take one final shot to try to tie the game. Russell passed in to K. C. Jones. The clock began. Before anyone could foul him, Jones passed to John Havlicek, who was standing downcourt with no Lakers nearby. Havlicek simply held on to the ball, and before any of the Lakers could get to him, time ran out, and the fans rushed onto the floor.

Milton Gross—whose motto was *Run with the pack and you'll read like the pack*—was always searching for that special angle that would distinguish his column from the straightforward game stories most of the sportswriters filed. In one of his most celebrated pieces, he had left the press box during the seventh game of the 1956 World Series, searched the locker room for Don Newcombe, the pitcher for the Brooklyn Dodgers who had folded under the pressure of the game, then accompanied him home and wrote a moving account of Newcombe's emotional distress called "Long Ride Home." Gross decided to reemploy this technique for Auerbach's last game, and once it was over, he hooked up with the coach to accompany him home.

When Auerbach and Gross finally left the Garden, Auerbach found a parking ticket under his car's windshield wiper. He'd had so much good luck, he told Gross, he figured he deserved a little bad luck every now and then. The two men went up to Auerbach's suite at the Hotel Lenox, with its ninth-floor view of the Boston Public Library. Auerbach, who hadn't eaten since he regurgitated that corned-beef sandwich at one o'clock, was ravenous. He called the Chinese restaurant from which he always ordered takeout and asked for wonton soup, egg rolls, chicken wings in oyster sauce, spare ribs, roast pork, and steak cubes. The person who had answered the phone at the restaurant asked who was calling. "Auerbach, who do you think?" he asked. "And hurry. I'm starving."

The suite was cluttered with accumulated memorabilia, the mantelpiece lined with bottles of Chinese noodles, jars of nuts, and the countless letter openers Auerbach collected. He sat down in a chair and rubbed his face. He was still tense from the game, and he was still wearing the clothes that had gotten soaked when the Celtics threw him into the shower.

"What would you have done if you had lost the game?" Gross asked.

"I don't know," Auerbach said. "I would really be down, but a lot would have depended on how we lost. If we went down swinging, it wouldn't be so bad. I wouldn't have said anything to the team. Certainly not about choking in the clutch. How could I have said anything after all these years?" He paused. "Where the hell's that food?"

"Before the game," Gross asked, "did you say anything to the team about this being your last game?"

"You mean, 'Win it for me'?" Auerbach asked. "Are you crazy? They're pros. I never mentioned myself and I never would."

Auerbach thought back on the long season he'd just completed, on all the coaches like Fred Schaus who had pursued him as if in some sort of vendetta and all the jeering, booing, Celtics-hating fans around the league who had prayed for his defeat. "If they were going to beat me, this was their shot," he said. "And they couldn't."

IN THE DRESSING ROOM after the 76ers' final playoff loss to Boston, Chamberlain had crossed the floor to Dolph Schayes and extended his hand.

"Great year," Schayes said.

"Great year for you, too," Chamberlain said.

And it was. At the end of the season, Dolph Schayes was voted Coach of the Year for winning fifty-five games and leading the 76ers, one of the worst teams in the league two years earlier, to their first-place finish in the Eastern Division. A few weeks later, however, Irv Kosloff fired him. Many sports-writers assumed that Chamberlain had had Schayes fired; one columnist, noting that Chamberlain had gone through five coaches in seven years, declared that he was "devouring them like aspirin tablets." Chamberlain's dissatisfaction was certainly a factor. "Wilt thought I was a rotten coach," Schayes recalled years later. Schayes always felt that his biggest problem was his failure to communicate with Wilt. But Chamberlain's dissatisfaction aside, Irv Kosloff also felt that, under Schayes, the 76ers were not going to become the championship team that, given their talent, they should be. And for whatever reason, Schayes had been unable to establish his authority over the team's star player.

Shortly afterward, Kosloff called Alex Hannum. Franklin Mieuli had fired Hannum because the year Mieuli had traded Chamberlain, against Hannum's advice, the Warriors had ended the season in last place in their division—in fact, the sixty-three games lost by the Warriors in 1964–65 set an NBA record for worst team performance—and followed that up with a second losing year. Still, Hannum had coached Chamberlain successfully once, and he was still the only coach in the league who had beaten Auerbach in a championship series in the last ten years. But Hannum considered Schayes a friend, since he had played with him and coached him on the Nationals, and he was uncomfortable talking about taking over a friend's job behind that friend's back. "Listen, he's gone," Kosloff said. "Either you're going to coach this team or someone else will."

Although Hannum realized that nothing short of a championship would satisfy Kosloff, he believed the team had the talent to win one, and he took the job. Chamberlain was, of course, the key to the team's championship ambitions, and since he had worked productively with Hannum three years earlier in San Francisco, both Hannum and Kosloff expected that he would look forward to renewing the relationship. But Chamberlain was unhappy with the contract he'd signed just the previous year. Bill Russell, who had been given a raise when named player-coach, was now earning substantially more than Chamberlain, and Wilt wanted a raise. Then, two weeks before the start of the 76ers training camp, a fire destroyed Chamberlain's San Francisco duplex, where he still stayed during the off-season. Distraught, he had gone down to live with his parents in Villa Chamberlain, the Los Angeles apartment building he'd built, and when the 76ers front office couldn't find him, the press reported that he was missing. Chamberlain eventually showed up in the middle of an exhibition match against the Knicks, overweight and unrepentant. "I wasn't missing," he said. "I knew where I was."

Chamberlain had just turned thirty and was at his peak as an athlete. He was also wealthy and independent. He had shrewdly invested in real estate and mutual funds, and had bought a Harlem nightclub, Small's Paradise, where he could be seen in the company of people such as the writer James Baldwin. He was perpetually dissatisfied and never seemed to go out with the same woman more than twice, but was also usually generous with fans, willing to spend time talking to sick children, and remained loyal and close to his childhood friends from Haddington, getting one of them, Vince Miller, a job as an assistant on the 76ers.

In 1959, when Chamberlain first joined the league, he had been willowy and graceful. But he had now filled out, entirely with muscle—his neck thicker, his shoulders and chest broader, his thighs and calves more muscular—and the impression he gave was not of an extraordinarily tall man but of a massive physical presence, a true giant who had the proportions of normal well-built men but loomed far above them. Chamberlain's exact height was a question of some dispute. He always maintained while a pro that he was seven feet one and one-sixteenth inches tall. As a freshman at the University of Kansas, the athletic department had listed him as seven feet two. But the fact was that he had never allowed anyone to measure him since high school, and some of the people in the NBA swore he was taller than seven-three. They pointed out that the entrance to the shower in the Detroit dressing room was seven feet three inches high, and Chamberlain had to duck to go through it. They noted that center Mel Counts, then with Baltimore, was seven feet tall and when Chamberlain played against him, he appeared several inches taller. They observed that while Chamberlain loved to bet spontaneously on just about anything—the number of birds on a wire, the number of miles from one arena to the next—he'd always refused any bets, and there had been plenty, that he was taller than seven feet one and one-sixteenth.* His weight was a similar mystery. He was officially listed at 250 pounds, but he conceded he was closer to 290, and many people felt he weighed considerably more than 300. "I don't even know how much he weighs," Hannum confessed to an acquaintance. "He won't get on a scale for me."

Most people who met Chamberlain felt intimidated, and that was how he

---

*In 1980, when Chamberlain returned to Philadelphia to be honored along with the other members of the 76ers' 1966–67 team, broadcaster Al Meltzer and Jack Kiser of the *Daily News* urged him to admit he was taller than he had always claimed. Chamberlain agreed to be measured and lay down on a table while the team's publicist, Harvey Pollack, produced a tape measure. The result: seven feet and one-half inch. Chamberlain was actually slightly shorter than he had always claimed; he just appeared taller.

had come to expect them to feel. Anyone challenging him seemed to be violating the natural order. That, however, was exactly what Hannum knew he needed to do. Since the 76ers had essentially the same team as the year before, it was the players, and particularly Chamberlain himself, who were going to have to change if they were to beat the Celtics. Hannum wanted Chamberlain to return, once again, to playing a team-oriented game, and Chamberlain said he was happy to comply. "You know, I can pass the ball as well as anyone in basketball," he told Hannum.

"Fine," Hannum said. "Let's see it."

But Chamberlain was less receptive to Hannum's idea that he play less than a full game. The coach, however, insisted. This team was more talented than the teams Chamberlain had played with earlier in his career, Hannum explained. The other players all wanted and deserved their minutes, and it was good offensive strategy to give the team a different rhythm from time to time. Chamberlain disagreed—a contest of wills with Hannum, at some point over something, seemed almost inevitable given Chamberlain's personality—and when the exhibition schedule got under way, he became surly and uncooperative. Hannum realized that, although he'd actually gone so far as to challenge Chamberlain to a fight in 1963 to get the man's respect, he was going to have to earn it again. Before an exhibition game in Sacramento, when Chamberlain was bad-tempered, Hannum ordered the other players out of the locker room and gave him a blistering lecture, and by the time they emerged, it was obvious to the other players that Hannum had asserted, and Chamberlain had accepted, his authority.

The team's first game of the season, against the Knicks, drew the biggest crowd the 76ers had ever enjoyed on opening night. They beat the Knicks decisively, in part because Chamberlain, who had to be taken out for a spell in the second period after the Knicks' Howie Komives gouged him in the left eye, checked his scoring and concentrated on passing. The 76ers also won their second and third games. They looked good, but they had not yet been seriously tested. Then in late October the Celtics, who were also undefeated, came to Philadelphia for the first matchup of the season between the two archrivals.

WHEN BILL RUSSELL was named player-coach back in the spring, his new contract provided him a salary of $125,000 a year, making him one of the highest-paid athletes and one of the richest black men in the country. His manner by then had become commensurately regal, suave, and even theatrical. In the summer he flew off to Liberia to oversee his rubber plantation and hunt in the jungle. Around Boston, he dressed in his impeccably tailored suits and wore a flowing dark cape that made him look, in the words of one sportswriter, "like the Phantom of the Opera." That year he published his memoir, *Go Up for Glory,* which Leonard Koppett, in his review in *The New York Times,* described as "heartfelt, angry, sometimes disquieting—and frequently instructive . . . a book that is only incidentally about basketball. Essentially it is about being a Negro in America in this generation."

For Russell, the central challenge of being a Negro in America was dealing with what he referred to as "white thinking." It was prevalent, he felt, in and around Boston and was the reason why, although he had been there for eleven years now, he continued to dislike the city. In fact, he'd decided Boston was probably the most rigidly segregated city in the country. Russell and his wife and three children still lived in Reading but had moved to a new house. It was in a more secluded area, on Haverhill Street, surrounded by open fields and trees, but Russell still felt threatened there. He bought his wife a pistol and installed floodlights on the grounds. Once, when he returned from a road trip in the middle of the night, he found Rose sitting up in the kitchen with the gun, frightened by strange noises she thought might be intruders.

After Russell was named coach, he began encountering even more examples of white thinking. Some sportswriters continued to go to Auerbach with their questions, as if he were still the one running the team. And if sportswriters did come to Russell, they often asked the stupidest questions. At his first press conference, one of them asked him if he thought he could judge white players purely on the basis of their ability. Russell treated the questioner politely, as if he had raised a legitimate point, but he was appalled. Other questions he started getting that season were just as bad. Did he become coach to help race relations? If he failed, would this reflect badly on the Negro race? And he continued to be asked about the ability of blacks to coach whites. *Bill, the Celtics all know you, but could a Negro go in cold and manage an unfamiliar team that's three-quarters white?*

In fact, unlike other players who were hired to coach their old teammates, Russell had very little trouble exerting his authority over the Celtics. His cold, remote manner helped. After Russell had taken the job, Auerbach had told him that he was going to be in the difficult position of coaching people who had once been his teammates, that they all knew he liked some of them better than others, that the ones he disliked would expect to be treated unfairly and the ones he liked might think they could take advantage of the friendship. It was therefore essential, Auerbach had said, that Russell treat all the players equally. And so at the breakup dinner at the end of the 1965–66 season, when Russell had had his first chance to address the entire team in his new capacity as coach, he had said that he intended to cut all his ties to the other players. From then on, he intended to act as a coach rather than a teammate.

In September, on the first day of training camp, one of the players decided it would be funny to hide the new coach's sneakers. Russell ordered the team to spend the day running, excusing himself from the exercise because he had no sneakers. As the season began, Russell found other opportunities to assert his authority. He fined one player for wearing a turtleneck sweater to a game and another for leaving gear in the locker room and a third for missing a team plane.

His on-court transition to the role of player-coach was more difficult. Russell had developed such intense concentration as a player that he sometimes was unaware that other players were tiring. On one occasion he simply forgot to relieve K. C. Jones, who ended up playing the entire game despite the fact that, at the age of thirty-four, he was simply too old to stay in for a full forty-eight minutes. Another time, playing the Knicks, Russell forgot he had taken out Havlicek and Sam Jones until someone asked him during a time-out why the team's two top shooters were sitting on the bench in the final minutes of a close game. "I thought you were in all along," Russell said to Sam Jones.

Red would have known, the players told one another on such occasions. But Russell was unfazed. All coaches made minor mistakes, and in any event the team won its first four games by an average of almost twenty points. Auerbach had always liked to start the season strong, build a rapid lead, and then hold it, and in their first year under Russell, the Celtics seemed on the verge of doing this. Then they flew down to Philadelphia for the opening encounter with the team they all knew would be their primary challenger that year.

"THERE'S NO BIG DEAL ABOUT THIS GAME," Hannum had insisted beforehand, but everyone knew that was not true. "This is THE game," Jack Kiser wrote in the *Philadelphia Daily News*. Almost 12,000 fans showed up, setting another attendance record for the 76ers. When the game started, the two teams at first kept pace with each other, but then, beginning in the second quarter, the 76ers for the first time revealed their true potential and went on a scoring rampage that stunned the Celtics, amazed the sportswriters, and stirred the Philadelphia fans into an unprecedented bloodlust. Everyone was scoring except Chamberlain, who devoted himself to rebounding and assists and ended the game with only thirteen points. When the 76ers' lead reached twenty, the crowd screamed for thirty, and when it reached thirty they screamed for forty. Red Auerbach, now the Celtics general manager and no longer entitled to sit on the bench, was in the stands among the Philadelphia fans he had always detested. He had never heard them louder or more charged up. The 76ers, he thought, were driving them into a literal frenzy.

Kill! the crowd screamed as the 76ers' lead continued to grow and the flummoxed Celtics trotted helplessly up and down the court. *Kill! Kill! Kill!* The Celtics' performance was so awful that Auerbach finally couldn't take it anymore, and left the hall before the game was over. The final score was 138–96, the margin of victory for the 76ers an astonishing forty-two points. As Russell walked off the court he glanced at the scoreboard and shook his head in disbelief. It was the single worst defeat in the history of the Celtics franchise, and none of the Boston players could really explain why it had happened. "We just got beat," Russell said after the game. "Beat bad. Beat every way you can get beat."

The 76ers won their next two games as well, which allowed them to argue that, counted with the eleven straight games they had won at the end of the previous season, they had now won eighteen consecutive regular-season games, a league record, although the Celtics and the defunct Washington Capitols, joint holders of the previous record of seventeen straight games, had both done so in a single season. Hannum, however, was more interested in the total number of victories the team was going to amass over the course of the season now under way. The league record at the time, set by the

Celtics in the season that ended in 1965, was sixty-two. Hannum wrote a series of ascending numbers up the side of the wall of the Philadelphia clubhouse, ending with the number seventy. That was the goal for the season total, he explained, and each time the team won another game, he checked off the appropriate number.

Boston later took a game from Philadelphia, but no sooner had the 76ers had their streak broken than they took off on another, going nine games before their second defeat of the season, and then twelve before their third, and then another twelve before their fourth. They went on to win forty-six of their first fifty games, setting another record, and putting them ten games ahead of the Celtics.

Russell thought the 76ers this season were unlike any of the other teams Chamberlain had played on. Until now, Chamberlain had always dominated his teammates in scoring. As a result, the Celtics had always played Wilt's teams by allowing him to get his points and containing his teammates. In the years past it had worked. But they could no longer do that, because now the 76ers had four players—Wilt Chamberlain, Billy Cunningham, Hal Greer, and Chet Walker—who could score consistently. That gave them a diversified game, since one of the four was always bound to have a hot hand.

Indeed, the 76ers called one aspect of their game "milk it," which meant everyone on the team fed the ball to the player with the hot hand. A hot hand could last not just for a run of a few minutes or for a quarter, but for an entire game or even for more than one game. In February, Chamberlain began a game against Baltimore having hit thirteen consecutive baskets at the end of the previous game. As the game progressed, Chamberlain made another sixteen field goals without a miss, which put him within three baskets of the all-time record of thirty-two consecutive field goals. With four minutes left to play, Hannum, unaware that Chamberlain was so close to breaking the record, took him out to rest him. The players informed their coach of what was at stake, however, and he immediately sent Chamberlain back in.

This raised the suspicions of Baltimore's new coach, Gene Shue, who leaped off the bench. "What's up here?" he shouted. "What are they trying to prove?"

A reporter at the press table told Shue how close Chamberlain was to breaking the record for consecutive field goals.

"Well," Shue said loudly, "that asshole isn't going to get any more records tonight!"

Shue ran along the side of the court. The 76ers were ahead of the Bullets by some thirty points—a humiliating margin—and Shue did not want to compound the humiliation by having Chamberlain break yet another record at the expense of his team. "Foul him!" Shue shouted at his players. "Foul the big guy! Don't let him stop to get a shot up! We've got to stop him from getting more baskets!"

Whenever the ball was passed to Chamberlain, the Bullets crowded around him, arms raised, but nonetheless he managed to score twice more before the game was over. Still, Shue had managed to deprive him, by only two baskets, of the satisfaction of setting a new record for consecutive field goals. When reporters gathered around Shue after the game, the coach was in a defiant mood. "He didn't get the record, did he?" he asked. "He needed four and he only got two because we wouldn't let him get four. Nobody but nobody is going to set a record against us if I can help it."

The foul line still plagued Chamberlain. In the beginning of the season, he had come up with yet another shot, moving from the center of the free-throw line to the side, and trying to drill the ball straight in, almost like a line drive. But the first game in which he attempted this, he made fewer than half of his free throws, and he soon returned to the cumbersome, childish underhand shot. His shooting percentage on free throws was so bad that other coaches ordered their players to foul him immediately if he got the ball, realizing that the 76ers were much less likely to score points with Chamberlain shooting fouls than field goals. *Grab him! Grab him!* went the shout from the opposing bench as soon as he received a pass.

Inconsistency with free throws, however, was a minor nuisance because Chamberlain, having submitted however reluctantly to Hannum's guidance, was playing team ball and playing it even more effectively than he had the year that he and the Warriors and Hannum had gone to the finals. Instead of moving into the low post, where he often clogged up the lanes and prevented his teammates from driving to the basket, he took up the high post, by the foul line, where he could pass off to teammates. Since he could easily hold the ball with one hand, he used ruses that resembled old Globetrotter gags, tucking the ball into one teammate's stomach like a quarterback faking a handoff, only to pass it to another. He took one-third as many shots as he'd taken the year he averaged fifty points a game, but he was hitting slightly more than 68 percent of his shots, a league record. And while he was not, for the first time in his career, leading the league in scoring, he had a record number of assists for a center.

One *Sport* magazine headline referred, inevitably, to "The Startling Change in Wilt Chamberlain," but this story, the "new new Wilt," was such a familiar one by now in Chamberlain's career that the writer, Leonard Shecter, tartly observed, "If there had been as many new Wilts in the past eight years as everybody said there were, there would now be a whole basketball team of Wilts—five to play, one to coach. That is, if the five playing Wilts could get along with the coaching Wilt. There is some doubt."

The main effect of Chamberlain's new style was to allow his teammates to put their considerable talents to use. With Chamberlain, Chet Walker, and Luke Jackson, the 76ers had a massive, muscular front line that no other team in the league could match. Jackson, arguably the most valuable player after Chamberlain and certainly the strongest, set picks for the shooters and handled rebounds if Chamberlain was out of position. Walker, a quiet, self-contained man off the court, became startlingly aggressive once the game began, and could take a pass at the baseline, then drive into the lane or swerve up the court to get open. Hal Greer, who had a superb mid-range jump shot and ran the fast break, provided what Hannum thought was a perfect backcourt pairing with veteran Larry Costello, whom sportswriters were fond of referring to as "the last of the two-handed set shooters." Billy Cunningham and Wally Jones came off the bench to contribute energy.

Sportswriters praised the 76ers for their diversified scoring, for their teamwork, for the willingness of players to make winning the game a greater priority than running up their individual statistics. Those had always been the hallmarks of the Celtics, the very qualities that had led sportswriters to argue that the Celtics of, say, the 1961 championship were the greatest team ever to play in the NBA. But as the 1966–67 season reached its midpoint, people were now beginning to say the very same thing about the 76ers. Bill Russell was asked by a reporter if he thought the 76ers were the best team ever to play the game. "They might be," he acknowledged. Others were less equivocal. "This was the best basketball team I ever saw and probably the best of all time," argued Merv Harris, a California sportswriter who had been covering basketball since the early fifties.

The 76ers were also an exceptionally close and harmonious team, by far the most harmonious team Chamberlain had ever played on. "Don't be afraid to praise your teammates," Hannum had told him shortly after arriving. He did, and his teammates, for the first time, felt appreciated and essential. They were no longer simply porters bringing the ball to Chamberlain. When Chamberlain had first joined the 76ers, it had, like most teams in the league, two racially distinct cliques. Whites such as Al Bianchi and Johnny Kerr formed one group, and the blacks—Hal Greer, Chet Walker, Luke Jackson—formed another. But now it became much more integrated, and Billy Cunningham, an Irish New Yorker, ended up as one of Chamberlain's best friends.

Members of other teams rarely saw one another between games—most of the Celtics went their separate ways—but the 76ers became a gang, heading over to Pagano's, an Italian restaurant on Chester Street, after most games, and inviting one another to their houses. Whites and blacks went to the movies together, pulled pranks, played golf, drank beer, and helped one another pick up women. A couple of days after that annihilating victory over Boston in late October, Chamberlain held a Halloween party at the Philadelphia apartment Hannum had persuaded him to occupy for the season. He dressed as an Arab sheikh. Hannum showed up wearing a ballerina's tutu.

IN JANUARY, during a game with Baltimore, Larry Costello, the veteran 76ers guard, wrenched the ligaments in one of his knees, and after the game the team's doctor placed him in a cast that ran all the way from his ankle to his thigh. Wally Jones, who'd played irregularly until then, began filling in for Costello. Jones, known as Wally Wonder, was a colorful player who liked to swing his arms windmill-style on defense and wave his hands after foul shots. During his distinctive jump shot, his legs scissored so far out in front of him that Andy Musser, who called the 76ers games for radio, referred to the move as "the jackknife." Jones, who would later convert to Islam and change his first name to Wali, was considered a crowd-pleasing substitute, capable of hot streaks but not entirely reliable, and Hannum at first feared that without the experienced Costello the team might begin to falter. Jones, however, surprised those who considered him little more than a court clown by running up remarkable scoring totals (thirty-three points in one game, twenty-one in another), and after beating Baltimore the night Costello was injured, the 76ers won their next eight games for another ten-game streak.

Philadelphia ended the regular season with sixty-eight wins and thirteen losses. That record was not only the best record in the league, it was the best in NBA history. It represented a winning percentage of .840, beating a record set by the defunct Washington Capitols back in the forties, before the modern game had evolved. And that was only one of many NBA records the 76ers broke that year. The 10,143 points they scored also set a new record. So did their field-goal percentage of 48.3. So did the fact that in all but one of the eighty-one games they played, they scored 100 or more points.

Because the league had expanded, the board of governors had changed the rules to allow four teams from each division to make it into the playoffs, which meant that the first-place team, instead of resting during the opening round, played the third-place team. Philadelphia faced Cincinnati, and after losing the first game, the team roared back to win the next three and take the series. Boston, meanwhile, polished off the Knicks, and the two great rival teams prepared to meet each other once again. The 76ers, feeling that overconfidence may have been in part responsible for their playoff loss to the Celtics the previous year, approached the series with grim determination. Despite leading Boston by eight games at the end of the regular season, Philadelphia had good reason for caution. The Celtics had proved that they were the only team in the league capable of containing the 76ers, winning five of the nine games the two teams played during the regular season. Both of the two home games the 76ers had lost had been to the Celtics. The one game in which they scored less than one hundred points had been against the Celtics.

Boston had by now won eight consecutive championships. In six of those years, before claiming the title, Russell and the Celtics had needed to get past Chamberlain and one of his teams, and each time, whether from luck or talent, from psychology or coaching or divine intervention, the Celtics seemed ordained to win. And so, as the series began, the one question for sportswriters and basketball fans was: *Will they do it again?* After all, things were different now. The Celtics still had Sam and K. C. Jones, Havlicek, and Satch Sanders, but the average age on the team was thirty-one. Most important, Auerbach, for the first time, would not be coaching. Russell had so far proved he could handle the job, but it was admittedly a disadvantage to simultaneously take part in the game, concentrating on the execution of your particular tasks, and study the moves of all the players on both teams, the way a coach sitting on the bench can do. At a crucial moment in a critical game, Russell might fail to notice a teammate's slight fatigue, or an opponent traveling, or a defender drifting out of position and freeing up the lane—the sort of details to which Auerbach had always been alert and which could lead to a substitution or complaint that could shift the balance of the game.

THE OPENING MATCH was played in Philadelphia at the Palestra because a circus had been booked into Convention Hall. In the first quarter, Chet Walker unintentionally hit Russell in the stomach when Russell closed in to stop his jump shot. Russell crumpled to the floor, vomited, and lay prone for four minutes before he rose, staggered to the bench, still retching, and wrapped a towel around his head. He returned at the start of the second quarter, but never completely recovered, and for every rebound he came up with, Chamberlain had two. Working from the high post, Chamberlain shot infrequently, instead feeding the ball out to the guards for jump shots or passing in to the forwards breaking across the lane. And when one of his teammates missed a shot, he moved in to grab the rebound and dunk. In the third quarter, the 76ers put together a twenty-five-point lead, and while the Celtics managed to narrow it to fourteen points, the outcome never really seemed in doubt.

That first game not only put Philadelphia up by one, it reversed the customary dynamic between the teams. In previous years, every time Chamberlain and one of his teams had met the Celtics in the playoffs, Boston won the first game, establishing a lead that it never relinquished. Now, for the first time, it was the Celtics who would have to come from behind. People had felt Boston had the psychological edge going into the series, but the edge now seemed to shift to Philadelphia.

The second game took place on the parquet floor of the Boston Garden. Chamberlain was playing with sore legs, the hard floor of the Palestra, with no give, having aggravated a case of shin splints. He continued to concentrate on defense while Chet Walker and Wally Jones did most of the scoring. The first half was close, but then Philadelphia surged in the third quarter. Hannum, who could taste victory, was up off the bench, holding his hands together in a gesture of prayer and imploring his players to maintain the momentum, shouting, *Get back! . . . Keep the pressure on 'em! . . . Run! . . . Control it!* On the Celtics, Sam Jones was cold, hitting only three for sixteen.

Bailey Howell, a veteran shooting guard who'd joined the team that year, had scored twenty-two points, but he had run up five fouls. So Russell took Jones and Howell out in the fourth quarter and replaced them with what he thought of as his little guys, Larry Siegfried and rookie Jim Barnett. The substitution of the Tiny Tots—as sportswriters called them—drew boos from the Garden crowd, but with less than five minutes left to play, Siegfried and Barnett helped the Celtics narrow the 76ers' lead from fourteen to one. At that point Hannum expected Russell to send Jones back in, but Russell decided to stick with his second string, which was fine with Hannum, since neither of the substitutes could score the way Sam Jones could if he recovered his shot.

The 76ers surged a second time, and the Celtics missed their last five shots. With Boston down by five and seven seconds left, Chamberlain blocked a desperate Celtics pass, punching the ball with his right fist so hard that it rose fifty feet up into the air, almost reaching the rows of Celtics championship banners dangling from the ceiling, before falling back to the floor. It was the first time a Philadelphia team had won a playoff game in the Garden since 1960. It also meant that the Celtics were now down by two games and needed to win the next game in Philadelphia or face the almost impossible challenge of taking all of the following four games.

After the game, Russell shut the door to the Celtics dressing room, and it remained shut for nearly half an hour as the team allowed the loss to sink in. When he finally unlocked the door, some two dozen reporters packed into the small room. Most of the Celtics were still in their sweat-soaked white-and-green uniforms. The atmosphere was grim. Don Nelson studied a stat sheet with a stony expression. Bailey Howell, saying nothing, pressed an ice pack to his right ankle. Sam Jones sat on the lip of the whirlpool bath, dangling his feet in the churning water. Wayne Embry, Russell's enormous backup center, slumped on a bench with his head in his hands. He seemed to be on the verge of tears. Auerbach sat next to Embry, holding his head in his hands as well.

"Realistically, Red," one reporter said to Auerbach, "what chance do you have, what chance of winning four out of five?"

"It's not over yet," Auerbach said. "Wednesday in Philly is the key game. We win that and we'll have momentum."

The sportswriters blamed Russell for the back-to-back defeats. Under pressure from Chamberlain, he seemed to have found it so challenging just to play his position that he had forgotten he was coach. During that Philadelphia surge in the third quarter, both John Havlicek and Bailey Howell had been shouting at Russell to call a time-out so the team could regroup, but Russell had failed to act. And although Howell had the best shooting hand that night, dropping in eleven out of fifteen shots, Russell had taken him out of the game so he wouldn't foul out before he was really needed, but then Russell left him on the bench, even when, at the end, Boston had drawn within one point of Philadelphia. It was a mistake, the sportswriters agreed, that Auerbach would never have made.

"Celtics Learn, Sadly, That Russell Is No Auerbach," ran the headline in *The Philadelphia Inquirer.* "For eight years, the Celtics have avoided mistakes in the key games," Jack Chevalier wrote in the paper. "They played like the Green Bay Packers and let the other team ruin its own chances. Now they look like the Yankees—a group of champions getting old. The Celtics dribbled on their toes, stepped on the out-of-bounds line, and missed lay-ups. They griped to the referees. Their fans walked out the door muttering excuses—just like race track losers." The Boston newspapers were just as harsh. "The Celtics do not deserve to win the playoffs for the ninth year in succession because in cold-blooded premeditation they handicapped themselves by making Russell, their meal ticket, handle two big jobs," wrote *Globe* columnist Harold Kaese. "The Celtics undoubtedly would have won Sunday's game if Auerbach had been coaching them." A radio announcer in Washington, D.C., speaking the morning after the game, summed up the general feeling: "The Celtics are dead."

WALLY JONES had been afflicted with tonsillitis and swollen glands since February, and on Tuesday after game two he woke up with a fever and a sore throat. When he went to practice that afternoon at Convention Hall, the 76ers trainer, Al Domenico, took his temperature. He had a fever of 102 degrees. Stanley Lorber, the team physician, determined that Jones had a respiratory infection and sent him home to bed. Jones's status for game three the following night, Lorber told Hannum, was questionable.

This was troubling news for Hannum. The 76ers had a number of minor injuries. Chet Walker was playing with a bruised hip bone and Chamberlain still suffered from the shin splints he'd picked up in game one from the rock-hard Palestra floor. But Walker and Chamberlain were playing magnificently, particularly Chamberlain, who since the series began had been labeled the Great Intimidator by one sportswriter and Captain Marvel by another. Larry Costello was still sidelined by his bad knees. Without Costello, if Wally Jones got sick the only players Hannum had left were Matty Guokas, a promising but raw rookie who played a total of only twenty minutes in the first two playoff games and scored only four points, and Bob Weiss, who'd been added to the team late in the season and had not had a minute of playoff time. Hannum knew he needed Jones. Wally was a streak shooter who could get a hot hand at crucial moments, and he had become a critical part of the team. In game one he proved decisive, driving in on Russell three times at a turning point to score three baskets in a row.

Jones stayed in bed for almost twenty-four hours, getting out at four o'clock on Wednesday afternoon, about an hour after the line started forming outside Convention Hall. When he reached the dressing room, Dr. Lorber decided he could play, and Hannum put him in the lineup. At the tip-off Jones felt extremely tired and looked it as well, but Hannum kept him in. In the fourth quarter he found his second wind, and he stopped a late Celtics surge by firing in successive jump shots that put the 76ers solidly back in the lead. It was a star-making performance—the reason that Jones had been nicknamed Wally Wonder and that basketball fans in Philadelphia had taken to wearing buttons that said "Wally Wonder for Mayor."

Alex Hannum was even more worked up than he had been in game two, leaping from the bench in his baby-blue sport jacket, his bald head gleaming, as he exhorted his players and shouted at the referees. He had only adopted the tactics Red Auerbach had pioneered and promulgated, but Auerbach himself was now consigned to the seats, and, with Russell playing full-time, the Celtics lacked a coach who was going to protest loudly and constantly to the officials. There was no one on the Boston bench to offset Hannum's lungs. It infuriated Auerbach. By retiring as coach, he had deprived his team of an undeniably potent weapon, his own mouth, and now, sitting in the stands, he saw the 76ers commit all sorts of uncalled infractions that no one on the Celtics bench protested. Every time the Celtics started gaining some momentum, it seemed to Auerbach, one of the 76ers, Billy Cunningham or Chet Walker, called an injury time-out and Boston's momentum faded. It was obviously phony, Auerbach thought, but no one was doing anything about it.

As they had in game two, the Celtics closed to within a point in the final minutes, then ran out of steam. The game ended with Philadelphia up by eleven, and at the final buzzer the fans began chanting, *Boston is dead! Boston is dead!* A sole spectator up in the balcony ceremoniously played "Taps" on a trumpet. Auerbach pushed through the crowd, under a balcony where a Philadelphia fan was leaning over the rail shaking a fist and screaming obscenities. He took the elevator up to the Celtics locker room. Outside the door a cluster of newspaper reporters was waiting, among them *Philadelphia Inquirer* columnist Frank Dolson. One of the reporters asked Auerbach if he was ready to concede that the 76ers were a great team. "They haven't won anything yet," Auerbach said. "Wait'll they win eight in a row. Eight *years* in a row. Then talk."

Frank Dolson always thought Auerbach was an angry, coarse, and arrogant man, and now, instead of showing some class and paying tribute to the team that had just beaten the Celtics three times in a row in the playoffs—an unprecedented occurrence—Auerbach began complaining about how the 76ers had called fake injury time-outs. "Real bush league!" Auerbach snapped. The Celtics could do it, too, he went on, but it would stretch the game to five hours and ruin basketball.

As Dolson watched, Auerbach, striding angrily back and forth in the corridor, took out a cigar and lit it. The cigar looked like the same type of cigar Auerbach loved to light up on the bench in the final moments of a Celtics win—the notorious and despised Victory Cigar. But Auerbach had not lit up this cigar any place where the crowd might see him, and Dolson decided that was because it was a Defeat Cigar, and though it may have looked identical to a Victory Cigar, it had a much more bitter taste.

AS THE FOURTH GAME approached, Russell's outlook was philosophical. He continued to talk about taking it a game at a time, but he knew how unlikely it was that the Celtics could win the next four in a row, as they would have to do if they were going to come back, and he had decided that, since he had been a good winner, he could be a good loser, too, if it came to that. Until the series was over, however, he was more than happy to make sly digs about Chamberlain. At a workout two days before the game, Russell told the collected reporters that he was impressed but not surprised by how well Chamberlain had been playing. He also said it was remarkable how thoroughly Chamberlain had changed his game, emphasizing defense and play-making. "But he's had a good teacher," Russell said, adding, "and I don't mean Hannum."

"Then who's the teacher?" a reporter asked.

"Me!" Russell shouted, and gave his famous cackle.

With the series now at 3–0, some of the 76ers fans were predicting a sweep. Their mantra was: *Win in four on the Boston floor.* But the players themselves were apprehensive. Wally Jones, still feeling the aftereffects of tonsillitis, was so fatigued that, except for practices, he spent the days following game three in bed. Hal Greer came down with a serious sore throat and had to take to bed as well. More significantly, the pain in Chamberlain's knees had grown worse with each game. Now the slightest bend in either knee sent an excruciating jolt through the leg, and he was forced to go up and down stairs sideways, to avoid bending his knees. When he arrived for practice on Friday, he could barely walk. Dr. Lorber examined him and realized that Chamberlain's knee-joint capsules had become inflamed. Lorber instructed Chamberlain to spend the entire day receiving heat treatment on his knees. He thought that if Chamberlain remained inactive, and received heat treatment that day and the next, the inflammation might subside enough for him to at least start on Sunday. Chamberlain spent several hours each day with his knees under an infrared heat lamp, but by Saturday afternoon, when the team was leaving for Boston, he was still walking stiff-legged.

That day, Alex Hannum's wife, who had remained for the season at the couple's house in Los Angeles, received several threatening telephone calls. The callers warned her that because of the large sums that had been bet on the upcoming game, her husband needed to be careful. They stopped there. Alarmed, Hannum's wife called the Los Angeles County Sheriff's Department, which regarded the threats as more than a prank. The 76ers had been favored to win, the police reasoned, but if they swept the series they would beat the point spread, which meant gambling syndicates stood to lose large sums of money. The calls may not have represented actual threats, they may instead have been attempts to intimidate or distract Hannum, but the Los Angeles Sheriff called the Boston Police Department, which assigned five plainclothes detectives to accompany the coach from his hotel to the Garden and remain with him until the team flew out of Logan Airport after the game. "Hannum never told us what it was about," recalled trainer Al Domenico. "We were guessing why these detectives were following him around."

By the time the game started, emotions in Boston Garden were raw, even ugly. ABC had planned to televise the game nationally, but the American Federation of Television and Radio Artists had declared a strike, and Chris Schenkel and Jack Twyman, who usually covered basketball for ABC, were honoring it. Chet Forte, the director, and Chuck Howard, the producer, volunteered to call the game, but the electrical workers' union at the Garden decided that this amounted to crossing the picket line, and they threatened to cut off the arena's power, throwing it into darkness in the middle of the game. Auerbach, however, warned them that he would take them to court, and when the electrical workers backed down, ABC was able to proceed with the broadcast.

Although both teams were fatigued and racked with injuries, the game was fiercely physical and high scoring, and the first half ended with the Celtics up 66–60. The antagonism on the court was heightened by Celtics fans in the upper balconies who bombarded the 76ers with coins and eggs, one egg splattering onto the suit the injured Larry Costello was wearing as he sat on the bench. Another fan tossed a firecracker into a 76ers huddle. The Celtics had their own distractions. Bill Russell was suffering such severe cramps in his left leg that he called time-outs on three occasions so trainer Joe DeLauri could massage it. Sam Jones twisted his ankle in the third quarter and had to go temporarily to the dressing room. Bailey Howell's four-year-old daughter, who was being watched by a babysitter while his wife attended the game, fell out of a second-story window as the game was going on, breaking a leg and suffering abdominal injuries, and with time still left to play, Howell had to throw a jacket over his uniform and rush to the hospital.

The tension felt by both teams erupted late in the fourth quarter. With Boston up by three, Sam Jones set out on a fast break down the court. The only man between him and the basket was the 76ers rookie Matt Guokas, who decided to foul Jones emphatically enough to prevent him from scoring. Guokas got both arms around Jones, who, with Guokas clinging to him, was unable even to try the shot, and the two men stumbled off the court ensnared with each other. Jones thought he could have put the game away, and was so frustrated at Guokas that he swung his fist at him. Guokas swung back. The roar of the fans became deafening as both teams surged up off their benches. A general melee broke out in mid-court, eggs hurled from the upper balconies hit Guokas, and then a Boston fan jumped out of the stands and onto the court and tried to throw a punch at one of the 76ers before the police wrestled him down.

In the final minute of play, Luke Jackson scored to bring Philadelphia within two. Russell received the inbounds pass and Chamberlain fouled him to stop the clock. Chamberlain's sore knees had hampered his running and jumping throughout the game, but he thought he should be able to rebound Russell's second foul shot if Russell, who had made only three of his seven free throws that night, missed again. Russell went to the free-throw line. A hush descended over the Garden. He aimed and sent the ball arching directly into the basket, then did the same with the second shot. That put Boston up by four, and the game ended with the Garden fans screaming, *We ain't dead! We ain't dead!*

THE 76ERS felt that they needed to finish off the Celtics in the fifth game. If Boston won again, the series would stand at 3–2, and the Celtics would return to their hometown with the momentum having shifted in their favor. One fan made the point by hanging a poster from the first tier of Convention Hall that read: "No. 4 NOW." For their part, the Celtics were determined to set the pace of the game, to establish an early lead and to press the 76ers for the entire forty-eight minutes. Bailey Howell had rejoined the team, having been assured that his daughter, who was in traction and wearing a cast, would recover completely, and that seemed like a good omen to Boston. So did the fact that it was the Celtics who scored first, when Russell flipped the opening tip-off to Havlicek, and he raced downcourt to make a quick layup. By the end of the first quarter, they had an eleven-point lead. Jack Ramsay, the general manager of the 76ers, had issued a plea to the Philadelphia fans to refrain from retaliating for the egg attack against their team in Boston, asking them to please leave all missiles at home. Inevitably, the fans had ignored Ramsay's request, only now, with the 76ers so far behind, it was their own team, not the Celtics, that they pelted with garbage.

But then the 76ers found their rhythm and began outscoring Boston, and by halftime they had narrowed the Celtics' lead to five. In the 76ers locker room during the halftime break, Billy Cunningham told Wally Jones that the reason Jones had missed several points was because he was failing to follow through on his shots. As the second half began, Jones adjusted, and the 76ers began outscoring the Celtics by a ferocious rate. In one long sequence in the third quarter, they were putting in more than three baskets for each one the

Celtics managed, and Jones made eight out of nine attempted shots. Chamberlain's knees still bothered him, but, ignoring the pain, he was everywhere, scoring, rebounding, and making assists.

Now the crowd pelted the Celtics with eggs, oranges, and coins. In the fourth quarter, as the Boston players looked increasingly weary and ragged, the fans began chanting, *Boston is dead! Boston is dead!* Some of them pulled out enormous cigars and lit them. With one minute to play, Philadelphia was up by twenty points. It was such a big lead that Hannum decided to take Chamberlain out, in order to allow him to receive a standing ovation. The crowd came to its feet, roaring approval, when Chamberlain walked off the court, but he refused to acknowledge it, taking a seat on the bench and sipping water from a paper cup.

Though clearly exhausted and hopelessly behind, Russell refused to give up, and with less than a minute left, he raced down the court to try to block a layup by Luke Jackson. Billy Cunningham, watching, thought that Russell was playing as if he didn't believe the scoreboard, as if he were still convinced that, regardless of the evidence, the Celtics simply never lost in the playoffs. But at the final buzzer, just seconds later, the final score stood at 140–116. The Celtics' unbroken eight-year reign, the single greatest team record in sports history, was over.

Once the 76ers reached the locker room, Hannum locked the doors. He wanted his players to have a few minutes by themselves, to savor their accomplishment and to acknowledge to one another the teamwork that had made it possible. Then he allowed the doors to be opened, and the reporters poured in, along with Irv Kosloff and Pennsylvania governor Raymond Shafer. Basketball teams in the playoffs usually reserved the champagne for the finals. Celebrating a mere playoff victory would under normal circumstances seem premature, but the win over Boston was so momentous that earlier in the day the 76ers front office had trucked in cases of champagne. Kosloff was not by nature a demonstrative man, but when Hal Greer drenched him with champagne, he responded by picking up a bottle, shaking it, and spraying the players.

In the midst of all the celebration, Chamberlain remained relatively subdued, sitting on the bench and smoking a cigarette. When a photographer came up to take his picture, he waved the man away. Beating the Celtics, his goal ever since he had joined the NBA eight years earlier, had left him strangely irritable and depressed. The fact was, in a situation like this, he sometimes felt he preferred losing to winning. When you lost you could put it behind you and move on, but when you won you only succeeded in ratcheting up the tension, because the thing about winning was that you had to keep doing it. Also, Chamberlain had never succumbed to the myth of Celtics invincibility. He was convinced that the defeats he and his teams had suffered in previous playoffs were due to nothing more than bad luck. If fortune had favored them ever so slightly, they might have come out ahead in two or three of those six playoff encounters, and the notion of Celtics invincibility would never have gotten started. It had taken all year for the 76ers to pierce this myth, but they had done it, had revealed that Boston was simply another team, a good team, for sure, but not a collection of godlike immortals, not *invincible*. By celebrating so ecstatically, however, it seemed to Chamberlain that the 76ers were in a way acknowledging that they had bought into the myth, that they believed they had toppled a dynasty, when all they had done was beat an aging team in the second round of the playoffs to clinch the Eastern Division title.

A few minutes later, Bill Russell entered the Philadelphia locker room, his black cape draped across his shoulders. He cut a path through the celebrating players until he reached Chamberlain and extended his hand. Chamberlain took it.

"Great," Russell said.

"Right, baby," Chamberlain said.

"Great," Russell said again. Then he turned and made his way back through the throng and out the door.

MUHAMMAD ALI, who had been drafted by the U.S. Army, had decided to go to prison rather than serve in Vietnam, and in early June 1967, a group of ten prominent black athletes held a secret meeting with him in Cleveland, at the Negro Industrial and Economic Union, to discuss his decision. The meeting was organized by Jim Brown, the Cleveland Browns fullback, and most of the athletes were football players, but Brown also invited Bill Russell, who had known Ali since 1962, back when he was still Cassius Clay. Russell went the meeting not to persuade Ali to change his mind but to tell him that he would support him whatever course he took. Ali had been stripped of his heavyweight title, with some people denouncing him as a traitor, and Russell felt that the attacks on him were one more indication of how rapidly race relations were deteriorating. Russell saw the election of California governor Ronald Reagan as another indication. Reagan had made attacks on welfare programs—and implicitly, it was clear to Russell, on the black people who depended on them—a centerpiece of his campaign. It seemed to Russell that more and more Americans were finding socially acceptable ways of expressing racial hostility.

That was particularly true in Boston. Russell supported the court-ordered busing program that had gone into effect there, and to his dismay the whites in South Boston and Charlestown—prototypical Celtics fans—were violently demonstrating against it. Louise Day Hicks, who was leading the fight against the desegregation of Boston's schools, had declared her candidacy for mayor the month before Russell's meeting with Ali. Her campaign slogan, "You know where I stand," was a particularly powerful example of the obvious but acceptably coded bigotry that Russell saw proliferating. When Martin Luther King, Jr., declared that Hicks's election would be a "tragedy," she responded by saying, "Dr. Martin Luther King is the real tragedy of our times."

But Russell had to admit that the increased tensions came from the fact that the country was making undeniable progress on some racial matters. In the fall of 1967, before the start of the regular season, he took the Celtics to play an exhibition game against the St. Louis Hawks in Alexandria, Louisiana. Russell's grandfather, who was still alive and living in Monroe, had never seen Russell play, and so Russell's father drove all the way from California to take him to the game. Aspects of Jim Crow segregation continued to exist in the Deep South—Louisiana courthouses, for example, still had different seating sections for "white" and "colored"—but integration had begun. When Russell's grandfather asked where the "colored" section of the Alexandria arena was, his son told him there was none; they could sit anywhere they wanted. And when, during halftime, Russell's grandfather said he had to go to the bathroom, his son told him that the arena did not even have a colored restroom, and they went and stood at the urinals right next to white men—something that would have been inconceivable just a few years earlier.

After the game, the two men joined Russell in the locker room. Russell's grandfather wandered off, and Russell found him standing by the showers crying. Russell, who had never before seen his grandfather cry, became alarmed, and asked what was the matter. "Nothing, I'm happy," Russell's grandfather said. He gestured to the showers, where John Havlicek and Sam Jones, a white man and a black man, stood side by side soaping up and discussing the game. "I never thought I'd see anything like that," he said.

The Celtics' exhibition tour also took them to Puerto Rico, and it was there that Russell called a meeting of the team's veterans to discuss the upcoming season. During the off-season, people had kept coming up to the Celtics—on the streets, in parking lots, in stores, and while standing in ticket lines at the movies—and asking, *What happened?* Havlicek, for one, got pretty tired of hearing that question. A number of the players felt that what had happened— the reason why they had lost the 1967 championship—was that Russell had simply been overburdened. It was too much to expect one man to simultaneously coach the team and play most of every game. Sam Jones had been telling people that Russell should give up one of the positions, and since he was more valuable as a player, and made most of his money from playing, what he needed to do was step aside as coach. It simply hadn't worked.

Russell was not about to do that. Resigning would have been an open acknowledgment that he had been a failure. But he had spent the off-season reviewing his performance. He decided that, because he had been overly aware of his own inexperience, and overly sensitive about it, he'd been too preoccupied with establishing his authority. Unwilling to appear indecisive, he'd failed to ask the other players for their suggestions and had paid little notice when they'd been made unsolicited. At times, while on the court, he'd also become so caught up in playing the game that he stopped paying attention to things that, as a coach, he should have noticed, such as whether one of his teammates needed a rest.

The six veterans that Russell had invited to his room in Puerto Rico for the private meeting were John Havlicek, Satch Sanders, Sam Jones, Bailey Howell, Don Nelson, and Wayne Embry. He told the players that this room at the moment contained a century's worth of basketball experience. He asked if they would let him tap into that knowledge and told them to feel free to criticize his own play if he deserved it. When the season got under way, the players began taking Russell up on his suggestion, particularly Havlicek, the team captain, who also served as a sort of assistant coach, there being no actual assistant coaches. As Russell had aged, he had developed a tendency, after rebounding the ball and passing it out, to jog up to half-court and watch the action unfold rather than hustling all the way down and plunging into it himself. If Havlicek was on the bench on such occasions, he began yelling, *Get down there, Russ!* and Russell would give a start and then move on downcourt.

JERRY WEST had broken his hand in the opening minutes of the first round of the Western Division playoffs in 1967, and the Lakers had been swept by the Warriors, who also beat the Hawks to win the Western Division title. The Warriors were now coached by former Celtic Bill Sharman and had, in Rick Barry and Nate Thurmond, the top scorer and the best young center in the NBA. The 76ers had beaten them easily in the finals, however, and Chamberlain had become, for the first time since he was in high school, a champion. *The Sporting News* named him Player of the Year, declaring, "The greatest point producer in basketball history, Chamberlain deliberately sacrificed what could have been his eighth straight scoring title in the interest of team play."

Despite the victory and the acclaim, Chamberlain became discontented in the summer of 1967. He always maintained that, in return for signing with the 76ers, Ike Richman had promised to give him an equity position in the team when he left the league. Such an arrangement would have violated NBA rules, but Richman was a shrewd and creative attorney who knew how to structure any deal so it satisfied all the legal technicalities. To circumvent the rules, Richman had never committed any such agreement to writing, and when he died, Irv Kosloff said he had no knowledge of an agreement, did not consider it legally enforceable, and would not honor it. "I know nothing about it and I can't do anything about it," he told Chamberlain. Kosloff also told Chamberlain that Richman's share in some harness horses that Chamberlain and Richman had bought together was actually the property of the 76ers. Kosloff's position infuriated Chamberlain, and although he still had one year to go on his existing contract, he refused to appear at training camp until it was renegotiated.

In the end, Kosloff agreed to give Chamberlain a lump sum for his putative share in the 76ers, throw out his current contract, and sign a one-year deal for $250,000. But by the time the deal was announced, Chamberlain had missed training camp and all but the final exhibition game. Alex Hannum declared himself pleased with the outcome, telling reporters he'd rather

have Wilt report a month late and come satisfied than arrive on time but unhappy. Hannum was afraid, however, that Chamberlain's eagerness to pick a
quarrel with Kosloff meant that the commitment to the team he'd shown the
previous year had faded. When Chamberlain finally did catch up with the
76ers, in Allentown, Pennsylvania, where they were playing the final exhibition match, the scheduled start of the game was only minutes away and the
locker room was deserted.

"Where is everybody?" Chamberlain asked Hannum.

"You've been away," Hannum replied dryly, "but basketball teams usually go onto the court to warm up before a game."

The huge size of Chamberlain's deal had already provoked some complaints among his teammates, who felt they had all contributed to the championship and that the rewards should have been distributed more equitably.
One player joked that Chamberlain should present each member of the team
with a check for $10,000, and Hal Greer demanded that his salary be raised
from $25,000 a year to close to $40,000. The championship the 76ers had
won the previous season, instead of uniting a tight team even further, was
pulling it apart. Chamberlain himself remained annoyed with Irv Kosloff despite the settlement, and this undercut his enthusiasm on the court. Also,
once the regular season began, Chamberlain felt that he had no particular
goal with which to motivate himself. Repeating as national champion
seemed insufficiently challenging; the Celtics had been easily beatable the
year before, and it was hard to see how, since they were all now even older
and slower, they could prove more difficult this year. And anyway, simply
winning games was not that rewarding to Chamberlain. Track and field had
been his first sport, and he had always retained the track star's passion for
setting records. Since Chamberlain had already set records in scoring and rebounding, there didn't seem to be much left to do, and so he decided he'd try
to lead the league in assists.

Never before had anyone other than a guard set the record for assists.
Guards brought the ball up the court, established the pace of the game, and
determined who got the ball for what play. As a result, one of a team's two
guards usually controlled the ball for 90 percent or more of the team's time
of possession. A center typically had the ball for little more than 5 percent of
the time. Chamberlain felt that if he could lead the league in assists, in setting up other players to score, while controlling the ball for such a short period of time, it would be the least predictable and therefore the most

impressive of his records. As the season progressed, Chamberlain stopped going to the basket very often and instead concentrated on passing off to his teammates, even if he was in position to make the shot himself. He became angry if teammates to whom he passed the ball then passed it to someone else, since that meant he would not get an assist on the shot taken, and he favored Billy Cunningham and Wally Jones, players who tended to shoot as soon as they got the ball. In one game, against San Francisco, Chamberlain did not take a single shot through all four quarters. He began to seem bored by basketball, and his play at times became almost criminally sloppy. In December, he set a league record by missing twenty-two free throws in a single game.

The 76ers were leading the Eastern Division, but not by the same margin as last year, and the Philadelphia press began to complain that Chamberlain needed to score more often if the team was going to win a second championship. Hannum had not endorsed Chamberlain's goal of leading the league in assists. To the contrary, he wanted Chamberlain to go to the basket consistently, but Wilt was ignoring his instructions. So Hannum decided he had to embarrass Chamberlain into shooting. In December, after a game with St. Louis, Hannum told a reporter he was afraid that since Wilt no longer used some of his old moves, he might actually have lost them for good. Wilt read the quote in the paper the next day, and on a plane to Chicago, he sat down beside Hannum and showed him the article. "Did you see this?" he asked.

Hannum said he had seen it.

"Did you say this?" he asked.

"If it's there, I guess I did," Hannum replied.

The next night, as Hannum had anticipated, Chamberlain made it his mission to prove Hannum wrong, and he scored sixty-eight points against the Bulls. He also ran up scores of forty-seven and fifty-three in the two following games. But Chamberlain was nonetheless irritated with his coach. He felt that, by pressing him to score, Hannum was thwarting his plan to lead the league in assists, and that turned him against the one coach who had led him to a championship. In mid-season, on a flight home after losing to the Celtics in Boston, Hannum tried to give the team a pep talk about the importance of winning, but Chamberlain interrupted him. "I think there are more important things than winning," he declared. "I think you have to learn how to lose, too."

Chamberlain went on to tell Hannum he disagreed with the coach's priorities and values. What particularly pissed him off, he said, was the fact that Hannum shook the hand of every player in the locker room after a game if the team won, but did not do so if the team lost. Chamberlain told Hannum he felt that, in doing this, Hannum failed to take into account individual effort. What if one player had a great night but the team lost? What if one player had a lousy night but the team won? Chamberlain said he didn't feel like he deserved a handshake if the team won but he had a lousy night. "It makes me feel like a hypocrite," Chamberlain said. "I think you're a hypocrite when you do it."

The atmosphere in the cabin turned frigid. "I have to place a premium on winning," Hannum explained. He said he was sorry that Chamberlain did not like shaking hands, but that he would go on extending his hand to Wilt after a win and Wilt could take it or not as he chose. The *Bulletin*'s George Kiseda, who was on the plane, witnessed the exchange and felt that after such open hostility it was going to be almost impossible for Hannum and Chamberlain ever to repair their relationship.

AT NINE O'CLOCK in the evening of Thursday, April 4, 1968, a gang of young black men stopped a car driven by a white man on Blue Hill Avenue in the Roxbury section of Boston. Martin Luther King, Jr., had been assassinated while standing on the balcony of a Memphis hotel an hour earlier, and the radios in the stores along Blue Hill Avenue were full of the news. As bystanders watched, the young black men pulled the white man from his car and beat him senseless; then, as he lay on the sidewalk, they began rocking his car back and forth, trying to overturn it.

That night and the following day, similar acts of violence broke out in forty-six cities across the country, a wave of shooting, rock throwing, assault, arson, vandalism, and looting that left fourteen people dead. Police set curfews, ordered liquor stores closed, and used tear gas to disperse rioting gangs. In Washington, D.C., alone, more than 350 people were injured and more than 800 people were arrested. Amid all the outpourings of grief and rage, the blanket news coverage, and the grim television images, most people forgot that the first game in the playoff series between Boston and Philadelphia was scheduled for that night.

For all the friction between Wilt Chamberlain and Alex Hannum, the

76ers had finished in first place in the Eastern Division. They had taken an early lead, had never been truly challenged by any other team, and had finished eight games ahead of the second-place Celtics. Chamberlain had led the league in both assists and rebounds, and since no other player had ever done so simultaneously, that in itself was another record. The 76ers had beaten the Knicks in the first round, the Celtics had done the same to the Pistons, and now, the day after Martin Luther King's assassination, they were supposed to begin the series to determine the Eastern Division winner.

Bill Russell was at home in Reading when he heard the news of King's murder, and he was so shocked by it that he was unable to sleep that night. He had known King. He and his wife had worked for the Boston chapter of the NAACP. He had been there when King gave his speech on the Boston Common, and he had been in Washington, D.C., when King gave his "I have a dream" speech. Russell had not agreed with King on everything, particularly his policy of nonviolence. The way Russell saw it, if the apostles of nonviolence were being gunned down in the streets, nonviolence didn't seem to be getting them very much. Still, Russell had a great deal of respect for King. It was as if King had been the last buffer holding back all the black rage, and now his death had unleashed it, and it looked like the whole country was going to go up in flames. Everything he had been saying all these years, it seemed to Russell, all the things that had earned him the label the Angry Negro, were coming true.

Auerbach called an emergency meeting of the Celtics early in the afternoon, before their plane left for Philadelphia for the opening game, to discuss whether the team should play that night. Downtown, in Post Office Square, a rally of 10,000 people protesting King's death snarled traffic, and the Celtics had difficulty getting to the Garden. Once they arrived they found that their reactions to the killing varied. While Russell and the other blacks were still in shock, Bailey Howell, who was white and from Louisiana, saw no reason to cancel the game. What was the big deal about Martin Luther King? he wanted to know. The man was just another minister. Would they cancel the game if Billy Graham or, for that matter, if the Pope died? Howell said he just didn't get it. Russell himself was in no mood to play, but he thought that with rioting still going on in Philadelphia and elsewhere, if they postponed the game at this late time, the 12,000 unruly fans might use that as an excuse to take to the streets. The other blacks on the team agreed, and the Celtics decided they would play.

Fog rolled through the streets of Philadelphia that afternoon, bringing traffic almost to a halt and hiding the signs of the sporadic rioting the city had endured. In the middle of the afternoon, Chamberlain had called the 76ers general manager, Jack Ramsay, to say he didn't want to play, but Ramsay pointed out that tickets had been sold, all the players had a contractual obligation to play, and if the game was canceled the crowd could turn ugly. Later in the afternoon, Chamberlain received a call from Russell saying the Celtics had decided to play, and the two men agreed that it would be a bad idea to risk angering the fans.

But unlike Red Auerbach, Alex Hannum did not call a special meeting to discuss the assassination. The 76ers had had no meeting or practice scheduled for the day—they were just supposed to show up before game time—and so when Hannum heard that the Celtics had voted to play, he decided on his own that the 76ers would play as well. Chamberlain learned how his teammates felt only when they all drifted in separately before the game. The Celtics also arrived, and when the members of the two teams discussed what to do, racial divisions cropped up. Bailey Howell pointed out that Martin Luther King wasn't the president of the United States. He wanted to know why King's death merited the cancellation of an NBA playoff game.

The remark incensed the black players. Seven of the twelve Celtics were black, and so were six of the nine 76ers. Both teams had fielded all-black lineups. The NBA was more integrated than any league in professional sports, and unlike eight years ago, in Southern cities its black athletes could now sleep in the same hotels as their white teammates. Those advances were in part the result of the civil rights movement that King had led. Maybe this game should be canceled out of respect to King or played as a testament to the fulfillment of his dreams, but either way, the black players felt, the matter should be deliberated.

Chamberlain became increasingly agitated. The Celtics, he felt, had had an opportunity to come together and decide as a team what to do, but the 76ers had had no such opportunity. And so, twenty minutes before game time, Chamberlain declared that the 76ers were going to put it to a vote, and ordered everyone except his teammates out of the dressing room. Once the staff people left, the atmosphere in the room turned dispirited. No one said much. None of the black starters wanted to play. But Hal Greer thought it was too late to call off the game, and Chet Walker, who was too depressed to consider the vote anything more than a charade, abstained. With only Chamberlain and Wally Jones actually voting against playing, the team decided to take the floor and silently filed through the door and out into the corridor.

Philadelphia was still under the limited state of emergency declared by Mayor James Tate, and there were nearly one thousand empty seats that night at the 76ers' new arena, the Spectrum Center. The fans who did appear gave the 76ers a standing ovation when they came onto the court, grateful to them simply for showing up, but once play began they were subdued, and more than half of them left before the end of the game. The 76ers, unable to muster any enthusiasm, put up almost no fight, and Boston defeated them solidly.

The second game was delayed for three days in honor of King, and both Russell and Chamberlain flew to Atlanta and joined the somber funeral cortege that followed the mule-drawn wagon carrying the body of the slain civil rights leader through the city's streets. When the series resumed on Wednesday night, the two centers were emotionally drained, and other players such as Chet Walker were still bitter about playing the opening game the day after the murder. King's death had made Walker feel enraged and helpless, and being forced to play a basketball game on the day when blacks across the country were grieving for their lost leader had only compounded it.

Despite the emotional turmoil of its black players, the 76ers were favored to win the series, and they did beat Boston in the next three games, creating an apparently unsurpassable 3–1 lead. No team in playoff history had come back from a 3–1 deficit, and a consensus existed among Boston sportswriters that the series was all but over. "The Celtics have seen the Garden for the last time until October," Cliff Keane wrote in the *Globe*. "When the Celtics fell three behind," said Tim Horgan in the *Herald-Traveler*, "I filed them under the W's for 'Wait 'til next year' and took myself off to Fenway Park."

Strangely enough, the size of the gap between the two teams became a source of inspiration for the Celtics, who became determined that if they were going to lose, it would at least be by a smaller margin. Before game five, Havlicek wrote the word PRIDE on the blackboard in the dressing room. Auerbach had never been one for inspirational talks before a game, and Russell was even more laconic, but before the game he told his team, "We've come so far, and I don't want to go home now." Then he turned to Don Nelson, whose hometown was Moline, Illinois. "Don, you don't want to go back to Moline yet, do you?" he asked.

The joke loosened up the Celtics, who were aware that the 76ers were not as invincible as the sportswriters seemed to think. Billy Cunningham was out, having broken his wrist in three places after colliding with Knicks rookie Phil Jackson in the first round of the playoffs. Luke Jackson, who had torn a hamstring muscle in that same series, had reinjured it against the Celtics. Wally Jones had an injured knee. Chamberlain had bruised his right big toe, the one he used to turn in the pivot. And he was also suffering from shin splints, as he did at the end of almost every season, the result of the cumulative pounding that his immense body gave his lower legs over the course of some one hundred games. On top of that, he was playing with his right knee wrapped after pulling his calf muscle in the opening tip-off of game three.

Boston, led by Havlicek, overcame the odds, outhustling the tired 76ers, and when game five was over they were out in front by a startling eighteen points. They had won after convincing themselves the Boston Celtics simply could never lose a playoff series by a margin of 4–1. The Celtics were taking it one game at a time, of course, but they had managed to find a logical imperative for victory in game five, and now they found a different logical imperative for game six. Game six was played in the Garden, and while they had lost both games played in the home arena so far, they felt they were destined to win at least one there. They pressed the faltering 76ers, who missed three out of every four field goals and lost by eight points. That evened the series and brought it to the seventh game, and the logical imperative to victory that now applied for the Celtics was that they never lost the seventh game.

In a long, exhausting series such as this, determination was critical, and the Celtics, having dug themselves out of the hole, also knew by now that they were simply more determined than the 76ers. The match took place in the Spectrum, where a banner hanging from the balcony said, *Boston is dead,* and it was close, but the Celtics were playing evenly and consistently, everybody contributing, while on the 76ers Chamberlain took only one shot from the field in the second half, and missed. Boston won by four, and when it was over, some of the team's fans who had come down for the game raised a green banner that said, *Celtics Rule Again.*

For the rest of his life, Alex Hannum blamed himself for the defeat. The 76ers had the better team, he thought, and they should have beaten the Celtics as easily as they had the previous year. Instead, they were thrown off by the King assassination, and then angered by being told they were going to go ahead and play game one. Hannum felt that if he had called a meeting like Auerbach had done, his team would have had a chance to collect itself and could have taken game one and possibly swept the series instead of losing it.

Sportswriters would later consider Boston's come-from-behind triumph over Philadelphia to be one of the greatest accomplishments of the Celtics dynasty. In the *Herald-Traveler,* Tim Horgan called it "more surprising than an American winning the [Boston] marathon; more amazing than the Bruins making the playoffs; more astounding than four successive Red Sox pitchers going the route at Fenway Park."* But the series was overshadowed by the upheavals of that tumultuous year—war, assassinations, riots, protests, the presidential election—and when the Celtics flew home from Los Angeles the following month after winning their tenth championship in twelve years, only seventy-five fans showed up at Logan Airport to greet them.

*On the same day the Celtics clinched the series, Ambrose Burfoot became the first American to win the Boston marathon since 1957.

22

TEN DAYS after the season ended for the 76ers, Alex Hannum announced that he was leaving the team and soon after that signed on to coach the American Basketball Association's new franchise in Oakland. Irving Kosloff needed to find a new coach, and Chamberlain, aware of the increased stature Bill Russell had acquired as player-coach of the Celtics, offered his services. He also wanted more money, a three-year contract, and some form of equity in the team. Kosloff turned him down and named Jack Ramsay, the general manager and former coach of St. Joseph's University, to be the coach as well. Chamberlain's one-year contract had expired, and even if he wasn't going to become coach, he wanted more money. But both Ramsay and Kosloff felt that Chamberlain had been overpaid as it was, and had no intention of raising his salary. In fact, as had Franklin Mieuli when Chamberlain was with the Warriors in San Francisco, Kosloff had come to the conclusion that regardless of the man's talent, he could not consistently produce championships, and what he brought in at the gate was not worth the aggravation and expense of keeping him on the roster. "You're free to go make any deal with any team you want," Kosloff told him.

Not only did Kosloff release Chamberlain, he actively tried to find him a new home. The year before, when he was planning to renegotiate his contract with the 76ers, Chamberlain had told the sportswriter Merv Harris that he might be interested in playing for the Los Angeles Lakers, and Harris, who knew the Lakers' new owner, Jack Kent Cooke, had passed this information along. Cooke had called Kosloff for his permission to approach Chamberlain, but Kosloff had said Chamberlain was not available. Now, a year later, Cooke was in his hotel room during a business trip to New York when he received a call from Kosloff, asking him if he'd be interested in acquiring Chamberlain.

Cooke had wanted to bring Chamberlain to the Lakers ever since he'd bought the team from Bob Short in 1965. In Jerry West and Elgin Baylor, Cooke felt, the Lakers had two of the most outstanding players the league had ever seen, but the team continued to be frustrated in its quest for a championship, at times by just a mere two points, because it lacked an outstanding center. Darrall Imhoff, the personable Lakers center for the last four years, played only a supporting role on offense but was good on defense and more than adequate during the regular season. What it came down to was that he did not have the firepower to take on Bill Russell in the finals. Now the greatest center ever to have played the game, the one man who'd beaten Russell, was being offered to Cooke, and not only that, his availability came at a most propitious time for the owner.

The Lakers' new arena, the Forum, which Cooke had spent $16.5 million to build, had opened in suburban Inglewood in the beginning of the year. It had bars and restaurants, elevators and air-conditioning, and space for 4,000 cars and 16,602 basketball fans. Some architecture critics thought that the building, with its arches and its columns and its circular shape, intended to evoke a Roman amphitheater, was in extremely bad taste, but Cooke was immensely proud of the place. "Never call it an arena," he wrote in a memo to his staff. "It's the Fabulous Forum or sports theater." The Forum was on the way to attracting more than two million spectators and grossing some

$15 million by the end of its first year, featuring auto racing, boxing, hockey, tennis, ice skating, horse shows, the circus, concerts—Cooke had made a standing offer of $200,000 to the Beatles, who had stopped performing, for a three-night engagement—and of course basketball. The Lakers had gone to the finals five times in the last seven years, and season tickets were selling at unprecedented levels. If the arena was only two-thirds filled for the Lakers' forty home games, Cooke stood to gross some $2.5 million in basketball revenues from ticket sales alone. That did not count television revenue, nor the revenue from the additional fifteen to twenty playoff games if the Lakers, as they almost undoubtedly would, went all the way to the finals. Those games, which would be close to sold out, could bring in upwards of an additional $1 million. The way Cooke saw it, Chamberlain could be a big draw in what was now among the largest arenas in the league.

With his side-vent suits and black knit ties, his booming voice and florid vocabulary and the relentless belief in himself that irritated people less singularly driven, Jack Kent Cooke had presence. Originally from Canada, he had started out selling encyclopedias, began buying and selling radio stations for the publisher Roy Thomson, and became a master at identifying undervalued assets, then revitalizing and flipping them. By the time he was in his mid-thirties he was worth a reported $20 million. One of the first investors to sense the huge growth potential in professional sports, Cooke in 1961 had bought a 25-percent interest in the Washington Redskins for $350,000 that would be worth $4 million ten years later. By the mid-sixties, the price of basketball franchises was rising exponentially. Ike Richman and Irv Kosloff had paid some $500,000 for the Nats in 1963; a year later the Baltimore franchise sold for $1.2 million; and in 1965 the Celtics had been sold by Marjorie Brown and Lou Pieri for $3 million. A few months later, on September 15, 1965, Cooke paid a record $5.175 million to acquire the Lakers. He had at that point never seen a live professional basketball game.

For all his buoyant optimism, Cooke was an unforgiving perfectionist, and turnover within his organization was constant. At the press conference announcing his acquisition of the Lakers, he had glanced purposefully at coach Fred Schaus and said, "I have never been able to announce why a pro basketball or baseball team cannot win every game." The message was clear: the new owner had a huge amount of money, and was willing to spend it, but he wanted—or demanded—a winning team. Though he knew virtually nothing about basketball when he bought the team, Cooke and his wife and his entourage of friends watched from courtside seats directly across from the Lakers bench, and they all cheered the players when they were ahead and castigated them when they fell behind. Cooke himself actually yelled more loudly and more angrily than Schaus, and also got into the habit of paying visits to the dressing room afterward, critiquing a player's game in front of other players. The players hated it. So did Coach Schaus. They all felt the pressure and got frantic about winning every single game. They could never just go out and *play*. But none of them dared criticize Cooke publicly until Rudy LaRusso spoke up, and he did so only after he was traded.

Cooke had since become more adept at handling his athletes, but he was still an interventionist, and instead of delegating the job of courting Chamberlain to his coach or general manager, he took it on himself, inviting the player to his Bel Air mansion, where they discussed their shared passion for English cars. Five other teams were interested in acquiring Chamberlain, and Seymour Goldberg, a Los Angeles attorney who had been recommended to Wilt by Ike Richman, handled the negotiations. Sam Schulman, the owner of the Seattle SuperSonics, made Chamberlain an offer 35 percent higher than Cooke's initial offer, but Chamberlain preferred Los Angeles to Seattle. He owned his apartment complex, the thirty-two-unit Villa Chamberlain in central Los Angeles, where his parents stayed part of each year. His father had cancer, and if he lived in Los Angeles he could spend time with him, so when Cooke agreed to match Schulman's offer, Chamberlain told Goldberg to take it.

But before the contract could be drawn up, Chamberlain received a call from Bill Sharman, who had become coach of the Los Angeles Stars, one of the teams in the new American Basketball Association. Attendance was dismal at the young league, but it had recently begun stealing players from the NBA—Rookie of the Year Rick Barry of the San Francisco Warriors was one—and some of the owners and coaches thought that if the ABA could attract Wilt Chamberlain, he might, all on his own, provide the star power to make the league a success. Since Wilt had no real desire to play in the new league, which was desperate enough to hire players who had been banned from the NBA, Goldberg advised him to consider it only if its owners agreed to pay him an exorbitant amount of money. "Wilt, I'm going to get you a million bucks," Goldberg told Chamberlain. The basketball player, stretched out on the floor in his living room, kicked his bare feet in the air with glee.

Chamberlain and Goldberg met with Jim Kirst, the owner of the Stars, and George Mikan, the commissioner of the ABA, at the Biltmore Hotel in downtown Los Angeles. Goldberg said that Chamberlain would not consider leaving the NBA for less than $1 million. If that was too large a sum for the Stars to shoulder alone, he said, the league's wealthy team owners could each contribute to a pool to make it up, since the entire league would benefit from Chamberlain's presence. "You'll make it back in no time," Goldberg said.

Mikan found the idea appealing, but before a formal offer could be made, all the owners in the new league would have to vote on the proposed $1 million pool. As Mikan was polling the owners to find out if they'd be willing to contribute to the pool, one of the owners opposed to the idea leaked the story, and on July 4, 1968, an article in the *Los Angeles Times* described the hitherto secret negotiations. That angered the other owners, disrupting the negotiations, and also jeopardized Chamberlain's unsigned deal with the Lakers. Jim Hardy, the manager of the Stars, later insisted that Wilt had made a handshake agreement to join the ABA but that when the story of the discussions broke, the NBA threatened to take him to court because the league's reserve clause prevented him from playing for any other professional basketball team, not just those in the NBA. Whether or not the clause was legally valid, the litigation would have been long and costly, and a court order might have kept Chamberlain from playing until it was resolved. Once the story broke, Hardy told the *Los Angeles Times,* "Chamberlain obviously was intimidated into believing his signing with us would have been extremely costly to him."

Chamberlain denied that he had made a handshake agreement with the ABA, and Cooke insisted no pressure had been brought to bear by the NBA, but they both moved quickly to complete their own deal and three days later announced it during a press conference at the Forum. Television cameras and news photographers surrounded Cooke and Chamberlain as they stood behind a podium set up beneath a basket on the court. Chamberlain looked snappy in an electric-blue suit and a matching tie and handkerchief. "The Celtics have been a team of specialists, and for the last three or four years the Lakers have been the same type of team," he said. "All they needed was a little more firepower at center."

In return for Chamberlain, the 76ers were receiving Darrall Imhoff, Archie Clark, and Jerry Chambers, three players who had certain talents but were not stars, and the consensus held that, as had happened when Frank Mieuli traded Chamberlain from the San Francisco Warriors in 1965, the new owner had gotten him for next to nothing in terms of basketball talent. "It is as if the Niblets people traded the Jolly Green Giant to Heinz for a soup recipe and two vats of pickles," Joe Jares wrote in *Sports Illustrated*.

The terms of the deal were not announced, but it was widely reported to be $250,000 a year for four years. Subsequent litigation revealed that Chamberlain had signed a contract to play for three seasons at $200,000 a season. In addition, Cooke gave him a loan at 4 percent to acquire a $100,000 interest in Cooke's cable television company, and a second loan to make investments in certain tax shelters. Over the long run, Wilt's attorney, Sy Goldberg, realized, these investments would prove much more lucrative for Chamberlain than the $1 million in cash he would have received from the ABA.

Chamberlain took great satisfaction in claiming that the contract made him the highest-paid athlete in the world. "It's for plenty of bucks, baby, plenty of bucks," he told his friend Milton Gross. Chamberlain's critics argued that he was overpaid and that his huge salary would create resentment among the other Lakers, particularly Jerry West and Elgin Baylor, but Chamberlain argued that his record-setting contract created a precedent that would allow all athletes to demand better salaries. "What I've done has been good for the other guys," he told Gross.

The deal did in fact make Chamberlain one of the three highest-paid athletes in the country. (The other two were Johnny Unitas of the Baltimore Colts and John Brodie of the San Francisco 49ers, both of whom had long-term contracts valued at $1 million.) It also meant the Lakers now had the biggest payroll in the history of the NBA. In addition to the approximately $250,000 Chamberlain was earning, Cooke was paying Elgin Baylor and Jerry West both $100,000. Rookie Bill Hewitt had received a $25,000 signing bonus and a three-year contract at $25,000 a year. "The payroll is a little scary," commented *Los Angeles Times* columnist John Hall.

But Cooke had also now assembled a team whose combined talent had no equal anywhere in the league. In fact, some sportswriters felt that the Lakers were now so manifestly superior that no other team could hope to truly challenge them. "The Los Angeles Lakers may be the first team to clinch the National Basketball Assn. championship five days after the fourth of July," George Kiseda wrote in the *Philadelphia Bulletin*. "With Wilt Chamberlain joining Jerry West and Elgin Baylor, Ronald Reagan and Doris Day could play the other two positions for them." But Jim Murray, the archly sardonic columnist for the *Los Angeles Times*, predicted trouble. "The only thing Wilt can't do is get along with his fellow players, owners, coaches, fans, and writers," he wrote. "That's why the Philadelphia 76ers are putting him out on a 'make-offer' basis. It's nothing personal with Wilt. It's just that his presence overwhelms everybody within a radius of fifteen miles. The rest of the act become spear carriers."

CHAMBERLAIN was joining a team with one of the most passionate, heroic, and admired players in the league, Jerry West. No one in the NBA was more dedicated or self-sacrificing. West had shown these qualities time and again, perhaps most spectacularly in a game more than a year earlier, on March 7, 1967. That day, against the Knicks, Willis Reed's elbow caught West in the nose, breaking it, and he was led off the court feeling dizzy and bleeding profusely. West refused to go to the dressing room, however, and the trainer put packing in his nose. "You swallow some blood and get nauseous," West said later. "That's the hardest part of it."

Once West came out of the game, the Lakers' lead dwindled, and then, with six minutes left, they were on the verge of losing it altogether. Coach Fred Schaus looked over at West. Back when he was a senior at West Virginia, West had broken his nose in a game against Kentucky—he broke his nose four times in college alone—but had had it packed in ice, and when Schaus sent him back into the game he had scored nineteen points. Now, just as he had done that day in the game against Kentucky eight years earlier, Schaus asked West if he was capable of playing. West nodded, stripped off his warm-up jacket, went into the game with padding on his broken nose, scored two quick field goals, and the Lakers won.

Even with efforts like that, the Lakers finished the 1966–67 season with a 36–45 record, their worst since moving to Los Angeles. Schaus was by nature one of the most restrained coaches in the league—he made suggestions rather than give orders and would protest an official's call by stamping his foot—and as he had gotten older, he had lost the ability, or the inclination, to drive his men. The Lakers had become a static team, content to coast on the natural gifts of West and Baylor, and by the 1966–67 season they had been overtaken in the Western Division by the Warriors. That year, they barely made it into the playoffs, and after West broke his hand, the Warriors took the series in three straight games. For Jack Kent Cooke, who was in his second year of ownership of the Lakers and also in the midst of building the Forum to showcase his new team, its dismal performance that year had been unacceptable. He decided he needed a new coach.

Cooke wanted to go outside the NBA, to find a fresh talent instead of signing a fired coach or some assistant. Cooke had retained his respect for Schaus, making him general manager, and when he saw a copy of *Sports Illustrated* with Bill Bradley's face on the cover, he asked Schaus who had coached Bradley at Princeton. Schaus told him the man was named Bill van Breda Kolff. Schaus, in fact, knew van Breda Kolff, who had played for the Knicks in the earliest days of the NBA, and he thought he would make a superb coach for the Lakers.

The son of a Dutch American stockbroker who had played on Holland's 1912 Olympic soccer team—which won a bronze medal—van Breda Kolff was an uncouth, fun-loving, beer-drinking former drill sergeant with big ears, a thick chin, and a bullhorn voice. He'd enrolled in Princeton, then flunked out and joined the marines. After the war, he returned to Princeton, but flunked out again, played for the Knicks, then coached basketball for eleven years at Lafayette and Hofstra before returning to Princeton for a third time, but now as basketball coach. Under his leadership Princeton became a basketball powerhouse, and in 1967 it was ranked the fifth-best basketball team in the country, becoming the first Ivy League school ever to make it into the top ten.

When van Breda Kolff joined the Lakers in the fall of 1967, sportswriters thought that with the same starting lineup and a new coach with no pro experience, the team would show little immediate improvement. But van Breda Kolff retooled the club, restoring discipline and emphasizing team ball. During games, Butch, as everyone called him, stood on the sidelines in a sport coat, his tie clipped to his white shirt, tugging up his pants and bellowing at the referees. *For Chrissakes, Manny! Can't you call one right just once in your life?* "Butch earns his technicals," Schaus became fond of saying. Van Breda Kolff was not particularly reflective. "All I care about is my family and the guys," he once said. "You play the game, you have a few beers, and you go home, that's it, that's life." But he was emotional and fair and honest. He did not play favorites or act the courtier to his stars. In fact, he had no hesitation about yelling at them, calling Baylor a "dum-dum" in front of the other players, who nicknamed him Fang and Crazy Horse. Nonetheless, van Breda Kolff was popular with his players, who appreciated his loyalty and enthusiasm, and the fact that he left his anger on the court; after cursing at them during a game, he was happy to go out for a beer afterward.

By mid-season, players and coach had jelled, and the Lakers had become a unified and cohesive squad relying on all five men. They passed sharply, set crisp screens, and moved smoothly from offense to defense in a rolling, fast-paced game that made the Forum fans delirious with joy. West thought they were the equal of any team in the league, particularly on defense, and in a nationally televised game against the Celtics in the Garden, they proved it. The Lakers led by thirty points at the half, built the lead to forty, and won by thirty-seven—handing the Celtics their worst defeat in two years.

The Lakers beat Chicago in the first round of the 1968 playoffs and then routed the Warriors 4–0, avenging the humiliating sweep of the previous year. Going into the finals against the Celtics in the spring of 1968, the Lakers felt they had the younger, stronger, quicker team. They figured the Celtics had to be exhausted from the grueling series with Philadelphia. But Boston proved unexpectedly strong, taking two of the first three games, and then West, diving for a loose ball in the final seconds of game four, even though the Lakers were ahead by thirteen points, collided with John Havlicek.

West had been absolutely bedeviled with injuries throughout the season. He'd been kneed in the thigh and hit in the face with a karate chop, had broken his left hand, bruised his hip, broken his nose twice, and pulled a groin muscle. Now, in the collision with Havlicek, he sprained his left ankle. Van Breda Kolff decided West was capable of playing, and sent him in bandaged, but the ankle was swollen and sore and he played awkwardly. With West limping, Baylor favoring his fragile knees, and Russell dominating the backboards, the Celtics could not be contained. They won the fifth game, and then, by a shocking score of 124–109, they won the sixth and final game.

After the game, van Breda Kolff kept the press out of the Lakers dressing room while the team absorbed the defeat. The players all sat for a while in silence, and then someone said, "When do we get our playoff checks?" West was appalled. It was as if the man had been playing only for money and didn't care whether the team won or lost. That was the difference between the Lakers and the Celtics, West decided, the determination to win. There were determined players on the Lakers, and West himself was one of the most driven, determined players in the league, but as a team they were not as determined as the Celtics. The Celtics no longer seemed the most talented team in the league, simply the most determined.

• • •

Butch van Breda Kolff was excited about bringing Wilt Chamberlain to the Lakers. For the longest time, the team had been in the market for a player who could stand up to Bill Russell, but because the Lakers always finished so well, they rarely had a shot at the top draft picks, and in any event, players with the potential to stand up to Russell were few and far between. In fact, throughout the league, the only player who had demonstrated the ability to do so consistently was Chamberlain. The team was less enthusiastic than the coach. Jerry West thought Chamberlain was incredibly talented, clearly the biggest, most talented center in the league. But if West could have had his pick of any player in the league, he'd have taken Bill Russell, even given Russell's advanced age. Chamberlain was stronger than Russell, in West's view, but he lacked Russell's flexibility and, more important, Russell's dedication to winning and ability to rise to the occasion when the occasion demanded greatness.

Some of the Lakers thought the acquisition of Chamberlain made little sense. It might give the team *too much* talent. After all, they told one another, there was only one ball. Darrall Imhoff, the Lakers' departing center, believed chemistry could become a problem. "I don't know if you can have any happiness with three superstars on a team," he told an acquaintance. A few of Imhoff's teammates worried that they were going to miss him. Imhoff was not a great rebounder, but he had worked smoothly with Baylor, setting up the pick-and-roll that allowed Elg to execute his favorite play, the drive in from the left wing. They also thought they were going to miss Archie Clark, an all-star guard who, if West was injured or fatigued, could take over and run up thirty points. This was a team that had dominated the Western Division and gone six rounds with Boston in the finals. But without Clark, and without Gail Goodrich, whom the Lakers had lost to Phoenix in the expansion draft, the team had much less bench strength, particularly in the backcourt.

"We just broke up a great team," one of the veteran Lakers complained to van Breda Kolff after the trade was announced. "We'd been to the finals. Why make a deal like that?"

"Look, we'll build another great team," van Breda Kolff said.

Despite his profane manner, van Breda Kolff had an almost poetic appreciation for basketball. He loved the movement of the game, the rhythm, the passing, the ingenuity and improvisation, the finesse, the explosion of a fast break, the moments of inspiration, the ballet of it all. It was what he called *the fluid game,* and he felt the fans instinctively appreciated it, too. That was what they came to see, that was what roused them so much more than mere scoring, particularly scoring by the big men—whom van Breda Kolff called the big bulls—when they simply overpowered smaller players by driving, or bulling, their way to the basket for a dunk.

Like Auerbach, another basketball aesthete, van Breda Kolff found the dunk an intrinsically ugly move. He felt that the dunk and the big bulls executing it were ruining basketball, and he had actually proposed that the NBA raise the basket and expand the court size so that they would reacquire the proportions they'd had to players when the league was started. But it was not merely the size of the athletes that dismayed van Breda Kolff. He also felt their attitude toward the game had changed. The good players, he thought, were interested only in their statistics—points, rebounds, assists—because that was what determined their salary. They had no motivation to play team ball. He felt that the owners, under the misguided impression that fans wanted scoring, had instructed referees to favor the big bulls in their calls, and as a result it had become almost impossible in the NBA to play defensive ball without being charged with fouling.

Van Breda Kolff had no hesitation about airing his opinions in public, and the year before, he had given an interview to a California newspaperman who wrote an article saying that in van Breda Kolff's view, "the officiating is ridiculous." Commissioner Kennedy fined van Breda Kolff $250 for abusing officials in public, but that had no deterrent effect on van Breda Kolff, who also criticized players, singling out Chamberlain as particularly lazy. "He can pass well if he wants to," he had told one reporter the previous season. "If he wants to he can play defense better than anybody in the league. If he wanted to he could be *two* Bill Russells on defense. But Wilt's always been celebrated; he doesn't know the word *work*. It's not his fault. That's just the way things are with him."

Now, in August, a few months after making that remark, van Breda Kolff flew out to New York and drove up to Kutsher's Country Club for a league-wide meeting of coaches and referees to discuss rule changes. The Maurice Stokes charity game was scheduled to coincide with the meeting, and Chamberlain was playing in it. Van Breda Kolff brought a Lakers jersey with him and asked Chamberlain to put it on for the photographer. But Chamberlain had been insulted by van Breda Kolff's comments, and, deciding to give the coach a taste of what it was like to try to handle him, he refused to put on the jersey. They went back and forth about it. Van Breda Kolff felt that Chamberlain was seeing what he could get away with, and Chamberlain felt the coach was trying to boss him around. He continued to refuse, and finally van Breda Kolff, insulted himself, had to give up. It was an inauspicious beginning.

THE LAKERS started their training camp in late September at the Loyola University gym. After a photo day, van Breda Kolff closed the workouts, explaining that the twelve players, including Chamberlain and four rookies trying to land positions, needed to become acquainted in private. That was a logical move, but with the heightened curiosity over Chamberlain, it inevitably led to speculation that van Breda Kolff was trying to hide something. According to one rumor circulated by reporters, he and Chamberlain were hardly on speaking terms. It was true that Chamberlain remained just as uncooperative as he'd been the previous month at Kutsher's. By the third day of practice, he had stopped running with the team, saying he needed to spare his knees. Van Breda Kolff felt it would be unfair, and create serious problems, if he allowed Chamberlain to loaf while forcing Baylor and West to work hard, but Chamberlain was so obviously unenthusiastic that the other players said they preferred to practice without him, and the coach gave up.

He had other concerns. It was obvious to everyone in the league that without Gail Goodrich and Archie Clark, the Lakers lacked bench strength, particularly in the backcourt. "The Lakers better shore up their backcourt or the glamour boys are going to have trouble," Auerbach told a friend. Schaus began calling other coaches to discuss the availability of their guards. One of those Schaus called was Bill Russell, to ask about Larry Siegfried, and Russell gleefully recounted the call to a Los Angeles sportswriter, explaining that he'd said he was willing to trade Siegfried for Chamberlain. "I told him I needed a backup center. He said, 'You can't have [Mel] Counts. He's not for sale.' I told him I didn't want him, I wanted the other center he had, Whatsisname, the one you got from Philadelphia. He'd make a good backup center.'"

At the end of training camp, van Breda Kolff formally added rookie Bill Hewitt to the roster. Hewitt was a gangly, imperturbable six-seven forward who could alternate with Mel Counts playing opposite Baylor in the front-court. Van Breda Kolff also acquired Keith Erickson, a large, quick-handed guard from Chicago, and Johnny Egan, a ballhandling backcourt man from the Milwaukee Bucks. At six feet tall, Egan had the distinction of being the shortest man in the league, and sportswriters almost invariably described him as "little Johnny Egan." But Egan could press and scramble. He used his small stature to advantage, darting around taller but slower men, and van Breda Kolff figured that all Chamberlain needed to do was pick up rebounds and get them out to Egan or West or Baylor—the three of them could run the fast break as well as anyone in the league.

With all the additions to the roster and the reconfiguring of existing play-ers, the Lakers felt to Jerry West more or less like an entirely new team. And they were as awkward as colts. In their first game of the season, in Philadel-phia, the 76ers destroyed them, running up a lead that for a spell exceeded thirty points because the way Chamberlain was playing, under the basket, impeded his teammates from scoring. When van Breda Kolff benched him, the Lakers rallied but failed to win, then went on to lose three of their first four games. The team was still out of shape and disorganized, but the main problem was the difficulty the other players were having in adjusting to Chamberlain's presence.

To the less important players such as Mel Counts, Chamberlain seemed moody, intimidating, and distant, but that was in large part due to the fact that Chamberlain's father was dying of cancer. In late October, his father fi-nally passed away, and Chamberlain became even more depressed. The de-pression exacerbated the usual problems he had with insomnia on road trips, slowed him a step or two on the court, and made him irritable around the dressing room. Chamberlain did get along with Jerry West, whose skills complemented his, but even so, West thought the Lakers were not ideally suited to Chamberlain, who seemed to work best on a team that played a slower game and had good outside shooters who could score from the perimeter and leave the paint to him. Chamberlain liked to set up in the low post on the left side, but when he did this he blocked Baylor's drive from the left wing to the basket, and that threw Baylor's entire game off.

Also, Chamberlain was used to being regarded by his teammates as the central figure in the dressing room, the dominant personality, the one the oth-ers turned to for validation and the final word in a crisis, and in Elgin Baylor he was facing a man who had for the last ten years been regarded as the leader of the Lakers. Baylor and Chamberlain quickly developed a competitive relationship marked by sarcasm and hostile humor. Baylor would tell Chamberlain he had hands like a blacksmith's and Chamberlain would taunt Baylor with his superior statistics. To make matters worse, they had political differences in a year of intense political polarization and upheaval. The 1968 presidential election campaign had begun in earnest after Labor Day, and Chamberlain supported Richard Nixon—he had been at the Republican convention in Miami—while Baylor was out campaigning for Hubert Humphrey. Van Breda Kolff, trying to make light of the matter, told an acquaintance, "If Jerry comes out for George Wallace, we'll be in trouble."

But Chamberlain's egotistical jockeying with Baylor was nothing compared to his mounting conflict with van Breda Kolff. The tension and suspicion that first surfaced at Kutsher's Country Club had increased during training camp, and once the season began, the two men were constantly at odds. The coach instructed Chamberlain to play the high post out by the free-throw line on offense, to free up the lane and make it easier for Baylor to drive. Chamberlain argued that this took him out of position for rebounding, and since he had readjusted his style of play away from heavy scoring, this was one of his key contributions in any game. Chamberlain also felt that, seeing as this was now his ninth season in the NBA and only van Breda Kolff's second, he simply had more experience than his coach and did not like being told what to do. During one practice, when van Breda Kolff criticized one of Chamberlain's moves, the player waved his hand dismissively at the coach and said, "I know what's best."

"Forget it!" van Breda Kolff shouted back. "Just forget I said anything!"

Instead of finding a means to demand Chamberlain's respect, as Alex Hannum had managed to do on two different teams, or of charming him and pretending to defer to him while actually guiding him, as Frank McGuire had done, van Breda Kolff continued with his futile confrontational approach, giving Chamberlain orders and then, when Chamberlain ignored them, acting disgusted but helpless. Van Breda Kolff's task, however, was complicated by the fact that Chamberlain now had no particular motive to cooperate with his coach. He was no longer desperate to prove he could beat Bill Russell and win a championship, since he'd already done that, and he was now making so much more money than his coach, and was so much more celebrated, that the idea of deferring to him seemed illogical.

A month into the season, Chamberlain's lack of respect for van Breda

Kolff had deepened into contempt, and he began complaining publicly about him to reporters. "I would think," he told one, "that with the experience a Wilt Chamberlain, an Elgin Baylor, or a Jerry West has in this league, a coach who has a lot less experience would want to take advantage of it and talk things over." But van Breda Kolff was just as outspoken, and he retaliated by hinting to reporters that the real problem was that Chamberlain was uncoachable. "They say when he wandered into the Palestra, in Philadelphia, back in the ninth grade, people asked him for autographs," van Breda Kolff told one sportswriter. "All the attention spoiled him." Once the two men began denigrating each other publicly, their personality clash became an open feud, and Chamberlain progressed from ignoring the coach's instructions to seeking opportunities to challenge him. Van Breda Kolff had a rule forbidding food in the locker room before a game, but Chamberlain, in open defiance, brought in chicken or hot dogs, and van Breda Kolff had no choice but to appeal to general manager Fred Schaus. In close quarters on road trips, tensions between the two became so high that on one occasion in November, Schaus had to fly in to effect a temporary reconciliation.

Jerry West found the whole situation demoralizing. He could understand how Chamberlain, with all his years of experience, would not like to be told to change his game. West himself would resent being told to change the way he shot. But at a certain point, he felt, a player needed to accept the fact that he was a player and not a coach and should surrender to the guidance of the coach. Why, he wondered, had Chamberlain started thinking no one had the right to tell him what to do? The merits of the argument aside, it seemed to West that both Chamberlain and van Breda Kolff had put their need to prevail in their feud over the interests of the team. The feud had created a palpable tension in the locker room. All the other players were drawn up into it, even those such as West himself who tried to avoid taking sides. For the first time in West's nine years with the Lakers, they were not a happy team, and it was affecting West's performance. All West wanted to do was play good basketball. Instead he went into one of the worst shooting slumps of his career, missing more than half of his field goals in one twelve-game stretch.

By December, the Lakers were leading the Western Division, but their 18–9 record was hardly impressive. While Chamberlain dominated the opposition on rebounds, he did not get the ball out quickly enough to set up the fast break. He also did not move out of the key to set screens for his teammates, and that encouraged them to simply pass to him and then stand around waiting for him to do something. The quickness and fluid harmony that was the trademark of the Lakers had disappeared, and their on-court efforts showed such a lack of enthusiasm and coordination that the hometown crowd began to boo them. Van Breda Kolff started taking Chamberlain out if he seemed cold and substituting Mel Counts, and when that happened, the fans cheered.

The team proved that it could play well when it felt like it. Before a packed house at the Forum, the Lakers trounced the Celtics 116–106, with Johnny Egan coming off the bench in the third quarter to lead a fast-breaking streak that gave his team thirty-one points. In Boston ten days later, the Lakers again beat the Celtics. But then, as if to prove that their problems were entirely the product of attitude, they lost to Chicago, the second-worst team in the Western Division, by a dismal score of 90–81. As the year wound down, the Lakers were having a tougher time with the bad teams than with the good ones. A big part of the problem, van Breda Kolff thought, was that his players were not thinking on court. It was as if the problems caused by Chamberlain's presence had deprived them of their intelligence. They ignored his instructions, forgot their assignments, and did—or tried to do—whatever they wanted.

Van Breda Kolff became so discouraged that he took to sitting on the bench in glum silence. The entire team was dispirited, which was ironic, van Breda Kolff thought, because it was in first place. At this time last year, the team had been in third place, yet everything had been sweetness and light. Van Breda Kolff did have several private conversations with Chamberlain in which he tried to reach an understanding. "There are three things we can do," he told Chamberlain on one occasion in early December. "One, we can have a fistfight, and I'm not about to do that, because you're bigger and stronger and could kill me. Two, we can take the whole thing to Cooke and tell him it's you or me and let him decide. Or, three, we can work this out together like gentlemen and do what's best for the team." But by that time, Chamberlain had become so deeply entrenched in his sullenness and pride that he had become unreachable. So van Breda Kolff decided to go public about the dispute, hoping that he could somehow bring the issue to a resolution. "I've reached the point where I don't give a blank," he told *Los Angeles Times* writer John Hall, one of his allies in the press. "It's coming to a head," he went on, adding, "it can't keep going on this way."

The open warfare between van Breda Kolff and Chamberlain was so alarming to the Lakers front office that the day Hall's column appeared, Fred Schaus held what was called a "peace conference." The one-hour meeting was more in the nature of a stern lecture. Schaus told the players and the coach that all teams had personality clashes, but most of those teams managed to confine their disagreements to the locker room. Because of the presence of the great stars on the Lakers, these inevitable conflicts were of considerable interest to the press, which picked up on them, and magnified and distorted them. Schaus said he was tired of hearing about the Lakers' problems from other general managers and of reading newspaper stories in which his players took shots at one another and their coach. He was not going to name names, he continued, but several people were responsible, and they knew who they were. From now on, he said, he wanted the Lakers' problems kept within the Lakers family.

Schaus also said that these problems were not insurmountable but that they did need to be addressed immediately. One of them seemed to be that certain players were not accepting van Breda Kolff's authority, and he wanted it understood that the coach's authority was final. Schaus said that when he was coach, neither the owner nor the general manager had interfered, and now that van Breda Kolff was coach, neither he—Schaus—nor Jack Kent Cooke would interfere with him. Although the team was leading the division by four games, Schaus said, it was simply not playing good basketball. Each player was expected to play as hard as he could, and the team needed to run. The fans deserved a hustling team that played interesting ball. The Lakers had spent nine years building from scratch an excited following for basketball in Los Angeles, and he didn't want to see that ruined in one season by a listless, overpaid, bickering team.

When he finished with his lecture, Schaus had no idea what effect it would have. The atmosphere in the room was grim and unforgiving. But there was one positive sign. Chamberlain, who had skipped the Tuesday and Wednesday practice sessions, practiced afterward with his team for the first time all week.

All the peace conference did was establish a temporary truce, one that fell apart again on February 3, 1969, after a game in Seattle. With the floundering SuperSonics in second-to-last place, it was not an important game—the *Los Angeles Times* had not even sent a reporter to cover it—but the Lakers had lost 114–107, and van Breda Kolff felt the defeat at the hands of such a patently inferior team was inexcusable. Chamberlain had contributed virtually nothing, and after the game, in the hallway on the way to the locker room, van Breda Kolff began complaining loudly about Chamberlain's bad attitude and lack of hustle. Chamberlain responded by complaining loudly about van Breda Kolff's poor judgment in substitutions, and then he called him the dumbest coach he had ever played for. Van Breda Kolff told Chamberlain to shut up, and Chamberlain replied that no one talked to him that way. The words got angrier, and the rest of the Lakers, listening to their coach and their star center attack each other with such savage language, felt mortified and humiliated. Suddenly, van Breda Kolff made a menacing advance on Chamberlain, who then stepped toward his coach ready for a fistfight, but at that point Baylor moved between the two and pushed them apart.

Fred Schaus was called, and he met the team plane at the airport. Many of the players who resented Chamberlain's overall attitude sided with van Breda Kolff, and that only further angered Chamberlain, who was saying he would refuse to play as long as van Breda Kolff was coach. Van Breda Kolff, for his part, was saying he was going to force Chamberlain to sit on the bench. Jack Kent Cooke, furious about the row, called the two men into his office and dressed them down. The fight had taken place out of the public eye, and Schaus told the players that anyone who discussed the matter with reporters would be fined $500.

BILL RUSSELL had spent the summer of 1968 in Hollywood, living at Jim Brown's house and hanging out on the set of a movie Brown was shooting. He was there when Bobby Kennedy was assassinated, and Kennedy's death, along with the riots in Chicago and the intensifying war in Vietnam, reinforced his view that American society, no longer able to sustain its own internal contradictions, was imploding. At the same time, Russell's marriage was breaking down. He had grown so distant from his wife, Rose, that the two of them no longer seemed to be able to have a conversation. Otherwise preoccupied, Russell didn't bother showing up at the league-wide meeting of coaches and referees at Kutsher's Country Club in August to discuss the rules. He was the only coach who failed to attend, and Commissioner Kennedy fined him $500.

But he did appear the following month at the Dome Room on the second floor of the Hotel Lenox to announce the signing of his new contract, which at $400,000 for two years represented a substantial raise but was still less than Chamberlain was making. To underscore the importance the team attached to the ceremony, all the Celtics were there, as was Auerbach and Celtics president Jack Waldron. Russell, however, seemed bored. He wore a black mohair suit with flared trousers and gold trim, sandals, and a large peace medallion, but he was fifteen pounds overweight, and as Auerbach and Waldron joked with reporters, he sat at the table eating a dish of ice cream. When one sportswriter asked what he thought of the contract, he shrugged and said, "It ain't no big thing."

The Celtics by then had the oldest team in the league. Russell—the only player from the Celtics' first championship season thirteen years ago who was still on the team—was thirty-four. Sam Jones was even older at thirty-five, while Bailey Howell was almost thirty-two, Satch Sanders thirty, and John Havlicek twenty-eight. Their age was offset by the fact that they had all played together for so many years. They all knew one another's idiosyncrasies and needed virtually no coaching. As usual, they started the season well, going up eleven and three. But then the other teams played themselves into shape, and adjusted to new teammates and coaches, and the Celtics began to slide. They were capable of brilliant nights—beating the 76ers 130–98—but they also seemed creaky and inconsistent, particularly Russell.

With the season only a month old, Russell already felt fatigued, not just physically but mentally. It was a new and different fatigue from any he had experienced before, and he could not shake it with bench time or a few days off and a good night's sleep. Nothing seemed to restore him, and he was playing mechanically and without fire. "His shooting touch is only a little better than a robot's," Dan Hafner noted in the *Los Angeles Times*. "He gives the appearance of being just too tired to continue." As the months went by, the feeling of fatigue deepened until it began to seem perpetual and bottomless. Russell felt almost like he was drowning in it. Then in early February, the day before Chamberlain and van Breda Kolff came to blows in Seattle, Russell was knocked to the floor in the final seconds of a game against the Knicks at Boston Garden. His right knee took the impact. It was his third game in forty-two hours, his thirty-fifth birthday was less than a month away, he'd been suffering from a heavy cold for two weeks, and he'd managed only five hours of sleep the night before. He tried to raise his head but then fell back, his teeth clenched, his hand covering his face as play continued around him.

Joe DeLauri, the Celtics trainer, was watching from the sidelines. He knew Russell had a high tolerance for pain—DeLauri had seen him stand impassive while DeLauri shoved a dislocated finger back into its socket—and he had never seen Russell in such pain before. DeLauri called for a stretcher while the team physician, Thomas Silva, hurried onto the court and knelt by Russell, who was lying on his back, his arms spread in a sacrificial position. When Silva tried to touch his knee, Russell jerked in agony, and the doctor had him carried on the stretcher into the dressing room and then taken by ambulance to Boston's University Hospital. Later that evening, Silva told the team that X-rays revealed Russell had not suffered any broken bones. Instead, he had acutely strained knee ligaments. "Plus," the doctor added, "complete physical exhaustion."

But even though he was old and worn out, Russell was still the key to the Celtics game. After his knee injury, Russell had to take himself out of the lineup, and Boston lost its next five games—its worst losing streak in two decades. Even though the injury was far from healed, Russell rejoined the team for the next game. Wearing a knee brace and limping, he scored the tying basket at the end of regulation play, and the Celtics won in overtime.

In late February, Auerbach and the Celtics arrived in Los Angeles to play the Lakers. Two days before the game, Auerbach, dressed in a striped sport coat and mint-green shirt, held a lunch for reporters at the Forum Club. He was sitting at the table smoking a cigar when Jack Kent Cooke joined the group.

"It's good to see you in your decline," Cooke said. The Lakers, despite their internal turmoil, were in first place in the Western Division while the Celtics were in fourth place in the East, trailing even the Knicks.

"No comment," Auerbach replied.

"The declining Celtics are still good for a sellout," Cooke said. "They tell me that our game Friday with you guys is sold out already."

"We're still magic," Auerbach said. "Not even Los Angeles can say that." Auerbach could not resist taking a dig at Cooke. "A few years ago someone said that Los Angeles was the basketball capital of the world," he went on. "Someone undoubtedly who had been sniffing brandy."

"I wouldn't be guilty of such a redundancy," Cooke said. "I assume that everyone knows it."

One of the reporters asked Auerbach what he thought of Chamberlain.

"I don't know what goes through his mind," Auerbach said. "He can be as good as he wants to be. But nobody can tell him what to do at this stage. All you can do is ask him. Now Bill Russell—you can talk to him and he'll listen."

"How many points does Russell score?" Cooke asked.

"We don't depend on him to score," Auerbach replied. "Defense is his game. That and getting the ball downcourt. He does that consistently well."

Cooke felt Auerbach was disparaging Chamberlain. "Wilt Chamberlain is the most intelligent athlete I've ever known," he said. "We've all seen Ted Williams go oh-for-five. Some nights it goes in, some nights it doesn't. I think that right now Chamberlain is playing as well as he's ever played for anyone. We're going to win it all."

"You're going to win it all if you don't play us," Auerbach said.

"Revenge," Cooke said and smiled.

"You'll be an old man before you get that," Auerbach replied. "Russell will be walking around the court on a cane. Chamberlain never could beat Russell." Auerbach stood to leave. "See you in the playoffs," he said.

We're still magic, Auerbach had said to Cooke. There was something about the phrase, and one of the reporters at the lunch had jotted it down. It seemed particularly apt two nights later, when Boston took to the court of the Forum for the game it had flown into town to play, because the fourth-place Celtics, who were trying to keep the fifth-place Royals from squeezing them out of the playoffs altogether, crushed the Lakers 124–102. Chamberlain scored thirty-five points, but Jerry West, once again injured—this time with a pulled hamstring—sat out the game, and it was the Lakers who seemed leaden and clueless. They had worked to within two points in the third quarter, but then Boston went on a 21–7 scoring spree that lasted into the fourth quarter and turned the game into an utter rout.

AS THE REGULAR SEASON drew to an end, the Lakers continued to hold on to their lead over the second-place Hawks while also continuing to play listlessly. Van Breda Kolff still had not decided on a consistent starting lineup, and Chamberlain was playing a different type of game almost every night. Those stories about the "new Wilts" used to come out every couple of years, but now his teammates never knew from game to game when a new "new Wilt" would appear. Chamberlain's main problem, it seemed to Jerry West, was that he had never made up his mind about the kind of basketball he wanted to play. In one match against the Royals, he scored only two points and took only three shots, devoting himself entirely to defense, and the Lakers won. But then, in another game against the Royals, he stunned the crowd and his teammates by scoring sixty points, even though he had not scored more than thirty-five in the previous fifty games. Van Breda Kolff, however, continued to take him out of the lineup if he was inconsistent, and when that happened, the Lakers tended to play better.

Mel Counts, Chamberlain's substitute at center, was a lanky young white guy from Oregon who, at seven feet, was almost Chamberlain's height, and while Counts lacked Chamberlain's strength and jumping ability, he was for a center an extremely talented outside shooter. He had played for the Celtics for two years, as Russell's backup, but saw little action, and then was traded briefly to Baltimore before winding up in Los Angeles, where he again played backup, this time to Darrall Imhoff. At the beginning of the year, van Breda Kolff, anticipating that Chamberlain would play a full forty-eight minutes, moved Counts to forward, where, with his shooting ability, he could add sixteen to twenty-four points to the team's total. When van Breda Kolff took Chamberlain out, he switched Counts to center, and by playing the pivot Counts freed up the middle, allowing Baylor to return to his trademark driving game. The substitution made the entire team click, all five men playing in the zone, and they suddenly resembled the fluid, rhythmic Lakers of previous years. In late-season games, with Chamberlain on the bench and Counts in the pivot, the Lakers managed to make up eighteen points against Phoenix and fifteen points against Baltimore. The players loved it and so did the fans.

But one aspect of Chamberlain's inconsistency was that he could prove, in any particular game, matchless. In one late-season game against the Celtics, he dominated Russell under the boards, bringing down forty-two rebounds, a league-wide season record, even though he was playing with a thick bandage on his bruised left hand. What helped power Chamberlain's performance that night was his anger at the ongoing criticism of his performance. No matter what he did, he felt, he could not get a break. When he concentrated on defense, the sportswriters took him to task for not scoring enough. And when he did score a lot, they accused him of being selfish. They also constantly complained that he was impeding the Lakers' celebrated running game, but Chamberlain did not feel that, despite the team's reputation, it was a running team any longer. The primary starters—Tom Hawkins, Johnny Egan, Baylor, West, and himself—were all over thirty years old, and could not hope to keep up with the twenty-five- and twenty-six-year-olds on the younger teams they played. They needed to slow the game and set up, Chamberlain felt, and that was the pace at which he played.

Chamberlain had also maintained throughout the season that the turbulence on the team was inevitable given the great difficulty the other players would have in adjusting to him, but that once they had done so the turbulence would fade, and as the regular season came to an end, that seemed to happen. After the incident in Seattle, Schaus had held another peace conference, and since then Chamberlain and van Breda Kolff had made a point of being civil. Then the players had held a meeting at which Chamberlain's teammates told him that ever since joining the Lakers he'd been aloof and irritable and none of them felt they had gotten to know him. Chamberlain had responded by trying to open up, kidding with the bench players, making nice to Baylor. To complete the turnaround, West recovered from his injuries and pulled out of his second shooting slump of the season. In one of the final games of the regular season, the Lakers beat Boston again, this time by thirty-five points, a humiliating drubbing for the Celtics that had fans in the Garden jeering and prompted Russell to administer a twenty-minute tongue-lashing to his team during which he threatened them with fines if they played so poorly again. It was now spring, but the Lakers at last looked alert, powerful, and integrated, Chamberlain and Baylor finally playing as if they knew each other's moves. Usually they set up, sometimes they ran the ball, but both offenses were finally working for them, and what before had seemed like inconsistency was now regarded as variety. They had won ten of their last thirteen games and ended the season in first place in the Western Division for the first time since 1966, with the best won-loss record (55–27) in their history.

Attendance at Lakers games was also the best on the record books. A total of 465,695 fans had bought tickets for Lakers games during the regular season. More than 11,000 spectators had showed up at each of the forty-one home games. In the upcoming playoff games, ten of which would take place at the Forum, they would sell another 160,958 tickets, which meant an average attendance of more than 16,000. For all the turmoil and dissension it had caused, Jack Kent Cooke's decision to sign Chamberlain had not only given the Lakers the best team they'd ever had, it had proven to be financially shrewd.

Boston, meanwhile, barely made it into the playoffs, finishing the season in fourth place with a 48–34 record—their worst finish since 1950, the year before Auerbach took over. The problem for the Celtics was that their fast break had fallen apart, and the fault was in good measure Russell's. Still feeling utterly fatigued, Russell was not rebounding enough, and other members of the team hung back to help him recover the ball rather than break down the court. That gave the defense time to get in position and forced the Celtics to try to grind out a set play. But after that last nationally televised defeat at the hands of the Lakers, Russell started hustling—*Move it, Russ!* Havlicek would shout if Russell showed signs of slacking off—and at the tail end of the season the team was able to return to the fast break.

Still, they all looked weary. It was widely believed, even among Boston fans, that the Celtics dynasty had peaked in 1966, that in 1967 it had succumbed to a superior team, that the 1968 championship had been a fluke due to the effect of the King assassination on the 76ers, and that by 1969 the team was an aging, fading shadow of its once glorious self. Sportswriters had taken to referring to Russell, who was now thirty-five, as "the old man." Sam Jones had turned thirty-six and announced he would retire at the end of the season. "As all schoolchildren know," Frank Deford wrote in *Sports Illustrated* as the 1969 playoffs began, "the Celtics are too old. Too old. Too old. This is a recording."

Age had certainly contributed to the Celtics' fourth-place finish in the Eastern Division. Back in the fall, just a few weeks into the regular season, Havlicek had realized that they clearly were not the strongest team in the division. Baltimore, New York, and Philadelphia were all younger, faster, and more powerful. Philadelphia, now coached by Jack Ramsay, still had the core of the team that had won the 1967 championship except for Chamberlain, plus Darral Imhoff and Archie Clark, who'd helped the Lakers get to the finals the previous year. In Baltimore, which had been in last place only two seasons earlier, rookie Wes Unseld had teamed up with Earl Monroe to create a formidable fast break that made the Bullets the most exciting team in the division, though at the end of the season they were plagued with injuries. "Four guards and not two good legs among us," Monroe complained. The

Knicks, who now included Walt Frazier, Bill Bradley, Willis Reed, and Dave DeBusschere, were the most promising team in the East, the team of the future, though in 1969 they still lacked experience.

During the long grind of the regular season, the Celtics simply could not keep pace with these younger, stronger teams. Russell's only goal had been to make it into the playoffs. Boston's rank at the end of the regular season did not matter as long as it was in the top four. Once the Celtics had clinched that spot, Russell allowed the team to coast, conserving its energy for the post-season and hoping to avoid any injuries that might ruin its chances there. The Celtics had enough championship experience to know that if they did make it to the playoffs, anything could happen.

TO PROTECT HIS KNEES, Bill Russell had played less than usual during the last couple of weeks of the regular season, so when the playoffs began he felt rested, as did his teammates, and they beat Philadelphia 4–1 in the opening round, then took on New York. The Knicks had beaten the Celtics in all but one of their seven games during the regular season, and they entered the series as five-point favorites. In the first game, the Knicks looked unbeatable and the Celtics were floundering, but then in the third quarter Russell called time-out and delivered a blistering lecture—"You'd have to write it all in exclamation points," Sam Jones said later—and Boston won by eight.

In game two in Boston Garden, the Knicks, who'd been dismissive of the Celtics prior to the series, became so unnerved by Boston's pressing defense—and particularly by Russell; under the basket they all had one eye on Russell's telescopic arms—that in one stretch they took thirty-three shots and made only three. It was such an embarrassing spectacle, with some of the Knicks' balls missing the hoop completely and some even missing the backboard, that at moments the Celtics fans literally erupted in laughter. The final score, 112–97, actually understated the magnitude of the disaster for the Knicks; Dave DeBusschere, normally a brilliant shooter, took nine shots and missed every single one. It was, he felt, the worst game he'd ever played in his life, and the only consolation he took from it was the certainty that he could never again play as badly. After that debacle, the outcome of the series was never in doubt. Boston won it in six and became, for the twelfth time in thirteen years, Eastern Division champions.

• • •

The Lakers had faced the Warriors in the first round. Chamberlain considered their center, his friend Nate Thurmond, more challenging than any other center in the league, including Russell. Thurmond was as tall as Russell, but stronger, and more of a threat on offense. Thurmond had been on crutches when the Lakers met the Warriors in last year's playoffs, but this time around he was healthy and playing well. The Warriors also had Jeff Mullins, an outstanding shooting guard and playmaker who served as his team's Jerry West. When the Lakers lost the first two games, van Breda Kolff adjusted the starting lineup yet again, taking out the veteran Tom Hawkins and installing rookie Bill Hewitt opposite Baylor in the front court. The team came roaring back for four straight victories, their fortunes helped when, just thirty-seven seconds into the third game, Jeff Mullins was floored with a crippling knee injury.

For the Western Division championship, the Lakers took on the Hawks, who had been sold by Ben Kerner to a group of Atlanta investors the previous summer. The Hawks were a strong, balanced team, well coached by Richie Guerin, an astute strategist of the game. But while they played physically bruising defense—it harked back to the NBA of the late forties—they lacked both a big center and a scoring superstar. The Lakers took the first two closely contested games, but with both West and Baylor in curious slumps, they lost the third. West, who was suffering from migraine headaches so intense they blurred his vision, took two shots that actually missed the basket altogether in one game, something he could never remember doing before. Afterward, van Breda Kolff asked Chamberlain, who'd been concentrating on defense, to revert to the high-scoring style that the coach had spent the season insisting he abandon. Chamberlain had been averaging only fourteen points in the post-season, but he racked up twenty-five in the next game, and the Lakers easily won it and the game that followed, taking the Western Division title. After the fifth game, someone wrote on the blackboard in the Lakers dressing room, *Boston Here We Come.*

AT THE OUTSET of the finals, oddsmakers in Las Vegas rated the Lakers nine-to-five favorites over the Celtics. They had the better regular-season record and, since they had won eight of the nine playoff games they'd just completed, momentum was on their side. They had the home-court advantage. They were younger and stronger and faster and more talented—West, Baylor, and Chamberlain having all averaged more than twenty points per game during the regular season and Chamberlain having led the league in rebounds. The only factor keeping the odds from favoring the Lakers even more heavily was that since 1959 the two teams had met six times for the championship, and the Celtics had won every time.

Elgin Baylor had been in a slump for most of the playoffs, but he had hit fourteen of eighteen shots from the field in the last game against Atlanta, and that streak had given him a psychic jolt that he felt carrying him into the showdown with Boston. Baylor had never doubted that the Lakers would make it to the finals, nor had he ever doubted that the Celtics would also make it. Baylor knew one thing about Boston: when it had to win, it won. Nonetheless, Baylor was convinced that this was the year the Lakers not only could but would finally beat the Celtics. A championship was the one goal that had eluded Baylor in basketball, and he desperately wanted to win. For one thing, he wanted revenge for that long string of losses to the Celtics in the finals. Also, he was thirty-four, and while his knees had recovered, he could feel his speed and strength and agility ebbing. He was afraid he might never get another shot at a title.

At a team meeting prior to the first game, Baylor told the other players that the one great advantage the Lakers now had over the Celtics was Chamberlain and the effect he would have on Bill Russell. No one could prevent Russell from performing brilliantly on defense, but where Baylor felt that Russell made a real difference—and one that was often overlooked by the writers heaping accolades on his defensive accomplishments—was on offense. So often in a game, Russ managed to run up as many as twenty points, often sneaky, overlooked points made on offensive rebounds but points that nonetheless amounted to the margin of victory. If Chamberlain prevented Russell from making those offensive rebounds, Baylor told his teammates, that could decide the series. Chamberlain agreed, and he was convinced he could do it. After all, how often had Russell gotten into double digits against him? The fact of the matter was, when the Lakers were playing the Celtics, Chamberlain loved to see Russell with the ball.

The day of the first game, the *Los Angeles Times* carried an article titled "It's Time to Find Out If Wilt's a Winner." The article, by Mal Florence, who had covered the Lakers all season, referred to the "whispering campaign" that characterized Chamberlain as a perennial loser. These critics kept alluding to the fact that, playing on three different franchises in his ten-year career, Chamberlain had met Russell and the Celtics seven times in either the playoffs or the finals, and had won only once. Chamberlain was of course well aware of the whispering campaign and was acutely sensitive about the charge that he was a loser. What Chamberlain felt his critics overlooked was the fact that Boston did not sweep any of these contests. Many were decided in the final seconds of the seventh game and could have gone either way.

Boston had won one of the final games by one point, two of them by two points, and another by four points. That represented a sum total of nine points—four baskets and a foul shot. Take away those nine points and the Celtics dynasty disappeared altogether, and instead you had Wilt Chamberlain with a handful of championship rings.

THE DAY of the first game, Jerry West felt tired and listless from the moment he woke up. He snapped at his wife, Jane, who knew better than to reply, and while he attended the pregame practice, he hardly did any running. After the practice he bumped into Bill Russell, who was leading the Celtics to their practice session.

"How you doing?" Russell asked.

"I feel like I got nothing in me," West said. "This season's been two years long."

"It'll be over soon enough," Russell said.

Once the game began, however, West shook off his nervous lethargy. He played for forty-six minutes without tiring—dribbling, running, spinning, taking his signature jump shot from beyond the perimeter—and scored a playoff record of fifty-three points. During a down moment in the third quarter, Russell came up beside him. "Empty, huh?" he said. "I'm getting so I just don't believe you country boys anymore."

But both teams played almost flawless basketball, intense and error-free. Neither team was ever more than seven points ahead. They were tied fifteen times and swapped the lead twenty-one times. Boston led at the half and at the end of the third quarter, but the Lakers took the lead with seven minutes left to play when Keith Erickson scored on a loose ball, and they never surrendered it. Chamberlain made a critical basket with twenty-three seconds remaining, and at the buzzer the score stood at 120–118. The sportswriters in attendance considered it one of the best—and most rousing—games ever played in the NBA. "It was a game that should be preserved for the ages," Mal Florence declared in the *Los Angeles Times,* "one that should be used in future textbooks as a classic example of the way pro basketball should be played." Russell, who thought the Celtics had played superb basketball, was surprised that his team could score 118 points and still lose a game, but the key for the Lakers had been West. He had taken—and made—so many shots that toward the end of the game he started to find it embarrassing, and began passing off to Egan and Baylor. In the dressing room afterward, his arm was so sore that the Lakers trainer, Frank O'Neill, had to ice it down as if he were a baseball pitcher.

Elgin Baylor knew that the Celtics' goal was to split the opening pair of games in Los Angeles. If they could force Los Angeles to lose one game at home and then head back to Boston where, with the home-court advantage, they might win two, they would be up 3–1 and almost impregnable. The Lakers' strategy represented the mirror-opposite of this approach. They hoped to win the first two in Los Angeles and split the second two Boston games to return home for game five with a 3–1 lead. And so, although it was early in the series, the second game appeared crucial to both teams.

After the breathtaking first game, interest in the series grew even more intense. Tickets for game two quickly sold out, and Forum officials arranged for it to be shown on closed-circuit television in two theaters in downtown Los Angeles and in the International Ballroom at the Beverly Hills Hilton. It was another close, nerve-racking match, even more physical than the previous game. The Celtics' Don Nelson hit his head on Chamberlain's chin and had to have six stitches, while the Lakers' Bill Hewitt, whose wife had given birth during game one, received a gash on his jaw that required five stitches.

Throughout the game, Chamberlain and Russell effectively neutralized each other. Since Russell, on defense, had to remain under the backboard to counter Chamberlain, he could not come out and contest the ball the way he usually did, and this freed up the Lakers' shooting stars. West rang up forty-one points and Baylor hit for thirty-two while Johnny Egan scored twenty-six. To Bill Russell's surprise and irritation, Egan—*the little guard*—was making a crucial difference in the series. He had a graceless, desperate shot, but he moved quickly, and each point he scored seemed to represent to the fans the triumph of the underdog. Van Breda Kolff had made Egan a permanent starter only during the playoffs, and at first the Celtics had ignored him, focusing all of their energies on West instead, but between West and Egan the Lakers backcourt was producing fifty to sixty points.

In fact, during the second game, the two guards together scored sixty-seven, more than half the team's total output, and the Lakers won 118–112. In the dressing room afterward, Chamberlain sat on a bench holding an ice bag against his jaw, which ached from the collision with Don Nelson. The score, he thought, was deceptive. The Celtics had played well, with the lead again changing hands constantly, until a late spurt led by Elgin Baylor, who scored the Lakers' twelve final points, put the team ahead.

Baylor, who felt that he had played better than in any other game in the playoffs, was more encouraged. Van Breda Kolff had rested him for a few minutes at the start of the fourth quarter, and that had enabled him to maintain an exceptionally fast pace when he went back in. Baylor thought that his final twelve-point rally, and his team's two surges in the third quarter when the Celtics twice built up ten-point leads, were the turning points in the game. They showed that the Lakers now knew how to come back, regardless of the advantage the Celtics had established. In years gone by, Boston had more often than not been able to prevent such rallies because they surged and then, instead of slacking off, maintained a level of intensity that allowed them to trade baskets with their opponents. But now, when the Celtics turned it on, the Lakers could ratchet up their own intensity and overtake them again, and as a result Boston had lost two straight. Twice in previous playoff matchups, it was the Lakers who had lost two straight, and this had created a discouraging gloom, an ominous sense of foreboding that no one acknowledged but that would dog the team for the rest of the series, right up to the final bitter defeat. Baylor now wondered if, this time around, the Celtics were starting to feel similarly discouraged.

Russell insisted that the series was far from over. Taking off his uniform in the dressing room afterward, he told reporters, "Yes, I will see you Thursday, for the fifth game." But he knew as well as they did that in the thirteen years since he had joined the Celtics, the team had never trailed 0–2 in a playoff series. They'd been down 3–1 in 1968, but they had that first victory to cling to. Furthermore, no team in the history of the NBA had ever come back to win the championship after losing the first two games. The hole was just too deep.

Some one hundred Lakers fans, including the actress Rhonda Fleming and her husband, producer Hall Bartlett, accompanied the team to Boston and watched from front-row seats just behind the Los Angeles bench, but they were drowned out by the packed stands of Celtics supporters noisily demanding victory. Responding to that energy, the Celtics blew out of the starting gate, running up an 11–2 lead while the suddenly perplcxcd Lakcrs wcnt almost four minutes without scoring from the field. For the first time in the series, the Celtics double-teamed West—an omission in the first two games that had struck the Lakers as curious. Both West and Baylor lost their range, and the team fell seventeen points behind at halftime. It surged to a three-point lead in the third quarter, but that effort was so exhausting that West asked to be taken out, and the Lakers again fell behind, this time by fourteen points. West returned, but, unlike game one, this time he really did have no strength left. Johnny Egan tried to take his place as the primary outside shooter. He scored fourteen of the team's sixteen points in one stretch, and the Lakers surged a second time. But the two rallies had drained them, and while they were able to narrow the final gap with Boston, they could not overtake the Celtics and lost by six points.

Game four would be decisive, giving the Lakers an almost insurmountable 3–1 lead or tying the series at two apiece. A number of retired Celtics such as Tommy Heinsohn, Jim Loscutoff, and K. C. Jones showed up to sit with Auerbach behind the team's bench. For the second time in a row, the Celtics blasted off at the opening, running up a quick ten points while the Lakers were unable to score until five minutes into the game. From then on out, both teams played badly, turning the ball over dozens of times, and enduring long scoreless stretches, but with seven seconds left, the Lakers had a one-point lead and felt the game was theirs.

Then Joe Gushue, one of the officials, ruled that Baylor had stepped out-of-bounds retrieving a misfired pass from Chamberlain. Baylor was certain he had not in fact stepped out of bounds, but Gushue simply pointed at the line, saying nothing, and giving the ball to the Celtics. In the Boston huddle, Larry Siegfried suggested a play they called "Ohio," a special triple-pick based on a play that Siegfried and John Havlicek had used when they were together at Ohio State. Before the playoffs, Russell had gone through the regular-season stats, and he realized the team had lost seventeen games by three points or less. The Celtics had not been closing the way they should. They needed a surprise last-second play, a buzzer-beater, but Russell let the players themselves come up with one, and so during a practice that Russell did not attend, Havlicek had introduced "Ohio" to his teammates, and they had it saved up for just such an occasion.

But the play was complicated, and the team had never used it in a game before, and as they went into motion, Sam Jones, who had the ball, collided with his teammate Bailey Howell. Jones was knocked off balance, ruining the play, and as he slipped, he threw up a high shot from twenty-two feet out.

Even before he released it he could tell that the ball was badly thrown, that it would fall short, and he felt certain it would miss. In the excitement of the moment he assumed that Russell was still in the game, and he tried to put some backspin on the ball, to make it pop up, so that if it did miss, Russell might tap it in.

Russell, however, was not in the game. He had taken himself out and put in Don Nelson so the Celtics would have one more shooter in the crucial final moments. Standing on the sidelines Russell also thought Jones's shot was going to miss. *Damn,* he said to himself.

Jones, watching his shot loop toward the basket, thought it wasn't even going to hit the front rim, but it did, then it bounced up because of the backspin, hit the back rim, and with one second left on the clock, it dropped in. Chamberlain, enraged at the idea of losing the game by one point on such a sloppy shot, jumped up and grabbed the ball with both hands as it fell from the net, but with one second left the Lakers could accomplish nothing and they knew it.

We're still magic, Auerbach had told Jack Kent Cooke earlier in the season, and so it would seem. That such a badly thrown ball—a brick, a clunker, a classic Hail Mary desperation bailout shot—would not only go in but would determine, by *one* point, the outcome of a critical game in a championship series, well, there was only one explanation for it, fans and sportswriters and the players themselves agreed, and that was Celtics luck. Whether you despised it or swore by it, everyone had to admit it existed. "I was very lucky," Jones said after the game. "Somebody Up There likes him," wrote Gerry Sullivan in the *Herald.* "Kiss the Blarney Stone," proclaimed Mal Florence in the *Los Angeles Times.* "Drag out the four-leaf clovers." Tom Heinsohn, for one, even subscribed to the not entirely facetious theory that Boston Garden had a resident leprechaun who favored the home team. "Didn't you see that little gremlin sitting on the hoop when Sam shot?" he asked one of the sportswriters. "I thought for sure you'd see it."

The Lakers, angered by that loss and with the crowd behind them back in Los Angeles, played game five in a ferocious state of mind. They outran, outshot, and outscored the Celtics, who seemed hapless and uncertain. But the game was not without its costs for the Lakers. Boston's Emmette Bryant, who was six-one and known as Little Em, stuck a finger in Chamberlain's eye in the third quarter, and Wilt's sight was blurry for the rest of the game.

Then, with less than three minutes left to play, Bryant, who was also known as the Pest, stripped the ball from Jerry West, and despite the fact that the Lakers had a solid lead, West lunged for the ball and felt a stab of pain in his left thigh.

West hated to be called injury-prone, but he accepted the fact that he was. In his nine years in the NBA, he had broken his nose eight times and his hands twice. He had torn and pulled and bruised muscles, he had strained ligaments, and he had sprained ankles, wrists, and fingers. Most of the time these injuries, as well as various illnesses, had not kept him from playing, but some of them had, and in those nine years in the league he had missed a total of 128 games—more than an entire season. In 1967–68 he had set his own record by sitting on the bench for thirty-one games. In the season just completed, he'd been prevented from playing for twenty-one games. By the time the playoffs began, he had felt fine, but then after game two his hand had swollen up when he hurt it in a fall.

Now, with two and a half minutes left in the fifth game, West hobbled to the bench and sat down while Frank O'Neill, the trainer, examined him. West had pulled a hamstring. What particularly irked him was not just that he was hurt but that he been so foolish as to injure himself on such a meaningless play, diving recklessly after the ball even though the Lakers had a comfortable lead. Even without West, however, Los Angeles won easily. After the game, Robert Kerlan, the team physician, injected West's leg with cortisone, but the doctor was unable to immediately determine the severity of the injury. He would have to wait until tomorrow, when the hamstring had tightened up, before evaluating it, and he was uncertain that West would be able to play in game six.

Chamberlain, still unable to see clearly, was nursing his sore, swollen eye in the dressing room. Despite the thirteen-point victory, his mood was grim, and he brooded over the vagaries of chance. Luck once again appeared to be asserting itself as a factor in the finals. First there was Sam Jones's very, very lucky shot in the last seconds of game four—a shot that by any measure simply did not deserve to go in. If the off-balance Jones had missed that shot, the Lakers would have won game four and with their victory tonight would have won the championship. Instead, there would be at least one more game, in Boston Garden, with West—the Lakers' highest scorer, who'd run off twenty-eight points in the second half of the game they'd just won—injured and possibly unable to play. A reporter asked Chamberlain if the team would be able to maintain its momentum if West was benched because of his injury. "I don't think so," Chamberlain said.

VINCENT CARTER, an associate of team physician Robert Kerlan, accompanied the Lakers to Boston for game six to treat Chamberlain and West. Chamberlain arrived wearing sunglasses to hide his swollen eye, his vision still blurry. West's thigh bothered him, but he walked without a limp. By this time, going into the sixth game of the series, both teams felt battered and drained. On the Celtics, John Havlicek had a pulled groin muscle and a gash on the bridge of his nose, and he had been wearing a bandage over his left eye after the Lakers' Keith Erickson stuck a thumb in it during game three. Larry Siegfried, the most grievously injured Celtic, had a pulled hamstring, a hip-joint injury, bruised knees, and a swollen left elbow. Even the uninjured players were exhausted. They were approaching their one hundredth game of the season, and their reserves were depleted. Because of the tension, many of them were unable to sleep. Havlicek felt his body weakening game by game.

By the afternoon of game six, Chamberlain's vision had cleared, but his eye was still sore and he had gone through practice wearing the sunglasses. West had kept his leg wrapped in hot packs during the day, and trainer Frank O'Neill set aside a heating pad on the bench for him to apply to his leg whenever he came out of the game. Just before it began, Dr. Carter gave West's injured leg a shot of Novocain, and O'Neill bandaged it heavily. "If I had to take a saliva test now," West joked, "I'd never get out of the starting gate." Tom Hawkins had injured his ankle during practice, and so while Carter was at it he gave Hawkins a Novocain injection as well.

Just as they had in the two earlier games in the Garden, the Celtics surged to an early lead and were up 55–39 at the half. West was not visibly limping, and in fact, as often happened, by the second half his hamstring had sufficiently loosened that he was able to pick up the pace, and he eventually scored a total of twenty-six points. Even so, van Breda Kolff could see that he was playing at only 75 percent of his capacity, and made him rest for ten minutes. Elgin Baylor, after playing so well earlier in the series, was once again off his game. But the largest disappointment, in van Breda Kolff's view, was Chamberlain. A large part of what justified the big guy's salary was the expectation that he would step up in crucial, high-pressure situations like this one—with the chance to finish the series at hand and the team's leading scorer injured—and make a difference. Van Breda Kolff made sure the other Lakers got the ball in to Chamberlain, but he did nothing with it, taking only five shots and making only one of them.

The Lakers had hoped to clinch the title this night and avoid a winner-take-all seventh game. But they could not make it happen. Instead, they played as if the outcome were a foregone conclusion, as if here in the Garden, this seedy, hot arena, with its musty, smoke-filled air, its beer-stained aisles and dangling white-and-green banners and overhanging balconies filled with rowdy fans, the Celtics could not lose, as if the series was destined to go to a climactic seventh game and there was no point in futilely expending energy in game six. Even when the Celtics lost their rhythm in the fourth quarter and missed twenty-one out of twenty-seven field goals during one stretch, the Lakers couldn't capitalize, and they went down 99–90.

Despite Chamberlain's poor performance, he predicted in the dressing room after the game that the Lakers would win game seven. And when one of the reporters went into the Celtics dressing room and repeated what Chamberlain had said, Russell snapped. Tensions had been building between Russell and Chamberlain throughout the series. There had been a lot of jostling in the pivot, the two men pushing each other harder and harder, and at one point during game three they briefly came to blows after an entanglement over a rebound. It also irritated Russell that Chamberlain had been telling reporters that the Celtics' run of championships was due to luck. The man, he thought, was a loser who had an excuse for everything. "Who cares what Wilt says?" Russell asked. "That's all I've heard over and over again through the years—'Wilt this and Wilt that.' I don't give a damn what Wilt has to say."

THE CHAMPIONSHIP SERIES was to end where it had begun, in the Forum. In previous finals, Boston had always won the seventh game, but it had always had the home-court advantage. Every single one of those seventh games had been played in the Garden. Now, for the first time, they'd be playing the concluding game on an opponent's court. So far in the series, neither team had won a game away from home, and the Vegas oddsmakers rated the Lakers three-point favorites.

When the Lakers returned to Los Angeles after game six, everyone in town seemed to be asking about Jerry West's condition. *Can Jerry go all-out in game seven?* The team practiced the day before the game and West's leg had improved, but he was still favoring it. He felt that whether the team won or lost was going to depend on whether his knee held up, and the day of the game he was so tense even the sound of his own children irritated him. But Baylor, Chamberlain, and the rest of the Lakers felt confident. They were on home turf, their Sunday workout had been loose, and they knew what they needed to do. This was their year.

Jack Kent Cooke, in fact, was so confident of victory that he stocked iced champagne in the locker room, strung nets across the ceiling filled with thousands of balloons in neat cellophane packages, and had the University of Southern California's marching band on standby, in the hallway outside the arena, to lead the victory celebration by playing "Happy Days Are Here Again." He had even gone to the expense of printing up a program for the victory celebration. In the dressing room prior to the game's start, van Breda Kolff told his team to anticipate the Celtics fast break and to run themselves, keeping the pace fast, keeping the game moving, but the Lakers knew that already, and as they walked up the corridor to the court, they felt that mentally and physically they were prepared.

Just before the game started, Russell came upon a copy of the victory program Cooke had printed up, and he decided to do something he usually avoided as coach—resort to a motivational ploy. As exhausted as he was, he believed the Celtics could win that night only if they ran the entire game, and that required starting and then playing at a level of intensity higher than whatever the Lakers could muster. It was simply a matter of determination. They'd have to will themselves up to the necessary level of intensity and then stay there, but it was only for one final game, and they were an experienced team and they knew they were capable of it. So Russell showed the Celtics the Lakers' victory program, pointed out that Jack Kent Cooke had the audacity to tempt fate by presuming his team would win, and told them that the very existence of the program made it inevitable that they, the Celtics, would win, but only if they ran and ran and ran. Then they too filed out to the court.

The deal Roone Arledge had struck five years earlier between ABC and the NBA had paid off beyond his expectations, and the network was planning to broadcast game seven nationally, in prime time. The stands were filled with men in jackets and ties—spectators not fans, as Alex Hannum had once derisively observed—but when Jerry West was introduced, they began clapping and cheering madly and then started standing up until just about all the people in the arena were on their feet, and the cheering continued for the frail, shy man from Kanawha County who refused to give up. West just stood there acknowledging it, but the truth was he hated that kind of thing and felt like hiding. All he wanted to do was play the game.

The two teams took the floor, the Lakers in their gold uniforms with blue trim, the Celtics in green with white trim, all the Boston players still wearing the black sneakers that Red Auerbach had declared compulsory back in the fifties on the grounds that they didn't show the dirt like white sneakers. Russell wanted the Celtics to get out ahead early, and they did, right out of the tip-off. With West injured, the Celtics stopped double-teaming him, and that undercut the effectiveness of Johnny Egan, the man left open when the Celtics sagged back on West. Sam Jones in particular was able to take advantage of West's bad leg, cutting, feinting, dropping in jump shots. By the second quarter a pattern was established, with Boston building up leads of ten or twelve points and the Lakers fighting back to close the gap without ever moving out ahead. The first half ended with the Celtics up by three. The Lakers tied the game in the third quarter, but immediately went into a slump, missing fifteen shots in five minutes, and by the fourth quarter the Celtics had established a twenty-one-point lead.

It was then that the Lakers finally found their rhythm. West's injured leg made each step painful, and he wasn't as quick on defense. But with only one man guarding him, he now made up for it on offense, shooting from the outside and scoring more points than anyone else on his team. The Lakers steadily moved closer to the Celtics, basket by basket, and with each point West became more intense. He was in the zone, practically every shot dropping in, and it seemed to Baylor that West was now playing as if his hamstring were perfectly fine. But suddenly, just as West looked as if he was taking over the game, he twisted his injured left leg and began hobbling again. Not long after that, Baylor sprained a muscle in his right leg, and that slowed him. Even so, the Celtics were slowing as well, as their age got the better of them, and the Lakers continued to narrow their lead.

Chamberlain was concentrating on defense, still jostling angrily with

Russell in the pivot. With five minutes left on the clock, and the lead cut to nine points, he went up for a rebound, his twenty-seventh of the game. He grabbed the ball but fell off balance when he dropped back, stumbling to the floor and striking his knee so hard against the floorboards that he felt the jangling sting throughout his body. The officials called for a standard twenty-second injury time-out. Trainer Frank O'Neill sprayed Chamberlain's knee with a numbing anesthetic. Chamberlain returned to the court, but his knee hurt so badly that he could only limp with a grimace, and when the clock was stopped after West was fouled, Chamberlain asked van Breda Kolff to take him out.

The request infuriated van Breda Kolff. All professional athletes were expected to play with pain from time to time, it was the price of glory, especially in the finals. West was limping up and down the court, but he hadn't asked to be taken out. Baylor was favoring a leg, and he hadn't asked to be taken out. Chamberlain, however, was insisting that he couldn't play, so van Breda Kolff took him out and replaced him with Mel Counts.

On the court, Bill Russell was astonished that Chamberlain had taken himself out of the game. Chamberlain had only banged his shin, it seemed to Russell, hardly a serious injury, and in any event, with the championship at stake, you played, injured or not. *There are no such things as injuries,* Auerbach had said at the outset of the playoffs. *If a player can walk, he can play.* At least that was the Celtics philosophy. Back in the final game of the 1965 championship series, Russell had insisted on playing with a hemorrhaging eyeball after Jerry West had jammed a finger in it. That was the way it was supposed to come down in the pros—a player refusing to take himself out of the game even when the coach wanted him out. After all, most of the players on both teams were nursing some sort of injury. The Celtics' Larry Siegfried had played throughout the series with a pulled hamstring, bruised knees, bruised hip, left-elbow contusion, and charley horse—though, as one sportswriter noted, he was wrapped tighter than Ramses II.

Not only was Russell surprised to see Chamberlain go out, he wanted him in the game, despite the fact that his own job became a lot easier with Wilt on the bench. The reason was that, though he had yet to announce it, this was Russell's last game. Halfway through the season, around the time he hurt his knee so badly that he had to be carried off the court on a stretcher, Russell had decided to make this season his last. His level of play was deteriorating, his moments of inspired basketball were fewer and fewer. One reason the Celtics had barely made it into the playoffs was that he had so rarely been able to ignite the team. His coaching responsibilities made it almost impossible for him to throw himself completely into a game, but he was also losing his passion for basketball. He had not lost it entirely, and he was determined that he would not allow that to happen, that he would not keep playing when his passion was gone and he was suiting up just for the money.

Russell had always remembered Bob Cousy's final season, with endless maudlin tributes in every city in the league, as if Cousy had died and all these crowds of people were mourning him. Russell had decided he did not want to go out that way, on a tide of raw emotion, so he had mentioned his decision to no one else except Oscar Robertson, after the playoff series with the Royals. But he did want to go out with one last championship victory, and he wanted Chamberlain in the game. To win his final game with Chamberlain sitting on the bench—instead of in the game, forcing Russell to earn it—would cast a cloud over the victory. Chamberlain, by asking to be taken out, was ruining Russell's final game, Russell felt, and like van Breda Kolff, he was infuriated.

Chamberlain was sitting on the bench, a towel around his shoulders, and after a minute his knee felt better and he signaled to van Breda Kolff. "I'm ready to go back in," he called.

But with Mel Counts playing center, the Lakers had narrowed the Celtics' lead to just three points, and van Breda Kolff decided to keep Counts in the game. "Wait," van Breda Kolff said. "Wait."

Chamberlain grabbed another towel and stalked to the far end of the bench. Most of the Lakers, he felt, had been playing miserably throughout the game. Baylor was eight for twenty-two, and Counts, despite the team's little surge when he took Chamberlain's place, was four for thirteen. Jerry West and Wilt himself were the only two players making more than a third of their shots. Chamberlain felt it was necessary for him to return to the game. He signaled to van Breda Kolff again and again, and when the coach did nothing, he approached him. "Put me back in," he said.

Van Breda Kolff now had a decision to make. Did he put his star center, a man considered by many to be the best basketball player in history, back in for these crucial final minutes? Or did he stay with Counts? Counts had a hot hand. He had just hit a jump shot from the foul line to bring the Lakers within a point. It was the closest they'd been in the entire fourth quarter. As had happened from time to time throughout the season, with Chamberlain on the bench the Lakers were playing better than they had at any other point in the game. Chamberlain had pulled down twenty-seven rebounds, but van Breda Kolff felt that all too often on defense, instead of moving around and blocking out, Chamberlain simply stood under the basket waiting for the ball to be shot so he could pick up the rebound. And since the Celtics were shooting so well, all too often there was no ball to rebound. Counts, on the other hand, was moving off Russell when Russell set picks and switching over to cover the unguarded Celtic with the ball. That had cut into Boston's scoring. And back in the first game of the Western Division championship against the Hawks, Counts had made a game-winning three-point play in the final seconds. Counts had proven that he could come in at the end and provide the jolt that put the team over the top. So van Breda Kolff made his decision. "I'm not putting you back in," he told Chamberlain. "We're playing better without you."

Chamberlain, enraged and humiliated, returned to the end of the bench and sat back down.

With less than two minutes to play, and the game very much in the balance, the tension on the court became almost unbearable. The noise from the crowd made it almost impossible for the players to hear one another, and both teams turned sloppy. West, his backcourt partner Keith Erickson, and Celtic Don Nelson all committed turnovers. Counts scored again to put the Lakers up by one—the first time the entire game they had been in the lead—but an official called him for traveling, and the basket was erased. Now there was little more than a minute left to play. Erickson blocked a shot, and the loose ball was recovered by Nelson, a former Laker, who made a wild, awkward shot from the top of the key. The ball struck the front rim and bounced a good three feet up into the air, and then, just as had happened with Sam Jones's lucky shot at the end of the fourth game, it fell into the basket.

The Celtics now had a three-point lead, but with forty-five seconds left, the Lakers felt they were still in the game. They recovered the ball after an offensive foul by Larry Siegfried. Counts tried to drive to the basket, but Russell blocked the shot. It had been a rough game, with both teams fouling each other heavily, and now Siegfried—the best free-throw shooter in the league—drew a foul. It was the ultimate pressure moment, but Siegfried, wrapped in bandages, stepped to the foul line and lofted in both shots. Then Havlicek was fouled and put the Celtics up by six with a free throw. Frustrated, desperate, having clawed their way back only to slip in the face of this final Celtics surge, the Lakers sank two free throws and made a final basket, but then they ran out of time, and, with Chamberlain watching angrily from the bench, they lost the game, the series, and the championship by two points.

As the fans filed out, ABC sportscaster Jack Twyman was interviewing Havlicek on the sidelines when Red Auerbach, cigar in hand, materialized beside him. Auerbach pointed at the ceiling. "What are they going to do with those goddamned balloons up there?" he asked. "They'll eat them!" he shouted and burst into giddy laughter.

In the Lakers dressing room, Chamberlain was angrier than he'd ever been in his life. He felt certain that van Breda Kolff had benched him as payback for all their quarrels. Motivated by spite, the coach had thrown away the game and the championship title, and publicly humiliated Chamberlain himself, in order to settle a score. Van Breda Kolff was just as angry. No true athlete, he believed, asked to be taken out of a championship game in a crucial moment—with the outcome in the balance and his teammates and fans depending on him—just because he got a little banged up. It was unprofessional, the equivalent of leaving the field of battle after a minor flesh wound. An argument broke out. Van Breda Kolff called Wilt a quitter and Chamberlain called him a liar, and the two men had to be physically restrained from attacking each other.

West sat on a bench in his sweat-soaked jersey, his injured leg propped up on a chair. He had given the game everything he had. In fact, he had played so hard—earning a triple-double, with forty-two points, thirteen rebounds, and twelve assists—that *Sport* magazine was to name him the Most Valuable Player of the series. But still his team had lost. They should have won, but they didn't. It seemed to Bill Libby, one of the sportswriters, that West was like a figure in a Greek tragedy, someone the fates had conspired to deprive of the one thing he truly wanted. The visitors' dressing room was next door, and as West sat resting his knee on the bench, the sounds of the Celtics' celebration could be heard through the wall. "I can't stand to listen to that," he said.

The Celtics, who had felt the heat of West's determination through all seven games, were aware how much he had wanted to win. They all admired him for his talent and for his character, and after a while Russell and

Havlicek came into the Lakers dressing room to pay him tribute. Russell, who was overcome with emotion and unable to speak, clasped West's hand for a long moment in silence and then turned away. Havlicek said, "I love you."

Russell and Havlicek returned to the visitors' dressing room. As the celebrations died down, the Celtics showered and changed and gradually made their way out to the street. Russell, one of the last to remain, finished putting on his lavender shirt and tan suit. Someone had left a single bottle of champagne next to his locker. Russell rarely drank, but he figured it would be nice to have a bottle of the champagne used to celebrate his final victory. He picked up the bottle with one hand and his battered suitcase with the other, and walked out the door. In the hallway, a young female usher stepped in front of him and held out a pen and paper.

"You've refused all these years," she said. "How about signing this now, just this once?"

Russell ignored her and continued down the hall.

IN RACIALLY TROUBLED BOSTON, the Celtics' unexpected victory touched off a frenzied celebration unmatched by any of their previous championships. Only seventy-five people had shown up the previous year to welcome the team back after winning the finals, but now a crowd of 2,000, including Governor Francis Sargent, was waiting when the Celtics arrived at Logan Airport, and they broke into cheers as the players appeared through the gate. The city's newspapers welcomed them just as enthusiastically. Under the headline "The Conquering Celtics," the *Herald*'s editorialist wrote, "Each game of the grueling playoffs seems to have its own hero, but the secret of the Celtics is that, unlike Los Angeles, they do not rely on super stars to save their games. The Celtics play and win as a team—a team that keeps Boston the home of champions and proud of them." *The Boston Globe* declared, "Some day in the far-off future, there'll be other great teams, no doubt. But they'll have no stature in Boston, where people will sneer: 'Aw, you shoulda seen the Celtics.' "

Two days later, on a cool and drizzling Thursday morning, 30,000 people gathered four and five deep along a parade route that ran from the Commons down Tremont Street and then up Washington Street and ended at City Hall, where Mayor Kevin White waited to hand out silver trays and Boston rock-ers to the members of the team. A flatbed truck, its sides lined with red, white, and blue bunting, pulled the Celtics slowly through the cheering, waving crowds. Auerbach wore a khaki raincoat and jovially scattered cigar ashes on his players. They were all there, the heroes of the series: Havlicek the team captain, Sam Jones the savior of game five with his off-balance final-seconds shot, Little Em Bryant, Satch Sanders, Bailey Howell . . . all of them that is except Bill Russell. It was the first time in their eleven championships that the city had honored them with a parade, but Russell—the man who played for the Celtics not for Boston, who said he owed the public nothing, who never heard the boos because he never listened to the cheers—declined to attend. Although no one knew it at the time, he was gone.

THE FINAL GAME of the 1969 championship series was the culmination of an epic ten-year rivalry between two of the greatest athletes of mid-century America. But it was more than that, too; it was the last battle in what had been an ongoing contest over how best to compete, a contest that had revealed to fans and to the players themselves the essence of athletic greatness in a team sport. And in the end it had turned on a single moment and a single choice—Chamberlain's request to be taken out—that seemed to reveal the issue at the very core of the rivalry: could determination trump talent? Milton Gross had watched the game closely. Both Russell and Chamberlain, he thought, were extremely complex individuals, but in the end what differentiated them on the court was that Russell was always able to make his players an extension of himself, while Chamberlain, for all his personal dominance, never truly became a part of a team. And in the end, that was the difference between winning and losing.

In the days after the game, the debate continued over van Breda Kolff's decision to keep Chamberlain on the bench for the final minutes. Some, like Milton Gross, blamed van Breda Kolff. His decision was tantamount to suicide, they said, and the upshot was that the Lakers had not been beaten by the Celtics but by their own coach. Many people, however, blamed Chamberlain for asking to be taken out of a championship game when he had teammates who were injured and still playing. It was, according to this line of thinking, the ultimate indication of Chamberlain's selfishness as a player, his refusal to sacrifice himself for the sake of his team, and if nothing else it proved that he was overvalued and overpaid. After all, back in 1966, with Darrall Imhoff at center, the Lakers had also lost the seventh game of the finals by two points, and that had been at Boston Garden, without the home-court advantage.

Chamberlain, who followed the coverage, continued to brood over the final game. He decided van Breda Kolff was the worst coach he'd ever played under, a rotten coach, utterly hopeless, a man ignorant of human nature. By keeping him out of the game, van Breda Kolff had humiliated him on national television and prevented the Lakers from winning the championship. It was true that Mel Counts had had a hot hand in those final minutes, Chamberlain reasoned, but van Breda Kolff could have sent Wilt back onto the floor and also kept Counts in, by moving him to forward. Russell had been playing with five fouls at that point, which restricted his aggressiveness on defense, and Chamberlain was sure he would have been able to score against him. Chamberlain talked to Milton Gross by telephone from his home in Los Angeles, just before visiting the doctor to treat his twisted knee. "The thing that kills me," he said, "is that we had the chance to win and he wouldn't put me back in. I don't see how he could have left me on the bench. I asked about ten times." The Lakers, he went on to say, were the better team and should have won the game but had been undermined from within, by their coach. "They didn't beat us," he said. "We beat ourselves. You don't mind too much being beaten by a really superior team, but to go out and beat yourself, it's a shame."

Van Breda Kolff, while not complaining as publicly as Chamberlain, took the position that if he had made any mistake, it was not in keeping Chamberlain out but in leaving him in as long as he had. The team that had finished the game, with Counts at center, had been in the midst of rallying from a deficit created by the team playing with Chamberlain. "If I had had fifteen minutes' practice with the team that finished the game," he told an acquaintance, "and if I had played them the whole game, I would have won the title."

The ongoing dispute, and the way it was played out in the papers, distressed the other Lakers. Jerry West felt that Chamberlain, by publicly blaming his coach for the loss to Boston, was only going to inflame matters, making it probably impossible for both men to remain on the same team come the following season. West wished Chamberlain had kept quiet until he gained a little perspective on the season, but that was not Chamberlain's way. The big guy was always going to sound off. A few days after the seventh game, West flew into New York to receive the Dodge Charger that *Sport* magazine was giving him for having been named Most Valuable Player. During the lunch at Leone's Restaurant, someone asked West if he saw a solution to the feud between Chamberlain and van Breda Kolff. "Yeah," West said, "one of those old-time duels."

AFTER THE SEASON ENDED, Bill Russell set out on the college lecture

circuit. During his talks, he spoke with little preparation, taking questions and candidly giving his opinions on whatever topic came up. Students asked him for his views on the Black Panthers, the military-industrial complex, and women's liberation. In late May, his tour brought him to the University of Wisconsin, and in the midst of political questions, one student stood up and asked why Russell was always compared favorably to Wilt Chamberlain when, as Russell himself well knew, Chamberlain was by far the superior player. The only reason the Celtics usually beat Chamberlain's teams, the student continued, was that he always had such weak teammates. The Celtics were just lucky, the student added, and would have lost the 1969 championship if Chamberlain hadn't been injured in the final minutes. "Why don't people see that?" the student asked.

Russell had faced tougher interrogators before, but he was nonetheless a little startled by the question. He pointed out that in Wilt's first year he had played with Paul Arizin and Tom Gola and Guy Rogers. "That's not bad," he said. On the 76ers, he continued, Wilt's teammates included Luke Jackson,

Chet Walker, Billy Cunningham, Hal Greer, and Wally Jones. "That doesn't seem bad company," he said. On the Lakers, he went on, Wilt started with Elgin Baylor, Keith Erickson, and Jerry West. "That's not bad either," Russell told the student. "I don't see how anybody can say he never played with anybody good. Now, you say he got hurt . . ."

As Russell began talking about Chamberlain's injury in the last minutes of the seventh game, he started to feel more and more exasperated. As he'd listed Chamberlain's genuinely talented teammates over the years, it had reminded him of Chamberlain's tendency to blame everyone but himself for his defeats. And now, when he got onto the subject of Chamberlain's supposed injury, all of the rage Russell had felt at Chamberlain for ruining what was Russell's final game came flooding back. Throughout his career, Russell had made it a practice never to publicly criticize another player, on his team or any other, but now he let loose.

"I want to tell you something," Russell said to the student. In the final game of the championship series, he went on, Wilt had hurt his leg when the Lakers were trying to catch the Celtics and asked to be taken out. But the Lakers kept the rally alive, and they fought back to within two points of the Celtics. "So Wilt made a miraculous recovery and wanted to come back into the game," Russell said. "Now, in my opinion, if he's hurt so bad that he can't play in the seventh game, he should go straight to the hospital. But if he's hurt and then five minutes later recovers, there's something wrong with that injury. You can't quit like that and win championships."

Russell told the student he sided with van Breda Kolff for keeping Chamberlain on the bench for the final minutes. "Wilt copped out in the last game," Russell said. "Any injury short of a broken leg or a broken back isn't good enough. When he took himself out of that game, when he hurt his knee, well, I wouldn't have put him back in the game either." Russell told the student that he himself had never said Chamberlain had no talent. "But basketball is a team game," he went on. "I go by the number of championships. I play to bring out the best in my teammates. Are you going to say he brought out the best in Elgin and Jerry?" Russell then said he thought criticism of Chamberlain as a loser was both justified and unjustified. By calling him a loser, people acted as if he should have been a winner. But that assumed he was greater than he actually was. On the other hand, Chamberlain invited the criticism because he was the one who made the loudest claims about his greatness. "He asks for it," Russell said. "He talks a lot about what he's going to do. What it's all about is winning and losing, and he's done a lot of losing. He thinks he's a genius. He isn't."

Russell was unaware that a local reporter was sitting in the audience, taking it all down. The reporter wrote a story highlighting the remarks about Chamberlain, the newswires picked it up, and it appeared around the country. The story did not dwell on the fact that Russell thought he was speaking off the record to a group of college students, and Chamberlain, whose knee was still so sore from game seven that he'd canceled a tour with the Harlem Globetrotters in Europe, was enraged. "He's been my house guest and he's broken bread with me," he told an acquaintance. "I'd like to jam a ball down his throat."

TWO DAYS after the Celtics had won the championship, George Sullivan, a reporter for the *Herald-Traveler,* dropped by Red Auerbach's office in the Garden to discuss the season. Sullivan asked Auerbach if he was satisfied with the job Russell had done as coach. "What are you talking about?" Auerbach asked. "Two days ago we won the world championship." Sullivan pointed out that with a different coach, the Celtics might have done much better during the regular season. Auerbach dismissed this reasoning, and when he called Russell to describe the conversation, Russell said, "Don't worry, Red, it doesn't make a difference, because I've made up my mind to leave."

Auerbach did not take Russell seriously. He thought that Russell just felt exhausted, and Auerbach was convinced he could get Russell to change his mind. Auerbach believed Russell had a good three years of top-caliber play left in him. Russell was aging, and his legs weren't what they used to be, but Auerbach was certain that his intelligence and his years of experience would more than compensate for that. Also, Auerbach knew that Russell was aware that without him, the Celtics would simply collapse. So Auerbach kept talking to Russell, trying to bring him around, and Auerbach thought Russell was going to do it, because when he asked why Russell wanted to stop playing, the answers he got seemed vague and unsatisfying.

"I don't feel like it," Russell said.

"Where's your logic?" Auerbach asked.

"I don't have any," Russell said.

• • •

Nonetheless, Russell's mind was made up, and during the summer he wrote an article for *Sports Illustrated* describing his decision. It appeared on the newsstands in early August, and for just about everyone in Boston, it was the first they'd heard the news. Many of the city's sportswriters, who had never liked Russell anyway, felt he had betrayed his team by hiding his decision to retire in return for a check from *Sports Illustrated,* reportedly in the amount of $10,000, for the exclusive story. Now, two months before the new season was to begin, the Celtics had neither a center nor a coach. And since Auerbach had gone into the college draft assuming that Russell would return, instead of drafting a center, he picked a guard named Jo Jo White.

One day that summer Russell climbed into his Lamborghini and drove to California, leaving behind his wife, Rose—their marriage had gone stale a good ten years earlier—and his three children and his house on Haverhill Street in Reading. He wanted to put every aspect of his life in Boston in the past. He had once said he planned to retire to Liberia to run his rubber plantation, in which he had invested $250,000, but it had gone bankrupt. His restaurant, Slade's, had gone bankrupt as well, and he defaulted on a $90,000 loan from the Small Business Administration he'd used to purchase it. He was in arrears on his taxes, too, and a few years later the IRS put a lien on the Reading house because he owed the federal government $34,430.

Unable to persuade Russell to change his mind, Auerbach named Tommy Heinsohn as the next coach. But without Russell the team finished the season 34–48, failing to make the playoffs for the first time in twenty years, and attendance plummeted. At the end of the season, Heinsohn realized that the team would need to be completely rebuilt, and he released three of the remaining players from the dynasty years: Emmette Bryant, Bailey Howell, and Larry Siegfried. (Four years later, Heinsohn coached a new Celtics team featuring John Havlicek, Dave Cowens, Don Chaney, Jo Jo White, and Paul Silas to another championship.)

In Los Angeles, Russell found an apartment near Hollywood, became a vegetarian, and took up serious golf. He tried to get into the film business, landing a few supporting-actor roles and appearing on some comedy-variety television shows, then he began working as the color analyst for ABC's basketball broadcasts.

Butch van Breda Kolff knew that after what had happened in game seven of the finals, he would be unable to coach Chamberlain any longer, and he quit his job and became coach of the Detroit Pistons. Jack Kent Cooke hired Joe Mullaney, who'd built Providence College into a national powerhouse, as his replacement. The following year, Chamberlain ruptured the patella tendon in his right knee during a game against Phoenix and was out for most of the season. He recovered by the playoffs, however, and the Lakers went all the way to the finals again, only to lose to the Knicks. The next year, Mullaney could get the Lakers only to the second round of the playoffs. So Cooke fired Mullaney and hired former Celtic Bill Sharman, and in 1972 the Lakers did finally win the championship, by beating the Knicks, though Elgin Baylor, his knees completely worn down, had retired early in the season and was not part of the team. In 1973, the Lakers again made it to the finals, to face the Knicks for the third time in four years.

The Knicks were now at the peak of their early-seventies greatness, with Earl Monroe and Walt Frazier in the backcourt, Jerry Lucas and Willis Reed sharing center, and Bill Bradley and Dave DeBusschere at forward. They lost the first game but took the next three. Bill Russell was covering the series for ABC, and he was back in the Forum for the fifth game. It was close, but both Chamberlain and West were well past their primes by then. The Knicks won by nine and clinched the series. After the game, Russell, wearing his gold ABC blazer, walked down the corridor toward the Knicks dressing room to interview the new champions. As he reached the door, it opened and out stepped Chamberlain, who had just been inside congratulating the winners and was still drenched in sweat and wearing his Lakers warm-up jacket. Russell and Chamberlain saw each other at the same time, their eyes met for a brief, hard moment, and then they walked past each other without nodding or speaking. The sportswriter Merv Harris witnessed the encounter and thought, *Cold, icy cold.*

By then Russell also had his own nighttime radio talk show, taking calls and conducting interviews. While most of his guests were athletes or sports figures, he never invited Chamberlain to appear, even though they were now living in the same city. A caller once asked him why. "It's hard to interview someone," he said with his trademark cackle, "when you're not talking to him."

IN 1973, Russell became coach of the Seattle SuperSonics and revived his war with the Boston press corps by telling Seattle reporters in his first press conference there that living in Boston had been a traumatic experience and had left him with scars and bad memories. Boston was the most rigidly segregated city in the country, he declared, and its sportswriters were some of the most egregious racists, complaining constantly that the Celtics had too many black players. Larry Claflin, a columnist for the *Boston Herald-American,* responded by describing his support for and celebration of black athletes, and concluded by saying, "I am not a racist sports writer. I suspect Russell is the racist."

Throughout the seventies, Russell remained angry and unpredictable. In 1972, he refused to appear at a public ceremony in Boston Garden retiring his number even though he was at the arena to broadcast the game, and Auerbach had to have the banner raised with just a few of the old Celtics standing around, before any fans arrived. In 1975, he refused to show up for the ceremony inducting him into the Basketball Hall of Fame. In 1977, despite his declarations earlier in his career that he disliked white people, he married one. His second wife was Didi Anstett, a striking, dark-haired woman who had been Miss USA in 1968 and was fourteen years younger than he was.

The marriage didn't last, and neither did his job with the SuperSonics. He brought the team into the playoffs three times, but had difficulty imposing his will on the new generation of players preoccupied with their salaries and statuses and uninterested in Russell's concept of team play. After four years, when the team fell apart and began losing at home as well as on the road, even the fans demanded Russell's departure, and it became inevitable.

Russell became a game analyst for CBS, but his commentaries were sometimes rambling and vague, and in 1983 the network replaced him with Tommy Heinsohn. His next job, as coach of the Sacramento Kings, lasted only eleven months. He was then made the team's vice president of basketball operations, but was fired from that job as well after a year and a half. Afterward, Russell went into seclusion. He stopped reading newspapers and watching television news. Selling the house he'd bought on a golf course in Sacramento, he retreated to his home outside Seattle on Mercer Island, hidden on a hillside, with a view of Lake Washington, and lived as a recluse, reading and watching *Jeopardy!* and golf on television.

THE NIGHT Chamberlain ran into Russell in the Forum he had played what turned out to be his final game in the NBA. He always liked statistics, and he had amassed plenty. He had played 1,045 regular-season games in fourteen years for a total of 47,859 minutes. He had scored 31,419 points and made 23,924 rebounds. He had played 160 playoff games for a total of 7,559 minutes, 3,607 points, and 3,913 rebounds. He had won seven divisional titles and two championships. The following year he became coach of the San Diego Conquistadors, a team in the still struggling American Basketball Association. Leonard Bloom, the owner of the Conquistadors, signed him for $1.92 million for three years, with the idea that he'd coach a year and then, when his playing contract with the Lakers expired, he'd play as well. But he missed practices and even games, and demoralized his players by criticizing them excessively. The team tied for last place and Chamberlain quit.

Over the next few years, various NBA teams tried to lure him out of retirement. In 1976, William Wirtz, the owner of the Chicago Bulls, offered him a salary and a cut of all tickets sold above the current average if he would join the team. The Knicks and the New Jersey Nets also made offers. So did the Lakers' new owner, Dr. Jerry Buss, who wanted Chamberlain to play backup center to Kareem Abdul-Jabbar, and 76ers owner Harold Katz, who launched a public campaign to try to lure him back to his hometown. Instead, Chamberlain coached a women's volleyball team, appeared in commercials when a company such as Volkswagen wanted to make a point about size, and acted in *Conan the Destroyer* with Arnold Schwarzenegger. But he seemed bored, restless, and lonely. He spent days on end watching giant-screen television in his mansion in Los Angeles. He complained to friends such as Al Attles and Eddie Gottlieb that they never called him, but the fact was they did call. Chamberlain, however, was notoriously difficult to reach. "When and where and I'll take it from there," the message on his answering machine said, but he hardly ever returned phone calls or replied to letters. The mailbox at his home was at the foot of a long driveway, next to the trash cans. Once, when he was leaving in his car with his attorney Michael Richman, the son of his old friend Ike Richman, he stopped, opened his mailbox, and threw all his mail into the trash can.

"What are you doing?" Richman asked.

"Nothing in there," Chamberlain replied.

By the early nineties, more than two decades after the 1969 championship series, Chamberlain and Russell were still not speaking, and Russell's criticism continued to gnaw at Chamberlain. "Bill Russell: Why do you find it so hard to apologize to me for that statement you made about me some twenty-odd years ago, that you later admitted was made in error?" Chamberlain plaintively wrote in a 1992 memoir. "For those of you who don't remember, after a championship series in which Bill's Celtics beat my Lakers, I sat out much of the fourth quarter—I was *taken* out. Russell was asked, in a post-game interview, why I wasn't put back in the game and, infuriated, he said, 'I would never have left the game with anything less than a broken back.' As if I *wanted* to sit down, as if I didn't *want* to play! I was furious. Years later, Bill admitted—but not to me—that his comment was out of line. Someone asked him if he'd ever apologize to me and he said, 'No, I can't apologize. I'm not that kind of guy.' "

Then, in 1993, almost a quarter of a century after their feud had started, Russell and Chamberlain were reunited. By then, a year after the Dream Team appeared in the Barcelona Olympics, the NBA had become a huge and fabulously lucrative sports business. Even weak franchises sold for hundreds of millions of dollars, and Michael Jordan was earning $30 million a year. Shaquille O'Neal, another one of the league's new stars, was to appear in a new commercial for Reebok sneakers, but to make the point that he was the latest in the succession of great NBA centers, the producers asked Russell, Chamberlain, Kareem Abdul-Jabbar, and Bill Walton to appear with him. The commercial was shot in Los Angeles, and Chamberlain was accompanied to the set by his lawyer Sy Goldberg, who at five-seven felt among all these seven-footers as if he were walking through a redwood forest. Russell and Chamberlain did not go into the issue that had divided them and Russell certainly did not apologize to Chamberlain, but the two men found it was possible to stand together in the same room and shoot the breeze as if nothing had ever happened.

Russell's mixed success in later life was softening him. "I don't care if I never go to Boston again," he had told a reporter in 1975, but now the memorabilia promoter Joie Casey lured him back to the city by signing him to an exclusive autograph contract. Since Russell had refused most autograph requests through the decades, his signature was extremely rare. Casey figured it was one of the five most valuable in the world, up there with the autographs of Fidel Castro, Mikhail Gorbachev, Pope John Paul II, and the Queen of England. By the terms of the deal, Russell was paid a reported $250,000 to sign five thousand pieces of memorabilia—jerseys, basketballs, photographs, cards—over two years. Casey then actually set up a reunion between Russell and Chamberlain, arranging for them both to spend a January afternoon in 1995—the year the Boston Garden was finally torn down—signing autographs at Boston College High School.

The two men, realizing that it was now habit more than bitterness that had kept them apart, that they were too old for feuds, sat in adjacent booths chatting with each other as well as with fans, Russell's distinctive cackle erupting periodically. Russell had always liked to be one up on Chamberlain, and he managed to accomplish that on this afternoon as well, signing some five hundred autographs for a reported $120,000, while Chamberlain, who'd given his autograph to almost anyone who asked over the years, signed one thousand but earned only $40,000. Russell, who left first, invited Chamberlain to dinner, but Chamberlain joked that Russell's tight schedule wouldn't give Chamberlain the opportunity to eat all the food he would want to order if Russell was paying the bill.

After that, the two men began talking from time to time by telephone—as regularly as a couple of old ladies, Chamberlain liked to tell people—the calls usually initiated late at night by Chamberlain, who would call Russell "Felton," while Russell called his old rival "Norman." Their conversations ranged over just about every conceivable topic, but they never discussed the question that almost invariably arose whenever either one of them was interviewed, or even just buttonholed in an airport by a fan: which of the two had been the greater player.

Then in 1997, Bob Costas jointly interviewed Russell and Chamberlain before the all-star game and Russell finally made a public but limited and oblique apology for calling Chamberlain a quitter almost thirty years earlier.

"I said something I shouldn't have said," Russell told Costas. "I was wrong."

"What was that?" Costas asked.

"I'm not going to go into it," Russell said. "What I said was wrong and injurious to him. I apologized to him."

Having made peace with Chamberlain, all that awaited Russell now was a reconciliation with his true antagonist, the city of Boston. From the mellowed vantage point of late middle age, Russell had begun to have different feelings about the city he had disliked as long as he had played there. In Boston he had been surrounded by teammates who had enabled him to be as good as he was and to win as often as he had. Had he played on any other team, he probably would not have been as successful as he was. That team—Cousy, Sharman, Heinsohn, K. C. Jones, and later Havlicek, Sam Jones, Satch Sanders—had perfectly complemented his daunting but limited talents. If the Rochester Royals or the St. Louis Hawks had drafted him, he might have been an also-ran, just as he might have ended up a shipyard welder if USF's scout Hal DeJulio had not happened to catch his final game for McClymonds High back in 1952. The NBA team he did wind up playing on was assembled by Red Auerbach, and so it was safe to say that without Auerbach there might have been no Bill Russell—at least the Bill Russell who the Professional Basketball Writers Association of America decided in 1980 was the greatest player in the history of the NBA. But without Walter Brown there would have been no Red Auerbach, and without the city of Boston there would have been no Walter Brown. So Russell now realized he had been wrong all those many years ago when he said he owed the public nothing. The city's fans—the Corner Boys—had supported the team through those precarious years in a way that the fans of a lot of those early clubs—Washington, D.C., or Chicago, to give two examples—had not supported their teams.

And so it came about in 1999 that Russell agreed to return to the Celtics' new arena, the FleetCenter, to have his number officially retired once again, this time in a public ceremony. Proceeds from the benefit would go to the National Mentoring Partnership, a foundation in which both he and his daughter, Karen, were involved. Some 10,000 fans bought tickets to the event, and special guests sat at sixty-five tables set up on the floor of the court. The tribute lasted three hours. Bill Cosby and Bryant Gumbel served as emcees, Cosby acknowledging that for most of the sixties, the Celtics had no equal on the court. "I have trouble saying this because I am from Philadelphia," he said, and when the name of the rival city provoked reflexive boos, he added, "I don't know why you're booing me. You won everything."

Johnny Mathis, Russell's old classmate from McClymonds High School, sang. Russell had bought Hal DeJulio's airplane ticket to Boston, and he listened from one of the tables. "Ladies and gentlemen," Cosby said at one point. "None of us would be here if it weren't for one man—stand up, Hal De-Julio!" Red Auerbach, who by then was eighty-one years old and still smoking cigars, sat nearby. Bob Cousy, Tom Heinsohn, and John Havlicek all offered tributes. Russell usually wore only two of his championship rings, from his first year, 1957, and from his last, 1969, and now members of those two championship teams appeared in the lights. So did Wilt Chamberlain. He had flown in on the red-eye from California, and he graciously deferred to Russell, pointing out that in eight postseason matchups with his great rival, Chamberlain had prevailed only once. "A man," he said, "can get an inferiority complex that way."

When Russell finally took the floor, as lanky as ever, his hair and goatee now completely gray, he was greeted by a five-minute standing ovation. Russell had been painfully embarrassed by all the effusive flattery at the beginning of the evening, but now he was overcome with emotion. He told the crowd that he had dreaded this moment because he was afraid he would cry. He particularly thanked Chamberlain. Wilt, he said, had been an integral part of his career, requiring him to improve as a player, and he had done so, just as his own presence had required Chamberlain to improve. Each had made the other better. He added that he had always tried to live the sort of life he thought he should live, and he thanked the audience for allowing him to be a part of their lives.

And then, from the upper balcony, a single voice called out, "We love you, Bill!"

The shouted declaration—reminiscent of that fan's legendary cry to Bob Cousy on the night of his farewell in the old Garden—echoed among the rafters. There was a momentary pause that seemed longer than it was, and then Russell, in a choked voice, broke it.

"I love you, too," he said.

FIVE MONTHS LATER, on October 12, 1999, Wilt Chamberlain's grounds-keeper, Joe Mendoza, arrived at ten-thirty in the morning at Chamberlain's hilltop mansion in the Bel Air section of Los Angeles. The house, built in the early seventies for $1.2 million, a price that at the time seemed astronomical, had redwood timbers, a soaring fieldstone chimney, geometric roof lines, cantilevered balconies, a chrome spiral staircase, a shower like a car wash, and a swimming pool that extended from the living room out to the patio. Now, however, the entire place was not only dated but worn and deteriorating; the redwood had dried out and split, the grout in the tiles was rotting, an earthquake had damaged the roof and cracked the pool and patio.

Mendoza let himself into the house and saw Chamberlain lying on his bed. Mendoza thought nothing of it, since Chamberlain was in the habit of staying up late and sleeping late, and the groundskeeper went about his work. But when he returned shortly after noon, Chamberlain had not moved. Mendoza, alarmed, checked his body, and found that Chamberlain was not breathing. Mendoza called 911, and the paramedics who arrived seven minutes later declared Chamberlain dead of what appeared to be cardiac arrest. Mendoza then called Chamberlain's attorney, Sy Goldberg, who immediately drove over to the house.

The news, while shocking and upsetting, did not come as a complete surprise to Goldberg. Chamberlain had turned sixty-three only two months ago, and to many people he had appeared to be a tower of vitality, still trim and muscular, still working out, still talking about the possibility of going back to the NBA and how he might match up against Shaquille O'Neal. But Goldberg was one of the few people who knew that, in recent months, Chamberlain's health had deteriorated sharply. He had a history of heart problems dating back to adolescence, and his heart had begun bothering him again earlier in the year. He had actually felt quite ill when he flew to Boston to attend the celebration for Bill Russell. In just the last two months, his heart had become so weak and irregular that he'd lost fifty pounds and was scheduled to have a pacemaker implanted.

On top of that, an osteoarthritic condition made him walk with a limp, and he was also scheduled to have hip-replacement surgery. And then there were the teeth, the ones that had been smashed into the roof of his mouth by Clyde Lovellette of the St. Louis Hawks, the notoriously dirty player who elbowed him—intentionally, Chamberlain always believed—in the chin during Wilt's rookie year. The treatment he received back then—removing some teeth but not others—was inadequate, and the teeth that had remained had bothered him ever since. Just five days before he died, almost forty years to the month after the incident occurred, he'd finally had additional teeth removed, but the operation, he told a friend, had caused him the worst pain he'd ever experienced and left him so weak he felt like he was falling apart. When he had some friends and family over for dinner on Saturday night, two days after the operation, he was so short of breath he couldn't climb the stairs without assistance. The body of the man considered by many to have been in his prime the best all-around athlete in the world was failing him rapidly.

By the time Goldberg reached Chamberlain's house, a local television station was reporting an unconfirmed story that Chamberlain had died, and the wire services immediately picked it up. The police, expecting reporters and curiosity seekers, were stringing yellow crime-scene tape across the driveway. Chamberlain's body had not yet been removed, and Goldberg was there with it, in the bedroom, when his cell phone rang. It was Bill Russell, calling from who knew where, saying he had heard the rumors but there had as of yet been no official statement from Chamberlain's family and he wanted to know from Goldberg: was it true?

Goldberg told him that it was. Wilt had died, he said, probably sometime during the night, of what looked to be a heart attack. Russell, Goldberg could tell, was absolutely devastated. If the biggest tree in the forest can fall, Goldberg thought, the smaller ones are going to have to face the fact that they too assuredly will. But Goldberg knew that it wasn't just the intimation of his own mortality that Russell found so shattering. He suspected there was also some remorse for his harsh criticism of Wilt thirty years earlier. Goldberg knew that the criticism had cut to the quick, wounding Chamberlain deeply, and when the two men did finally start talking again, just a few years earlier, it seemed to Goldberg as if they were pretending to be friends without having repaired the damage. Chamberlain, Goldberg knew, had never forgiven Russell. So maybe, Goldberg thought, Russell's grief was tinged with a little guilt. And then there was the simple fact that Chamberlain and Russell had each made the other who he was.

Russell was in Boston on business when he had heard the news, and he called Goldberg. He was too shaken to talk to any of the reporters who telephoned the office of the Boston Celtics asking for comment. And not just shaken, but damaged in a way that felt irreparable. Chamberlain, who was two years younger than Russell himself, had always seemed larger than life, both literally and figuratively, a vigorous, tireless, opinionated giant—a good two and a half inches taller than Russell—with supernatural athletic abilities, a gargantuan ego, and stunning appetites, but also a man who could be truly generous, loyal, funny, approachable, and unpretentious.

But the loss Russell felt was not simply at the untimely death of an occasional companion and, on the basketball court, a formidable opponent. In a strange way, Russell felt that Chamberlain was the only person who had ever really understood him, and that he was the only person who had ever really understood Chamberlain. No one else had gone through what the two of them had gone through. No one else knew what it was like to be, all at once, a black man, and so tall that newspaper reporters regularly referred to you as a giant, and the best at what you did, and wealthy and famous—the first black superstar athletes outside of boxing—but at the same time to live in a segregated society, where in one entire region of the country, when the two of them were starting their careers, they couldn't stay in the same hotel as the white rookie benchwarmers who carried the equipment, and where, even in their hometowns, they knew that some of the fans rooting for them wouldn't want them living next door. No one else had ever been through all that.

A few days after Chamberlain's death, a memorial service was held at the City of Angels Church of Religious Science in the Marina del Rey section of Los Angeles. Some eight hundred people attended, and ushers set up giant television screens outside the church to accommodate the overflow crowd. Inside, bouquets of flowers crowded the altar, along with oversize photographs of Chamberlain in basketball uniform. Jazz played on the church's speakers as the mourners filed in. Jerry West was seated up front near Elgin Baylor. Chet Walker and Billy Cunningham were there from the 76ers team that had given Chamberlain his first championship, and so was Alex Hannum, its coach. Nate Thurmond, who played with Wilt during his stint on the San Francisco Warriors, and Al Attles, who'd been on Wilt's team the night he scored the one hundred points in the game against the Knicks, both came, and so did Bill Walton and Jim Brown. Then Bill Russell filed in, dressed formally, moving slowly and deliberately, as regal as ever.

Meadowlark Lemon, who'd been a Harlem Globetrotter the first year Wilt toured with the team, had become an ordained minister, and he led off the service. He told the mourners that Wilt Chamberlain had been a happy man who loved life, and so the service was to be not a sad occasion but a happy one, a celebration. Various speakers joked about Chamberlain's argumentativeness, his late-night phone calls, his claim to have slept with twenty thousand women, which, as every male in America who had done the calculations knew, worked out to an average of 1.5 women a night every night of every year from the age of fifteen onward. Barbara Lewis, one of his four sisters, said he had been a big mouth even as a small child, once asking a freeloading neighbor why she always dropped by at dinnertime. Tom Hawkins, a former Laker, said Wilt Chamberlain, not Michael Jordan, owned the record book. In addition to the one-hundred-point game, he said, there was, just to mention two of the more choice statistics, the season Wilt averaged more than fifty points a game and because of overtimes played an average of forty-eight minutes and thirty seconds per game even though a regulation game has forty-eight minutes.

Throughout the recollections, Al Attles, one of Wilt's closest friends dating back to the days when they both played for Eddie Gottlieb's Philadelphia Warriors, wondered what Bill Russell would say. Not only had Attles played in some of the epic battles between Russell and Chamberlain, he was well aware of the long, bitter feud between the two men. As far as Attles knew, Russell had never uttered the genuine, heartfelt apology that Chamberlain felt he was owed, and when finally Russell rose to speak at the service, he did not offer one now. But, without referring directly to the feud, he said that he and Chamberlain had talked regularly in recent years. Age had made them both more forgiving.

Pausing, Russell looked out at the audience. It was true, none of his and Chamberlain's disagreements mattered now. What mattered, what remained, were those moments of intensity on the court thirty to forty years earlier, when he and Chamberlain each pushed the other to play harder and go higher than either had ever played or gone before. Russell had always insisted on viewing life from his own particular, even contrary, perspective, and he now said that while some people thought he and Chamberlain had made for the greatest rivalry in sports history, the truth was that they had not actually been rivals at all. Rivals tried to best each other, he explained, and neither he nor Chamberlain had been out to do that. They each had different objectives. Chamberlain was interested in statistics and he, Russell, in victories, and both of them had reached their respective goals without doing so at the expense of the other. The fact was, they loved playing against each other more than anything. They loved the competition. "The fierceness of that competition," Russell said, "bonded us for eternity."

ACKNOWLEDGMENTS

In previous books—whether about a corporate takeover battle, a murder trial, or a contemporary marriage—I have explored the psychology of conflict, and that was the issue that initially drew me to the story of the rivalry between Bill Russell and Wilt Chamberlain. But I soon became convinced that it also had the form of a classical epic, beginning in 1959, building through various reversals and shifting alliances over a ten-year period, and reaching a climax in the last minutes of the 1969 finals. It coincided with and was in good measure responsible for the growth of the NBA from a minor to a major league. It produced the first iconic black superstar athletes—outside boxing—and played a role in advancing race relations in the sixties. It involved the top players and coaches of the age, all extraordinarily vivid personalities with conflicting values. Finally, it gave me the opportunity to investigate the tension between talent and teamwork that is at the heart of all team sports.

The narrative of the rivalry has never been the subject of a book before. Books, most long out of print, have been written about the Celtics, but they also cover the post-Russell years, and the rivalry is usually relegated to a chapter analyzing the relative strengths and weaknesses of Russell and Chamberlain. Several sports memoirs, similarly out of print, also discuss the rivalry in passing. My goal was to capture these men and their teammates, opponents, and coaches, to explore the forces that motivated them all, and to convey the spirit of the times, the atmosphere of the arenas and dressing rooms, and the heat and smoke of the combat.

Numerous people were interviewed for this book: players, coaches, trainers, sportswriters, the family members of owners. Interviews were conducted in person, on the telephone, and in writing. Elgin Baylor described how he came to be the first black player to boycott an NBA game to protest segregation. Tom Heinsohn explained the narrowly averted strike he organized as head of the players association during the 1964 all-star game. Wilt Chamberlain's sister Barbara Lewis told me about their father, who moved from rural Virginia to Philadelphia at the age of eighteen. Dolph Schayes discussed the perils of coaching Chamberlain. The 76ers trainer Al Domenico recalled the time the team's bus was attacked by crazed Celtics fans. Wilt's teammates Joe Ruklick and Al Attles recounted the night Wilt scored one hundred points. Michael Gross described his father Milton Gross's journalistic creed: run with the pack and you'll write like the pack. Sy Goldberg described the deal to trade Chamberlain to the Lakers and Bill Russell's reaction to Chamberlain's death. Some of the people who figure in the narrative, such as Tom Heinsohn, Dolph Schayes, Elgin Baylor, Bob Cousy, and Al Attles also read sections of the manuscript. While they had no power of approval over it, I wanted to give them the opportunity to confirm the material and point out any inaccuracies.

But a number of people, such as Frank McGuire, Alex Hannum, Guy Rogers, and of course Chamberlain himself, are now dead. Others were too elderly or too ill to sit for extensive interviews. Some people, including Bill Russell, simply declined to talk, and others talked but, unwilling to speak critically about teammates or opponents who have passed away or are aging in retirement, insisted that the controversies and personality conflicts that give the narrative its drama were manufactured or exaggerated by outsiders. "Wilt never missed a practice," one of Chamberlain's teammates assured me. "That's because we never practiced," another explained. In any event, the sunset reminiscences of retired players and coaches are not infallible. Red Auerbach has claimed for years that Walter Brown arranged for the Ice Capades to play in Rochester in return for information crucial to the Russell trade, and this has simply been asserted as fact in certain books, but the truth is the Ice Capades had already been performing in Rochester. Brown and Lester Harrison, the owner of the Rochester Royals and the man who might have acquired Russell in the 1950 draft, were friends and fellow owners in a struggling league who depended on each other, and previously Brown had helped resolve a dispute between Harrison and the management of the Rochester arena over scheduling the Ice Capades. Similarly, Bob Cousy in recent years has claimed that after he graduated from college he had decided that if he was not drafted by the Celtics he would not play in the NBA, but in his own 1957 memoir, *Basketball Is My Life,* he describes how, after Boston passed him over in the 1950 draft, he signed a $9,000 contract with the Tri-

Cities Blackhawks. Rather than rely on solitary voices, I have tried to draw on multiple accounts of events and cross-check them with contemporaneous sources.

Since the NBA continued to struggle into the sixties, its teams were eager for the publicity that newspapers could provide, and sportswriters then had a level of access that is the envy of contemporary journalists. I am particularly indebted to the dozens of reporters and magazine writers in Boston and Philadelphia and San Francisco and Los Angeles—Milton Gross, Bud Collins, Joe Looney, Jack Kiser, George Kiseda, Ed Linn, Leonard Shecter, Arnold Hano, Dick Friendlich, Mal Florence, Bob Ottum, to name a few—who watched the games courtside, visited the dressing rooms afterward, rode the buses and planes with the teams, and ate and played cards and went drinking with the players.

I am grateful to Michael Richman, his son Ike Richman, and Joe Ruklick for introducing me to players as well as answering my questions; to Robin Deutsch of the Basketball Hall of Fame for allowing me access to its archives, which included notes and correspondence; to Ed Kosner, former editor of the New York *Daily News* for allowing me to do research in its files; to the staffs in the microfilm rooms of the New York Public Library, the Library of Congress, the Boston Public Library, and the Philadelphia Public Library; to Shirley Figgins for passing questions to her ill boss, Franklin Mieuli; to Bob Cousy's assistant, Helena Hacket; to Laura Planklett in Jerry West's office; and to my editor, Jon Karp, and my agent, Jennifer Rudolph Walsh, for their support. Most of all I'd like to thank my wife, Jeannette Walls, for her enthusiasm and encouragement.

The literature on the National Basketball Association in the fifties and sixties includes memoirs—and sometimes multiple memoirs—by Red Auerbach, Wilt Chamberlain, Bob Cousy, Tom Heinsohn, John Havlicek, Bill Russell, and Jerry West, among others. All authors are indebted to those who have preceded them, and these memoirs were extremely useful to me, as were Dan Shaughnessy's *Seeing Red,* Bill Libby's *Goliath,* George Sullivan's *Wilt Chamberlain,* and two oral histories, Charles Salzberg's *From Set Shot to Slam Dunk* and Terry Pluto's *Tall Tales.* Through the Freedom of Information and Privacy acts, I was able to obtain the FBI files on both Wilt Chamberlain and Bill Russell. Statistics, scores, and pertinent facts were checked with *The Official NBA Encyclopedia.*

NOTES

The archives at the Basketball Hall of Fame include newspaper clips, press releases, team memoranda, and correspondence. Not all of this material is dated, and when I have drawn from undated or unpublished sources, I have cited them BHFA.

CHAPTER 1

3   The citizens of Boston: *Boston Herald*, Nov. 2–4, 1959; "The Big Collision," *Sport*, Dec. 1959.

5   "Just trying": "When Wilt and Russell Meet," *Sport*, March 1960.

5   "Pro basketball will be": "The Big Collision," *Sport*, Dec. 1959.

5   Chamberlain had attracted: "Can Basketball Survive Chamberlain?," *The Saturday Evening Post*, Dec. 1, 1956.

6   Russell had eaten: "When Wilt and Russell Meet," *Sport*, March 1960.

7   Russell considered himself: Russell, *Second Wind*, 95.

7   People had been feeding: Bill Russell int. in *Deseret News*, May 20, 2001.

7   Chamberlain had spent: "Great Moments in Sport," *Sport*, Nov. 1963.

7   Pro ball was more violent: "Pro Basketball Has Ganged Up on Me," *Look*, March 1, 1960.

8   Naulls had chased him: Chamberlain, *Wilt*, 106.

8   In mid-court: Bill Russell int. in *Deseret News*, May 20, 2001.

9   The referee tossed: "The Tall Ones in Boston," *Sports Illustrated*, Nov. 16, 1959; "When Wilt and Russell Meet," *Sport*, March 1960.

10   Russell thought: *Los Angeles Times*, Oct. 19, 1999.

10   Auerbach had first: Auerbach, *Winning*, 96.

10   He rationalized: Auerbach, *On and Off*, 168.

11   "He incites": "A Master's Touch," *Sports Illustrated*, April 5, 1965.

11   "When I first": Cited in Auerbach, *Red*, 267.

11   "the challenging": Manchester, *Glory*, 877.

11   kidnapped Mack Parker: Branch, *Parting*, 257.

12   never even bothered to vote: Shaughnessy, *Seeing*, 17.

12   Brooklyn's Williamsburg section: Willensky, *When Brooklyn*, 36.

12   street moniker: "A Master's Touch," *Sports Illustrated*, April 5, 1965.

12   Red and his friends: Shaughnessy, *Seeing*, 29–30.

13   "Da People's Cherce": Willensky, *When Brooklyn*, 36.

13 "requires a good": Cited in Riess, *City Games*, 107.

13 At the Eastern District: Red Auerbach int. in *Herald Traveler and Boston Record American*, Dec. 20, 1972.

14 "He was lucky": Salzberg, *From Set Shot*, 12.

14 Auerbach read a newspaper: Auerbach, *Red*, 47.

14 Ned Irish: "Basketball's Big Wheel," *The Saturday Evening Post*, Jan. 15, 1949.

14 This convinced him: *The New York Times*, Jan. 22, 1982.

15 Irish came up with: Koppett, *Twenty-four Seconds*, 9.

15 move the Empire State Building: "Basketball's Big Wheel," *The Saturday Evening Post*, Jan. 15, 1949.

15 Veterans were streaming: Manchester, *Glory*, 409.

15 baseball was the sport: Halberstam, *Summer*, 12.

15 Max Kase, sports editor: Koppett, *Twenty-four Seconds*, 13.

15 Harry Truman had signed: Manchester, *Glory*, 401.

16 When Red Auerbach read: Auerbach, *Red*, 47.

17 Auerbach made his case: Auerbach, *Management*, 15.

17 Ned Irish brought in: Koppett, *Twenty-four Seconds*, 22.

18 Going into his first: Red Auerbach int. in *Herald Traveler and Boston Record American*, Dec. 20, 1972.

18 "If you get obnoxious": "A Master's Touch," *Sports Illustrated*, April 5, 1965.

18 He hated hearing: Auerbach, *On and Off*, 67.

18 He wanted it understood: Red Auerbach int. in *Herald Traveler and Boston Record American*, Dec. 20, 1972.

19 Many early games: Pluto, *Tall Tales*, 18.

19 "I'll give these customers": Auerbach, *Red*, 69.

20 He had never been able: Walter Brown int. in *Boston Record*, Jan. 29, 1962.

20 "Walter, I think": *Boston Herald*, March 23, 1950.

20 Joe Looney: *Boston Herald*, March 24, 1950.

21 Brown told: Ibid.

21 Some of the reporters: Auerbach, *Red*, 84.

21 The photograph: *Boston Herald*, March 24, 1950.

22 a "gimmick": Walter Brown int. in *Boston Record*, Jan. 29, 1962.

23 "I don't know anything": *Boston Herald*, Sept. 9, 1964.

23 "Walter, what's going": Marjorie Brown int. in Auerbach, *Red*, 83.

24 "Are you kidding": Walter Brown int. in *Boston Record*, Jan. 29, 1962.

CHAPTER 2

26 "How the hell": "The Boston Collection," *Sports Illustrated*, Oct. 6, 1997.

26 Walter Brown also assumed: Walter Brown int. in Carey, *High Above*, 56.

26 "Walter, I've seen": Auerbach, *Winning*, 66.

27 Don Barksdale: Ashe, *Hard Road*, 24.

27 "Boston takes": Auerbach, *Red*, 92.

27 "Abe's gonna go crazy": Shaughnessy, *Seeing*, 88.

27 "It's a white dollar": Pluto, *Tall Tales*, 75.

28 "Do you realize": Auerbach, *Red*, 92.

28 "Thank you": Shaughnessy, *Seeing*, 87.

28 "hair is now": *Boston Herald*, April 28, 1950.

28 "I don't give a damn": Cousy, *Basketball*, 105.

29 SENTIMENT OUT: *Boston Herald*, April 28, 1950.

29 Cousy himself was stunned: Cousy, *Basketball*, 103.

29 People joked: McPhee, *A Sense*, 62.

30 "We need height": Cousy, *Basketball*, 105.

30 Accepting the fact: "The Wonderful Wizard of Boston," *Sport*, Feb. 1960.

30 "The secret auction": "Why They're After Podoloff's Neck," *Sport*, June 1959.

31 "I'm sick and tired": "The Wonderful Wizard of Boston," *Sport*, Feb. 1960.

31 As he read Cousy's: Walter Brown int. in ibid.

32 Cousy, staying with his parents: Cousy, *Basketball*, 110.

32 "To me, he's just": Carey, *High Above*, 58.

32 "I hope you make": Cousy, *Basketball*, 112.

34 "This is what": *Boston Herald*, Oct. 18, 1950.

34 "the knights of the keyboard": Auerbach, *Management*, 152.

35 "the inventor of the automatic choke": Halberstam, *Summer*, 183.

35 "We know now": Cited in "Hothead on the Boston Bench," *Sport*, Feb. 1956.

36 "Syracuse flu": Salzberg, *From Set Shot*, 217.

36 "I'll put fifty": Ibid., 217.

36 "We have to be careful": "Is the NBA Big League?" *Sport*, Jan. 1957.

37 "those New York refs": Ibid.

37 "Hey, we doubled": Pluto, *Tall Tales*, 21.

38 Murray Mendenhall: Los Angeles *Daily News*, April 11, 2002.

38 "When fans are walking": "Is the N.B.A. Big League?" *Sport*, Jan. 1957.

38 Biasone was alternately: Danny Biasone int. in *The New York Times*, BHFA.

38 "Take your time": Pluto, *Tall Tales*, 30.

39 "Movement is no longer": "Is the NBA Big League?" *Sport*, Jan. 1957.

CHAPTER 3

41 "That's a lot": "Farewell to Bob Cousy," *Sport*, March 1963.

41 "I hold him": "Hothead on the Boston Bench," *Sport*, Feb. 1956.

41 The first time Auerbach saw Chamberlain: Libby, *Goliath*, 23.

42 "Why don't you go": "My Life in a Bush League," *Sports Illustrated*, April 12, 1965.

42 "This is the most": Auerbach, *Winning*, 81.

42 "If that kid even thinks": Auerbach, *Red*, 273.

43 "I'm Joe Lapchick": Libby, *Goliath*, 15.

43 "It was a manhunt": "Wilt vs. the NBA," *Sport*, April 1959.

43 "About the only place": "Why I Am Quitting College," *Look*, June 10, 1958.

44 Wilt Chamberlain grew up: Auth. int. of Barbara Chamberlain Lewis.

44 "Wilt worked": Ibid.

45 Brown thought Wilt's legs: Libby, *Goliath*, 19.

45   he'd lock the rec-center: Blinky Brown int. in *The Philadelphia Inquirer*, Oct. 21, 1999.

45   Wilt the Stilt: Sullivan, *Wilt Chamberlain*, 20.

45   "Where does he shoot": Philly.com, Oct. 13, 1999.

46   "They didn't want to wreck": Libby, *Goliath*, 25.

46   "This time, I benefit": "Wilt. vs. the NBA," *Sport*, April 1959.

47   "to violate the Lindbergh kidnapping law": "Can Basketball Survive Chamberlain?," *The Saturday Evening Post*, Dec. 1, 1956.

47   "Nobody will believe": Ibid.

48   *Born is going to make:* "My Life in a Bush League," *Sports Illustrated*, April 12, 1965.

49   "the Negro talking": "Can Basketball Survive Chamberlain?," *The Saturday Evening Post*, Dec. 1, 1956.

49   "And they wanted to win": Libby, *Goliath*, 31.

49   "godfathers" privately assured him: *The New York Times*, Oct. 18, 1985.

49   "Why does a Philadelphia boy": "Can Basketball Survive Chamberlain?," *The Saturday Evening Post*, Dec. 1, 1956.

49   "We couldn't afford that boy": Sullivan, *Wilt Chamberlain*, 35.

49   "I feel sorry": "Can Basketball Survive Chamberlain?," *The Saturday Evening Post*, Dec. 1, 1956.

CHAPTER 4

50   Three years before: Auth. int. of Hal DeJulio.

52   "Negro job": Russell, *Go Up*, 11.

52   Charles Russell became: "The Ring Leader," *Sports Illustrated*, May 10, 1999.

53   run and jump, Powles saw: "They Make Rules to Stop Russell," *Sport*, April 1956.

53   "What good will it do?": "I Was a 6′9″ Babe in the Woods," *The Saturday Evening Post*, Jan. 18, 1958.

54   "If you play": "Bill Russell's Private World," *Sport*, Feb. 1963.

54   Every year, a man named Brick Swegle: Russell, *Second Wind*, 68–79.

56   His adrenaline was pumping: Bill Russell int. in *The New York Times*, Dec. 28, 1955.

56   "We didn't think": Harris, *Lonely*, 20.

56   San Francisco was his one chance: "Bill Russell's Private World," *Sport*, Feb. 1963.

57   "lousy coach": "Unstoppable San Francisco," *Sport*, April 1964.

57   once been a football powerhouse: Maraniss, *When Pride*, 90.

57   "Homeless Dons": Rappaport, *Classic*, 102.

57   "jackrabbit basketball": "Unstoppable San Francisco," *Sport*, April 1964.

58   Regarding his athletic scholarship: "I Was a 6′9″ Babe in the Woods," *The Saturday Evening Post*, Jan. 18, 1958.

58   stayed in the gym until midnight: Russell, *Russell Rules*, 116.

58   They broke down basketball: Russell, *Second Wind*, 93.

58   "A real mass of muscles": "Bill Russell's Private World," *Sport*, Feb. 1963.

59 "When Bill Russell registered": "Unstoppable San Francisco," *Sport,* April 1964.

59 "smart feet": Russell, *Russell Rules,* 116.

59 "Now where in the world": Hirshberg, *Bill Russell,* 37.

60 "They are scarcely representative": "Unstoppable San Francisco," *Sport,* April 1964.

61 Heinsohn . . . was flabbergasted: Auth. int. of Tom Heinsohn.

61 "This is like a one-man volleyball game": "They Make Rules to Stop Russell," *Sport,* April 1956.

61 Russell's wingspan, which had never been measured: *The New York Times,* Dec. 28, 1955.

61 wrapped his fingers around: "The Man Who Must Be Different," *Sports Illustrated,* Feb. 3, 1958.

61 when Woolpert saw: Rappaport, *Classic,* 103.

61 "Did you ever see": "They Make Rules to Stop Russell," *Sport,* April 1956.

61 "We weren't planning": Ibid.

62 "The rest of us": "Unstoppable San Francisco," *Sport,* April 1964.

62 "This is the greatest": Ibid.

CHAPTER 5

63 Auerbach felt uncertain: "A Master's Touch," *Sports Illustrated,* April 5, 1965.

64 "Try to get this guy": Red Auerbach int. in *Herald Traveler and Boston Record American,* Dec. 19, 1972.

64 "Red, he can't shoot": Ibid.

65 the president singled him out: "They Make Rules to Stop Russell," *Sport,* April 1956.

65 "I was just another black boy": Russell, *Go Up,* 37.

66 The owner of the Harlem Globetrotters: Nadel, *The Night,* 82.

67 *You want to talk to Woolpert:* Bill Russell int. in "I Owe the Public Nothing," *The Saturday Evening Post,* Jan. 18, 1964.

67 "How ya doin' ": Bill Russell int. in New York *Daily News,* Nov. 3, 1996.

68 Harrison knew Abe: Lester Harrison int. in *USA Today,* April 22, 1983.

68 "I'm going to have to pass": "Bill Russell's Private World," *Sport,* Feb. 1963.

69 Kerner knew St. Louis: "Old Days and Changed Ways," *Sports Illustrated,* Nov. 25, 1968.

69 trading Macauley bothered Auerbach: "A Master's Touch," *Sports Illustrated,* April 5, 1965.

70 "Red, I need bodies": Pluto, *Tall Tales,* 124; Red Auerbach int. in *Herald Traveler and Boston Record American,* Dec. 19, 1972.

70 one historian would later: Halberstam, *The Fifties,* 696.

70 *God, I've traded away:* "Sportsman of the Year," *Sports Illustrated,* Dec. 23, 1968.

71 "If he intends": Russell, *Go Up,* 46.

72 Gross was a dry: Auth. ints. of Vic Ziegel and Michael Gross.

72 Ike Gellis, was a gambler: Auth. int. of Vic Ziegel.

72 a "digger": New York *Daily News,* May 11, 1973.

72 Madison Square Garden: Riess, *City Games,* 29.

73 "This ain't possession basketball": Account of game in *New York Post,* Dec. 19, 1956.

74 "Not even pro baseball": "Education of a Basketball Rookie," *The New York Times Magazine,* Feb. 24, 1957.

74 "Russell, are you worried": Bill Russell int. in *USA Today,* May 4, 1999.

75 "Bill Russell's Buildup": "Bill Russell Is Better Than Ever," *Sport,* Jan. 1961.

75 Russell . . . became stuck: *Boston Herald,* Dec. 23, 1956.

75 "Just try not to let": "I Was a 6'9" Babe in the Woods," *The Saturday Evening Post,* Jan. 18, 1958.

75 "Doesn't this guy": Ibid.

75 Auerbach, watching from the sidelines: "Sportsman of the Year," *Sports Illustrated,* Dec. 23, 1968.

76 "You'll have to forgive me": Carey, *High Above,* 101.

76 "After waltzing effortlessly": *Boston Herald,* Dec. 23, 1956.

77 "It's certain that the increased receipts": "Education of a Basketball Rookie," *The New York Times Magazine,* Feb. 24, 1957.

77 "Boston Forming 'Dynasty' ": *New York Post,* Dec. 28, 1956.

77 "If you let the names": "I Was a 6'9" Babe in the Woods," *The Saturday Evening Post,* Jan. 18, 1958.

77 "putting the question": Koppett, *Twenty-four Seconds,* 67.

77 "What do you do": "I Was a 6'9" Babe in the Woods," *The Saturday Evening Post,* Jan. 18, 1958.

77 "Russell, what's the matter": Fitzgerald, *Championship,* 54.

78 Russell felt that the . . . fine: "I Was a 6'9" Babe in the Woods," *The Saturday Evening Post,* Jan. 18, 1958.

78 "What the hell": Shapiro, *Bill Russell,* 60.

78 Years later, Auerbach would decide: "The Winning Ways of Red Auerbach," *Sport,* March 1965.

79 "Hey, Bill!": Harris, *Lonely,* 22.

79 blocked as "Wilsonburgers": "We Are Grown Men Playing a Child's Game," *Sports Illustrated,* Nov. 18, 1963.

80 "In one beautiful": Fitzgerald, *Championship,* 52.

80 "In a single generation": "Basketball Is for the Birds," *Sports Illustrated,* Dec. 8, 1958.

CHAPTER 6

82 "When one player": *New York Post,* Dec. 28, 1956.

82 "I've never seen anything": Ibid.

83 "I feel sick": "Can Basketball Survive Chamberlain?," *The Saturday Evening Post,* Dec. 1, 1956.

83 "And what is that?": *New York Post,* Dec. 29, 1956.

83 "Wilt Chamberlain's the greatest": Chamberlain, *Wilt,* 68.

83 "Allen—and 14,000 others": Enid (Oklahoma) *Daily Eagle,* Nov. 19, 1955.

83 "It took me": Chamberlain, *Wilt,* 51.

84 Allen worked personally: "Why I Am Quitting College," *Look,* June 10, 1958.

84 "Why isn't Chamberlain": "Can Basketball Survive Chamberlain?," *The Saturday Evening Post,* Dec. 1, 1956.

84 "He played here": Ibid.

84 years later Chamberlain admitted: Chamberlain, *Wilt,* 60.

84 The decision left Allen: Libby, *Goliath,* 34.

85 "He scored at will": Auth. int. of Joe Ruklick.

85   "I'd enjoy the next": Sullivan, *Wilt Chamberlain*, 42.

85   During the games: "Why I Am Quitting College," *Look*, June 10, 1958.

86   "The trouble seemed": Sullivan, *Wilt Chamberlain*, 46.

86   "I told Phog": "Can Basketball Survive Chamberlain?," *The Saturday Evening Post*, Dec. 1, 1956.

86   Although Chamberlain's team: "How We Became the Champs," *The Saturday Evening Post*, Dec. 14, 1957.

87   "We're playing Wilt": Chamberlain, *Wilt*, 67.

87   "We're a chilly club": Rappaport, *Classic*, 113.

87   *Is this coach crazy?:* "How We Became the Champs," *The Saturday Evening Post*, Dec. 14, 1957.

88   Quigg was nervous: Rappaport, *Classic*, 111.

89   it wasn't his fault: Chamberlain, *Wilt*, 68.

CHAPTER 7

90   The team's offense: Auth. int. of Tom Heinsohn.

91   "If you play for me": *Boston Record American*, Feb. 16, 1965.

91   Throughout the season: Auth. int. of Tom Heinsohn.

91   His teammate Jim Loscutoff: Fitzgerald, *Championship*, 98.

91   "You bunch of chokers!": Auerbach, *Red*, 317.

91   Tensions existed: Auth. int. of Tom Heinsohn.

92   "Russ, this is my cousin": Auth. int. of Tom Heinsohn. Also Heinsohn, *Heinsohn*, 76.

92   this struck Russell: Russell *Go Up*, 128.

93   "I think you ought": Auth. int. of Tom Heinsohn. Also Heinsohn, *Heinsohn*, 92.

93   Cousy had a hot hand: Cousy, *Basketball*, 172.

94   "Coon!," "Black nigger!": Russell, *Go Up*, 94.

94   "The hatred between": Auerbach, *Winning*, 186.

94   "You're all stealing": "I've Barely Begun to Fight," *Sports Illustrated*, Nov. 18, 1968.

94   "Make it five": Pettit, *Bob Pettit*, 56.

95   "What the hell": Pluto, *Tall Tales*, 138.

95   "Look at that": Ben Kerner int. in *Boston Herald*, Jan. 2, 1985.

95   "I must ascertain": Auerbach, *Red*, 135.

95   "From all I hear": Shaughnessy, *Seeing*, 127.

95   The team's locker room: Auth. int. of Tom Heinsohn.

96   *Don't be throwin':* Auth. int. of Tom Heinsohn.

96   "Defense and dollars": Greenfield, *World's Greatest*, 149.

96   he still felt so nauseated: Hirshberg, *Bill Russell*, 10.

97   Auerbach told the team: Auth. int. of Tom Heinsohn.

97   "Shut up, Russell": Auth. int. of Tom Heinsohn.

97   Heinsohn didn't want to leave: Auth. int. of Tom Heinsohn.

98   Hannum put himself: "Old Days and Changed Ways," *Sports Illustrated*, Nov. 25, 1968.

98   It seemed to Ben Kerner: Pluto, *Tall Tales*, 127.

98   Hannum liked to sit around brainstorming: "Old Days and Changed Ways," *Sports Illustrated*, Nov. 25, 1968.

99 Ed Macauley wondered: Pluto, *Tall Tales,* 131.

99 Auerbach, watching: Auerbach, *Winning,* 5.

CHAPTER 8

100 "I have no definite proof": Sullivan, *Wilt Chamberlain,* 35.

101 When he first arrived: "Why I Am Quitting College," *Look,* June 10, 1958.

101 "It was nice talking to you": Ibid.

102 "glandular infection": Chamberlain, *Wilt,* 74.

102 Chamberlain had begun: "Why I Am Quitting College," *Look,* June 10, 1958.

102 Chamberlain figured: "The Real Wilt Chamberlain," *Sport,* March 1961.

103 "Very early": Pluto, *Tall Tales,* 101.

103 "You might as well": Chamberlain, *Wilt,* 101.

103 "idly palming": *The New York Times,* June 19, 1958.

103 In almost every city: "Wilt vs. the NBA," *Sport,* April 1959.

103 He was astonished: Chamberlain, *Wilt,* 90–91.

104 After touring Europe: Auth. int. of Michael Richman.

104 "a wonderful little guy": *The New York Times,* Jan. 13, 1980.

105 "He pumped the house": Auth. int. of Joe Ruklick.

106 "What can I tell you": "Wilt vs. the NBA," *Sport,* April 1959.

CHAPTER 9

107 *You dumb schvartzeh!:* Shaughnessy, *Seeing,* 115.

107 "If I can't yell": *Boston Herald,* Jan. 31, 1984.

108 "Do you think": Russell, *Go Up,* 69.

108 "Russell, what do we": Shaughnessy, *Seeing,* 115.

108 Russell had to put up: "Growing Up with Privilege and Prejudice," *The New York Times Magazine,* June 14, 1987.

108 trouble finding a job: "Oscar Robertson at the Peak," *Sport,* April 1964.

109 Cousy knew it was out: Cousy, *Celtic Mystique,* 55.

109 Russell was coolly rebuffed: "The Man Who Must Be Different," *Sports Illustrated,* Feb. 3, 1958.

109 broken into twice: "The Unknown Side of Bill Russell," *Sport,* March 1966.

109 Russell liked the house: "I Was a 6'9" Babe in the Woods," *The Saturday Evening Post,* Jan. 18, 1958; "We Are Grown Men Playing a Child's Game," *Sports Illustrated,* Nov. 18, 1963.

109 It seemed obvious: "I Owe the Public Nothing," *The Saturday Evening Post,* Jan. 18, 1964.

110 "The crowds won't stand": Russell, *Go Up,* 73.

110 "a permanent fixture": Branch, *Parting,* 203.

111 *It stood out:* Russell, *Go Up,* 14.

111 "Mike, I just worked": Auth. int. of Michael Richman.

112 Gottlieb and Chamberlain announced: *Philadelphia Daily News,* May 31, 1959.

112 One of the first things: "The Real Wilt Chamberlain," *Sport,* March 1961.

113 Then, in a game: "The Tragedy of Maurice Stokes," *Sport*, Feb. 1959.

114 they were surprised: "The Big Collision," *Sport*, Dec. 1959.

114 It was time, he decided: Chamberlain, *Wilt*, 102.

CHAPTER 10

115 He micromanaged his players': Maraniss, *When Pride*, 223.

116 *I'm not running a union:* Auerbach, *Red*, 172.

117 it was said of Jones: Greenfield, *World's Greatest*, 117.

117 "Red, . . . there's a colored kid": Ibid., 116.

117 "Had he attended": "The Man Who Replaced Bob Cousy," *Sport*, Nov. 1964.

118 "You're a Yankee": Halberstam, *Summer*, 23.

118 Auerbach, too, insisted: "A Master's Touch," *Sports Illustrated*, April 5, 1965.

118 his players liked to joke: Maraniss, *When Pride*, 331.

118 He once estimated: Auerbach, *Red*, 215.

118 "stupid and incompetent": Shaughnessy, *Seeing*, 139.

119 "I won't go": Russell, *Go Up*, 98.

119 Edward Finke, who: Havlicek, *Hondo*, 137.

119 "He guarantees the integrity": Cited in "Hothead on the Boston Bench," *Sport*, Feb. 1956.

119 "No coach is so violently": Cited in Shaughnessy, *Seeing*, 131.

120 "He will dominate": "The Big Collision," *Sport*, Dec. 1959.

120 "both beautiful": *The New York Times*, Oct. 25, 1959.

120 "the finest debut": *New York Herald-Tribune*, Oct. 25, 1959.

121 "The Age of Wilt": *Philadelphia Daily News*, Oct. 26, 1959.

121 How do you defend: "Wilt Chamberlain As We Knew Him," *Sport*, Aug. 1960.

122 preferred to play: "Pro Basketball Has Ganged Up on Me," *Look*, March 1, 1960.

122 "probably the greatest": "Doing Just Fine, My Man," *Sports Illustrated*, Aug. 18, 1986.

122 Every day, he ate: "Pro Basketball Has Ganged Up on Me," *Look*, March 1, 1960.

122 Tommy Heinsohn decided: Auth. int. of Tom Heinsohn.

123 "If we let": Pluto, *Tall Tales*, 226.

123 "They're getting away": Libby, *Goliath*, 64.

123 Ruklick, Chamberlain's white backup: Auth. int. of Joe Ruklick.

123 a thirty-three-year-old juvenile delinquent: Havlicek, *Hondo*, 87.

123 "Clyde said": Auth. int. of Cal Ramsey.

124 Ball was surprised: *Philadelphia Daily News*, April 26, 1979.

124 "If I punch someone": Sullivan, *Wilt Chamberlain*, 73.

125 "There were less than a hundred": Auth. int. of Al Domenico.

125 "There are days": "Walking Wounded Everywhere," *Sport*, Feb. 1960.

126 "Suddenly, housewives": "When Wilt and Russell Meet," *Sport*, March 1960.

127 "What do they mean": *New York Post*, March 21, 1960.

127 "You do that again": Auth. int. of Tom Heinsohn.

128 "Believe it or not": Carey, *High
  Above*, 131.

128 Chamberlain's knuckles: *New York
  Post*, March 21, 1960.

128 "They have momentum": *New York
  Post*, March 23, 1960.

129 "Is it true": *New York Post*, March
  25, 1960.

CHAPTER 11

130 The first was television: Manchester,
  Glory, 584–86, 877.

131 That 1958 game: "The Best Football
  Game Ever Played," *Sports
  Illustrated*, Jan. 3, 1959.

131 commercial jet travel: Manchester,
  Glory, 818, 1002.

132 "an overweight ghost": Cited in
  Koppett, *Twenty-four Seconds*, 104.

132 The Lakers struggled: Auth. int. of
  Elgin Baylor.

133 "If he had turned": "Elgin Baylor: One
  Man Franchise," *Sport*, April 1959.

133 "He never broke": Cited in Pluto,
  Tall Tales, 171.

133 His one idiosyncrasy: Auth. int. of
  Elgin Baylor.

134 In the opening seconds: "Elgin
  Baylor: One Man Franchise," *Sport*,
  April 1959.

134 Baylor also had: Account of Baylor's
  boycott from auth. int. of Elgin
  Baylor; also "Life with Elgin
  Baylor," *Sport*, March 1963.

136 "Never before had a": "Elgin Baylor:
  One Man Franchise," *Sport*, April
  1959.

136 The army, more than happy: Auth.
  int. of Elgin Baylor.

137 The owners voted again: Pluto, *Tall
  Tales*, 181.

137 Baylor found out: Auth. int. of Elgin
  Baylor.

138 "He has arms": *Los Angeles Times*,
  April 27, 1969.

138 Schaus finally started him: West, *Mr.
  Clutch*, 81.

CHAPTER 12

140 "He loved Saperstein": Auth. int. of
  Seymour Goldberg.

140 Owners around the league: "Wilt
  Chamberlain As We Knew Him,"
  Sport, Aug. 1960.

141 "He never seemed": Auth. int. of Joe
  Ruklick.

141 Johnston's biggest problem: Auth.
  int. of Joe Ruklick.

142 "I'm trying to rebound": "The
  Master Plan to Change Wilt
  Chamberlain," *Sport*, March 1962.

142 "From then on": Auth. int. of Joe
  Ruklick.

142 "Every player should be": Sullivan,
  Wilt Chamberlain, 91.

142 "Chamberlain's view was": Auth.
  int. of Paul Arizin.

142 the players cruelly joked: Auth. int.
  of Joe Ruklick.

143 Chamberlain blamed the problem:
  The Philadelphia Inquirer, March
  18, 1991.

143 *Don't let it bother you:* Sullivan,
  Wilt Chamberlain, 87.

143 "You're not a team!": Libby,
  Goliath, 96.

143 Chamberlain, for his part:
  Chamberlain, *Wilt*, 123.

144 "That's enough": Auerbach, *Red*, 279.

145 "The best public relations man":
  "McGuire Raises a Standard," *Sports
  Illustrated*, Oct. 30, 1961.

145 McGuire talked: Ibid.

145 "never before": Ibid.

146 Frank McGuire was: Auth. int. of
  Joe Ruklick.

146 He kept files: "How We Became the Champs," *The Saturday Evening Post*, Dec. 14, 1957.

146 McGuire figured: Libby, *Goliath*, 81.

147 "Fifty?" Chamberlain protested: *Philadelphia Daily News*, April 27, 1959.

147 "I have two goals": "The Master Plan to Change Wilt Chamberlain," *Sport*, March 1962.

147 McGuire could not believe: Auth. int. of Al Attles; also Pluto, *Tall Tales*, 229, and "McGuire Raises a Standard," *Sports Illustrated*, Oct. 30, 1961.

148 "If my scoring average": *Philadelphia Daily News*, April 27, 1979.

148 "Frank was a more": Auth. int. of Paul Arizin.

148 "Wilt," he joked: Libby, *Goliath*, 107.

149 "Some day soon": Wolf, *Great Moments*, 129.

149 "The game seemed": McPhee, *A Sense*, 6.

150 "Basketball, professional basketball": "Elgin Baylor and Basketball's Big Explosion," *Sport*, April 1961.

150 "On a hot night": Ibid.

151 The game was seen: Auth. int. of Harvey Pollack.

151 In the years to come: *Philadelphia Daily News*, April 27, 1992.

151 "Let's run 'em": Ibid.

151 Phil Jordon, the Knicks' starting center: Auth. int. of Joe Ruklick.

151 "You're all I've got": *The New York Times*, March 1, 1987.

152 It seemed to Imhoff: *The Washington Times*, March 2, 1987.

152 "Why don't you": *Associated Press*, Oct. 13, 1999.

152 *Give it to Wilt!: The New York Times*, March 1, 1987.

153 Chamberlain's friend and teammate: Auth. int. of Al Attles.

153 "There's no way": Libby, *Goliath*, 104.

153 Donovan ordered: *USA Today*, March 2, 1987.

153 It was an ironic reversal: Auth. int. of Paul Arizin.

153 This game, it seemed to Guerin: Pluto, *Tall Tales*, 223.

154 "He's going for one hundred": *The New York Times*, March 1, 1987.

154 Wilt shot, missed: Auth. int. of Joe Ruklick.

154 "This ball is a relic": Auth. int. of Harvey Pollack.

155 "I never thought": Auth. int. of Al Attles; also Pluto, *Tall Tales*, 223.

CHAPTER 13

157 The award gave Russell: Libby, *Goliath*, 76.

158 "the fiercest private war": "Bill vs. Wilt—Basketball's Epic Battle," *Life*, Dec. 1, 1961.

158 "All season Russell": *The Philadelphia Inquirer*, March 24, 1962.

158 a "new" Wilt: Ibid.

159 *What are you doing?: The Philadelphia Inquirer*, April 2, 1962.

159 "There would have been more": *Boston Herald*, April 2, 1962.

159 "The brawl had": *The Philadelphia Inquirer*, April 2, 1962.

160 Russell, who had suffered: *The Philadelphia Inquirer*, April 7, 1962.

160 They had no game plan: *The Philadelphia Inquirer*, April 6, 1962.

160 When Sam got the pass: *Boston Herald*, April 6, 1962.

161 a "malfunction" in the clock: *Boston Herald-Traveler*, April 8, 1969.

161 McGuire was so infuriated: Libby, *Goliath*, 111.

161 "Who beat you?": *Boston Herald*, April 6, 1962.

161 "You remember": Chamberlain, *Wilt*, 140.

161 He thought it was: Fitzgerald, *Championship*, 116.

161 "the hardest earned": *Boston Herald*, April 6, 1962.

161 "If it were baseball": Ibid.

161 Both teams had been playing: West, *Mr. Clutch*, 93.

163 Whenever Hano watched: "Jerry West's Burden," *Sport*, March 1962.

163 Tweety Bird: Pluto, *Tall Tales*, 189.

163 Despite his modest height: "Unpredictable All-American," *The Saturday Evening Post*, Jan. 9, 1960.

164 it pained the coach: "Unpredictable All-American," *The Saturday Evening Post*, Jan. 9, 1960.

164 West decided: West, *Mr. Clutch*, 78.

165 West thought the policy: Ibid., 47.

166 Hundley came to hate: "Hot Rod Hundley," *Sport*, Dec. 1962.

167 "Mr. Clutch": Harris, *Fabulous*, 61.

167 the ultimate trophy moment: West, *Mr. Clutch*, 105.

168 Schaus thought Selvy: *Los Angeles Times*, April 16, 1962.

168 West himself had wanted: West, *Mr. Clutch*, 106.

169 Russell, watching: Fitzgerald, *Championship*, 117.

169 Auerbach, standing: *Los Angeles Times*, April 20, 1962.

169 *I missed it: New York Post*, April 19, 1962.

169 He'd made up his mind: *Boston Herald*, April 19, 1962.

170 "I'm glad that's over": Fitzgerald, *Championship*, 118.

170 "I missed the big one": *Boston Herald*, April 19, 1962.

CHAPTER 14

172 "The Celtics conjure": *Boston Herald*, Jan. 9, 1966.

172 Corner Boys: *The New York Times*, BHFA.

172 Dolph Schayes: Auth. int. of Dolph Schayes.

173 Over the years: Auth. int. of Tom Heinsohn.

173 "Johnny, I got": Carey, *High Above*, 141.

173 For all the aura: Auth. int. of Tom Heinsohn. Also "The Master's Touch," *Sports Illustrated*, April 5, 1965.

174 To Havlicek: Havlicek, *Hondo*, 82.

174 the Celtics' training camp: Auth. int. of Tom Heinsohn.

174 one fat center: *The Boston Globe*, Sept. 24, 1968.

174 Auerbach rode: Auth. int. of Tom Heinsohn; also Cousy, *Last*, 126, and Auerbach, *Red*, 189.

175 *Gentlemen, you are: Boston Herald*, Sept. 28, 1984.

175 Chamberlain and a friend: Chamberlain, *Wilt*, 143.

176 Gottlieb made numerous: *San Francisco Chronicle*, Oct. 13, 1964.

176 The investors acquiring: Auth. int. of Shirley Figgins, Franklin Mieuli's assistant.

177 Gottlieb complained: Gottlieb correspondence, BHFA.

178 "Frank McGuire must have": Ibid.

178 In fact, Ben Kerner: Ben Kerner int. in *Boston Herald*, Jan. 2, 1985.

178 *Red, give 'em:* Auerbach, *Winning,* 161.

179 "How come the people": "The Master's Touch," *Sports Illustrated,* April 5, 1965.

179 he was feeling: Auerbach, *Winning,* 197.

179 "He could sit there": Cited in ibid., 210.

179 "a bleeding shark": Cited in ibid., 215.

179 "a ham actor": *Los Angeles Times,* Jan. 16, 1963.

179 While Auerbach was: Auerbach, *Winning,* 217.

180 "I suppose you people": Harris, *Fabulous,* 69; Auerbach, *Winning,* 215.

180 "Cousy and Big O": *Los Angeles Times,* Jan. 17, 1963.

181 he'd felt that the pressure: Cousy, *Basketball,* 177.

181 He suffered from nightmares: Cousy, *Last,* 16.

181 "Not since that memorable day": *Boston Herald,* March 18, 1963.

181 "I'm the guy who didn't want": Ibid.

182 *We love ya, Cooz!" :* Greenfield, *World's Greatest,* 48.

182 "The long reign": Cited in Cousy, *Last,* 37.

182 Game six was in: Account of trip and game day from Cousy, *Last,* 39–257; *Boston Herald,* April 25, 1963.

185 "You don't have fans": *Los Angeles Times,* Jan. 16, 1963.

185 Russell, who was so fatigued: Russell, *Go Up,* 140.

187 "With a farewell performance": *Boston Herald,* April 26, 1963.

CHAPTER 15

189 He had of course heard: "Old Days and Changed Ways," *Sports Illustrated,* Nov. 25, 1968.

189 "Does Chamberlain demand": "Meet the New Wilt Chamberlain," *Sports Illustrated,* March 12, 1964.

190 Since the season was: "I've Barely Begun to Fight," *Sports Illustrated,* Nov. 18, 1968.

191 "What the hell": "Sarge Takes Philly to the Top," *Sports Illustrated,* Feb. 1, 1967.

191 The Warriors, he thought: "The Fight to Remodel Wilt Chamberlain," *Sport,* Feb. 1964.

191 he had urged Dolph: Auth. int. of Dolph Schayes.

191 "You don't raise": "The Fight to Remodel Wilt Chamberlain," *Sport,* Feb. 1964.

192 The tension built: "The Waiting Made It Sweeter," *Sports Illustrated,* May 8, 1967.

192 "You've been fighting me": "The Startling Change in Wilt Chamberlain," *Sport,* March 1967.

192 One article: "The Fight to Remodel Wilt Chamberlain," *Sport,* Feb. 1964.

192 "You've got to bow down": "How Guy Rogers Moves the Warriors," *Sport,* Dec. 1964.

193 "a neurotic need": *Boston Herald,* Sept. 28, 1984.

193 the most selfish, surly: Greenfield, *World's Greatest,* 99.

193 Sanders and Jones decided: "Bill Russell's Private World," *Sport,* Feb. 1963.

194 "I thought the only people": Russell, *Go Up,* 135.

194 A month later, however: *The Washington Post*, May 26, 1999.

194 And the worst part: "We Are Grown Men Playing a Child's Game," *Sports Illustrated*, Nov. 18, 1963.

194 Like other black Americans: Bill Russell int. by UPI, in BHFA; *Christian Science Monitor*, Feb. 12, 1975.

195 Bill Russell had been tempted: "We Are Grown Men Playing a Child's Game," *Sports Illustrated*, Nov. 18, 1963.

195 "by standing in the schoolhouse": Branch, *Parting*, 821.

195 an "explosive situation": Ibid., 832.

195 Russell flew to Jackson: Russell, *Go Up*, 165.

195 "I consider playing": "We Are Grown Men Playing a Child's Game," *Sports Illustrated*, Nov. 18, 1963.

195 "Hey Russell, I'm white": "The Ring Leader," *Sports Illustrated*, May 10, 1999.

196 "Isn't that sweet": "I Owe the Public Nothing," *The Saturday Evening Post*, Jan. 18, 1964.

196 "I'm so great": Hauser, *Muhammad*, 83.

196 "an arrogant Negro": "Growing Up with Privilege and Prejudice," *The New York Times Magazine*, June 14, 1987.

196 When the Russells returned: Ibid.

CHAPTER 16

198 the biggest storm: *Boston Herald*, Jan. 14, 1964.

199 While the owners were meeting: Auth. int. of Tom Heinsohn.

199 "I've never had": Cousy, *Basketball*, 130.

199 "the kid forever": Cited in Fitzgerald, *Championship*, 205.

200 The association remained weak: Auth. ints. of Tom Heinsohn and Al Domenico.

200 "We sat cooling": Auth. int. of Tom Heinsohn.

200 "I don't even have": Ibid.

201 By five o'clock: *New York Post*, Jan. 15, 1964.

201 Shortly before six: *The New York Times*, Jan. 15, 1964.

201 "You can't do this": Auerbach, *Winning*, 58.

202 Heinsohn refused: Auth. int. of Tom Heinsohn.

202 The players took a vote: *New York Post*, Jan. 15, 1964.

202 "You go tell": Auth. int. of Tom Heinsohn.

202 "If any of my players": Russell, *Go Up*, 66.

203 "You can't do this": Pettit, *Bob Pettit*, 160.

203 A number of the players: *New York Post*, Jan. 15, 1964.

203 Even though catastrophe: *Boston Herald*, Jan. 17, 1964.

203 Brown himself had given: *Boston Herald*, Jan. 15, 1964.

204 "Whenever we win": *Boston Herald*, Jan. 17, 1964.

204 "No, I wouldn't": Ibid.

204 Heinsohn had: Auth. int. of Tom Heinsohn.

205 "Tom Heinsohn told me": *Boston Herald*, Jan. 18, 1964.

205 Baylor knew: Auth. int. of Elgin Baylor.

206 "It's sad to speak": Cited in Harris, *Fabulous*, 78.

206 Some seven doctors: Auth. int. of Elgin Baylor.

206 "The Lakers are ruining": "Elgin
Baylor: A Career in Danger," *Sport*,
April 1964.

206 "What about the claim": Ibid.

207 Finally, the Lakers arranged: Auth.
int. of Elgin Baylor.

207 "Take a vacation": "Elgin Baylor: A
Career in Danger," *Sport*, April 1964.

207 "muscle and hustle": Harris,
Lonely, 49.

207 "I told them": Sullivan, *Wilt
Chamberlain*, 151.

208 "I want to tell you": "How Guy
Rogers Moves the Warriors," *Sport*,
Dec. 1964.

208 Havlicek loved to watch: Havlicek,
Hondo, 132.

209 He once wrote: "How I Psych
Them," *Sports Illustrated*, Oct. 25,
1965.

209 It seemed to Russell: Russell,
Second Wind, 181.

210 Russell did wonder: Libby,
Goliath, 88.

210 going into the finals: "The Winning
Ways of Red Auerbach," *Sport*,
March 1965.

210 He hated the travel: Russell, *Second
Wind*, 248.

210 "You know," Hannum told
Chamberlain: "Old Days and
Changed Ways," *Sports Illustrated*,
Nov. 25, 1968.

211 "Get back, Red": Russell, *Go Up*, 105.

211 Chamberlain, finally losing it:
Boston Herald, April 21, 1964.

211 "I want Wilt": Pluto, *Tall Tales*, 239.

212 "Wilt's right cross": *Boston Herald*,
April 21, 1964.

212 At the Celtics' breakup dinner: Auth.
int. of Tom Heinsohn.

212 "I would like to say": *Boston
Herald*, April 28, 1964.

CHAPTER 17

215 "We will utilize": Arledge,
Roone, 30.

215 "ABC Sports gained": Ibid., 83.

216 On Labor Day: *Boston Herald*, Sept.
8, 1964.

216 "The Celtics—the very name": *The
Boston Globe*, Sept. 9, 1964.

216 "the personification": *Boston
Herald*, Sept. 12, 1964.

216 He initially suspected: Sullivan, *Wilt
Chamberlain*, 152.

217 He ordered Chamberlain: *San
Francisco Chronicle*, Sept. 23, 1964.

217 "Dr. Good News": *San Francisco
Chronicle*, Sept. 30, 1964.

217 "The only heart attack": *San
Francisco Chronicle*, Oct. 3, 1964.

217 Lorber told Chamberlain:
Chamberlain, *Wilt*, 160.

218 "It's a little strange": *San Francisco
Chronicle*, Oct. 14, 1964.

218 Chamberlain, Mieuli thought: *San
Francisco Chronicle*, Oct. 24, 1964.

218 For his part, Hannum worried: *San
Francisco Chronicle*, Oct. 15, 1964.

219 Chamberlain was greeted: Auth. int.
of Shirley Figgins, Franklin Mieuli's
assistant.

219 "What's this piece": "I've Barely
Begun to Fight," *Sports Illustrated*,
Nov. 18, 1968.

220 "At times": *San Francisco
Chronicle*, Nov. 17, 1964.

220 "playboy bachelor": "The World at
His Fingertips," *Sport*, Nov. 1965.

221 recognized two trends: *San
Francisco Chronicle*, Nov. 28,
1964.

222 "I now believe": Branch, *Pillar*, 404.

222 he took the passage: Chamberlain,
Wilt, 162.

222　Some people, including Bob Feerick: *San Francisco Chronicle,* Dec. 16, 1964.

223　"Boston plays all over you": *New York Post,* Dec. 17, 1964.

223　"the Late, Late Show": *San Francisco Chronicle,* Dec. 11, 1964.

223　Chamberlain didn't think: *New York Post,* Dec. 16, 1964.

224　"Poor Wilt": Sullivan, *Wilt Chamberlain,* 160.

224　"I've heard enough": Fitzgerald, *Championship,* 146.

224　McSweeney was wrong: "The Master's Touch," *Sports Illustrated,* April 5, 1965.

225　"You'll have to put": "The Winning Ways of Red Auerbach," *Sport,* March 1965.

226　The day after the Warriors: *San Francisco Chronicle,* Dec. 18, 1964.

226　Chamberlain had begun hassling: Chamberlain, *Wilt,* 164.

226　some of the investors: *San Francisco Chronicle,* Jan. 6, 1965.

227　Mieuli hoped to keep: *San Francisco Chronicle,* Dec. 24, 1964.

227　By that point, Mieuli: Auth. int. of Michael Richman.

227　Richman was a gregarious: Auth. ints. of Michael Richman, Harvey Pollack, and Al Domenico; also Lynch, *Season,* 1–14.

230　"He can do": *Los Angeles Times,* Jan. 14, 1965.

230　Hannum felt as anxious: *San Francisco Chronicle,* Jan. 6, 1965.

230　Thurmond was so discouraged: "Old Days and Changed Ways," *Sports Illustrated,* Nov. 25, 1968.

231　As the all-star game: *San Francisco Chronicle,* Jan. 15, 1965.

231　He urged the city's blacks: Branch, *Pillar,* 559.

232　"I don't want you": Halberstam, *October,* 55.

232　voted to boycott: *San Francisco Chronicle,* Jan. 12, 1965.

232　"Are you sure": *The Philadelphia Inquirer,* Jan. 15, 1965.

232　Chamberlain had been entitled: *New York Post,* Jan. 14, 1965.

232　Richman was not: Auth. int. of Michael Richman.

233　"I'm not leaving St. Louis": Chamberlain, *Wilt,* 164; "Old Days and Changed Ways," *Sports Illustrated,* Nov. 25, 1968.

233　The Lakers' Bob Short: *Los Angeles Times,* Jan. 14, 1965.

233　He had hoped Ned Irish: *New York Post,* Jan. 14, 1965.

234　"Chamberlain's been traded!": *New York Herald-Tribune,* Jan. 15, 1965.

234　he thought he could fit them: *San Francisco Examiner,* Jan. 14, 1965.

235　"What would it take": *New York Post,* Jan. 14, 1965.

235　"At midpoint, the pro-basketball": "Another Big Bluff by Big Wilt," *Sports Illustrated,* Jan. 25, 1965.

235　"one of the weirdest": "The Startling Change in Wilt Chamberlain," *Sport,* March 1967.

235　"The San Francisco Warriors": *Los Angeles Times,* Jan. 15, 1965.

CHAPTER 18

236　Ike Richman realized: Auth. int. of Dolph Schayes.

236　"Don't let any": *The Philadelphia Inquirer,* Dec. 5, 1965.

237　"My sales went up": Lynch, *Season,* 51.

237　"By the river": Philadelphia *Evening Bulletin,* Jan. 22, 1965.

237   "And now": Sullivan, *Wilt Chamberlain*, 167.

238   The two games against the Celtics: Auth. int. of Dolph Schayes.

239   he'd responded by writing: "Wilt Chamberlain as We Knew Him," *Sport*, Aug. 1960.

239   Schayes now felt: Auth. int. of Dolph Schayes; also "Trials of the Tall Men," *Dell Sports*, Feb. 1962.

240   "Why did this": Libby, *Goliath*, 132.

240   Schayes would later: Auth. int. of Dolph Schayes.

240   While the older players: "My Life in a Bush League," *Sports Illustrated*, April 12, 1965.

241   "Bring on the Celtics!": Sullivan, *Wilt Chamberlain*, 173.

241   "a snakepit": *Boston Herald*, April 7, 1965.

242   What kind of fan: Havlicek, *Hondo*, 100.

242   Auerbach would have paid: Fitzgerald, *Championship*, 148.

242   Dolph Schayes thought: Auth. int. of Dolph Schayes.

242   "Oh, man, this is going": "My Life in a Bush League," *Sports Illustrated*, April 12, 1965.

242   The other 76ers: *Boston Herald*, April 19, 1965.

243   "interjected many unauthorized": *The Philadelphia Inquirer*, April 10, 1965.

243   "It appeared that Wilt": *The Philadelphia Inquirer*, April 9, 1965.

243   Schayes, for his part: Auth. int. of Dolph Schayes; also *The Philadelphia Inquirer*, April 9, 1965.

243   Chet Walker felt that: Walker, *Long Time*, 162.

244   "Pressure! Pressure!": *Boston Herald*, April 15, 1965.

244   "You never knew": Auth. int. of Al Domenico.

245   Chet Walker felt like: Walker, *Long Time*, 163.

245   In the pregame huddle: Auth. int. of Dolph Schayes.

245   Red Auerbach had a saying: Havlicek, *Hondo*, 126.

246   "There's this guy": Shaughnessy, *Seeing*, 157.

246   "Have you ever seen": Carey, *High Above*, 142.

246   Country Boy: *New York Post*, April 29, 1969.

246   Havlicek would work up: Havlicek, *Hondo*, 126.

248   "Oh my God": Russell, *Go Up*, 115.

248   Strom also had a core: Shaughnessy, *Ever Green*, 111.

248   Schayes immediately: Auth. int. of Dolph Schayes.

249   "Let's make the play": Salzberg, *From Set Shot*, 213.

249   "I blew it": Pluto, *Tall Tales*, 260.

249   Auerbach seemed at a loss.: *Boston Herald*, April 7, 1965.

249   "Play defense": Libby, *Goliath*, 138.

249   Havlicek started counting: Havlicek, *Hondo*, 128.

250   *"Havlicek stole the ball!"*: Carey, *High Above*, 155.

250   "You were great, Wilt": Sullivan, *Wilt Chamberlain*, 179.

250   A Boston Garden work crew: *Boston Herald*, April 17, 1965.

251   If Russell was the heart: *New York Post*, April 29, 1969.

251   In mid-winter: Auth. int. of Elgin Baylor; also "The Elgin Baylor Miracle," *Sport*, Nov. 1967.

253   "They used to say": *Los Angeles Times*, April 11, 1965.

253   Normally, it would never: West, *Mr. Clutch*, 119.

253 The grudge he bore: "The Winning Ways of Red Auerbach," *Sport*, March 1965.

254 In game five: *Boston Herald*, April 27, 1965.

254 It was Tommy Heinsohn's final game: Auth. int. of Tom Heinsohn.

254 DON'T LEAVE US, HEINIE: *Boston Herald*, April 26, 1965.

254 Since it was probably: Auth. int. of Tom Heinsohn.

255 "You want to know": *Boston Herald*, April 26, 1965.

CHAPTER 19

257 *My God, do I look:* Auerbach, *Management*, 174.

257 John Waldron: *New York Post*, April 18, 1966.

257 "I'm announcing it now": Heinsohn, *Give 'Em the Hook*, 104.

257 "They want them to lose": "A Last Cigar for a Last Hurrah?" *The Saturday Evening Post*, March 26, 1966.

258 "Do me a favor": Ibid.

258 On December 3: Auth. int. of Michael Richman.

258 Despite the strains: Auth. int. of Dolph Schayes.

259 "Can't you give me": *The Philadelphia Inquirer*, Dec. 5, 1965.

259 At breakfast on the morning: Auth. int. of Al Domenico.

259 yelling nonstop: Lynch, *Season*, 3.

259 Suddenly, five minutes: Auth. ints. of Al Domenico and Dolph Schayes; also *The Philadelphia Inquirer*, Dec. 4, 1965, and Lynch, *Season*, 3, 4.

260 "Tell the team": Auth. int. of Al Domenico.

261 "whole new set of smoldering problems": Cosell, *Cosell*, 126.

261 "Bluntly put to you": "Pro Basketball's Hidden Fear," *Sport*, Feb. 1966.

262 "I'm only being realistic": Ibid.

263 Back in April: Lukas, *Common Ground*, 130.

264 "The [Celtics team] offers": *Boston Herald*, Sept. 12, 1965.

264 When Auerbach thought about it: *New York Post*, April 18, 1966.

265 Auerbach thought Frank Ramsey: *Boston Herald*, Jan. 18, 1966.

265 his anxiety had caused: Cousy, *Killer Instinct*, 36.

265 Tommy Heinsohn, despite his reputation: Auth. int. of Tom Heinsohn.

265 Russell was an obvious possibility: *Boston Herald*, Jan. 18, 1966.

266 "How would you like": Bill Russell int. in *New York Post*, April 19, 1966.

266 After the operation: Auth. int. of Elgin Baylor; also "The Elgin Baylor Miracle," *Sport*, Nov. 1967.

268 "The old pro": *Los Angeles Times*, Feb. 3, 1966.

268 Sam Jones thought Billy Cunningham: "Billy Cunningham and the Good Times," *Sport*, July 1966.

269 "Maybe if we press the kid": Auerbach, *Winning*, 349.

269 In Schayes's mind: Auth. int. of Dolph Schayes.

270 it seemed to Joe McGinniss: "Billy Cunningham and the Good Times," *Sport*, July 1966.

270 Russell still wouldn't commit: *New York Post*, April 19, 1966.

270 he liked the idea: "Where the Negro Goes from Here in Sports," *Sport*, Sept. 1966.

270 "Being something of a nut": *Boston Herald*, April 19, 1966.

271 "Once he had contended": *New York Post,* April 18, 1966.

271 "I wasn't offered the job": *New York Post,* April 19, 1966.

271 *This is the day: New York Post,* April 29, 1966.

272 "You hear me good?": Auerbach, *Winning,* 359.

272 That was a lot of money: *New York Post,* April 29, 1966.

273 Milton Gross—whose motto was: Auth. int. of Michael Gross.

273 When Auerbach and Gross: *New York Post,* April 29, 1966.

CHAPTER 20

275 "Great year": *Philadelphia Daily News,* April 13, 1966.

275 "devouring them like aspirin tablets": Cited in Chamberlain, *Wilt,* 175.

276 "Wilt thought I was": Auth. int. of Dolph Schayes.

276 Hannum considered Schayes: "I've Barely Begun to Fight," *Sports Illustrated,* Nov. 18, 1968.

276 "Listen, he's gone": Pluto, *Tall Tales,* 319.

276 "I wasn't missing": Lynch, *Season,* 62.

277 "I don't even know": "The Startling Change in Wilt Chamberlain," *Sport,* March 1967.

278 "You know, I can pass": Pluto, *Tall Tales,* 321.

278 Before an exhibition game: Philadelphia *Evening Bulletin,* Oct. 12, 1966.

279 "like the Phantom of the Opera": "Bill Russell's Most Trying Season," *Sport,* April 1967.

279 "white thinking": "Where the Negro Goes from Here in Sports," *Sport,* Sept. 1966.

279 he'd decided Boston: Russell remarks in press conference, *The Seattle Times,* June 6, 1973.

279 Once, when he returned: "The Unknown Side of Bill Russell," *Sport,* March 1966.

280 It was therefore essential: Auerbach, *Management,* 138.

280 at the breakup dinner: "Bill Russell's Most Trying Season," *Sport,* April 1967.

280 In September: Russell, *Russell Rules,* 76.

280 "I thought you were in": "Bill Russell's Most Trying Season," *Sport,* April 1967.

281 "There's no big deal": *Philadelphia Daily News,* Oct. 29, 1966.

281 "We just got beat": *Philadelphia Daily News,* Oct. 31, 1966.

282 Hannum wrote a series: "The Startling Change in Wilt Chamberlain," *Sport,* March 1967.

282 "milk it": "The Waiting Made It Sweeter," *Sports Illustrated,* May 8, 1967.

282 "What's up here?": *Philadelphia Daily News,* Feb. 25, 1967.

284 "If there had been": "The Startling Change in Wilt Chamberlain," *Sport,* March 1967.

284 "They might be": Lynch, *Season,* 80.

284 "This was the best": Libby, *Goliath,* 143.

284 "Don't be afraid": Ibid., 142.

285 the 76ers became a gang: Chamberlain, *Wilt,* 176.

285 Chamberlain held a Halloween party: Lynch, *Season,* 68.

288 Tiny Tots: *Boston Herald,* April 3, 1967.

288 "Realistically, Red": *The Philadelphia Inquirer,* April 3, 1967.

289 "For eight years, the Celtics": *The Philadelphia Inquirer,* April 4, 1967.

289 "The Celtics do not deserve": *The Boston Globe,* April 4, 1967.

289 "The Celtics are dead": *Boston Herald,* April 4, 1967.

289 Wally Jones had been afflicted: Auth. int. of Al Domenico.

290 the Great Intimidator: *Boston Herald,* April 3, 1967.

290 Captain Marvel: *The Philadelphia Inquirer,* April 6, 1967.

290 taken to wearing buttons: "Wally Wonder for Mayor," *Sport,* Sept. 1967.

290 It was obviously phony: *Boston Herald,* April 6, 1967.

291 "They haven't won anything yet": *The Philadelphia Inquirer,* April 7, 1967.

292 "But he's had a good teacher": *Boston Herald,* April 8, 1967.

292 Lorber examined him: *The Philadelphia Inquirer,* April 8, 1967.

292 Alex Hannum's wife: *Boston Herald,* April 10, 1967.

292 "We were guessing": Auth. int. of Al Domenico.

294 *We ain't dead!: Boston Herald,* April 10, 1967.

294 Cunningham told Wally Jones: *The Philadelphia Inquirer,* April 12, 1967.

295 Cunningham, watching: Lynch, *Season,* 140.

295 Chamberlain remained relatively subdued: *The Philadelphia Inquirer,* April 13, 1967.

295 The fact was: "The Fight to Remodel Wilt Chamberlain," *Sport,* Feb. 1964.

296 "Great," Russell said: "The Waiting Made It Sweeter," *Sports Illustrated,* May 8, 1967.

CHAPTER 21

297 a secret meeting: "I Am Not Worried About Ali," *Sports Illustrated,* June 19, 1967.

298 "You know where I stand": Lukas, *Common Ground,* 134.

298 "Dr. Martin Luther King": Ibid., 135.

298 When Russell's grandfather: Russell, *Second Wind,* 51.

298 "Nothing, I'm happy": "The Ring Leader," *Sports Illustrated,* May 10, 1999.

299 Havlicek, for one, got pretty tired: Fitzgerald, *Championship,* 180.

299 Sam Jones had been telling: Springfield [Mass.] *Daily News,* May 11, 1967.

299 He told the players: "Sportsman of the Year," *Sports Illustrated,* Dec. 23, 1968.

300 "I know nothing about it": Auth. int. of Seymour Goldberg.

301 "Where is everybody?": Libby, *Goliath,* 152.

302 Chamberlain felt that if he could lead: Chamberlain, *Who's Running,* 108.

302 "Did you see this?": "Win One for the Dipper," *Sport,* March 1974.

302 "I think there are more important things": Lynch, *Season,* 211.

303 At nine o'clock: *Boston Herald-Traveler,* April 7, 1968.

303 That night and the following day: *Boston Herald-Traveler,* April 6, 1968.

304 The way Russell saw it: Bill Russell int. in *The Philadelphia Inquirer,* April 6, 1968.

304 Bailey Howell, who was white: Walker, *Long Time,* 198.

304 Russell himself was in no mood: *The Philadelphia Inquirer,* April 7, 1968.

306 King's death had made Walker feel: Walker, *Long Time*, 201.

306 "The Celtics have seen": *The Boston Globe*, April 15, 1968.

306 "When the Celtics fell": *Boston Herald-Traveler*, April 21, 1968.

306 "We've come so far": "Sportsman of the Year," *Sports Illustrated*, Dec. 23, 1968.

307 "Don, you don't want": Havlicek, *Hondo*, 104.

307 *Celtics Rule Again: Boston Herald-Traveler*, April 20, 1968.

308 Hannum blamed himself: Alex Hannum int. in *Philadelphia Daily News*, May 1, 1979.

308 "more surprising than an American": *Boston Herald-Traveler*, April 21, 1968.

CHAPTER 22

310 "You're free to go make": Auth. int. of Seymour Goldberg.

310 Cooke was in his hotel room: "Wilt, West, and Baylor," *Sport*, March 1969.

310 "Never call it an arena": *Los Angeles Times*, Dec. 30, 1968.

311 He had at that point: Havill, *Last Mogul*, 142.

311 "I have never been able": *Los Angeles Times*, Sept. 30, 1968.

312 They all felt the pressure: Harris, *Fabulous*, 105.

312 Five other teams were interested: Auth. int. of Seymour Goldberg.

312 "Wilt, I'm going to get you": Auth. int. of Seymour Goldberg.

313 "Chamberlain obviously was intimidated": *Los Angeles Times*, July 12, 1968.

313 "The Celtics have been a team": Ibid.

314 "It is as if the Niblets people": "The Beard Moves into a New and Ticklish Pad," *Sports Illustrated*, Oct. 14, 1968.

314 Over the long run: Auth. int. of Seymour Goldberg.

314 "It's for plenty of bucks": *New York Post*, July 9, 1968.

314 "The payroll is a little scary": *Los Angeles Times*, Sept. 26, 1968.

314 "The only thing Wilt can't do": *Los Angeles Times*, July 12, 1968.

315 "You swallow some blood": "Pro Basketball Almanac," *Sport*, 1968.

316 when he saw a copy: Pluto, *Tall Tales*, 353.

316 "Butch earns his technicals": "Wilt, West, and Baylor," *Sport*, March 1969.

316 "All I care about": West, *Mr. Clutch*, 178.

316 he had no hesitation: "On Top—But in Trouble," *Sports Illustrated*, Jan. 27, 1969.

317 "When do we get": West, *Mr. Clutch*, 184.

318 West thought Chamberlain was incredibly talented: West, *Mr. Clutch*, 123.

318 "I don't know if you can": *The Boston Globe*, July 23, 1968.

318 "We just broke up": Pluto, *Tall Tales*, 354.

319 *the fluid game:* "Hedonist Prophet of the Spartan Game," *Sports Illustrated*, Sept. 23, 1968.

319 "the officiating is ridiculous": Ibid.

319 "He can pass well": Ibid.

320 Van Breda Kolff felt that Chamberlain: Pluto, *Tall Tales*, 354.

320 van Breda Kolff closed the workouts: *Los Angeles Times*, Sept. 26, 1968.

320 "The Lakers better shore up": *Los Angeles Times*, Sept. 24, 1968.

320 "I told him I needed": *Los Angeles Times*, Nov. 19, 1968.

321 players such as Mel Counts: Mel Counts int. in *The Boston Globe*, March 22, 1981.

321 West thought the Lakers: West, *Mr. Clutch*, 191.

322 Baylor and Chamberlain quickly developed: "On Top—But in Trouble," *Sports Illustrated*, Jan. 27, 1969.

322 Baylor would tell: Libby, *Goliath*, 189.

322 "If Jerry comes out": *Los Angeles Times*, Sept. 26, 1968.

322 "I know what's best": "Wilt, West, and Baylor," *Sport*, March 1969.

323 "I would think": Libby, *Goliath*, 183.

323 "They say when he wandered": "Wilt, West, and Baylor," *Sport*, March 1969.

323 Jerry West found the whole: Jerry West int. in *New York Post*, May 11, 1968.

324 A big part of the problem: Bill van Breda Kolff int. in *Los Angeles Times*, Dec. 17, 1968.

324 "There are three things": *Los Angeles Times*, Dec. 11, 1968.

325 a "peace conference": *Los Angeles Times*, Dec. 13, 1968.

326 van Breda Kolff began complaining: "The Wilt Chamberlain Controversy," *Sport*, Aug. 1969.

CHAPTER 23

327 Bill Russell had spent the summer: *Boston Herald-Traveler*, Aug. 22, 1968.

327 Russell's marriage was breaking down: Russell, *Second Wind*, 268.

328 "It ain't no big thing": *The Boston Globe*, Sept. 24, 1968.

328 "His shooting touch": *Los Angeles Times*, Nov. 19, 1968.

329 Joe DeLauri, the Celtics trainer: *The Boston Globe*, Feb. 3, 1969.

329 In late February: *Los Angeles Times*, Feb. 20, 1969.

331 Chamberlain's main problem: West, *Mr. Clutch*, 192.

331 No matter what he did: Wilt Chamberlain int. in *Los Angeles Times*, March 9, 1969.

332 the players had held a meeting: "The Wilt Chamberlain Controversy," *Sport*, Aug. 1969.

332 prompted Russell to administer: *Los Angeles Times*, March 17, 1969.

333 "As all schoolchildren know": "Comebacks All Over," *Sports Illustrated*, April 16, 1969.

333 Havlicek had realized: Havlicek, *Hondo*, 108.

333 "Four guards and not two": "Comebacks All Over," *Sports Illustrated*, April 16, 1969.

334 the worst game he'd ever played: Dave DeBusschere int. in *New York Post*, April 10, 1969.

335 suffering from migraine headaches: *Los Angeles Times*, April 16, 1969.

335 *Boston Here We Come*: *Los Angeles Times*, April 29, 1969.

CHAPTER 24

337 Baylor had never doubted: "Elgin Baylor's Playoff Diary," *Sport*, July 1969.

337 Chamberlain agreed, and he was convinced: *Los Angeles Times*, April 23, 1969.

338 "How you doing?": *New York Post*, April 25, 1969.

338 "It was a game": *Los Angeles Times*, April 24, 1969.

339 To Bill Russell's surprise: *Los Angeles Times*, April 27, 1969.

340 Baylor, who felt that: "Elgin Baylor's Playoff Diary," *Sport*, July 1969.

341 a play they called "Ohio": *The Boston Globe*, April 30, 1995.

341 Before the playoffs: Russell, *Russell Rules*, 202.

342 Even before he released it: *Boston Herald-Traveler*, April 30, 1969.

342 "Kiss the Blarney Stone": *Los Angeles Times*, April 30, 1969.

343 West hated to be called: West, *Mr. Clutch*, 205–7.

343 What particularly irked him: *Los Angeles Times*, May 2, 1969.

344 Havlicek felt his body: *Los Angeles Times*, May 4, 1969.

344 "If I had to take": *New York Post*, May 5, 1969.

345 "Who cares what Wilt says?": *Los Angeles Times*, May 5, 1969.

346 He felt that whether: West, *Mr. Clutch*, 199.

346 van Breda Kolff told his team: "Elgin Baylor's Playoff Diary," *Sport*, July 1969.

346 Just before the game: Russell, *Russell Rules*, 190.

347 West just stood there: West, *Mr. Clutch*, 200.

347 it seemed to Baylor: "Elgin Baylor's Playoff Diary," *Sport*, July 1969.

348 his knee hurt so badly: *Los Angeles Times*, May 7, 1969.

348 *There are no such things: Boston Herald-Traveler*, March 18, 1969.

348 tighter than Ramses II: *Boston Herald-Traveler*, April 29, 1969.

348 Not only was Russell surprised: Russell, *Second Wind*, 192–230.

349 "I'm ready to go back in": Wilt Chamberlain int. in *New York Post*, May 7, 1969.

350 Chamberlain had pulled down: Bill van Breda Kolff int. in *Los Angeles Times*, May 7, 1969.

351 "What are they going to do": *Los Angeles Times*, May 6, 1969.

351 Chamberlain was angrier: Chamberlain, *Wilt*, 218.

351 An argument broke out: Libby, *Goliath*, 194.

351 he had played so hard: "Jerry West Wins *Sport*'s First NBA Award," *Sport*, July 1969.

351 "I can't stand to listen": West, *Mr. Clutch*, 218.

352 "I love you": Havlicek, *Hondo*, 115.

352 "You've refused all these years": *Los Angeles Times*, May 6, 1969.

352 "Each game of the grueling playoffs": *Boston Herald-Traveler*, May 7, 1969.

352 "Some day in the far-off future": *The Boston Globe*, May 7, 1969.

352 Two days later: *Boston Herald-Traveler*, May 9, 1969.

CHAPTER 25

354 Milton Gross had watched: *New York Post*, May 7, 1969.

355 He decided van Breda Kolff: Chamberlain, *Wilt*, 212.

355 "The thing that kills me": *New York Post*, May 7, 1969.

356 "If I had had fifteen minutes'": "The Wilt Chamberlain Controversy," *Sport*, Aug. 1969.

356 "one of those old-time duels": *New York Post*, BHFA.

356 After the season ended: Account of Russell's lecture-circuit remarks, from Russell, *Second Wind*, 277–78;

"The Wilt Chamberlain Controversy," *Sport,* Aug. 1969; Harris, *Lonely,* 37; Libby, *Goliath,* 194.

358 Two days after: *Boston Herald-Traveler,* May 7, 1969.

358 "Don't worry, Red": Russell, *Russell Rules,* 208.

358 Auerbach did not take: Red Auerbach int. in *Herald Traveler and Boston Record American,* Dec. 19, 1972.

359 their marriage had gone stale: Russell, *Second Wind,* 246.

359 it had gone bankrupt: *Boston Herald American,* Sept. 16, 1973.

359 he defaulted on a $90,000 loan: *Christian Science Monitor,* Feb. 12, 1975.

359 the IRS put a lien: *Springfield Union,* June 9, 1973.

360 *Cold, icy cold:* Harris, *Lonely,* 34.

361 revived his war: *The Seattle Times,* June 6, 1973.

361 "I am not a racist": *Boston Herald American,* June 8, 1973.

362 "When and where": New York *Daily News,* April 8, 1990.

363 "What are you doing?": Auth. int. of Michael Richman.

363 "Bill Russell: Why do you": Chamberlain, *View from Above,* 185.

363 Russell and Chamberlain were reunited: Auth. int. of Seymour Goldberg.

363 "I don't care if I never": *Boston Herald Advertiser,* March 2, 1975.

364 Casey figured: *Boston Herald,* Jan. 19, 1995.

364 The two men: Auth. int. of Seymour Goldberg.

364 a couple of old ladies: *The New York Times,* Oct. 30, 1996.

364 they never discussed: Bill Russell int. by Chris Matthews, *Hardball,* MSNBC, June 6, 2001.

365 Had he played: Bill Russell int. in *Philadelphia Daily News,* Oct. 30, 1996.

365 "I have trouble saying this": *Boston Herald,* May 27, 1999.

366 Russell had bought Hal DeJulio's: Auth. int. of Hal DeJulio.

366 "We love you, Bill!": *The Boston Globe,* Dec. 30, 1999.

CHAPTER 26

367 Five months later: Auth. int. of Seymour Goldberg; *City News Service,* Oct. 12, 1999; *Philly.com,* Oct. 13, 1999; *The Seattle Times News Service,* Oct. 13, 1999; *Los Angeles Times,* Oct. 13, 1999.

369 But the loss Russell felt: Account of Russell's feelings taken from his remarks at Chamberlain's memorial service, *The Washington Post,* Oct. 17, 1999.

370 A few days after Chamberlain's death: Auth. ints. of Al Attles and Seymour Goldberg; *Houston Chronicle,* Oct. 17, 1999; *Los Angeles Times,* Oct. 17, 1999; Lynch, *Season,* 233.

BIBLIOGRAPHY

Arledge, Roone. *Roone*. New York: HarperCollins, 2003.

Ashe, Arthur. *A Hard Road to Glory: Basketball*. New York: Amistad Press, 1988.

Auerbach, Red, and Ken Dooley. *MBA: Management by Auerbach*. New York: Collier Books, 1991.

———, with Joe Fitzgerald. *On and Off the Court*. New York: Macmillan, 1985.

———, and Joe Fitzgerald. *Red Auerbach*. New York: Putnam, 1977.

———, with Paul Sann. *Winning the Hard Way*. Boston: Little, Brown, 1966.

Branch, Taylor. *Parting the Waters*. New York: Simon and Schuster, 1988.

———. *Pillar of Fire*. New York: Simon and Schuster, 1998.

Carey, Mike, with Jamie Most. *High Above Courtside: The Lost Memoirs of Johnny Most*. Sports Publishing LLC, 2003.

Chamberlain, Wilt. *A View from Above*. New York: Signet Books, 1992. First published, New York: Villard Books, 1991.

———. *Who's Running the Asylum?* San Diego: ProMotion Publishing, 1997.

———, and David Shaw. *Wilt*. New York: Macmillan, 1973.

Cosell, Howard. *Cosell*. Chicago: Playboy Press, 1973.

Cousy, Bob, with John Devany. *The Killer Instinct*. New York: Random House, 1975.

———, and Al Hirshberg. *Basketball Is My Life*. New York: J. Lowell Pratt, 1963.

———, with Edward Linn. *The Last Loud Roar*. Englewood Cliffs, N.J.: Prentice-Hall, 1964.

———, and Bob Ryan. *Cousy on the Celtic Mystique*. New York: McGraw Hill, 1988.

Fitzgerald, Joe. *That Championship Feeling*. New York: Charles Scribner's Sons, 1975.

Greenfield, Jeff. *Television*. New York: Crescent Books, 1977.

———. *The World's Greatest Team*. New York: Random House, 1976.

Halberstam, David. *The Fifties*. New York: Villard Books, 1993.

———. *October 1964*. New York: Villard Books, 1994.

———. *Playing for Keeps*. New York: Random House, 1999.

———. *Summer of '49*. New York: HarperCollins, 2002. First published, New York: William Morrow, 1989.

Harris, Merv. *The Fabulous Lakers*. New York: Lancer Books, 1972.

———. *The Lonely Heroes*. New York: Viking Press, 1975.

Hauser, Thomas, and Muhammad Ali. *Muhammad Ali: His Life and Times*. New York: Simon and Schuster, 1991.

Havill, Adrian. *The Last Mogul*. New York: St. Martin's Press, 1992.

Havlicek, John, and Bob Ryan. *Hondo*. Englewood Cliffs, N.J.: Prentice-Hall, 1977.

Heinsohn, Tommy, and Joe Fitzgerald. *Give 'Em the Hook*. New York: Prentice-Hall, 1988.

———, with Leonard Lewin. *Heinsohn Don't You Ever Smile?* Garden City, N.Y.: Doubleday, 1976.

Hirshberg, Al. *Bill Russell of the Boston Celtics*. New York: Julian Messner, 1963.

Koppett, Leonard. *Twenty-four Seconds to Shoot*. Kingston, N.Y.: Total/Sports Illustrated, 1999. First published, New York: Macmillan, 1968.

Libby, Bill. *Goliath*. New York: Dodd, Mead, 1977.

Lukas, Anthony J. *Common Ground*. New York: Vintage Books, 1986. First published, New York: Alfred A. Knopf, 1985.

Lynch, Wayne. *Season of the 76ers*. New York: St. Martin's Press, 2002.

Manchester, William. *The Glory and the Dream*. Boston: Little, Brown, 1973.

Maraniss, David. *When Pride Still Mattered*. New York: Simon and Schuster, 1999.

McPhee, John. *A Sense of Where You Are*. New York: Farrar, Straus and Giroux, 1965.

Nadel, Eric. *The Night Wilt Scored 100*. Dallas: Taylor Publishing, 1990.

Pettit, Bob, with Bob Wolff. *Bob Pettit: The Drive Within Me*. Englewood Cliffs, N.J.: Prentice-Hall, 1966.

Pluto, Terry. *Tall Tales*. Lincoln: University of Nebraska Press, 2000. First published, New York: Simon and Schuster, 1992.

Rappaport, Ken. *The Classic: The History of the NCAA Basketball Championship*. Kansas City, Mo.: Lowell Press, 1982.

Riess, Stephen. *City Games*. Urbana: University of Illinois Press, 1989.

Russell, Bill, and Taylor Branch. *Second Wind*. New York: Ballantine Books, 1980.

———, with David Falkner. *Russell Rules*. New York: Dutton, 2001.

———, and William McSweeny. *Go Up for Glory*. New York: Berkley Medallion Books, 1966.

Salzberg, Charles. *From Set Shot to Slam Dunk*. New York: Bantam Doubleday Dell, 1987.

Shapiro, Miles. *Bill Russell: Basketball Great*. New York: Chelsea House, 1991.

Shaughnessy, Dan. *Ever Green*. New York: St. Martin's Press, 1990.

———. *Seeing Red*. New York: Crown, 1994.

Sullivan, George. *Wilt Chamberlain*. New York: Grosset and Dunlap, 1966.

Walker, Chet, with Chris Messenger. *Long Time Coming*. New York: Grove Press, 1995.

West, Jerry, with Bill Libby. *Mr. Clutch*. New York: Grosset and Dunlap, 1970.

Willensky, Elliot. *When Brooklyn Was the World*. New York: Harmony Books, 1986.

Winship, Michael. *Television*. New York: Random House, 1988.

Wolf, Dave, and Bill Bruns. *Great Moments in Pro Basketball*. New York: Random House, 1968.

INDEX

as Olympic sport, 44, 48, 363
pickup, 44–45, 60, 101, 112, 155, 216
player trades in, 19, 33–34, 64, 67, 68,
    69–71, 226–35, 240, 245, 276,
    310–15
as professional sport, 74, 130–31, 146,
    173, 198–99, 213, 214–15, 363
rookie players in, 5, 10, 68, 71–80,
    90–99, 108, 113, 120–29, 174, 191,
    200, 239, 264, 268–70, 312, 356, 358
rules of, 6, 38–39, 46–47, 49, 61–62,
    78, 79–80, 82–83, 84, 90, 100–101,
    102, 105, 120, 129, 140, 286, 319,
    327, 365
running game in, 17, 73, 174–75, 183,
    184, 332
salaries in, 40–41, 49, 68, 74, 120, 200,
    203
scoring records in, 5, 10, 45, 51, 60–62,
    64–65, 68, 73, 78, 83, 85, 120, 121,
    122, 126, 129, 142–43, 146–58, 170,
    176, 182, 189, 191–92, 208–9, 210,
    221, 230, 234, 238, 258, 278, 281,
    282–85, 294, 301–3, 307, 321, 322,
    330, 331–32, 335, 336, 337, 354–58,
    362, 370–71
team finances in, 17–19, 21–28, 30–31,
    130–31, 200, 363
team owners in, 3–10, 20–24, 26,
    27–28, 104–6, 110, 140, 198–205,
    212–13, 242, 312–13
team travel in, 125, 131, 147, 180–83,
    199, 225
tempo of, 37–39, 41, 73, 75–76, 78, 79,
    87
ticket sales for, 5, 134, 185, 261–64,
    305, 332–33, 339
training in, 33–35, 90, 91, 107–8,
    116–17, 122, 146, 147, 163, 165,
    174–75, 200, 210, 216, 219, 266–67,
    276, 300–301, 315, 320, 329, 338,
    343
violence of, 19, 35–36, 73–76, 122–25,
    127–28, 129, 159, 162, 222

winning margins in, 118–19
see also National Basketball
    Association
Basketball Association of America
    (BAA), 16, 19, 105, 175
Basketball Hall of Fame, 361
Basketball Is My Life (Cousy), 30*n*, 181
basketballs:
    passing of, 29, 39, 45, 55, 76, 79, 89,
        97, 98–99, 102, 103, 109, 121, 125,
        128, 142, 153–54, 160–61, 162, 168,
        207, 208, 248–50, 317
    recovery of, 121, 333, 338
    spin on, 134, 143, 160, 164, 342
baskets, guarding of, 79, 95, 127–28, 162,
    244, 319
Baylor, Elgin, 112, 133–39, 148, 149,
    150, 153, 161–70, 180–86, 198,
    201–7, 249, 251–54, 266–68, 272,
    310, 314–23, 326, 331–41, 344–48,
    357, 360, 370
Baylor, Ruby, 266
Bemoras, Irv, 97, 98
Bianchi, Al, 259, 285
Biasone, Danny, 31, 36–37, 39, 140, 228
Big Seven tournament, 81–82, 83, 85
Big Ten, 47
Bishop, Joey, 258–59
Bloom, Leonard, 362
Bockhorn, Arlen, 222
Bolyard, Bucky, 164
bonuses, 112, 135, 189, 203, 272
Boozer, Bob, 223–24, 226
Borgia, Sid, 36, 95
Born, B. H., 48
Boston Braves, 69, 136–37
Boston Bruins, 173, 204, 263, 308
Boston Celtics:
    aging players of, 328, 333, 347
    attendance figures for, 63–64, 75, 77,
        173, 178, 245, 262–64, 359
    Auerbach as coach of, 5, 10–12, 20–42,
        63–65, 91, 96, 107–8, 110, 115–20,
        126, 130, 136, 159, 161*n*, 169,

Boston Celtics *(cont'd)*:
178–80, 181, 183, 184, 185, 189,
201, 204, 209, 223, 224–25, 245,
246–47, 248, 249, 250, 254–58,
264–66, 269, 270–71, 276, 280,
286–87, 289, 290, 319, 333, 347,
348, 365

Auerbach as general manager of, 281,
286, 288, 290, 293, 304, 305, 306,
308, 328, 329–30, 341, 342, 351,
353, 358, 359, 361

basic plays of, 33–34, 174–75,
341–42

black players on, 110, 262–64,
303–8

Boston as hometown of, 3–5, 21,
28–29, 40–41, 108, 127–28, 181–82,
244–45, 263–64, 268, 298–99,
352–53, 361, 363–66

defense of, 41, 51, 55, 57–58, 59, 74,
77, 78, 79–80, 90, 96, 97, 98, 118,
120, 161, 210, 212, 246, 249, 330,
334, 337, 339, 350

draft choices of, 26–32, 41–42, 67–71,
359

in Eastern Division playoffs, 41, 63,
90–93, 119, 157–61, 182, 241–51,
268–70, 285–96, 303–8, 317,
333–34, 359

fans of, 3–5, 21, 28–29, 30, 32, 34, 37,
40–41, 63–64, 75, 91, 118, 126,
127–28, 168, 172, 173, 181–82, 183,
193, 196, 211, 242, 244–45, 248,
250–51, 254, 262–64, 273, 289,
293–94, 307, 332, 333, 340, 345,
352–53, 365–66

fines against, 74, 77–78, 118, 332

home-court advantage of, 3–10, 21–23,
95–99, 171–73, 244–45, 260, 268,
287, 307, 339, 342, 345

injuries sustained by, 71, 73, 96, 157,
171, 183–84, 191, 206, 210, 212,
253–54, 287, 293, 328–29, 334,
348–49, 368

locker room of, 95–96, 199–200, 212,
298–99

Los Angeles Lakers as rivals of,
161–62, 167–70, 178–80, 182–87,
270–74, 317, 329–53

media coverage of, 20–21, 34–35, 72,
161, 169, 170, 172, 186–87,
270–71, 288–89, 291, 306, 308, 338,
342

mystique of, 3–10, 21–23, 77, 95–99,
119–20, 148, 171–73, 250–51, 272,
289, 291, 295–96, 306–8, 317, 329,
333, 337–38, 342

NBA championships won by, 3–10, 11,
77, 93–99, 100, 119–20, 148,
167–70, 171, 175, 178–79, 181,
182–87, 189, 191, 216, 235, 253–55,
270–74, 308, 317, 336–58, 359

offense of, 41, 54–55, 56, 58, 59,
90–91, 120, 170, 208, 209–10, 211,
222–23, 291–92, 299–300, 337

ownership of, 3–10, 20–32, 34, 38,
40–41, 42, 63, 68, 71, 76, 91, 95,
100–101, 110, 173, 181, 200, 201,
202, 203–5, 212, 216, 224, 255,
256–57, 365

Philadelphia Warriors as rivals of,
3–10, 41, 125–29, 146–47, 157–61

playing style of, 33–34, 64, 69–70, 74,
78–79, 90, 96–97, 115–20, 126,
157–58, 170, 174–75, 209, 211,
222–23, 293, 332, 333–34, 346

retired members of, 194, 210, 341,
348–49, 353, 358–59, 360, 361–62

Russell as star of, 6–10, 64, 67, 71–80,
90–93, 113, 116, 117, 157–61, 167,
171, 179, 193, 194, 210, 251,
262–63, 348–49

salaries for, 64, 66–67, 68, 73, 74,
76–77, 78, 96, 133, 258*n*, 272,
278–79

San Francisco Warriors as rivals of,
176, 177, 208–12, 222, 223

starters for, 169, 173–74, 359

Chamberlain, Wilton Norman "Wilt"
(cont'd):

coaches for, 141–49, 158, 189–92, 210–11, 230, 238–40, 242, 243, 258, 275–76, 284–85, 291–92, 300–304, 319–26, 328, 330–32, 344–45, 347–50, 351, 354–56, 360

college career of, 7–8, 41–42, 46–49, 81–89, 100–103, 112, 122, 129, 133, 144–45, 189, 233, 277

contracts of, 102–4, 111–12, 233, 235, 258, 276, 300, 301, 305, 312–15, 328, 362

death of, 155n, 367–71

as defensive player, 221, 331, 350

diet of, 122, 241

as draft choice, 41–42, 46–49, 56, 102, 121

dunking by, 8, 85, 89, 123, 148, 152, 209, 238, 287

education of, 5, 42, 44, 49

European tours of, 103–4, 106, 111, 140–41, 175, 216, 358

eye injury of, 342–43, 344

fans of, 81–82, 83, 85, 120, 233, 235–38, 277, 331, 332–33, 364

field goals scored by, 282–83, 307

financial situation of, 46–47, 49, 84–85, 100–101, 102, 111–12, 144, 312, 314

fines against, 243, 327

fouling of, 122–25, 127–28, 129, 142–43, 150, 152, 154, 210–12, 240, 283

free throws by, 122–23, 142–43, 148, 150, 152, 153, 155–56, 248, 283, 302

goatee of, 223, 242

groin injury of, 101–2

guarding of, 82, 83, 86–89, 102, 126, 127–28, 129, 152, 160, 210–12

hands and legs of, 5, 8, 45, 121

as Harlem Globetrotter, 102–4, 106, 111, 114, 140–41, 144, 175, 216, 228, 283, 358, 370

heart condition of, 217, 368, 369

height of, 5, 7, 8–9, 41–42, 43, 44, 45–46, 82, 87, 121–23, 138, 143, 150, 162, 191–92, 221, 277, 370

injuries of, 101–2, 124, 128, 141, 143, 223–24, 232, 233, 234, 237, 287, 289, 292, 294, 331, 339, 342–43, 344, 347–50, 351, 354, 355–58, 368

jump shot of, 148, 150, 152, 154, 208–9

knee injuries of, 143, 347–50, 351, 354, 355–58

lifestyle of, 102, 112, 175–76, 222, 240–41, 276–78, 312, 367–68

on Los Angeles Lakers team, 310, 312–15, 318–26, 328, 330–32, 335, 337, 344–45, 354–55, 357

mask worn by, 223–24, 237

media coverage of, 5, 6, 9, 42, 47, 49, 81, 85, 89, 100, 103, 112, 120–21, 124, 128, 129, 140, 143, 158, 191, 192, 210, 234–35, 239, 240–43, 261–64, 276, 284, 300–301, 302, 313, 314–15, 324–25, 331–32, 337–38, 343–44, 345, 355–56, 368–69

memoir by, 363

memorial service for, 370–71

as Most Valuable Player, 89, 126

"moves" of, 83, 103–4, 114, 146, 158, 220, 283, 322, 332

movie role of, 362

in NCAA championships, 86–89, 101–2

"new Wilt" image of, 192, 209–10, 230, 284, 330–31

one-hundred-point record of, 151–56, 370

pancreatitis of, 216–19, 232, 240, 241

passing abilities of, 121, 122, 123, 238, 278, 287, 301–2, 323–24, 341

personality of, 7–8, 82, 102, 112, 140, 191–92, 219, 223, 232–33, 239, 276–78, 295–96, 321–26, 331–32, 355, 362–63

on Philadelphia 76ers team, 231, 233,
235–38, 241, 249–50, 251, 260,
282–83, 289–90, 295, 300, 309–10,
313–14, 356–57, 370
on Philadelphia Warriors team, 100,
106, 111–12, 120–29, 141–49,
157–61, 175–76, 227, 228, 229, 233,
371
playing style of, 6, 7, 8–9, 189–92,
207–8, 236–37, 283–84, 321–26,
330–31
as professional player, 82–85, 100–104,
106, 111–12, 114, 120–29, 140–41,
228, 295–96, 348–49
as "quitter," 129, 140–41, 232–35, 240,
258, 351, 356–58, 364–65
racism experienced by, 83, 85–86, 103,
123, 124, 221–22, 261–64, 370
rebounds by, 120, 122, 129, 142, 148,
150, 182, 192, 234, 236–37, 244n,
281, 287, 321, 322, 323, 331, 348,
350, 362
record album of, 151, 237
as Republican, 322
reputation of, 5, 7, 41–43, 47–48,
81–85, 85, 100–103, 104, 112, 129,
140–41, 144, 149–50, 176, 230, 242,
276–78, 289–90, 300–303, 309–15,
319–26, 337–38, 354–58, 369–71
retirement of, 362–63, 368
as Rookie of the Year, 126
rookie season of, 5, 10, 120–29, 239,
356, 368
Russell compared with, 3–10, 56, 64,
81, 82, 84, 112, 114, 208–10,
291–92, 330
Russell's criticism of, 356–58, 360,
363–65, 369, 371
Russell's rivalry with, 3–10, 126, 128,
131, 136, 157–58, 161, 208–10, 215,
216, 238, 242, 282, 286, 287, 288,
291–92, 294, 296, 310, 318, 319,
320, 322, 330, 331, 337–38, 339,
345, 354–58, 366, 369–71

salary of, 121, 141, 142, 148, 176, 189,
210, 218, 226–27, 231, 234, 235,
258, 300, 301, 309–10, 312–15, 345
as San Diego Conquistadors coach, 362
on San Francisco Warriors team,
175–76, 189–92, 207–8, 226–35,
248–49, 283, 313, 356, 370
scholarship awarded to, 46–49
scoring by, 5, 10, 45, 83, 85, 120, 121,
122, 126, 129, 142–43, 146–56, 158,
176, 182, 189, 191–92, 208–9, 210,
221, 230, 234, 238, 278, 281,
282–84, 301–3, 307, 321, 322,
331–32, 335, 336, 362, 370–71
shooting ability of, 10, 82, 84, 86–89,
103–4, 148, 189–92, 208–9, 230,
231, 282–83, 302–3, 335
shots blocked by, 114, 126
as team player, 283–85, 300–303, 310,
314–15, 321–26, 344–45, 354–58
technical expertise of, 83, 84, 102,
103–4, 189–92
trading of, 226–35, 237, 240, 276,
310–15
training by, 122, 146, 216, 219,
300–301, 320
weight of, 122, 162, 191, 216, 219, 277
as "Wilt the Stilt," 45
Chambers, Jerry, 313–14
Chappell, Len, 224
Chicago Bulls, 120, 302, 317, 324, 362,
366
Chicago Stags, 30–31, 32
"choking," 86, 89, 91, 118, 152, 274
Cincinnati Royals, 113, 119, 120, 134,
137, 148, 182, 190, 229, 241, 257,
259, 268, 269, 286, 330, 331, 349
civil rights movement, 11–12, 49, 111–12,
194–96, 210, 297–99, 303–8
Claflin, Larry, 361
Clark, Archie, 313–14, 318, 320, 333
Clifton, Nat "Sweetwater," 28, 124
"clutch," 51, 54, 89, 160, 166–69, 173,
248–50, 255

235, 242, 245, 249, 251, 258,
  268–70, 286, 303–4
expansion of, 130, 157, 286, 318
formation of, 15–16, 19, 130
franchises in, 3–10, 20–24, 26, 27–28,
  67–68, 104–6, 110, 112, 120, 130,
  131, 136–37, 140, 157, 178,
  198–205, 212–13, 226, 242, 286,
  311, 312–13, 318
publicity for, 41, 103, 121, 203
racial quota system of, 109–10, 196,
  261–62, 271
rules determined by, 6, 46–47, 61–62,
  79, 80, 102, 105, 120, 140, 286, 319,
  327
team playoffs for, 39, 41, 63, 93–99,
  100, 119, 135, 139, 200, 242, 285–96
team relocations in, 131, 136–37,
  175–76, 178, 199, 230, 233
Western Division of, 67, 93, 137, 139,
  161, 178, 180, 201–2, 207, 249,
  252–53, 286, 300, 315, 318, 323–25,
  329, 330–33, 335, 350, 360
see also specific teams
National Basketball League (NBL), 16, 19
National Collegiate Athletic Association
  (NCAA), 6, 26, 47, 49, 61–62,
  65–66, 82–89, 99, 100–102, 144–45,
  165, 176, 264
National Football League (NFL), 131, 215
National Invitational Tournament (NIT),
  27, 50, 57, 60, 133
National Mentoring Partnership, 365
Naulls, Willie, 8, 73, 124, 230, 263, 264
NBA Players Association, 198–205,
  212–13
NBC, 131, 202, 215
Negro Industrial and Economic Union,
  297–98
Nelson, Don, 288, 299, 306–7, 339, 342,
  350
Neumann, Paul, 234
neutral courts, 35–36, 106, 110, 132, 134,
  137, 151, 152

Newcombe, Don, 273
Newell, Pete, 57, 59, 163
New York Giants, 131, 132
New York Herald Tribune, 120–21
New York Knickerbockers, 8, 17, 31, 43,
  72, 77, 120, 121, 124, 144, 148, 150,
  151–56, 226, 276, 280, 286, 307,
  315, 316, 329, 334, 360, 362, 370
New York Metropolitan Basketball
  Writers Association, 36, 126
New York Post, 72, 77, 119, 124
New York Times, 77, 103, 120, 172
New York World-Telegram, 13, 14, 15
New York Yankees, 15, 117–18, 171, 176,
  231–32, 289
Nichols, Jack, 41, 96
North Carolina, University of, Tar Heels,
  86–89, 144–45, 146, 147
Nucatola, Johnny, 36–37

Oakland High School, 50–52
"Ohio" play, 341–42
Olsen, Harold, 17, 18
Olympic Games, 22, 44, 48, 65, 67–68,
  69, 70–71, 73, 74, 84, 99, 165, 316,
  363
O'Neal, Shaquille, 363, 368
O'Neill, Frank, 251, 339, 343, 344, 348
Ottum, Bob, 240–41
Overbrook High School, 5, 45, 46, 112
overtime, 88–89, 97–99, 149, 169–70,
  273, 329, 371

peripheral vision, 29
Pettit, Bob, 69, 73, 75–76, 92, 93, 94, 96,
  97, 98, 99, 106, 126, 127, 148, 191,
  200, 201, 222, 232
Philadelphia Daily News, 121, 229–30,
  281
Philadelphia Inquirer, 151, 158, 229–30,
  258, 289
Philadelphia 76ers:
  attendance records for, 229, 231, 258,
  281, 305

rebounds, 6, 8, 26, 37, 41, 55, 58, 61, 64,
  69, 73–76, 79, 92, 97, 98, 112, 113,
  120, 122, 126, 129, 139, 142, 148,
  150, 167, 169, 170, 180, 182, 185,
  192, 234, 236–37, 244n, 248, 254,
  268, 273, 281, 287, 299–300,
  321–23, 331, 337, 348, 350, 362
Reed, Willis, 315, 334, 360
referees:
  coaches and, 11, 18, 95, 118–19, 126,
    144, 161, 162, 259, 316, 319
  fan harassment of, 36–37, 162, 272
  height of, 122–23
  judgment calls by, 123, 127, 129, 162,
    242, 247–48, 289, 316, 319
  rule changes and, 319, 327
  violence regulated by, 53–54, 222–23
Reinhart, Bill, 13–14, 64, 117
reserve clause, 213
Rice, Grantland, 72, 187
Richman, Ike, 111–12, 226, 227–30,
  232–35, 236, 237, 240, 241, 242–43,
  258–60, 300, 311, 312, 363
Richman, Michael, 111, 229, 362–63
Ridings, Gordon, 13, 14
"rifling," 76, 120
Risen, Arnie, 75
Rizzuto, Phil, 117–18
Robertson, Oscar, 101, 112, 120, 137,
  138, 148, 165, 180, 182, 198, 200,
  201, 202, 222–23, 241, 349
Robinson, Jackie, 27, 49, 196, 222, 271
Rochester Royals, 67–68, 98, 112, 365
Rogers, Guy, 8, 125, 128, 148, 158, 159,
  177, 192, 207–8, 212, 220, 356
Rookie of the Year, 68, 92–93, 113, 126,
  312
Rosenbluth, Lennie, 86–87
Ruklick, Joe, 85, 105, 123, 141, 142, 153,
  154n
running out the clock, 88, 98, 160–61, 273
Ruppert Knickerbocker Brewery, 256, 257
Russell, Charles, 52, 65
Russell, Charlie, 53

Russell, Didi Anstett, 361
Russell, John "Honey," 21
Russell, Karen, 108, 365
Russell, Katie, 52
Russell, Rose Swisher, 65, 71, 76, 109,
  196–97, 210, 279, 327, 359, 361
Russell, William Fenton "Bill":
  as ABC color analyst, 359, 360
  aggressiveness of, 73, 75–78
  as all-star player, 180, 201, 202
  as athlete, 6, 64–65, 76, 158, 194
  Auerbach replaced by, 264–66, 270–71,
    279–80, 286–87, 289, 358
  Auerbach's relationship with, 63–80,
    107–8, 110, 193, 264–66, 279–80,
    358, 359, 365, 366
  autograph of, 352, 364
  background of, 51–54, 99, 183, 194
  as black coach, 271, 278–80
  as black player, 8, 11, 52, 53–54, 60,
    65–66, 92–94, 107–11, 134, 193–97,
    210, 262, 271, 279, 297–99, 303–8,
    361, 370
  Boston as viewed by, 108, 263–64, 268,
    353, 361, 363–66
  on Boston Celtics team, 6–10, 64, 67,
    71–80, 90–93, 113, 116, 117,
    157–61, 167, 171, 179, 193, 194,
    210, 251, 262–63, 348–49
  as CBS game analyst, 361
  celebrity of, 70–71, 81, 177, 193
  as center, 64, 70–71, 72, 174, 208, 259,
    310, 335, 359, 363
  Chamberlain compared with, 3–10, 56,
    64, 81, 82, 84, 112, 114, 208–10,
    291–92, 330
  Chamberlain criticized by, 356–58,
    360, 363–65, 369, 371
  Chamberlain's rivalry with, 3–10, 126,
    128, 131, 136, 157–58, 161, 208–10,
    215, 216, 238, 242, 282, 286, 287,
    288, 291–92, 294, 296, 310, 318,
    319, 320, 322, 330, 331, 337–38,
    339, 345, 354–58, 366, 369–71